A Celebration of Poets

Atlantic
Grades 4-12
Spring 2011

A Celebration of Poets
Atlantic
Grades 4-12
Spring 2011

An anthology compiled by Creative Communication, Inc.

Published by:

PO BOX 303 • SMITHFIELD, UTAH 84335
TEL. 435-713-4411 • WWW.POETICPOWER.COM

Authors are responsible for the originality of the writing submitted.

All rights reserved. No part of this book may be reproduced or transmitted in any form or by any means, electronic or mechanical without written permission of the author and publisher.

Copyright © 2011 by Creative Communication, Inc.
Printed in the United States of America

ISBN: 978-1-60050-429-7

FOREWORD

Dear Reader:

Hope. In today's negatively laced headlines, hope seems to be lost to the back pages. Amid the struggles of the world with the economy, civil unrest, and just everyday living, hope seems to be waning. However, our youth provide a bright spark. They are not weighed down with the world on their shoulders. In reading the writing of today's youth, there is an optimistic light that shines through. A light that tells the story of love for friends and family. The story of spring emerging and creating a new green world. A story that does have the trials of a student's life, but also the joys of learning and moving past them. These students are aware of the problems of the world, but are not consumed with them. They still take the time to enjoy and write about the simple pleasures in life.

Each year as we publish the best student writing, I am amazed at the stories that are told, the feelings that are felt, and the lives that are shared with us through the safety of words. We are pleased to again offer this book as a testament of the hope these students have.

We have been working with student writers for over 18 years. Each year, we have students and teachers who take the time to write to us telling us of the hope that we share in providing our contests and books. We are glad that we are here to provide a creative outlet and give these students a spark to motivate their writing.

These students have taken the time to give a bit of themselves. We invite you to read what they have shared.

Sincerely,

Thomas Worthen, Ph.D.
Editor
Creative Communication

WRITING CONTESTS!

Enter our next POETRY contest!

Enter our next ESSAY contest!

Why should I enter?
Win prizes and get published! Each year thousands of dollars in prizes are awarded throughout North America. The top writers in each division receive a monetary award and a free book that includes their published poem or essay. Entries of merit are also selected to be published in our anthology.

Who may enter?
There are four divisions in the poetry contest. The poetry divisions are grades K-3, 4-6, 7-9, and 10-12. There are three divisions in the essay contest. The essay divisions are grades 3-6, 7-9, and 10-12.

What is needed to enter the contest?
To enter the poetry contest send in one original poem, 21 lines or less. To enter the essay contest send in one original non-fiction essay, 250 words or less, on any topic. Please submit each poem and essay with a title, and the following information clearly printed: the writer's name, current grade, home address (optional), school name, school address, teacher's name and teacher's email address (optional). Contact information will only be used to provide information about the contest. For complete contest information go to www.poeticpower.com.

How do I enter?

Enter a poem online at:
www.poeticpower.com
or
Mail your poem to:
  Poetry Contest
  PO Box 303
  Smithfield UT 84335

Enter an essay online at:
www.poeticpower.com
or
Mail your essay to:
  Essay Contest
  PO Box 303
  Smithfield UT 84335

When is the deadline?
Poetry contest deadlines are December 6th, April 12th and August 15th. Essay contest deadlines are October 18th, February 15th, and July 18th. Students can enter one poem and one essay for each spring, summer, and fall contest deadline.

Are there benefits for my school?
Yes. We award $12,500 each year in grants to help with Language Arts programs. Schools qualify to apply for a grant by having 15 or more accepted entries.

Are there benefits for my teacher?
Yes. Teachers with five or more students published receive a free anthology that includes their students' writing.

For more information please go to our website at **www.poeticpower.com**, email us at editor@poeticpower.com or call 435-713-4411.

TABLE OF CONTENTS

POETIC ACHIEVEMENT HONOR SCHOOLS   1

LANGUAGE ARTS GRANT RECIPIENTS   7

GRADES 10-11-12 HIGH MERIT POEMS 11

GRADES 7-8-9 HIGH MERIT POEMS 49

GRADES 4-5-6 HIGH MERIT POEMS 137

INDEX 203

STATES INCLUDED IN THIS EDITION:

DELAWARE
DISTRICT OF COLUMBIA
MARYLAND
RHODE ISLAND
VIRGINIA

Spring 2011 Poetic Achievement Honor Schools

*Teachers who had fifteen or more poets accepted to be published

The following schools are recognized as receiving a "Poetic Achievement Award." This award is given to schools who have a large number of entries of which over fifty percent are accepted for publication. With hundreds of schools entering our contest, only a small percent of these schools are honored with this award. The purpose of this award is to recognize schools with excellent Language Arts programs. This award qualifies these schools to receive a complimentary copy of this anthology. In addition, these schools are eligible to apply for a Creative Communication Language Arts Grant. Grants of two hundred and fifty dollars each are awarded to further develop writing in our schools.

Battlefield Elementary School
Fredericksburg, VA
Elena Danigelis*

Cape Henry Collegiate School
Virginia Beach, VA
Tina V. Howard*
Shannon Plank
Marieke Vanderwerff

Carson Middle School
Herndon, VA
Barbara S. Adams
Ellen Bickford
Allison D. Carey
Tiffany Estrella
Carla Gibson
Susan Miles*
Theresa Palmer
Barbara Poole*
Leigh C. Toweson*
Victoria Wuerful

Charles Barrett Elementary School
Alexandria, VA
Mya Akin
Carrisa Sumner

Charles City County High School
Charles City, VA
Natasha Rustchak*

Charles Shea Sr High School
Pawtucket, RI
George Grimes
Pat Winiarski*

Church of the Redeemer Christian School
Gaithersburg, MD
Toni Morris*

Corkran Middle School
Glen Burnie, MD
Carol Brinkley
Denise Calabrese*
Lydia Snyder
Mrs. Zipay

Courthouse Road Elementary School
Spotsylvania, VA
Brenda Nettles
Michelle Sims

Crestwood Elementary School
Richmond, VA
Diane Bivins*

Delaware Military Academy
Wilmington, DE
Brittany Carson*
Tara Dick*
Najma Landis

E Russell Hicks Middle School
Hagerstown, MD
Anne Kendall*

Featherbed Lane Elementary School
Baltimore, MD
Erin Lundberg*

Floyd T Binns Middle School
Culpeper, VA
Charissa Hollyfield*
Kellie Mahoney
Lindsay McFarland

Forest Park High School
Woodbridge, VA
Laura Dowling*

Forestville Military Academy
Forestville, MD
Loretta Adih*
Darnell Sarpy

George E Peters Adventist School
Hyattsville, MD
Myrna James*

Greenville Elementary School
Nokesville, VA
Susan Robertson*

Immaculate Heart of Mary School
Towson, MD
Kathy Zoppo*

Kenmore Middle School
Arlington, VA
Judith D. Freeman*

Kilmer Middle School
Vienna, VA
Barbara E. Appling*
Mary Kay Folk
Jim McElveen
Joseph McElveen
Taheerah Stewart

Linwood Holton Elementary School
Richmond, VA
Mary-Curtis Smart*

Magnolia Elementary School
Lanham, MD
Terri Childress
Camille Dorsey

Marshall Middle School
The Plains, VA
Sandra P. Simpson*

Mary Walter Elementary School
Bealeton, VA
Patricia Baker*

Monelison Middle School
Madison Heights, VA
Kristi Masencup
Melissa Ragland*
Lynette Smith*

Most Blessed Sacrament Catholic School
Berlin, MD
Cris Kaczmarczyk*

Mount St Charles Academy
Woonsocket, RI
Donald Hogue*
Ms. Tessier
Denise Turcotte*

Poetic Achievement Honor Schools

Norfolk Christian Middle School
Norfolk, VA
Paula Ross*

Norfolk Collegiate Middle/Upper School
Norfolk, VA
Ms. L. Belle*
Charles E. Cook*

Nottingham Elementary School
Arlington, VA
Sara McClellan*

Page Middle School
Gloucester, VA
LeeAnn VanVranken*

St Christopher's School
Richmond, VA
Cynthia Brown
Linda DiLucente
Deborah Epes
Renee Fraine*
Margaret Frischkorn
Marion Halladay
Carrie Hoge
Cabell Jones
Glorietta Jones
Paula Jones
Susan Kirk
James Morgan
Jen O'Ferrall
Sandra Oakley
Alisa Pava
Ellen Sands
Dorothy Suskind
Betsy Tyson
Wanda Vizcaino
Christie Wilson
Nancy Young

St Clement Mary Hofbauer School
Baltimore, MD
Simone Chappell
Christine Godlewski*

St Clement Mary Hofbauer School (cont.)
Baltimore, MD
Linda House*
Wendy Parker*
Susan Ritmiller
Catherine Urban

St Columba School
Oxon Hill, MD
Aliya Jones*

St Jane De Chantal School
Bethesda, MD
Shannon Cron
Eileen W. Theim*

St John Neumann Academy
Blacksburg, VA
Rachael Beach*
Sophia Leece
Jenny Mishoe
Sarah Pickeral
Mrs. Thurman

St Joseph School-Fullerton
Baltimore, MD
Katherine Diggs
J. Delores Keefer*
Carol Mackechnie

St Mary School
Cranston, RI
Jane Bowry*

Stevensville Middle School
Stevensville, MD
Kelly N. Sell*

Trinity School
Ellicott City, MD
Debby Moulding*

Waller Mill Fine Arts Magnet School
Williamsburg, VA
Sherrie A. Geyer*

Western Heights Middle School
    Hagerstown, MD
        Julie Cardenas
        Natasha Whetsell*

Woodbridge Sr High School
    Woodbridge, VA
        Catherine Hailey*
        Andrew McCarthy
        Joseph Potente
        Brittany Powell
        Ann Ragsdale

Wyman Elementary School
    Warwick, RI
        Elaine Houle*

Language Arts Grant Recipients 2010-2011

After receiving a "Poetic Achievement Award" schools are encouraged to apply for a Creative Communication Language Arts Grant. The following is a list of schools who received a two hundred and fifty dollar grant for the 2010-2011 school year.

Adolph Schreiber Hebrew Academy, Monsey, NY
August Boeger Middle School, San Jose, CA
Bedford Road School, Pleasantville, NY
Benton Central Jr/Sr High School, Oxford, IN
Birchwood School, Cleveland, OH
Blue Ball Elementary School, Blue Ball, PA
Bonneville High School, Idaho Falls, ID
Cedar Ridge High School, Newark, AR
Corpus Christi School, San Francisco, CA
Crestwood Elementary School, Rockford, MI
Dodson Elementary School, Canton, MI
Dr Howard K Conley Elementary School, Chandler, AZ
Eastport Elementary School, Eastport, ME
Emmanuel-St Michael Lutheran School, Fort Wayne, IN
Fannin County Middle School, Blue Ridge, GA
Fort Recovery Elementary School, Fort Recovery, OH
Frank Ohl Intermediate School, Youngstown, OH
Frenship Middle School, Wolfforth, TX
Gateway Pointe Elementary School, Gilbert, AZ
Greencastle-Antrim Middle School, Greencastle, PA
Greenville High School, Greenville, AL
Hancock County High School, Sneedville, TN
Holy Child Academy, Drexel Hill, PA
Holy Cross High School, Delran, NJ
Holy Family Catholic School, Granite City, IL
Interboro GATE Program, Prospect Park, PA
John E Riley Elementary School, South Plainfield, NJ
Joseph M Simas Elementary School, Hanford, CA
Lee A Tolbert Community Academy, Kansas City, MO
Malvern Middle School, Malvern, OH
Merritt Central Elementary School, Merritt, BC
Metcalf School, Exeter, RI
Norfolk Christian Middle School, Norfolk, VA

Language Arts Grant Winners cont.

Pioneer Career & Technology Center, Shelby, OH
Providence Hall, Herriman, UT
Ramsay School, Ramsay, MT
Reuben Johnson Elementary School, McKinney, TX
Round Lake High School, Round Lake, MN
Sacred Heart School, Oxford, PA
Selwyn College Preparatory School, Denton, TX
Shadowlawn Elementary School, Green Cove Springs, FL
St Elizabeth Catholic School, Rockville, MD
St Lorenz Lutheran School, Frankenmuth, MI
The Oakridge School, Arlington, TX
Tomlin Middle School, Plant City, FL
Vista Fundamental School, Simi Valley, CA
Walsh Elementary School, Walsh, CO
Washington County Union School, Roper, NC
Woodland Intermediate School, Gurnee, IL
Woodward Granger High School, Woodward, IA

Grades 10-11-12 Top Ten Winners

List of Top Ten Winners for Grades 10-12; listed alphabetically

Sarah Bauer, Grade 10
Valley Christian High School, CA

Katie Borne, Grade 10
Commonwealth Connections Academy, PA

Jake Fortner, Grade 10
Jennings County High School, IN

Linda Kou, Grade 11
Collège catholique Franco-Ouest, ON

Kiki Lawson, Grade 12
Crosstimbers Academy, TX

Nolan Mackey, Grade 11
Rock Hill High School, SC

Alison Malee, Grade 11
Loyalsock Township High School, PA

Rachel McDaniel, Grade 12
Evangelistic Temple School, OK

Lauren Wingenroth, Grade 12
First Flight High School, NC

Maggie Zhang, Grade 11
Fayetteville-Manlius High School, NY

All Top Ten Poems can be read at www.poeticpower.com

Note: The Top Ten poems were finalized through an online voting system. Creative Communication's judges first picked out the top poems. These poems were then posted online. The final step involved thousands of students and teachers who registered as the online judges and voted for the Top Ten poems. We hope you enjoy these selections.

Delaney and Madison

Delaney's a peach at eight ripe years old
she's muscle to her tip toes and does what she's told
cooky, not perfect, she's creative and smart
teaching others her language through smiles and art

what she doesn't know yet as she snores safe and sound
is her sister's got issues weird and profound
Madison Lynne worries and frets
over trivial things her Delaney barely gets

though the blonde can't walk straight and rarely brushes her hair
she's immune to the world's cruel remarks and harsh stare
her sister feels these things hoping straight to her gut
that Delaney will maneuver, that she'll stick it and strut

writing this now, Madz sees very clearly
she'll make it in life like her sis if only wearily
they'll sing brush karaoke, paint their fingers and toes
as for the rest…we'll see how it goes!

Madison Goebel, Grade 10
Delaware Military Academy, DE

Alzheimer's

Can you fight the dark of your situation?
When there is no light and senses have gone
Habit is the lone instinct you can count on
When thoughts are swallowed by a conflagration
When recollection is hesitation
The stories I share, you forget anon
Do you forget it all when it breaks dawn?
Is every day a reincarnation?

It seems your memory's been corrupted
Like a computer, there are files not found
Is it that your brain has been abducted?
Because it seems as if it's not around
Does every day you live remain the same?
I ask, will you ever remember my name?

Kyle Holmes, Grade 11
Liberty High School, MD

Why Is My Life So Sad

My days are so lonely with you so far away
I think about you since then and every day
How the memory of your eyes still floating in my mind
Because its brightness is unique, there is no other kind
I could wait a lifetime for you, or maybe die before I get by your side
At least the moments of my life that I spent with you were with pride
You are where I belong
You are the ache I feel all day long
You are the cure for this loneliness
Please come to me, and be brave to take away all this sadness
One more day, I will be dead
Why is my life so sad

Ivanildo Gomes, Grade 11
Charles Shea Sr High School, RI

Evolving Repetition

When we run out of things to say.
And there are no more different feelings to feel.
And run out of creativity to upgrade.
What will be our purpose be?
Everyone wants to experience.
But most people steal our opportunity of joy.
Personally, I don't wanna die young.
When most of us stop believing in the Greater.
And not only our bodies start to deteriorate on us.
Will we still have chance for living, forgiveness, and recovery.
I believe, I feel, I see sagacity.
I know, I title, I call man's prosperity.
When all feels at fault that's just another lesson to be taught.
The bright side is there is always a bright side.
So let the light outshine the struggling fight.
Humans mind is a heavy matter, don't be fooled it does not flatter.
Success is our destination and genuine is who we become.
Change is just better into best, and takes away room for rest.
Mankind is mankind and happiness is actually our goal.
One reason or another we fit our perfected evolved role.
Goodnight.

Claudia Peters, Grade 12
Loch Raven High School, MD

Survive

My mind flies with the stars in the sky
If he could feel the pain that I feel lord knows he would cry

Every moment I'm with him a part of me dies
I'm just at that point where I'm tired of all the lies

I'm starting to despise him
Now he's acting like it's a surprise

He should now realize
That it's time to say goodbye

I don't want to feel this way anymore
I don't want to have to strive to be alive

Cause I'm at the stage now
Where only god knows if I'll survive.

Stephaine Hood, Grade 12
Northwestern High School, MD

New Year

365 days have gone by
It's such a wonder how time flies
I've done so much this past year
and it's so sad that the last day is here.
I'm glad I spent time with the people I care about
and I know that I will love them forever, without a doubt.
They've helped me through two thousand and ten
and gave me someone to call "Friend."

Victor Garcia, Grade 10
Woodbridge Sr High School, VA

A Year and a Half
His pearly white teeth
His light brown golden curly hair
His big brown observing eyes
His little hands
Smaller than three years old
Bigger than two years old
Only a year and a half

It's amazing what a difference
One person can make
How much someone can change you
For the better
As a matter of fact
I could stare at him for days
Everything he does amazes me

If you met him, my son
I'm sure you'd fall in love as well

Steffany Galdamez, Grade 12
New Directions Alternative Education Center, VA

Carpe Diem
Let's seize the day,
Let's throw caution to the wind today.

Let's take all the risks we can bear,
For the paradise we see today, tomorrow may not be there.

Let's chase all of our dreams, because
They can't live forever.

Let's hold on to what we love,
Before it all slips away.

Carpe Diem
Carpe Diem
Carpe Diem

Christopher Boyd, Grade 12
Nansemond River High School, VA

War
I pray as I am in danger
The loud shots flying through the air
I pray that I might make it
As bombs stir up my ground
I pray to my Lord to save me
As men run toward me
I pray for my family
As the shots get closer
I pray to save my life
As the bombs get stronger
I pray as the men come closer and closer
I look to the sky as a big bright stream of light awaits me
I close my eyes and I am gone

Maria Bayzie, Grade 10
Commonwealth Academy, VA

I Am
I am independent and intelligent
I wonder about my future
I hear voices telling me to keep my head up
I see a great future coming
I am independent and intelligent

I pretend I'm all right sometimes when I'm not
I feel like I'm on clouds floating
I touch the sky
I worry about my schoolwork and grades
I cry when I see my mother crying
I am independent and intelligent

I understand that I may struggle in life
I say that I'm BLESSED!
I dream that I will become a millionaire one day
I try to get along with all my peers
I hope I will achieve all my goals
I am independent and intelligent

Whitney Bradby, Grade 12
Charles City County High School, VA

To a Boy in My Spanish Class
There's a boy in my class, his smile makes me weak
I stumble upon my own two feet,
I wish I could blurt out I LOVE YOU on the top of my lungs
Or even get the courage to ask where are you from?
But I guess my face will just turn red, embarrassed and shy,
Because I think your once cool guy

But you'd never notice a girl like me
I'm not as smart as I could be.
I'm frail, pale and a tid bit glad,
But I feel something special, it makes me so mad
I could just ask you if you feel the same way,
But I'm to nervous of what you would say
I'll never take that chance I don't want to be hurt
I feel like the mud on your shoe or lower than dirt.
I press my heart on your sleeve
If I could just open my mouth and breathe.

Samantha Ubago, Grade 11
New Directions Alternative Education Center, VA

Lost Poem
I want to write a poem but the words are not there
It's been too long pen and paper
My thoughts are clogged
My brain is exploding
Words like depressed and troubled stay clear
When am I ever going to get over this?
A memory reappears a situation calls upon my thoughts
My brain is twirling, my hand is twitching
My paper is calling
It's time Lost Poem

Ariel Blankenship, Grade 10
Brooke Point High School, VA

Beauty

A myth within itself;
A paradox of the earth
To be represented by those who posses it;
By those who understand
What good it is to be themselves.

And yet it's there, this myth.
Gift and curse and wonder in one.
There to be seen, to be understood
By those it graces with its touch.
Those lucky few it graces with its touch.

The rest are alone. Left to be themselves
Without the wonder of its favor
While it mocks them forevermore in those faces
Lucky enough to receive its blessing.
Those lucky few who receive its blessing.

Courtney Woodard, Grade 10
Douglas Southall Freeman High School, VA

The Moon and the Stars

Full moon
Shining a ghostly glow
High above, looking down
Gazing away from the crowd,
The view of the pitiful commoners
Your regal air lights up the sky
Making the viewers pass the subtle ones by
Taking up the spotlight
With your obnoxious ego
Everyone already knows that you are beautiful
Not many notice the little ones
But in a moment of pity
The maker said "Full Moon, you shall disappear for a few days,
For subtlety must have a turn to reign"
And even now every so often the Moon is pushed away
So the little stars can have their turn
To shine and be praised

Jessica Jones, Grade 12
Forest Park High School, VA

American Memories

Mom, pop, and apple pie.
Peanuts and Cracker jacks at the ballgame.
Saturday mornings.
Cartoons and comics.
Fireworks and little American flags.
Christmas Eve and Easter Sunday.

Fishing on a clear lake.
Camping in the mountains.
Taking a dip in the swimming pool.
Backyard barbecues.
These are my American memories.

Colin Ryan, Grade 12
Homeschool Plus, VA

Mother

You persist through heaps of waste unknown
  Spinning, a nimble ballerina on tippy toe
Your children's affections have yet be shown
  Your wrath, one day, will let them know
The pain you've been forced to forever suffer
  For allowing them a place to lay their head
You were kind and giving, a loving mother
  Rivers of water, crops for bread
If only they knew of your wasting away
  They'd end their foolishness once and for all
They'd be forced to remember what led them astray
  Human corruption shall be their downfall
I wish people would realize Mother, what you're really worth
  I wish they could see, there's only one Earth.

Mary Tadlock, Grade 12
Turner Ashby High School, VA

Turbulent Desire

His dreams were forever gone
Whirling by in the wind
Destined to fail from the start.

Taken from sight
Swept up from under his feet
His dreams were forever gone.

No care left in his mind
His desires crumble to Dust
Destined to fail from the start.

His ambition falling apart piece by piece
Like leaves floating away
His dreams were forever gone.

The kite of his life drifting away
Untethered from his hand
Destined to fail from the start.

Carelessness flowing through him
Like the breeze of a cool summer night,
His dreams were forever gone
Destined to fail from the start.

Nicholas Riehl, Grade 11
Annapolis Area Christian School, MD

Beach

The salty breeze blows
Wet sand clings between my toes
The foam-rimmed waves crash
Seashells line the beaten shore
Seagulls, in the air they soar

Riviera Boatman, Grade 10
Norfolk Collegiate School, VA

It's Me...Casey Jennifer Louise Callahan Anderson

I am from a delicious bowl of ice cream every night before bed, from Arizona Skinny Jeans and Converse shoes.
I am from the blow up pool, to the mixture of brown and green grass, from the warmth of the fireplace in the windy winter.
From Grammy, Daddaddy, and Daddy, from Uncle Paul, Aunt Rachel, Paulie, Zach, and Bryce.
Constantly laughing at people who fall, and going to church and youth group every Tuesday and Sunday.
From "Don't eat the gum under the table!" and "Get out of the clothes rack!"
I am from Grace Baptist Church, Working in the toddler nursery, VBS, and music performances.
From hearing stories of my dad getting his head stuck between the railings on the staircase.
From my Uncle getting a rev-up toy car stuck in his hair, and the times I would frequently pretend to be a mannequin in department stores.
My family is different. We have our moments...like any other family, but we have the ability to put up with each other.
Although we all have different personalities, beliefs, political views, and different ways of dealing with certain situations.
We all fit in. All of our differences make us who we are. We're stuck on each other, we're stuck like glue, and we wouldn't change a thing!

Casey Anderson, Grade 10
Grace Brethren Christian School, MD

In the End...

No one would have ever thought, the day would come, when we'd be no more.
Every day that passed brought more memories and every day that passed brought new tears.
Every day that passed made us really think about what's to come.
The days went on for years and years,
Never thinking to hold on, never considering this could be gone.
After years of ups and downs and pure confusion,
You realize those little moments, were the moments you wish you held on to.
You start to realize how different everything is and how you would do anything to get it all back.
All you think about is how much you wish you realized earlier what you had when you had it.
But in the end these moments, these memories, these wishes, they only made you stronger.

Lexus Walsh, Grade 10
Delaware Military Academy, DE

A Painting Named Happiness

The hues in the water reflect the degrees of my happiness.
It's increasing lately, you know.
I should climb the tree, wrap myself around.
Hide in the bushes — so beautiful — someone is sure to search.
It's incredible, young artist, that you could capture the colors of my soul, the safe place imagined in my head.
I shall dip my toes in the water; completely forget my shades of sadness.
Immerse myself in the water — I'm sure,
My happiness will swallow me whole.
Regurgitate a flower, fresh-faced and wide-eyed,
Grinning — I know.

Amber Short, Grade 12
C. Milton Wright High School, MD

Trees

We planted it the first day it arrived. It has grown with me ever since then. Stretching up to the sky, challenging the limits of the world.
I walk around this tree every day. Hug it; feed it; cherish it. Others do not love this tree.
They call it a corruption to their yards because of falling leaves.
No matter what they say, I will continue to help this tree grow. By the end of its days it will have a strong base.
It will branch out its limbs, shading the ground underneath.
This tree is and always will be my better half.

Benton Evans, Grade 11
Christiansburg High School, VA

The Battle of Evermore

I'm going to become an inmate in my mind, this empty prism that I have come to know so well.
I wonder if I will be stuck here for eternity.
I wonder if I will ever get out.
Am I dead or am I floating. Am I dreaming or hallucinating.
Like a dope I binge on sorrow, on false hopes, on dreams.
Like a drunkard I fall, I stumble, and wander aimlessly through my mind.
Will I carry out the deed tonight?
Will I finish without a fight?
Will I end the race at the start?
Will I continue through the fog?
Is there anyone out there now, that understands my cry?
Does anyone know what I scream out into the night?
And can they not see me in that light?
What has happened to my flight?
Will I crash and burn, I might?
Is the end coming near,
Do you really care my dear?
Have you decided against my will?
Or have you ended all your might?

Adam Link, Grade 11
Walsingham Academy Upper School, VA

Dance of the Universe

The universe's incandescent inhabitants are constantly locked in a slow, beautiful celestial dance around nothing
Stars greet each other, twinkling and genuflecting ever so slightly
As they began to twirl, their shimmering dust drifts

up
down
and out,

softly kissing the other sleepy bright ones around them, awakening them, beckoning to them to join in
And they do
Shining ever so luminously as the moon draws closer to them on its smooth, oblique orbit
The beautiful lunar body's quiet radiance complements those dazzling pinpoints of light, enveloping them in a loving glow
And they burn like a thousand candles
in their infinite graceful movement
The supernovas, in the meantime, only enhance the gorgeousness of the symphony of light
and interstellar explosions flare throughout the solar system,
sending pulses of energy from dancer to dancer,
dissipating into shining bits of nothing
But the dancing never stops.

Ellen Nguyen, Grade 11
Thomas Jefferson High School for Science and Technology, VA

Missing You

Waking up with the sound of a rooster was magical.
Smelling the strong smell of homemade coffee my grandmother Rosa used to make for the family was a daily routine.
Walking out of the house feeling the warm breeze bursting into my face made me feel safe.
The sapphire berry sky with it soft clouds looking like cotton balls remind me of my childhood.
The cottonseed rays from the sun passing through the clouds made me admire nature.
As I walk by myself I look at the wavy sea and it reminded me of my grandmother's lifetime.
The crystal green myth shore reminds me of her early life, and the lagoon deep end
Reminds me of the last time we spend together, but it also hurts me because it separate us.

Erika Reyes, Grade 12
Charles Shea Sr High School, RI

Blood

His blood, that is the flame.
O, His worthy name!
See His head hang.

That blood He shed for thee
Casts our sins aside
And strength
Arrives.

For through Jesus
There is strength,
Powerful strength!

He gave His soul to God, you see
So people, simple people
Drowning in sin
Could look upon that Cross
To be free again.

But pay attention!
You might lose sight
Of the loss of His life,
That very brave sacrifice —
The blood that casts us free!!

Julia Shumate, Grade 12
Huntingtown High School, MD

I Am

I am smart and kind
I wonder if angels cry
I hear loud voices
I see intelligent seniors
I am smart and kind

I pretend to like others
I feel amazing
I touch soft skin
I worry about education
I cry about death
I am smart and kind

I understand life
I say good things
I dream reality
I try to succeed
I hope for billions
I am smart and kind

Chanell Christian, Grade 12
Charles City County High School, VA

Come, Dreams

The soft breath of silence,
the pounding beat of rain,
the darkness needs no license
for it to call my name.

The birdsong keeps me waking;
the owls song of night.
The darkness keeps on taking
the starry beams of light.

Into my dreams I enter
a world that dares draw near,
a silent inner center,
where only I am here.

No one keeps my company —
I am myself alone.
No one is there to comfort me,
but in my head I'm home.

Shiona Clark, Grade 11
Forest Park High School, VA

Pink Tiger Lily

I see it as it looked,
That flower slowly blooming,
Day by day it gets fuller,
Brighter and taller,
It reaches its peak,
The most beautiful thing
Anyone has seen,
Comes to an end,
As it shrinks,
Starts to welt and become dry,
People wonder,
Will it survive?
The sun and water,
Can't seem to bring it back.
The flower slowly starts to die,
Comes back to almost beautiful
And keeps this process,
Until the cold comes along
And kills it.

Janelle Hall, Grade 11
Woodbridge Sr High School, VA

Tongues

they are lithe and quick.
twisting
oily and unctuous
I am milk.

your connoisseurship of
gesture (I thank you so
for your lies) benefits me
like a snail on a salt lick.

why must I endure this
jagged fraudulence as it
slithers nonchalantly forth
translucent and glistening
blackly.

hide your dead and
fetid words in the acquiescing
earth and I will turn
(because your syllables
cause my blood to unravel)
finally unable to see the
faint alphabet of your discourse
fade.

Morgan Nakroshis, Grade 12
Eleanor Roosevelt High School, MD

Society's Creation

I am the monster,
The bloodsucker
Creeping under your bed,
Squeaking your staircase

I am the monster,
Outcast of society
Laughter
Rejection

I am the monster,
Looking for nourishment
Hiding in your closet
Refuge

I am the monster,
Branded by society
Forever isolated...
Dare to be different

Nicole Bragg, Grade 11
Forest Park High School, VA

One Time

The lives we live
Are filled with the voices
Of people who warn us
About our choices
They tell us "be careful"
Like we can decide
Whether to be safe
Or to risk our lives
But we must heed their warnings
We'll remember one day
The things they have taught us
The things they say:
"One time to live
One time to die
One time to fight
One time to cry
One time to choose
What could affect our lives"
If only we listened,
If only we tried

Kyle Lamberti, Grade 11
Annapolis Area Christian School, MD

Block

Across from me in a sober state
Pupils congealed to ebony slate
Your cigarette placed tenderly
'Twixt fragile, arid plains

And were mine sky
How I wish that I
Could lie them tangent;
Amalgamate a horizon

While sparks produce flame
Brilliant, fickle, untamed
Crisp sun connects —
The panorama now nirvana!

Yet,
This place is chisel-chipped
Your face still nondescript
Desperate star soon fizzles
And with night, comes yearning.

Louise Gretschel, Grade 12
Montgomery Blair High School, MD

Reality

From a peek comes curiosity,
from a hug comes comfort,
and from a kiss comes everlasting love.

Nicole Foxwell, Grade 11
MorningStar Academy, MD

By Moonlight

What a waste I make of the day.
I have been so disillusioned to ever imagine that it could be contained.
So it flourishes beneath the surface, howling like a wolf and pounding —
Like a door, it becomes closed forever.
And again it festers within my very depths.
I find self satisfaction within the suppression
And I inflict fresh pain upon already salted wounds.

It's a snarl. It's a reason. It has consumed me. It is me.
A terror rises up against the tide,
But I'm stuck beneath the surface. And oh, how my breath becomes thin.

Feel it take, feel it call, feel the water
Encompassing my body as the sky becomes tainted.
Bubbles rise to the surface, as I gasp in for life.
It is not the air I seek, but an escape.

The last bubble blossoms at the surface,
And the sun has left its place in the ever glowing sky.
The waste I make of my day,
Is nothing compared to my nights.

Sarah DelSanto, Grade 12
Portsmouth High School, RI

Happy

Happy, innocent, waltzing through life without a care.
Crushed by those you thought friends.
Slowly beaten into submission until you're broken, abandoned, depressed.
No longer looking for the happiness you knew, just sitting, waiting in the gloom.
No cheerful ray or blissful memory.
Pain.
Pain.
Only pain.
You were once so full of life, yet now you long for none.
Is there a way to bring back that once vivacious carefree person?
No, while stuck in gloom your soul was torn in two.
In its place a new life, a new person steps into your shoes.
You can no longer see the world through rose-colored glasses.
All you see is the pain and evil through this new person's eyes.
All you want is to go back, yet that person, that life no longer exists.

Brendan Cornely, Grade 11
Salesianum School, DE

My Little Boy

I could not ask for anything more, you are my little boy,
I must say, yes I am young I may not be the best mom.
But you saved my life from all my faults, people have so much to say.
But I couldn't ask for anything else on this day.
Being an 18 yr old mom, how could it be you are all I ever needed to make me whole.
I promise you the world I will always try my best, I will never rest.
I am your daddy and your mommy. I love you with every inch of my heart.
There is a reason for everything, but this one no one can explain.
God gave me a gift when he gave me you my little boy I will always love you.

Meghan Arena, Grade 12
Charles Shea Sr High School, RI

I Am

I am outgoing and smart…
I wonder am I going to be successful…
I hear birds…
I see heaven…
I am outgoing and smart…

I pretend to be a nurse…
I feel loved…
I touch my heart…
I worry about my father…
I cry when bad things happen to my family…
I am outgoing and smart…

I understand that I can be anything if I put my mind to it…
I say that I am beautiful in and out…
I dream to be a nurse…
I try to be my best all around…
I hope to be successful…
I am outgoing and smart…

Brittany Wade, Grade 12
Charles City County High School, VA

I Am

I am young and intelligent…
I wonder where I would be in 5 years…
I hear success knocking at my door…
I see my hopes and dreams coming true…
I am young and intelligent…

I pretend to be happy when I am at my lowest…
I feel angels walking with me through tough times…
I touch people's hearts when they're in need of a friend…
I worry if sadness would conquer my goals…
I cry when the thoughts of my late family cross my mind…
I am young and intelligent…

I understand that I am not perfect…
I say work your hardest to achieve your goals…
I dream of being a successful person in adulthood…
I try my best at everything I do…
I hope my future will be bright…
I am young and intelligent…

Shane White, Grade 12
Charles City County High School, VA

Leaving the Past Behind

Going through ups and then some downs
Flying high then trampled into the ground
Pieces put together just to be broken again
Always hoping but never getting to the end
Why live my life anyway?
When I can barely make it through a day
Always wanting what I can't have
Can't touch it, can only look at
It's mostly a depressing life
Filled with drama and strife
But throughout this roller costar
All the little pieces are put together
I learned from my past mistakes
And I am able to wipe the tears from my face
I found the light in the dark abyss
No longer surrounding myself with darkness

Stephanie Walters, Grade 12
James River High School, VA

A Finch in Rostov, Russia

A Finch in Rostov, Russia flying in the sky
Through the clouds he flew he sure was really high

A metal bird he saw flying in the sky
Through the clouds it rumbled he sure was really high

Approaching him quite quickly it stared him in the eye
Getting closer every second he sure was really high

Down the little Finch flew passing others by
Avoid the metal bird he did he shouldn't have flown so high

He regretted from this moment he couldn't say goodbye
To his precious mother he shouldn't have flown so high

Woken from his slumber no bird, just a guy
His name was that of Finch descent he never was so high

Robert Paul Finch and Joseph Rostov, Grade 12
Norfolk Collegiate Upper School, VA

What Do You Do?

What do you do when you've lost all hope?
Where do you go? How do you cope?

What do you do when you're screaming out loud,
but there's no one to hear you, because no one's around?

What do you do when you're lost in the dark?
Well the light never moved — you go back to the start.

No one can help you, you're too far away,
turn around and find the light that keeps the darkness at bay.

Jenna Capobianco, Grade 12
Middletown High School, MD

A Friend Over a Boy

I didn't know she liked him
She never told me his name
So now I'm stuck between the two, what do I do?
Life is based on choices,
Do I choose my best friend,
Or do I choose him?
Even though we have had our ups and downs,
She has always been there for me.
I can't let a guy destroy our friendship
She means way more to me than he does!

Desiree Poosson, Grade 12
Menchville High School, VA

I'm Not Much of a Poet

I'm sitting in the back corner
Head palming my desk
No point in talking
Head palming my desk

I listen as the class talks
When is school going to end? I think
Head palming my desk.
When is school going to end? I think

Time freezes for a second
Head palming my desk
When is school going to end? I think
I'm living a repeated life

What are you doing? Someone asks
Head palming my desk
When is school going to end? I think
I'm living a repeated life
Eileen Fournier, Grade 11
Menchville High School, VA

These Woods Are True

These woods I wander,
Dark and deep;
These woods are not my own
To keep.
Though I wander
Through and through,
Over yonder trees
I do.
Yet still these woods
Are not my own;
How I long
To call them home.
But wandering
Is all I do,
For dark and deep,
These woods are true.
Rebecca Henenlotter, Grade 11
Oakton High School, VA

Hiding

I don't know you,
but I've seen you enough
to hold your eyes
underneath my fingernails
and taste that they
are blue as I
chew on them,
eyes stained to the sky;
wondering why we can't
see shooting stars
in the day.
Shalah Lock, Grade 11
Bel Air High School, MD

I'm Sorry

I'm sorry I don't have a 4.0 GPA, I'm happy with my 3.5
I'm sorry my life isn't perfect, I'm just glad to be alive
I'm sorry I'm not drop dead gorgeous from my head to my toes
But I'm not in the acting industry, therefore I don't put on shows

I'm sorry I don't come from a wealthy family, not everything is just placed in my hand
I'm sorry I have a unique personality not many people understand
I'm sorry everyone thinks I'm supposed to do what they say
What they fail to realize is that God is the only person that I truly obey

I'm sorry I can't always run to mommy and daddy to make everything ok
All I have is my pride and faith to help me along the way
I'm sorry that I sometimes say things to people that may seem incoherent
I'm sorry that everyone seems to think that they're my parents

I'm sorry that I'm the type of person that can easily speak their mind
And nowadays a person like me is truly hard to find
I'm sorry that not many people like me and think I'm stuck up
But unless you've taken the time to get to know me, then please shut up

I'm sorry that some people refuse to accept what my future plans are to be
But now I refuse to keep apologizing for simply being me
I'm done pouring my heart out, I am now wiping my tears
I'm done being sorry because I've been sorry for sixteen years
Alexis Robinson, Grade 11
Forestville Military Academy, MD

Maintaining a Fire Is a Risky Business

It's happened once; it's happened a million times before
Expecting each time to "be better, for sure"
Lie in our beds, stare straight through the ceiling
Wondering if the other shares the same feeling
Too afraid to take the leap, but too afraid to continue in the loneliness we weep
Remembering what the last times brought upon us
Are we willing to take the risk?

Too afraid to say what we want to say
Afraid you just might run away
But your heart is in my hand
Turn the glass, cross fingers it'll never run out of sand

Thoughts coming in through every direction
Better ones lost as if bad communication
We can blame miscommunication
Every right move seems to be the last one
Every night seems to be longer than the first one
We swore this would never happen again
But promises were meant to be broken
Love isn't always a liar
Maybe this time I could maintain this fire
Ian Bruce, Grade 10
Delaware Military Academy, DE

White

Snowflakes flutter endlessly
Each snowflake is like a person
Our color is white
Because we haven't
Decided what color
We are supposed to be
It's like a blank page
A story yet to be written
Our story
The tales of our lives
Start out by being white
Blank
Endless
There is no depth
But when the words are written
There is depth
There is no more white
There is an ending
Hailey Edsall, Grade 10
Colonel Richardson High School, MD

A Battle Worth Fighting

The north and the south,
Two separate divisions,
Soldiers fallen in trenches,
A nation of collisions.

Blood pricked skies,
The confederate flag held high,
The road to redemption,
The shouts and the glory cries.

The dead lay silent,
So many stories kept inside,
A battle worth fighting,
For the country they died.
Jesse Wooleyhan, Grade 10
Delaware Military Academy, DE

The Truth About Love

Love is but a bitter pain,
Leaving its victims with a broken heart
When eyes are vacated of a lover's flame
And without hesitation, departs.
Love is an endless black hole
Ruining all fools it devours
With a river of tears, takes its toll
Until its final dying hour.
Love is an evil tempter of fate,
Luring all pride to a great demise
Using sweet promises as bait.
Though some it may despise,
To others it grants a gift untold
That few may ever behold.
Kiersten Gausman, Grade 11
Madison County High School, VA

Rodents

The hue of the sunset was unbelievably true,
About as orange as a third of the Irish flag

It settled and settled for minutes on time,
I didn't believe for such time it could drag

It's now getting late, let's no longer wait,
hop on father's bike and ride right into the outskirts of the inner city

When we arrive
we'll contemplate
my house or your house
in the morn be my spouse
We can move to the cottage
and go from a rat to a mouse

It's again getting late, so no longer must we wait
It's now my own bike so let's ride right into what's now yours and mine.
Cristobal Montano, Grade 11
Woodbridge Sr High School, VA

Childhood Memories

When I was a child I counted the days, climbed the Etruscan green trees,
Ran in the warm earthy dirt, counting stars, afraid of the dark,
And, today I want to confess that childhood fascinates me…
And I'd give it all…
To stand again, little.
Played with butterflies of all colors, changed shoes,
A child is a divine being,
Full of peace and curiosity,
Bringing joy and happiness
In the innocent smile,
Today I am a child…tomorrow I don't know what I'll be…
I don't know if I'll be fine, do not know if I win what I ever wanted…
I know that today I have to do…I have to learn…and maybe teach tomorrow…
Today we do not have an opinion.
Antonia Lobo, Grade 12
Charles Shea Sr High School, RI

My Mama Told Me

My Mama told me
there was no difference.
But when I look at your flowing
hair I don't see naps.
When I see your smooth hands,
I don't see your ancestors' years in the field.
When I look at your back
it is straight and proud,
not slouched from ridicule.
When you speak, the words flow perfectly,
you don't stumble with the accent of your home.
When I look at your creamy white skin, I don't see
the pain my dark skin has brought me.
Catherine Turner, Grade 11
Appomattox Regional Governor's School for Arts and Technology, VA

Meant to Be

As it is very clear to me,
I really wish that you could see,
The us, the we,
What we were meant to be.

I fall, you stand,
I fly, you land,
In my heart,
But we stand apart.

I'm all alone,
My love for you is unknown.
With my heart,
I'm not too smart,

I have loved you from the very start,
I never thought we'd be apart,
And end up here, why can't you see,
That we were always meant to be.

Ashley Pennington, Grade 10
Elkton High School, MD

I Am

I am beautiful and intelligent
I wonder what my future holds
I hear whistling in the wind
I see a bright future
I am beautiful and intelligent

I pretend to care about drama
I feel like a new woman
I touch the sky
I worry about being unsuccessful
I cry when I don't get my way
I am beautiful and intelligent

I understand life
I say good things come to those who wait
I dream about being rich
I try to do my best at everything
I hope to see my name in lights
I am beautiful and intelligent

Shania Tyler, Grade 12
Charles City County High School, VA

My Wonderful, Terrible Place

As my mind wanders through space,
it takes me to a place
that is weird, but interesting and fun.
There are dragons and trolls
that stay tucked in their holes
and trees that grow bubble gum.
The world's not all smiles,
there's mean crocodiles
that gobble you up in one bite,
and the witches that snicker
and gossip and bicker,
can take you away in the night.
Let's not stay on the bad side,
let's go to the glad side
where the warm sun caresses your face,
and the daisies sing
such beautiful things
in my wonderful, terrible place.

Cynthia Gana, Grade 11
Forest Park High School, VA

The Window

It's ten o' clock in the morning,
I jump into the car,
Staring out that window,
Hoping it's not too far,
Wondering what it will be like,
To lay on the golden beach,
To splash into the ocean,
With the crisp sand at my feet,
Bare feet on the pavement,
Staring at the sky,
Walking on that boardwalk,
Watching summer days fly by,
I've looked out that same window,
Through all the passing years,
Praying that golden beach
Never disappears.

Erin Nicole Barger, Grade 10
Norfolk Collegiate Middle/Upper School, VA

Definition of Poetry

Poetry is lame
For those who can't be blunt
Decide to hide behind words, what a shame
Looking for emotions on a hunt
Just say what needs to be said
Because no one wants to decipher you
Your indirect feelings are a source of dread
I don't want to know, if that's all you do
So drop the rhyme scheme
And your fancy style
It's time to dream
If not only for a while.

Christina Byers, Grade 11
Grassfield High School, VA

I Am

I am funny and unique
I wonder why life is so hard
I hear spirits talking
I see ghosts
I am funny and unique

I pretend to be mean
I feel love
I touch people in a good way
I worry about my brother
I cry when I see love and basketball
I am funny and unique

I understand everything can't go my way
I say stuff I don't mean
I dream of a great life
I try to make everybody happy
I hope my life is long and good
I am funny and unique

Demaj Frazier, Grade 12
Charles City County High School, VA

I Am

I am smart and beautiful…
I wonder what's my purpose in life…
I hear people cheering my name…
I see money…
I am smart and beautiful…

I pretend that I'm famous…
I feel excited about my future…
I touch the lives of others…
I worry that I'll fail in life…
I cry when people do not support me…
I am smart and beautiful…

I understand love…
I say whatever I feel…
I dream to find love…
I try to be an inspiration…
I hope to live life to the fullest…
I am smart and beautiful…

Jazmyn Miles, Grade 12
Charles City County High School, VA

I Am

I am outgoing and like to have fun…
I wonder why people take other people for granted…
I hear my daddy talking…
I see my daddy smiling…
I am outgoing and like to have fun…

I pretend that I don't care…
I feel that I will be very successful in life…
I touch the moon and the stars…
I worry that my little sister will be okay…
I cry when I reminisce about my daddy…
I am outgoing and like to have fun…

I understand what people go through…
I say 'one love'…
I dream that I will have a big happy family and get married…
I try to be the best man I can be…
I hope for a better day…
I am outgoing and like to have fun…

Rodney Bradby, Grade 12
Charles City County High School, VA

Forgotten Dreams

Streaming sunlight through
fogged attic windows, blurred with age.
Lonely, solitary.
Gray fluff snowflakes shimmer
in the sunlight,
a streamline of past ideas,
memories forgotten,
lost.
Rusting oak chests litter the
blanketed floorboards, hinges cracked.
Inside,
dreams, neglected, put away for later.
Dreams that linger in the warm attic air, like
an ancient perfume.
A perfume deadly and powerful;
Lost dreams
are the most
cogent
of poisons.

Joanna Morelli, Grade 11
Walsingham Academy Upper School, VA

Tired

Blank, empty, washed-out, colorless;
In essence, dead, while living…
Motionlessness, quiet, peace —
Things wanted — rarely achieved at that moment.

Hallucinating, paranoid, schizophrenic,
So much sensory input but
Unable to respond to the stimuli…
Or too far gone to care.

Late nights, early mornings,
Mental and physical strain from
Before dawn to after dusk.
So much straining, eventually something snaps.

Mindless repetition,
The hurt gone beyond the level of feeling,
To where all that is left is pain and the work to be accomplished,
Just waiting to stop, and let the darkness wash over you.

Amndeep Singh Mann, Grade 10
Thomas Jefferson High School for Science and Technology, VA

Blind Sight

I stare desperately, trying to see beyond the film
my eyes cast over the world.
To pull it back, for a moment,
to have all revealed in its purest form,
would be ecstasy.
My pupils dilate as light floods over me.
It is merely a glimpse of the blinding truth.
I cannot bear to see things as they really are.
It comes in flashes and then is gone.
Everything is as it was.
As it was when the lightning struck,
and I heard no thunder, felt no tingling in my bones.
As it was when the seas heaved beneath me,
and no qualm beset my fragile nerves.
My eyes blind, my ears deaf, and my touch weakened.
No feeling penetrates the guard of my soul,
nothing encroaches upon my wall of woven ignorance.
The storm rages and the world resounds with cries,
but I am safe deep within the niches of my being.

Katelyn Pryor, Grade 11
Forest Park High School, VA

Beach

The sun warms the sand
The sand is yielding and warm
It falls to the ocean
The ocean falls on the shore
The ocean and land meet

Nathaniel Andrew Miller, Grade 10
Norfolk Collegiate Middle/Upper School, VA

Lost Love

Sunshine warms her soul,
On the grass she lays her head.
She thinks of nothing,
But dreams of love in her heart,
The only thing missing now.

Hannah A. Sacks, Grade 10
Norfolk Collegiate Upper School, VA

Marine

The darkness of the night
Is his best friend.
The silence of his movement
Will strike the enemy with fright.

From 1000 meters he lies and waits
A single shot
Will take his target out
As the question remains what will be his fate

Shall he live to see another day
Or shall he dine behind hell's gates?
His life lies in the hands of his squad
And for their safety they pray.

For the safety and freedom of their country
They exchange words of encouragement
But non shall be more reassuring
Than those three short words
"SEMPER FI MARINE"

Shayne Jackson, Grade 10
Harford Technical High School, MD

The Void

Before a human may receive a name,
Before a man may learn to walk and speak,
Before a female may be taught in school,
Before the fetus sees the light of day,
All consciousness, all mem'ries, were naught but
Perpetu'l nothingness, without joy, nor
The icy clutch of sorrow, to be felt.
The rosy tinge of life could not be seen,
The morbid thought of death could not be known.
This place cannot be recognized or found,
It has defining features none, but starts
And ends the lives of those we knew and know.
This place is truly home to all of life,
The heav'n about which poets write and songs
Are made and all creation aims to find.
But life can never enter here without
Exper'encing its own demise, it sleeps.
But, still, this place, so undefined, will wait
For all of life to come back to its grasp,
For all of life to return to the void.

Robert Rust, Grade 11
Walsingham Academy Upper School, VA

Drifting

Dandelions sway in the tired breeze
Thousands of unanswered prayers trapped on your eyelashes
"Make a wish," you tell me
"Soon we'll be somewhere else."
Little feathers tiptoe away from me
And in a heartbeat, an exhalation of breath
They're gone
Drifting, drifting away
Into a burning sky that swallows wishes
One by one they disappear
There's a dull look in your eyes
Silver that hasn't been polished in years
A coffin that has been closed and nearly buried
Drifting, drifting away
But we anchor each other to this world
Where the sky and the future loom over our tiny wishes
Somewhere they'll take root
Somewhere half-formed dreams won't vanish in seconds
So you smile and blink at the sky
And the prayers ascend and drift away.

Rachel Chuang, Grade 11
Thomas Jefferson High School for Science and Technology, VA

I Am

I am outgoing and a very happy person
I wonder when I will die
    and when I will see Joseph Alexander Tabb again
I hear my father talking to me sometimes
I see bad things every day
I am outgoing and a very happy person

I pretend my father is still alive
I feel pretty good
I touch women
I worry about a dead man walking
I cry about death
I am the man

I understand what it takes to be a man
I say I am the man of the hour too sweet to be sour
I dream about my father
I try to do my best
I hope to succeed
I am outgoing and a very happy person

Joe Tabb, Grade 12
Charles City County High School, VA

Looking Up

Dark clouds far behind,
Sunshine shining up ahead,
Footsteps in the grass,
Beside me, you are holding
My hand leading me forward.

Ally G. Arbogast, Grade 10
Norfolk Collegiate Middle/Upper School, VA

Watery Grave

The refreshing plunge
as its blue surface breaks way
its glass appearance
shattered by my body grasping
pulling down to peaceful sleep

Dennis Lindberg, Grade 12
Forest Park High School, VA

Dead Railroad

Waiting for the end to come.
You my parental guidance.
You taught me how to hide.
You taught me how to seek.
You taught me how to ride my bike
In the front yard.
You kissed my knee
When it was scraped.
But you stopped dead in your tracks.
Your engine stalled.
And the coals burned out.
You don't talk anymore.
You don't listen anymore.
You sit there
And look at me like I'm inhuman.
So just stay out.
Stay in that place.
Stay out of my life
I don't need you anymore.
Just stay away I saw the end come
And the pain that came with it isn't worth the trouble.

Jamie DuVal, Grade 12
Delaware Military Academy, DE

A Day of School

We start our day with a simple bell ring
When all are here the hallways ring

The teachers are smart much knowledge they posses
To college we will go and hopefully impress

Our grades must be great we study all day
The tests we must take get us hopefully an A

Half through our day we all meet for lunch
We must wait in line and then we can munch

Back to class we go even though it is slow
We all sit quietly unless you're a bro

The day comes to a close when the last bell rings
All students are out the hallways sing

Christian Asam and Andrew Maynard, Grade 12
Norfolk Collegiate Middle/Upper School, VA

Sabi

Mind adrift,
her steps are silent
on the path littered with soft, perfect petals.
Layers of cloth so sheer
form a white gown that whispers over her skin.
She is hoping to greet spring.
When the cherry blossoms bloom.

Daphne Fong, Grade 11
Thomas Jefferson High School for Science and Technology, VA

I Am

I am a blue circle of light,
the iris that hides out of fear and fright.
From death I shall leap into the comfort of my own,
behind enemy lines I'd rather not call home.

I am familiar to where the willows do weep,
where whispers sing and shadows creep.
But see through the smile and into the mind
of a girl whose secrets are all locked inside.

I am a piano with a tune as mad as mercury
awaiting a maestro to tame this panicked fury.
There is a voice within, clear as a Pavlovian Bell,
screaming to be uncaged from its internal forlorn cell.

I am the one whose mouth forms the word
of a world unknown, dying to be heard.

Renee Lafond, Grade 12
Cranston High School East, RI

Mirror

Mirror, mirror on the wall
You watched my rise and you watched me fall
But what about you scares me so,
Is it the scars on me you show?
Or the mistakes I've displayed through time?
While others forgave me, I've still lost my shine
Do you know the pain I've felt?
That others have caused and evil has dealt
That made me who I am today?
It blows my mind and causes me to fray
So pardon if it makes me seem rude
But now you know why I avoid you
Because you bring to light my greatest fear
Dealing with the truths you mirror…

Amy Cunningham, Grade 12
Forest Park High School, VA

A Soul Bereft

My countenance falls as you stroll away.
Should not I be the one who is bereft?
Though I have always known that I would pay,
I cannot imagine this sort of theft.
So improbable, so clever and cruel.
Stab my breaking heart, oh my wicked one,
Please deride your naïve but constant fool.
What disappears but the fiery sun?
There is only coldness in this harsh land,
Grieving for the dreary grave of my heart.
Salt and honey too taste so very bland,
My feelings and desires do depart.
On the shore will the calming waves still swell,
On this treachery I promise to dwell.

Hannah Bendfeldt, Grade 12
Turner Ashby High School, VA

I Am

I am cunning and awesome
I wonder if you knew that
I hear roars in agreement
I see a crowd
I am cunning and awesome

I pretend to speak in front of a crowd
I feel power
I touch water
I worry it will boil
I cry because I have tremors
I am cunning and awesome

I understand to be conservative is to have common sense
I say democrats are communist
I dream everyone sees the light
I try to inform all
I hope to become big
I am cunning and awesome

Dale Hutchinson, Grade 12
Charles City County High School, VA

The Seasons

the leaves fall slowly
as the new year dies
the leaves grow slowly
the only ones to survive.
the water flows swiftly
Ice in liquid form
veins frozen
cracked
with blood.
grass cut
bruised and sweet
like apples of bygone years
the sun blazes through deserts of joy
and the year dies again.

Margaret Hu, Grade 11
Thomas Jefferson High School for Science and Technology, VA

My Monarch, My Viceroy

My graceful monarch, my handsome butterfly flies
From milkweed to more, so lovely, colors so bright
How I love to watch as he flutters by my sill.
Even the birds look, looking with their beady eyes,
They would love to make a snack of my butterfly.
They don't, they look on, for my monarch is poison,
Even I am careful, my monarch is dangerous.

My viceroy flies, my handsome butterfly lives,
Hopping plant to plant, he is not troubled by birds.
He is like my monarch, just as gracefully handsome,
Colors just as bright. I love my viceroy much more
For though they look the same, only he cannot hurt me.

AnnaLea Clayton-Schwartz, Grade 10
Forest Park High School, VA

Happy Birthday

Today is the day you become another year older
Beautiful and smart but so much bolder.
Shining as bright as the stars in the sky
Today is your day set your standards high.

Higher than you ever have before
Get all dressed up so everyone can adore.
Adore your beauty when your night begins to start
Hope all your happiness and smiles feel your heart.

I want this day to be the best day ever
I don't want you to forget it not now, not ever.
I hope you love all the presents you get
And hope you enjoy and appreciate all of it.

So from me to you I say Happy Birthday
I hope you enjoy every second today.
Just want you to know I Love You
And hope you feel the same way too!

James Langham, Grade 11
Forest Park High School, VA

Empty

Silence is golden,
Many would say.
A window is open.
Memories flown away.

Plastic covers a living room,
Not a sound, not even a boom.
Dust, spider webs, a mother's nightmare,
Slight movements others are not aware.

Silence is golden,
Many would say.
Once a home, where no cobwebs were woven,
Now a grave, where no one will lay.

Thao Huynh, Grade 11
Woodbridge Senior High School, VA

Stand for Love

I take back everything I've said,
The thoughts that occurred in my head
Such pain in my heart
I plead for a clean start
Eyes revealing the pain
Love so true, can something remain
How could love bring so much pain
Here I am

Here I stand, back at point one
I fight, me and love, one on one

You're not like anyone

Katherine Arnett, Grade 11
New Directions Alternative Education Center, VA

High Merit Poems – Grades 10, 11, and 12

Road to Adulthood

As I open my eyes, every single day, I'm one step closer to my own predestined freedom. But with such a great accomplishment comes a great responsibility. As my family realizes that this "birdie" is ready to take his flight. Ya know momma bird isn't all right. As I soar to greatness and follow my own passage, and make a Mrs. Birdie with little birdies, no matter how old, far, or productive I can and will be. This birdie will always know you have been there for me. As I turn that legal age and walk across that stage, and leave the nest so I can construct my own, I'll have my own insight for what I think is best, for my family, myself and anyone else.

DeAndre Weaver, Grade 12
Dinwiddie High School, VA

Art Work

my fingers shake as the ink drips off
the lines are fluid but hasty looking
rushed and imperfect, just like me

the ink bleeds deep into my pores,
turning the luscious peach skin
into a dark and twisted structure

my muscles are rigid like a statue —
a perfect representation of my heart
sculpted from the hands who hurt me the most

thoughts have bled onto my body
words oozing out of every crack in my skin
words of ugly, shameless thoughts

every stroke of the mental brush
is so dull, so colorless, so ugly…

art is supposed to be beautiful,
but how can it be beautiful
when the one who created the art is ugly?

my body is my canvas,
full of ink already from my past
so wash my skin clean and make me new
for i yearn to be a beautiful piece of art

Victoria Shuklis, Grade 11
Dinwiddie High School, VA

Mother Lake

The baby duckling is now born
Her first push in, the water is torn
The first time she gets wet she isn't afraid
Because she knows her life, you will safely aid
You will carry her as she floats and she will not drown
Easily, with no trouble, as if she weighs less than a pound
You will protect her as you did her mother
No mammal can reach her, or any other
Your love for her is a motherly love
Sent to you straight from the heavens above
You rock her in your arms until she's ready to leave
And bring back a family of her own, is what you believe
You clean her off and watch her grow
All this you think as she travels slow

Marquita Mitchell, Grade 11
Southampton High School, VA

The Silent Scream*

The chilling ocean is restless and ominous,
The flaming orange sunset seeps into the sea,
An aged wooden pier stands sturdy and brawny,
The ultimate picture of life's simplicity.

But what is on the pier with a face so distraught?
The face that portrays uncertainty and fear,
The face that provokes trepidation,
The face that is on the pier.

The face on the pier belongs to a man,
Whose cries seep into the sea,
His screams are silent in the imminent evening,
Without a soul to hear his plea.

The picture feverishly exhibits,
The feeling of uncertainty that people of society face,
The need of security — a helping hand,
The need of a warm fiery embrace.

The screaming man is iconic,
Spreading the need for change within the outlook on life,
Allowing society to know one is not alone,
With regard to facing the world of strife.

Hailey Lane, Grade 10
Midlothian High School, VA
*Analysis of Edvard Munch's "Painting the Scream"

Unrequited Love

Bright golden illumination; pale creamy glimmer
A hot wildfire; a cool waterfall
Splashes of color; shades of monochrome
Loud and playful; silent and sober
Life and vitality; sleep and lethargy
Deer frolicking; crickets chirping
A rushing river; a trickling stream
A lack of feeling; a shortcoming of hope
Longing for his sweetheart; yearning for her soulmate
Glimpsing her delicate shine; admiring his strong rays
Over the seas; over the mountains
Never to meet; doomed by fate
A constant desire; an eternal love
Wasted on the world; thrown to the lands
Meant for his moon; intended for her sun
Unrequited love; unrequited love

Megan Anderson, Grade 11
Millbrook High School, VA

I Am

I am a great DJ and a unique dancer…
I wonder how my future will turn out…
I hear my turntables scratching…
I see a great future ahead of me…
I am a great DJ and a unique dancer…

I pretend that I am the greatest DJ alive…
I feel my heart beating to the music I play…
I touch my mixer:
I cry when I miss my aunt and uncle…
I am a great DJ and a unique dancer…

I understand life is complicated…
I say I am going to school for music…
I dream that I am a marvelous drummer which I am…
I try to keep my attitude under control…
I hope I have a great future…
I am a great DJ and a unique dancer…

Gregory Cotman, Grade 12
Charles City County High School, VA

Nice Guys Finish Last

Nice guys finish last
Debts repaid are things of the past
To be nice is to be forgotten
Being used will leave you a taste that is rather rotten
Like a vampire youth
People will suck you dry
Thinking of only their personal gain
They leave you to die
At the bottom of the pile
All you will ever know, the bowels of hell
Lend me your ear curious listener
I have a secret to tell
Being kind is not a crime
As for being too nice
I did my time

Kyle Sulecki, Grade 10
Delaware Military Academy, DE

The Noise

thunder
a battered textbook hitting the floor
the locker being slammed in an empty hallway
a glass vase
falling
shattering into seven jagged pieces on the floor
crickets chirping
a truck blaring its horn
traveling down a bustling street
centered in a restless night
The Noise
like the ocean smashing against jagged rocks
it roars in her ears

Sharmayne Miller, Grade 11
Eleanor Roosevelt High School, MD

Salty-Sweet

Hands gliding like the wind across its stiff amber skin,
I begin to reminisce.
Once climbed and relaxed in the crevice of its sweet
sugar smelling trunks,
reminding me of a warm winter time breakfast.
I hold on to its comforting memory.
    SNAP!
The memory and bark break from my hands.
This bark that was rough at the surface is now
Soft and flimsy in my hands.
It has apologized for not being the shelter
It once was,
And has brought me to reality.
Disappointed, I descend the tree.
Amongst looking back, I take in its halo of blacks, grays, and green
Roots spreading every which way into the frail earth.
Burrowed into the ground, arms extending above, never ending,
It calls me for an embrace once more.

Nkongho Beteck, Grade 12
Wicomico High School, MD

Moon's Heart

As Moon rises in the darkened night sky,
A lonely heart beats for one far away.
Insides feel empty, as though they might die.
Wind whispers through the trees as if to say,
"Love will return but not this night or day."
Moon sleeps and stars appear frozen in time,
Watching from above; chased by Sun's bright rays.
He left me empty, I thought he was mine.
Young and restless; in the peak of our prime,
With him I was happy, nothing was barred.
When together, passion, nothing sublime;
Without him I'm lifeless, a forest charred.
    It seems like forever we've been apart.
I hope someday, Moon, you will heal my heart.

Sarah Kramb, Grade 11
Liberty High School, MD

The Purest Love

My love for you is like a river that never ends
It sprawls and grows every day
Winding and turning around bends
I know it will never go away
It swirls through my head like a fog of smoke
Coiling and twisting around
I feel like it is my only blanket of hope
Because it's the purest love I've found
You're my only sense of security
My only sense of protection
My only hope in its purity
Everything else has been a product of deflection
I know I'll never ever lose it,
My love and passion for my music

Nakia Solomon, Grade 10
Turner Ashby High School, VA

I Am

I am funny and down to earth…
I wonder why humans can't break the laws
 of what's real and what's not…
I hear voices…
I see angels…
I am funny and down to earth…

I pretend to be a boxer…
I feel an angel touch…
I touch people's souls…
I worry about getting hurt…
I cry over lost life…
I am funny and down to earth…

I understand how life goes on…
I say mother…
I dream about girls…
I try to graduate…
I hope for my mother to get better…
I am funny and down to earth…
Wilbert Walker, Grade 12
Charles City County High School, VA

Graveyard Bleach

Silent whispers of the past,
Continue to speak to nothing but the wind.
All was forgotten by us who can breathe.
Unknown by the light,
The restless spirits of the night.

Forever they lay in the dark time of death,
Not to be seen by humans again,
For they are just a memory.
Lost in death's evil laugh and grin,
The ghost of the soul of one sin.

Crying out to be heard,
Those who never lived,
Those who create a fog.
The only place they can reach,
Is within the silent Graveyard Bleach.
Eliza Kulick, Grade 11
Forest Park High School, VA

Never Ending Game

Lies are spread over the table,
 you take your pick,
 I pick my own, though,
 when I'll use them is as mysterious
 as when you will.
This game hurts us both,
 but we can't wait for the next round,
 hoping the cards will be better
 and in turn, so will our façades.
Elena Rivera, Grade 11
Forest Park High School, VA

Nightmare

Screaming, panting, as I rushed into the woods
Chased out of my resting place
By the sounds of the disturbing night, my bare feet snapping branches
As the pain went through me
Calling out for help
But all that returned to me
was the fearful echoes of my cries in the distance
So I run, run to escape the fearful grip of death
My mind must be playing games
Playing a movie that brings evil memories
But I am in it, and there is no way out
Voices of the dead, principalities
And powers of the air, wailing in my head
I cannot get it out; they seem to have control of me
I just want everything to go away, I want to go home.
They surrounded me, putting an end to my escape
Ready to feast on my flesh, my screams pull me out
Screaming, panting, as I jerked out of bed
Falling into the waiting arms of my mother
Who assures me of safety
But this tale of horror, only I could tell.
James Adenekan, Grade 12
Charles Shea Sr High School, RI

The Dream

Passion.
A necessity in any type of situation.
Without passion there is no love, and without love,
We have nothing.
Everyone has their inspiration,
Their reason for existence.
My day revolves around a single purpose, a motif.
For every note that I play,
Every concert that I perform,
Every audition that I succeed,
I strive for my future,
My dream,
My life.
When I see myself as a middle aged and gray haired woman,
I see a darkness, yet blinding white lights.
Surrounded by midnight black dresses and tuxedoes,
The instruments of the symphony will reflect and shine bright beneath the spot lights.
This is a whole new level.
Gone is the high school level,
Gone is the collegiate level,
Welcome, to the professional level.
Genevieve Salamone, Grade 12
Forest Park High School, VA

Embracing Our Comrades (Sijo)

A life willing, a life breathing, as their own world struggles.
Their eyes shed tears. Their passion is lost. Mourning. They cry alone.
Yet we still love, we can still help, those who have given up. Embracing.
Richard Buka III, Grade 12
Forest Park High School, VA

I Am

I am a rapper and explorer...
I wonder what's out there in the world...
I hear waves...
I see new surroundings...
I am a rapper and explorer...

I pretend to rap on a large stage...
I feel drawn to something...
I touch something new...
I worry that I want to be the one...
I cry in the inside...
I am a rapper and explorer...

I understand there's a difficult road...
I say believe in yourself...
I dream for a new world for me...
I try to make something happen...
I hope to get there one day...
I am a rapper and explorer...

Quentin Williams, Grade 12
Charles City County High School, VA

Grasping the Unreal

Each dawn brings a new possibility.
As I stand alone in peaceful serenity,
The dew springs forth from weeping grass.
I do not want the moment to pass.
The gentle breeze kisses my face,
This will be my final resting place.
My hair dances in the air around my head.
No word must be said, instead,
I close my eyes and breathe in slow.
Please don't make me go.
I open my eyes and see the truth,
The cruel and twisted terrible truth.
The noises break through my thoughts.
I struggle to break free but all for naught.
Fear grips me to the heart,
And slowly drags me to depart.
So I'm left gasping, grasping the unreal.

Shaune Young, Grade 10
Harford Christian School, MD

Red

As I sleep in my bed
All I see is red
The blood of my ancestors generation
That lives through my eyes
The secret spies of their life
Of how they were slaves
But brave enough to live
In the under caves
So as I see my eyes filled of red
I remember that I am in my bed

Katelyn Bowman, Grade 10
Forestville Military Academy, MD

Cancer

Little by little you have taken my strength away
you make me feel as weak as a cornered prey when chased by its predator,
I want to escape but you have me surrounded.
I feel like I can't take it anymore, like I can't go on,
Then look at myself in the mirror and my skin as white as fallen snow.
Feels like you're my enemy, but this is not a nightmare
I won't wake up, I won't stand up, and the worst is that I won't escape
I try to take a breath, but it's like my lungs don't work anymore
I want to explain how I feel but you would never know.
Tired of asking myself what I've ever done to deserve this illness,
That seems too bad, this is a battle that I won't give up to fight,
I got to give my everything to stand up and face
Face what I really have.
Some people survive this
I wonder if I am
Because many people died too
I wonder if I would be one
I try not to be negative, but is hard to forget, that you
killed my father, my mother, and my friend.
This is a feeling that I can't express maybe I would be remembered
I would never know maybe people would forget that I was even born.

Lady Brito, Grade 11
Charles Shea Sr High School, RI

Let's Show Our Appreciation

Come with me on this beautiful rainy day
Where clouds are big black and gray
I ask myself
Why aren't the children out today?
I understand we normally come out when the sun is present and play
But let's be different and enjoy nature while we can
And allow the rain to hit our faces when we stand
Because no one is really sure how long we have left on this wonderful land
Nowadays many eccentric events are occurring mainly because of man
We know what we need to do
But steadily using new technology and old ways
Instead of separation and killing our nature, we need to congregate these days
Nature is crying and warning us and we constantly take it for granted
The causes are coming from our hands
We need to quickly enforce change for the sake of the land

Donae Owens, Grade 11
Benjamin Banneker Academic High School, DC

Depression

the feeling of depression settles into your soul.
walking around, head down, hands in your pockets, feeling nothing.
headphones in music up, holding back the tears,
passing your friends in the hall, no energy or happiness to say hi.
deep breaths trying to breath.
hoping and wishing for the pain to leave.
searching for the happiness I once had.

Jordan Correll, Grade 10
Johnston Sr High School, RI

Mystery
Mystery moves the soul and the mind
Stimulate the tiny moments in the brisk of time
Chaos and winds seems so equal and true
the time between loving and hating you
The time when unknown is quite evident
Is this living hell or heaven sent?
Has mystery blinded me of the depth of time?
Mystery the elapse of unfortunate thoughts in minds
Trickery yet beautiful as a day of joy
Scenery and young souls with flowers and toys
Time grabs you with both hands and chokes your spirit
The mystery of life is just as beautiful as ballad lyrics
Smooth crisp emotionally obtained
Spills out the love the hurt the shame
But if only mystery could be understood
And well get the point only mystery could
It makes no sense yet it's a lesson learn
To grasp the attention mystery earns
For everyone to yearn to understand you
And to hold back the truth like mystery can only do.
Emoni Matthews, Grade 11
Woodbridge Sr High School, VA

That Special One
Throughout a lifetime,
Of happiness and treachery;
People come and go,
Erasing from your memory.
Family members, lovers,
All evolving into your past;
Dreaming, wondering, wishing,
Why couldn't they all last?
On the upside of things,
You might find that special one;
Who makes you think to yourself,
"I've finally won."
They make you laugh,
They make you cry;
In all actuality,
They help you to survive.
It will take time,
To find that perfectly perfect person;
But when you do,
Always know that you will never lose, only win.
Holly Horsky, Grade 10
Delaware Military Academy, DE

Regrets
I forgot to tell him
How much I always loved him
Just how much I care
Wonder if he's figured out
I'm not me when he's not there
Kira Jersild, Grade 10
Norfolk Collegiate Middle/Upper School, VA

I Am
I am fun and respectful…
I wonder how college will be…
I hear the voices of people telling me to do the right thing…
I see a bright future for myself…
I am fun and respectful…

I pretend to be happy even when I'm not…
I feel my granddad watching over me…
I touch the key to my future…
I worry about how my anger affects people…
I cry when I think about my granddad…
I am fun and respectful…

I understand that everything happens for a reason…
I say that attitude is everything…
I dream about my future…
I try to treat people how I want them to treat me…
I hope that people can see God in me…
I am fun and respectful…
Amber Adkins, Grade 12
Charles City County High School, VA

I Am
I am quiet and smart…
I wonder why I am so short…
I hear sea waves splashing together…
I see me in the past…
I am quiet and smart…

I pretend it is actually the last day of school…
I feel bad for homeless people…
I touch…
I worry about my family…
I cry when I'm mad or sad…
I am quiet and smart…

I understand that you need to study to pass…
I say what don't kill you makes you stronger…
I dream about meeting Lebron James…
I try to pass all the tests I come to…
I hope I graduate high school this year…
I am quiet and smart…
James Earley, Grade 12
Charles City County High School, VA

The Love of a Mother
The love a mother is like
The peace of a nature, is like
The nature is the second mother
Like the green forest ridge and
The deep royal lagoon and the air
Like a kiss of a mother during sleep
And the white clouds with the
Sky sail blue is a place to have peace.
Omar Mejia, Grade 12
Charles Shea Sr High School, RI

Waving Hands

Red and black and blue and green ink stains dry skin
and smears into sinuous trickles,
and flows across the flat plains of flesh,
and sweetly glistens on the subtle ridges of my fingertips.

A tsunami of fingers,
the froth crowned by stubby fingernails,
gleaming with the stain of stubborn nail polish,
crashes onto the flesh colored shore
before the tide ebbs and my fingers stretch up.

My hand stretches skyward,
the ridges and soft abrasions jutting into sharp relief,
every tributary and stream open to inspection from my eagle eye,
the aerial view of the Everglades.

Underneath the mottled landscape of red and white,
an underground river flows;
pooling from the placid lagoons near my fingertips, as blood,
and therefore touch,
and therefore love,
flows from its peaceful confines
towards the rushing waterfall of my heart.

Chandini Jha, Grade 11
Walt Whitman High School, MD

'Til Death Do Us Part

The touch of your lips
Brings me closer to you
With your hands on my hips
Oh what things we do

I hold on no matter what we go through
Because you're my king
I feel I have nothing to prove
With you I can do anything

Now when that bell rings
And it's your time to go
I'll hold on to everything
And let no emotions show

We vowed that time and death would do us part
So the love I have for you is forever in my heart

Jenn'Asia Wheeler, Grade 12
Franklin Military School, VA

Memories

The best memories reach the heart
so you know you and your friends are never truly apart
it brings a smile to your face
to think of you all at your special place
way back when on some magnificent day
when you and your friends used to play

Amy Phillips, Grade 12
Menchville High School, VA

No Objection

Okay, let's talk about candy
and spiders.
Why?
Because they're
provocative. Horrifying. Tantalizing.
If you found spiders in your candy,
you'd scream, wouldn't you?
Jump back and trip, fall.
Scramble onto the counter.
Yell the name of a husband or father or brother
to get in here and squish them, squish them, squish them dead!

Spiders are hairy and long-limbed,
true, but what I fear about them most is the way they disappear —
one minute they're there, coming dangerously close,
and the next it's gone, until someone whispers
it's on your head/shoulder/leg —
and suddenly nowhere is sacred, nothing is safe.

Candy, on the other hand, is sweet.
Delightful and subtly poisonous.

Madeline Monk, Grade 11
Woodbridge Sr High School, VA

I Am

I am very strong minded and inquisitive
I wonder why people take things for granted
I hear a classmate talking about a whole lot of nothing
I see better days in my future
I am very strong minded and inquisitive

I pretend to listen when my mother YELLS!
I feel overwhelmed
I touch the cool air blowing
I worry about too many worthless things
I am very strong minded and inquisitive

I understand why students go completely off on teachers
I say I will be successful and mean it
I dream of walking the street and handing out money
I hope my dream comes true
I am very strong minded and inquisitive

Kanesha Jones, Grade 12
Charles City County High School, VA

Spring of 2004

The beautiful, yellow honeysuckles,
They flow in the wind and the scent goes with it.
The girls, Summer and Autumn, breathe in
The scents, as they dance in the
Yard along the fence.
Their lips were puckered and red,
From sucking the juice out of the
Honeysuckles.

Hana Meyer, Grade 10
Woodbridge Sr High School, VA

The Zen War

When do you let go
Of all you all you have become,
All you've come to know,
Of all you've ever done?

How do you turn out
The stars shining so bright,
Helping see past doubt,
And guiding through the night?

Why do you leave behind this world
Which you have grown to love,
Letting its image become swirled,
And your soul become void of?

What do you have to share,
Final words before you fade,
Truths that you've come to bear,
And secrets you'd never say?

But I've one final question
Before you turn to leave,
Has this all just been a lesson,
Or do you still believe?

Tavia Burden, Grade 10
Liberty High School, VA

Make You Smile

Dearest Love,
I will always be here for you.
When you have no one left to count on,
I'll be the single thing you can rely on,
I promise to always make you smile.

I'm never far away,
I'll always be right by your side,
So whenever you need me,
You'll know right where to find me,
I promise to always make you smile.

I hope you can feel the love,
As it rushes from my veins to yours.
I hope you feel the happiness,
Like rainbows shooting through you.
I never want to see you down,
I promise to always make you smile.

Cassandra Hagan, Grade 10
Harford Technical High School, MD

Summer

The soft breeze spreads heat.
There is nothing but free time.
The bright sunlight glows.

Becca Lynn Robinson, Grade 10
Norfolk Collegiate Middle/Upper School, VA

Cheers to All

Cheers to the lies you manifest in your head. The assumptions that let words go unsaid
Cheers to the years you let slide away, because you were off somewhere else
You refused to stay. Cheers to the faces in the halls
That go unnoticed until they seem to disappear all in all.
Cheers to the millions of dollars thrown away, instead of using them in
Africa or in some other way. Cheers to the boldness in my voice,
As I choose to voice my voice, because I have a choice.
Cheers to the silence that seems to creep in the middle of the night
The silence so strong you feel as though you can no longer hold on.
Cheers to the family torn to pieces because of lust the must of reason.
Cheers to the children without a mom or dad.
The ones who've gone through the hell of being an orphan.
To being adopted by a mom who shouldn't be a mom.
Cheers to the depressed kids with no one who understands.
Because being depressed is a disease that seems to be contagious
So easy to catch as the flu with a sneeze.
Cheers to me and you,
Cheers to him and her,
Cheers to the speechless left in my voice.
Because you left me speechless
With no voice.

Sara Urquia, Grade 11
Woodbridge Sr High School, VA

I Don't Understand

I don't understand
Why the world's great, climate of hate, rages unrestrained
Pulling us in while it tosses us out
I don't understand
Why all of the good times, always pass us by, leaving us far behind
Trying to play catch up but getting knocked down
Yeah I don't understand
Just why I must, be forced to give up, all of the stuff
That makes me who I am
I don't understand
Why a country that's stolen, has no problem rollin', in to stop you from strollin'
After certain hours of the night
I don't understand
Why I can't give a hug, to someone that I love, just because I'm in public
These are some of the things that I don't understand.

Darius Bergeron, Grade 11
Forest Park High School, VA

The River of My City

The old structured red bricks, stand quiet and lonely.
The buildings are beside the angry river, rushing down all the streets of the city,
with the black silver and greenish color from the nearby trees.
The rolling river offering the city many natural resources for the enjoyment of the people,
and inspired by its creator, Samuel Slater, and the old valuable Slater Mill.
For me it, isn't just a river.
It symbolizes the harvest in the old days and the hearth of the city.
It shows how men used creativity and hard work to avail the natural resources of nature.
A river that gave hope to my city.

Ieltsin Dias, Grade 11
Charles Shea Sr High School, RI

I Am

I am smart and loud…
I wonder why gas prices are so high…
I hear crickets chirp…
I see me in the future…
I am smart and loud…

I pretend to ride dirt bike…
I feel sad for some people…
I touch my dreams every day…
I worry about people that are sick…
I cry for people that suffer for no reason…
I am smart and loud…

I understand that life is short…
I say what don't kill me makes me stronger…
I dream about me being successful…
I try to be successful…
I hope to graduate…
I am smart and loud…

Herman Miles, Grade 12
Charles City County High School, VA

I Am

I am outgoing and funny…
I wonder about my future…
I hear the sound of my drum…
I see the batter as I pitch the baseball…
I am outgoing and funny…

I pretend that I care…
I feel that I am the best at whatever I do…
I touch my drum sticks…
I worry about nothing…
I cry when I'm hurt…
I am outgoing and funny…

I understand that I have a gift…
I say that I can do whatever I put my mind to…
I dream about life…
I try to succeed…
I hope I will achieve my goals…
I am outgoing and funny…

Jeffrey Johnson, Grade 12
Charles City County High School, VA

What Is Peace

What is peace when there's war?
What is love when there's hate?
Why is it that people betray?
Why can't this world be a perfect place?
Why is this lifetime such a struggle?
but why so many questions
and we're left with blanks
People stare into your secrets
whispers so loud and screams so quiet
Although happiness is rare,
anger overrules and chaos erupts inside my eyes
Rage is what my life has become
but the one thing that bothers me the most
is why can't anyone answer the questions
that I want to know the most?

Breanah Cole, Grade 10
Independence Secondary School, VA

Dove Isabeau

With her, my heart hurts the very least.
A magnificent beauty; fell in love with the beast.
Though she has left, in a fashion
My heart still burns with a fiery passion.
The stereotypical angel from above,
I'll forever give her my undying love.
Her humor is undying,
Together, I feel like I'm flying.
Her gaze is ever blaring,
And though it seems like she's uncaring,
Her personality is that like none before
Her heart, to me, is an open door.
With the eyes of a lion and the heart of a knight,
With sorrow, crying, she'd still get up and fight.
And in her eyes, I will start and finish there, too.
For as long as I see them, to HER I'll be true.

Isabeau Hickman, Grade 11
Forest Park High School, VA

Cliffhanger

Learned my lesson
Won't go there again
Done trying
A path too worn
Last time I traveled it I fell off
Time before I caused an avalanche
Broke my own legs
Near dug my own grave
Time for a new mountain
Too bad this one's too big to see past
And the ones behind me are too much trouble
Mistakes not to be made again

Jeremiah Watts, Grade 10
Leonardtown High School, MD

Image in a Mirror

I stand there
Looking at the image that stares back at me.
I stare harder,
And the image seems invincible
All I can think of there and then,
Is how unconquerable this image appears to be.
The strangest thing is that the image tries to overcome my moves
And the worst fact is,
The image succeeds.
So I decide to walk away,
From the image that never goes astray.

Nana Asihene, Grade 11
Forest Park High School, VA

I Am

I am odd and out of place…
I wonder what's for lunch…
I hear night fairies laughing…
I see dragons in the stars…
I am odd and out of place…

I pretend I am anywhere but here…
I feel the scrape of fangs on my skin…
I touch the soft fur of a chupacabra…
I worry about normality…
I cry when Darth Vader dies…
I am odd and out of place…

I understand that no one understands me…
I say the dark side has cookies…
I dream of total world domination…
I try to do what I like…
I hope one day to defeat Bowser…
I am odd and out of place…

Sara Miles, Grade 12
Charles City County High School, VA

I Am

I am smart and beautiful…
I wonder how the future will be…
I hear fairy dust falling all around…
I see rainbows…
I am smart and beautiful…

I pretend I'm a millionaire…
I feel the glitter of the stars raining down on me…
I touch the clouds way up high…
I worry about my mother passing away…
I cry about my pass…
I am smart and beautiful…

I understand that life isn't easy…
I say heaven is a beautiful place…
I dream about being successful…
I try my best in wanting to pass…
I hope to see nick soon…
I am smart and beautiful…

Brittany Ferguson, Grade 12
Charles City County High School, VA

The Stargazer

The eye crinkled shut foretells
Worlds far apart, and yet so near
And what wonders shall be beheld
In that great brass looking glass
Held so dear.
And the lips slightly parted reveal,
The night is favorable to thy gaze,
Far into realms a lifetime away.

Kaitlin O'Brien, Grade 12
Forest Park High School, VA

Why Me

Rebels stormed their own land
Killing sinful and innocent souls,
Women and young girls getting raped.
Forced to watch my family get killed
Turned me to a child soldier and drugs.

I followed orders and just kill on sight.
Killing more people than my age (ten)
Destroying my motherland for no reason.
But finally the war came to an end.
There is so much pain in my heart,
Am now left alone in the dark.

I know it's too late to reverse the past,
It's too late to blame it on faith.
Money cannot restore what I had before
I have been through too much, I cry no more,
So much regrets run through my mind.
I always ask God why me.

Sheku Janneh, Grade 12
Osbourn High School, VA

The Afghani Girl

A young girl,
Her face hidden beneath scarves,
Watches her world fall apart.

A boy throwing
Jagged stones at his sister,
No respect left for her.

Battle noises in
The distance,
Men meeting God or Allah.

Her mother falls
To her knees,
Begging her husband not to strike her.

And the girl,
Wrapped in scarves watches,
And she listens, as her life leaks from her eyes.

Kaitlyn Allen, Grade 11
Dinwiddie High School, VA

Summer Seas

Pretty colored seas
That are dark, clear, and blue
In the summer air
The new house by the sea
With the blue sea behind it.

Arnold G. Budagov, Grade 10
Norfolk Collegiate Middle/Upper School, VA

I Am

I am caring and strong...
I wonder what is the meaning of everything...
I hear the wind singing to me...
I see ponies dancing in the rain...
I am caring and strong...

I pretend to be a movie star...
I feel the sun rays against my skin...
I touch the heart of a loved one...
I worry that it won't be a good day...
I cry because my grandmother is gone...
I am caring and strong...

I understand nobody is perfect...
I say forgive but never forget...
I dream for peace, joy, love, and happiness...
I try to succeed in life...
I hope for a better tomorrow...
I am caring and strong...

Whitney Branch, Grade 12
Charles City County High School, VA

Ashes

Light peeping through the blinds
paints stripes on the sliver of incense
in my dark, dim room.

My finger swirls through the thread of smoke.
It caresses me, then
unweaves,
giving rise to scores of silvery strands.

Longing, sinewy fingers reach up,
diffusing into a hoary haze,
specks of sunlight shimmering throughout.

I blow on the faint orange ember below.
It brightens, but, just as suddenly,
disappears.

All that's left is
ashes

Jane Plummer, Grade 12
St. Elizabeth High School, DE

False Idols

I believed in you
I held you high
You took in the form of a halo
On your sacred pedestal
Did it hurt when you fell to the ground?
I watched you shatter into pieces, fragments, lies
We built you up
Only to watch you crumble and break
Everything I once knew has vanished
Starting anew
I learned my lesson
Never again will I trust your bold faced lies
You spit them out so sincerely
Sick to see who you deceived
They cry out in pain
But I won't shed a tear for you

Zoe Cain, Grade 12
Forest Park High School, VA

The Skin I'm In

There are days that I hate it,
This skin I'm in.
It itches
It chafes
It just feels so wrong.
Some days it's too uptight,
Won't budge an inch
Won't let me breathe
It feels like it's trying to suffocate me.
Some days it stretches too far out,
Pulling me in every direction one can possibly imagine
Stretching me past the points of my limits with no end in sight.
There are never any days when it feels 'just right'
Like it belongs on me, to me.
Can't someone help me find a skin that belongs to no one but me?

Erin Mabray, Grade 12
Forest Park High School, VA

My Future

So the good guys win the war
So the military was there for us
They were always ready to fight for us
Willing to lay their lives down for us
Every day of their lives
Ready at a moments notice
To defend the USA
I will join them
Ready to fight
To serve my country
Waiting, poised at cliffs edge

Tim O'Connor, Grade 11
New Directions Alternative Education Center, VA

how

how do you live life feeling alone
how can you breathe when you're on your own
can your heart bear to be lonely
have you ever wondered who is your one and only
the answer is that you want out
you think of love and you're filled with doubt
your heart is heavy it weighs a ton
you wonder why what have you done
you feel abandoned there's no where to turn
craving love and forever yearn
for a body to hold
not two but one makes it amazingly cold

Anthony Mikulskis, Grade 10
Johnston Sr High School, RI

The Faceless Man

I walk along my street often
More than once I encounter a man
He wears a long tan trench coat with a tan hat
His head is always faced down I never see his face

I encounter him wherever I go
He follows close behind me but says nothing
When I approach him he disappears
I am determined to discover him

One day he was following close behind me
I swiftly turned to catch him
He was there
Staring into my face
He had no need for eyes, a nose, a mouth or ears

As he stared my head began to ache
I heard loud screaming delivering to me agonizing pain
I blacked out
When I awoken I looked into my mirror

I have no face
No eyes, no nose, no mouth or ears
I search frantically for that man
But he is gone

Kyle Bauer, Grade 12
Meade Sr High School, MD

Of Thunder

Of thunder they came
With lightning they struck
In thrashings they harnessed the whippings of us
Toiled in pain
Tormented insane
We felt the power of pain
And were justly enraged

Of thunder they came
Took me and my brothers away
Enslaved we were sold
To households of gold
Held captive we worked until the day grew old

I've lived alive but was always dead inside

Of thunder I will come
Not afraid of whom I ever was
From my home to the field
I will step to heavens gate
To the show the thunder that has burned inside me
And the lightning that has scarred my body
To tell God of my story
Of thunder and pain

Gaston Touafek, Grade 10
Bishop Hendricken High School, RI

Love's Revenge

Night is here,
But you are not.
I trace the thought.
I wonder if you know
You stole the beating of my heart.
Do you keep track of things like that? Or do you just move on?
Another girl, another night, and the same old, same old song.
You broke something that can't be fixed,
Can't be seen or held.
You chipped away at the piece of me
Destined for someone else.
If I find the one that was to be mine,
But not so anymore,
I'll find the dungeon in which you reside,
And like darkness I will glide
Until I'm standing at your side
Looking down.
Silence is my cloak of choice,
But may you see my face.
Know that in this cold, hard world,
Karma still has a place.

Alexa Marshall, Grade 10
Home School, MD

Fly Away

Sometimes, I want to fly away.
Fly away, from all the hurt, pain, and despair.
I want to escape my rainy days,
and the fear that nobody cares.
I dream of fleeing my struggles and trials,
and overcoming my storms.
I long to escape this jungle of my life,
because I feel torn.
I wish I could leave it all behind,
all the burdens that I bear.
I wish my mind could be at peace,
and I could forget all my worries and cares.
I desire to be happy, joyous, and free,
able to live, instead of exist, and finally have peace.
Hopefully, one day, this wish will come true,
but until that day,
I will continue to wish to fly away.

Amber Gardner, Grade 10
Warwick High School, VA

Future

One window is all I need…
    to see what my future has in store for me
    to see if all the changes will be worth it
    for a chance to still connect with the dead
    to see my wife and kids someday
    to see the world from the home I built
    and finally realize it's all worth it

Matt Bernard, Grade 10
Delaware Military Academy, DE

At Best

He left me there on the dock next to the boats,
He left me there on the starched white dock,
He who had once brought me blood-red roses,
He who had gotten down on his knee.
There was a locket, carved with our initials,
And a ring, sparkling like ice in the wintry morning.
The wind bit my face, sharp as the roses' thorns,
Slapped at my skirt, wound around my feet.
The metal ring was cold in my palm.
I should have known then
It would leave a scar at the base of my finger.
I should have known, when I watched him carry
My suitcase into the white, empty room,
That he would strew his luggage around in my heart,
And leave the room still empty, still white.
As for that locket, it is now out of harm's way,
Far from the wind, in a drawer, where dust
Settles on letters as frost encases the dock,
Pushing the boats against creaking pylons,
And I am invulnerable, at best.

Meghna Khosla, Grade 11
Thomas Jefferson High School for Science and Technology, VA

My Teddy Bears

I love my little teddy bears
Each one different, short and tall, their fur so fluffy and soft
There's pink or orange, blue or grey
I couldn't choose so they all had to stay
I have one teddy bear that reminds me of the rainbow
I have another bear that likes to tango
Cuddling is what I love to do
And because of them my wish comes true
I have one big teddy bear named Andre
Reminds me of my friend he's very furry
My bears never make me mad or sad
Their the ones I go to for a joke or a laugh
Let's face it, they're like the best friend I never had
Brownie is my favorite bear of all
He's so cute, chocolate and all
Makes me hungry every time I see him
All because he smells like sugary sweets
Then there's a bear who plays music
Those are most of my bears, so pretty, cute and all
Will I ever give them up oh maybe; no way at all!

Ebony Davis, Grade 11
New Directions Alternative Education Center, VA

Ars Poetica

Poetry is clay
in your manipulative mind
molding thoughts throughout
Empty tolls of time
filled up with soapy bubbles
from the brainwash
Society has gotten to cure
imagination, inspiration, dedication
to the world of literature.
Strong thoughts flow premature
to the obstacles — conformity
molding of your mind — silly putty
But your mind is the manipulator
poetry is the putty more often than normally
mold it fervently, fantastically, enthusiastically
Throughout empty tolls of time.
Make it yours, theirs, mine.

ShaJhea Wilson, Grade 11
Forest Park High School, VA

I Hope to Soon Meet Charon

Silence; only silence will save my soul —
Siphon my life and breathe it in again
With the shadows that carry like feather
Unto the union of light and night.

Silence will break my essence from its whole,
Bring my shattered remnants into the glen
Where His shadow makes me but a beggar;
His mercy will my spirit save or smite.

Under His gaze: logos, thymos, eros
Become one anew by His powers sent,
Return my salvation's hope to glimmer
Against that final stretch of slim twilight.

But alas! My dreams of silence are marred —
Time has not yet let me rise unto stars.

Chin Yi Chow, Grade 12
Saint James School, MD

Distance

Through the distance,
I think about you,
and think about all that we been through.
How we argue and fight,
and I know that things will be fine by midnight.
Our love is so incredibly strong,
that sometimes it feels so wrong.
Knowing that you are not by my side
but I will be fine through this ride.

Nimra Naeem, Grade 10
Forest Park High School, VA

Mightier

They say that the pen is mightier than the sword,
But has anybody ever looked at a pencil?
It is the hero you would never expect,
But as sturdy as the one you would,
The shiny metal a mirror,
Reflecting your every thought,
And the soft pink eraser,
The window to a blank page,
Waiting to be rewritten.

Sarah Kerr Watts, Grade 12
Forest Park High School, VA

Wait

Every day the same pattern
Time is a numbing feeling
Watching the waves wake in the morning
The same old fog clouding my view
As I wait, wait

The silver ocean, like crystals forming together, masking my sight
The mist on my skin tickles my nose
But with a sigh I look back out
And see a faint light among the gray clouded audience
And I wait, wait
For him to return

Another day passed still he is not in my vision
Time passes by me but I will wait for him till I die
Another day sulking in gray colors
Again a little light cuts down the top of the sky
Hope still running through my veins but walls of water separate us
I hear a sound in the distance, a ship has found port
I smile and wait, wait
He has finally returned home

Shannon McKenna, Grade 11
Middletown Sr High School, MD

Ragged Stars

You sat outside
Looking out into the distance
I sat at your side
Living a moment that seemed only an instance,
And I wondered, what you were seeing,
I wondered, what you were feeling,
And I wondered, if you saw the same things I did,
I know we were just kids, but it seemed like we were past that
I sat there next to you not knowing what I was going at
I sat there watching crooked skies and ragged stars
Wondering if you were wondering just where we are
If there's a place for us in the midst of those spaces so vast
I wondered if you saw the things I saw first, last,
Perhaps you saw neat skies and straightedged stars,
Perhaps you were wondering if the dark's inside the light
Or if the light's inside the dark,
I sat there, watching the same as you
Looking at the same things
But from different sides,
We saw different things,
But I still sat at your side.

Emmanuel Flores, Grade 11
Bowie High School, MD

Dread, Wrath and Fire

First in dread did he shed tears,
And in those tears showed fears,
Then he soon would change to wrath,
Of which a fire soon would hath.

Megan Gazzelli, Grade 12
Forest Park High School, VA

To Live

I sit in reminiscence of my past and quiver
at the very thought
of how fast life has gone by.
Not yet an adult but
no longer a child.
Peaceful memories of my childhood
are interrupted by the
truth of reality.
I think back about all of the time
I have let slip by,
never thinking about how to use it wisely.
All of the breath that I
have wasted on angry words and
all the precious moments that
I never realized were there.
Every time I think about it I find myself in shame.
All of the times I let
great opportunities pass me by
and never thinking of them
once more.
It's a shame I never realized what I was living for.

Miranda Patterson, Grade 10
Clintwood High School, VA

Shattered

Thoughts of theories flow through my head
Like a river rushing by
Wondering if truth will ever surface
Upon this fast past train of thought
So many lies start to float by
With the truth thrown around the whirlpool
In the center of my mind
Picking out the pieces with a net
Because finding some comfort is better than none
All the stress that comes from the words I pull
Cause me to stay up late at night worrying
If the fast river of thoughts have tricked me
Trying to slow the river to find sleep easier
So I can process the fears and hopes I have
Not knowing how to reach the other shore
Everything being pulled by the strong current
Wondering how to get across to find a different life
Trying to break free of the world that has been created for me
But in the very end
I realize that I will truly be
Nothing more than defeated

Leah Dimeck, Grade 12
Grassfield High School, VA

Endless

I am still waiting
I forgot why, so I wait
Till I remember

Nicole Nachtman, Grade 10
Norfolk Collegiate Middle/Upper School, VA

I Am

I am beautiful and intelligent
I wonder what the college life is like
I hear voices telling me I'm something
I see my heart flutter within my chest
I am beautiful and intelligent

I pretend to care about what people say
I feel the weight of the world
I touch my goals and my dreams
I worry about losing my grandpa
I cry about the thought of losing family
I am beautiful and intelligent

I understand death is part of life
I say I don't care
I dream of becoming a famous photographer
I try always to do my best
I hope I will succeed in my dreams
I am beautiful and intelligent

Rickala Crewe, Grade 12
Charles City County High School, VA

When I Was Little

When I was little
My world was wonderful
And the sun was shining my way
My dreams were blue and pure
My house was the center of my life
And my parents were the gods of my universe.

Innocence flooded my soul
With the cartoons of Hanna-Barbered
Time passed slowly
Without my noticing.

That outside of my beautiful paradise
People were killed and others died of starvation
Withstanding the pain of the journey!
Feet were injured,
Eyes were empty of hope.

Cintia Pires, Grade 11
Charles Shea Sr High School, RI

Life as We Know It

Life is what you make it,
It is full of surprises.
All of us have a different journey, different paths as we go on
Always resting along side of the roads,
We all are meant to learn something,
For some the journey is fast, but for some is slow,
Sometimes the steps are hard
So we must do our very best;
No one can deny the power of the word life —
Life is not to be survived, but to be enjoyed and cherished.

Mirian Alves, Grade 11
Charles Shea Sr High School, RI

I Am

I am intelligent and charismatic…
I wonder how my future will turn out…
I hear bells ringing…
I see…
I am intelligent and charismatic…

I pretend like I am a movie star in Hollywood…
I feel very confident about myself…
I touch the sky…
I worry about my grandmother and my mother a lot…
I cry when I have a lot of stress on my mind…
I am intelligent and charismatic…

I understand that your life is what you make it…
I say that I will be successful…
I dream that I can someday make my family happy…
I try my hardest all the time…
I hope that I can graduate from college successfully…
I am intelligent and charismatic…

Tashauna Robinson, Grade 12
Charles City County High School, VA

Without

Without your arms
Who would hold me?
Without your ears
Who would listen to me?
Without your lips
Who would kiss me?
Without your lovely words
Who would make me feel good?
Without your hand
Who would fill in the empty space in between my fingers?
Without your eyes
Who would notice me?
Without your love
Who would love me?
Without you
Who would I be?

Waleska Negron, Grade 11
John Dickinson High School, DE

My Soul Is Yours

My soul is yours,
Your soul is mine.
This mutual agreement progressed with the essence of time.

They intertwine,
Wrapping in each other's arms ever so tightly.
Dreaming and hoping for the future that could be.

No melody, no sound.
Together, they create the sweetest music ever heard.
With just the uttering of those three powerful words.

Mykia Allen, Grade 12
Forest Park High School, VA

The Unreachable Face

It's you
You're the unreachable face
The beautiful chime I hear in my sleep
The sunshine kiss hair I long to stroke

On my way to you,
In the hall, on the bus, the train station
The unreachable face
I breathe, heavily
Over time,
I could see you wanted someone else
Feeling foolish and I guess I always knew
Thinking you were for me
And I was for you
Separated because of waiting
Scared to tell you the truth
How I feel about you
The unreachable face

Caley Lareau, Grade 10
Beacon Charter High School, RI

Looking Back

Floating down the aisle,
Silent smiles shifted.
Familiar faces surround me,
Memories flash through my mind.
From classes we won't forget,
To teachers who inspire us.
Laughs and tears,
First loves and best friends,
Mistakes made but no regrets.
The tassel will be treasured,
We'll slowly drift apart,
The pictures will fade,
Memories will stick with us.
Caps and gowns say it all,
As we share our goodbyes.

Briana Silva, Grade 12
North Providence High School, RI

Growth

Between summer mornings and
sweet spring rain
they stepped
into love
a light
in which winter gardens thawed
from their gray blue nights
as though freezing cold snow
was a dream for the year
and now
flower season
blossoms
the fruit of life

Madeline Cochran, Grade 11
C Milton Wright High School, MD

The Window

I see a window.
Through this window, I see an alternate world.
This alternate world, is not bad at all.
In this alternate world,
There is no such thing as war.
There is no such thing as violence.
Through this window,
I see man and nature coming together as one,
and just living.
No pollution,
no "global warming,"
no undrinkable water,
no landfills,
no nuclear power plants,
no jammed highways filled with machines to destroy the atmosphere,
and taint our air.
Through this window, I see nothing like what the world is today,
but what I hope is there tomorrow.

Nathan Buethe, Grade 10
Delaware Military Academy, DE

The Treachery of the Troubadour

I've told a tale of many a brave man who accomplished feats of great
but I'm the one of who I've sung and thus hath filled my plate

From St. John the brave to St. Stephen the quick
Their names replaced with my own a testament to my wit

With speed of thought and sleight of hand
I spread my name across the land

From lowest of paupers to grandest of kings
On the tongues of the people my glory it sings

No longer the weak no longer the serf
My name now strengthened from another's worth

For the sins I've committed have been out of vein
For not one single feat could I truthfully lay claim

Jarad Deans, Daniel Delaney, and Jacob McCormick, Grade 12
Norfolk Collegiate Middle/Upper School, VA

The Great Beyond

There is only pitch black
No sound, no light, no sense, no self
There is light, but only a speck
The speck surges and grows as it is noticed
The speck surges and grows until it consumes the dark and illuminates
The brilliance of Paradise is apparent
The speck is lost, darkness consumes
Eye must stay keen to the light
So when only emptiness remains a path can be found
There is only pitch black
No sound, no light, no sense, no self

Jamie Howard, Grade 12
Saint James School, MD

I Am

I am kind and outgoing
I wonder if I am getting a new car
I hear whistling
I see summertime at the beach
I am kind and outgoing

I pretend to be mean
I feel confident about myself
I touch the cool air
I worry about life
I cry when I think about my car accident
I am kind and outgoing

I understand why students fight in school
I say I would move out of this state
I dream about money and happiness
I try to be successful
I hope to be rich one day
I am kind and outgoing

Keirra Charity, Grade 12
Charles City County High School, VA

Baby Eats a Berry

Sweet baby growing so gently
With hair so golden, and cheeks so smooth
Waiting with pink plump lips so patiently
As I set down a plate of berries
She feels the berries prickly and frizzy
Then runs them, slimy, through her fingers
Poking the rough to make them juicy
Letting them on her plate to linger
Then in her mouth one goes
Immediately to make a sour face
She pushes them from her territory
To be alone in her place
She sits there delightfully
Then looks up for something new
Sweet little memories
Of baby's first time with berries

Heather Gosnell, Grade 12
Menchville High School, VA

Can You Imagine

Can you imagine…
A world without love
No help from "above"
Bombs fill the air
People no longer stare
Gun fire lights the night
Oh, isn't it such a sight
Cities lie in pieces
People searching for releases
A world without love
A world soon upon us

Brittani Carter, Grade 11
Forest Park High School, VA

True Love and Its Measures

I sorely wish the word could be elated
Or bliss but no perfection
For every spoken word, I am in truth fated
But if only truth was spoken out every interjection
I speak to you in the gist of things
Hanging onto you as though I am dragging down your wings
For we have never spoken one word
But my thoughts of you continue to be slurred
I know I know that watching you is yet another foolish dream
That once I let go I'll be the one ripping from seam to seam
That before you pull my mentality off, I thought I'd find my calling
For your love is my love and I fear I am falling
And as you walk away
I fear my mouth has lost the words to say
My heart is at a rate that's never bending
To the truth that speaks to me that says true love holds no happy ending

Nhu-Phuong Duong, Grade 11
Benjamin Banneker Academic High School, DC

The River by My House in the Winter

The river is so majestic and beautiful this time of year,
Not because it is particularly pretty,
Nor because all of the plastic ghosts and metal skeletons have washed away,
No, that may never happen,
But because water never dies like all these trees do.
Their death-inspired trance, their barren glares, their morbid stance,
They haunt the landscape, faded gray ghosts of the lush springtime.
Unlike these obelisks to hopelessness, water merely flows,
And in doing so, it does an incredible thing.
It ignores the destruction, the calamity around it.
Defiant of Death and his sentinels of bereavement.
It is so beautiful to me, because…
Envy paints with the most vibrant colors.

Dylan Tuck, Grade 11
Christiansburg High School, VA

Of Things Undone, of Things Not Begun

Of pieces unwritten, of tales hidden
Of adventures unknown, of journeys only one's own
Of compositions unfinished, of works diminished
Of endeavors undiscovered, of habits recovered
Of ambitions unfulfilled, of effort given still
Of thoughts unspoken, of influence broken
Of statutes unquestioned, of not so much as a whisper mentioned
Of people unaffected, of audiences disconnected
Of beings untamed, of sheep inane
Of society and evolution, of morality and devolution
Of the ascension through age, of turning the page
Of things undone, of things not begun, what lies ahead can only be one.

Ross Peterson, Grade 12
Walt Whitman High School, MD

I Am

I am smart and pretty…
I wonder about Tashauna…
I hear Trey Songz singing to me…
I see me being successful…
I am smart and pretty…

I pretend to have friends…
I feel very thankful and blessed…
I touch the sky…
I worry is my grandpa going to be ok…
I cry when I'm very mad…
I am smart and pretty…

I understand I'm very loved…
I say I'm the best I can be…
I dream I'm on top of the world…
I try to be the best friend I can be…
I hope to be successful…
I am smart and pretty…

Keyonia Williamson, Grade 12
Charles City County High School, VA

Kerri Lynn

Kerri Lynn
Kerri Lynn
Wherefore art thou Kerri Lyn
We Miss you
We Love
We want you home
You were the best
You took me to see *Finding Nemo*
It was the last time I saw you
You got into an Accident
Was in Pain
Then you went into a coma
Now you're home with God
Why did you have to get into that accident
I want you back
Please come home

Shawn Butler, Grade 10
Delaware Military Academy, DE

Tall and Strong

There are times when I feel weak
When I want to let my emotions show
But I know down deep inside
I have to stay tall and strong
Can't let the fear show
Can't let the sadness rise
I have to bury it down deep
To keep my composure
I have to stay tall and strong
For that is who I am
This is what I am

William Walsh, Grade 10
Delaware Military Academy, DE

My Reason to Live

Gracious
Tolerant
Supportive
Carefully, she carried me for nine months
Gracefully, she gave me life
With pain, after tender hours
She had the happiness of carrying me in her arms.
She says children grow too fast
Children need a mother when they cannot do something by themselves
My mother cares, as I am important
Children make mothers proud even though they weren't waiting for it.
She gets upset
She wants to see progress in my life
She wants to witness my success
She wants to thank me for all I will do
She does everything for that little human being
So little, but big enough to take all her attention.
The child grows, and the mom is getting old
The days are passing, and she cannot do enough
The years left behind cannot ever come back.

Karine Barreto, Grade 11
Charles Shea Sr High School, RI

Women Worry

The hollowed wind's wildly ways worry women,
Into completely avoiding the situation,
Roaming righteously but violently rampaging corrupts temptation.

Upon evacuation but not suffering damnation, women worry.
Wondering why women worry, without a wasteful displeasure,
But a peaceful leisure ensures the holy treasures.

Sights of such an anticipated series of sounds.
Swinging stupidly with sightless frowns.
Women worry, but rational thinking obstructs an irrational thought,

To disrupt a conventional gesture.
Completely undermining the wonderful feeling of sensational pleasure.
As fear takes over a fearless sound,

A faint hymnal plays all around.
Women worry, but only a worried person can see,
With sightless eyes electrified motion induce chemically.

Justin Forrest, Grade 12
Milford Mill Academy, MD

Living in the Moment

Dwelling on the past
Reminiscing on those moments, those moments
That won't ever last
Those moments that were given to those that did not deserve
Those moments that were taken
From those whom acquire my love
Have left me, Left me relentless
Hopeless but yet hopeful
Staining with that mellifluous
But oh so sweet desire
These are the moments, the moments that leave scars on your heart the moments you will never forget
Some of those moments are forever scorning
You look back and you ponder, you relive those moments
You wonder, you wonder what would've, could've, or should've been
But these thoughts will always remain moments
Moments in the past
As you relive that last moment of that perfect painted picture
You realize you were, you were living in the moment
Not for today, tomorrow, or yesterday or the day before
Or for that hour, minute or second, that second that would always last
It would always last and forever be just living in the moment

Whitney Barfield, Grade 11
Woodbridge Sr High School, VA

Midwinter

The book has been sent to publishing
I regret nothing
Except that you never got to read it
(Which might have changed the ending
so that now we would be walking outside our small circles and the day would seem far less cold.)
I don't know why I can't let you go,
You never called me
back or beautiful all those times the air was thick with silence.
An obscure sort of mystery who wanted someone more than I,
not being sure who I am, besides
the person you once saw something to look closer for.
This will turn out like all the others no doubt,
— No — Such talk won't get the bitterness out.
See how that was? I'm moving on and making fresh starts and making no sense at all
Because one day something shifted and the truth just stopped me in my tracks mid sentence.
Midwinter. A catatonic trudge.
Here though you are not, bringing numb toes and fingers aching from overexposure.

I'm going bleak from overexposure, like a frozen statue or a ruined photograph.
Someone excise these thoughts from my tired mind. Exorcise me.
Resuscitate me, you just might be the only one who can lift the colorless curse of the frozen and of those without regrets.

Jessica Fournier, Grade 10
North Kingstown Sr High School, RI

Show Scheme

As you flash your teeth on stage in a snaggled tooth way, I watch and see your victims swoon around your knees. The lights slide off your body and glide along the floor as you shiver across the room. Silver tends to sparkle around your chest, to distract them from the hole in your heart. Down your waist the red ribbon bends, seeming to invite the lost men. Binding arms wrap endlessly around them and I see the failure in your eyes because you cannot hold onto them forever.

Lisa Luck, Grade 11
Padua Academy, DE

London Night

"These cruel, wanton, indiscriminate bombings of London are, of course, a part of Hitler's invasion plans. Little does he know the spirit of the British nation, or the tough fiber of the Londoners." — Winston Churchill (1940)

The sun escapes the blitz
just as the siren is sounded.
Its dissonant cry pierces the cool air the
chilling wail screams its caution warning
beneath the alarming call;
a low rumble encroaching
provokes the danger. Coming to destroy.
Persistent staccato beats until each bomb
is released like a black balloon exploding
from the sky: city lights turn to fiery lights and
gray smoke chokes the air. Trying to find cover,
sheltered from the danger, some lay on the metal mattress
of the Morrison Table where they wait
the night, clinging to steel wire. No hope
for those who never made it to shelter.
Then the all-clear siren is sound and the sun
peeks slowly out. Children walk through shambles,
gas masks in hand, eager to find out,
which mates survived the night.

Katie Franzel, Grade 12
Lake Braddock Secondary School, VA

Tired

The body is tired
I make the same motions
Day after day after
The heart is tired
The burden of everyday life
Crushing it
It knows no rest
The soul is tired
It cannot distinguish between
The light and darkness
Night bleeds into day
And day fades into night
More tests and trials tomorrow
And the day after that
And the day after —
My life shall ever wind like this
Until my being knows life
No more

Natalia Mikutina, Grade 12
Douglas Southall Freeman High School, VA

Memory Box

I am from organized chaos,
A neat array of nothing important and everything vital.
I am from oak brown piano benches,
Warm honey ham and feather soft finger rolls.
I am from four inch pecan pies divided for ten people.
I am from Papa Gino's and China Man Buffet.
I am from nine o'clock phone calls and Joe's Playland,
Farmers Markets and two feet of snow Christmas Day.
I am from Duck Bridge with breaths held tight.
I am from Zagnut Bars and Fenway Park.
I am from the blue-shuttered playhouse and hummingbirds
I am from TV repairmen and golf carts,
T-ball, weeping willow canopies and swing set melodies.
I am from Catholic School,
Hiding under my desk for a week to avoid a nun's harsh ruler.
I am from Superman pendants and Spiderman comic strips.
I am from a gun in a dirt floor cottage in Ireland,
And Miss America in England.
I am from the beat up rusty car with no heat, A/C, or running boards.
I am from newspaper routes and 10K runs.

I am the memory box of my family.
And the three-decker over the railroad tracks.

Meghan Burke, Grade 12
W.T. Woodson High School, VA

Old Friend

and I know where I've been.
not where I'm going.
I know too much about loss.
I've lost her more than once.

and for every timid tremor.
to take my hand.
a sort of saddening gloom.
creeping in like an old friend.
and makes me wish I was still again.
death, tuck me in
I know I shouldn't, but
I just miss an old friend.

James Wells, Grade 11
Woodbridge Sr High School, VA

Sadness

Sadness is when the world has become gray.
    All of the bright colors have disappeared.
Clouds dominate the sky on a rainy day,
    No rainbow waiting for you at the end.

Cheerful summer has lost her glow, so now
    You are doomed to lasting, freezing winter.
No hot chocolate to keep you warm, and no soft, playful snow.
    Leftover from summer, in your finger, lays a horrible, painful splinter.

Music has completely ceased to play,
    No more ups and downs of a melody.
You remember a tune, but all you hear is static.
    From the barest, dull sounds, you try to create harmony.

No more color, no more music.
    The more you try to create it, you lose it.
No more laughter, no more smiles.
    Let's hope you're not trapped for more than a while.

Lydia Bubniak, Grade 10
Foxcroft School, VA

Grades 7-8-9 Top Ten Winners

List of Top Ten Winners for Grades 7-9; listed alphabetically

Adela Baker, Grade 7
Clague Middle School, MI

Aimee-Lee Belzile, Grade 9
Ecole Secondaire Catholique Horizon, ON

Elizabeth Daley, Grade 7
St David Junior High School, AZ

Kendra Donahue, Grade 7
Sandwich Middle School, IL

Diana Harmata, Grade 9
West Jr High School, MO

Emily Murphy, Grade 9
Trinity High School, NH

Michael San Juan, Grade 8
Palmer Catholic Academy, FL

Brian Simonelli, Grade 8
Hanson Middle School, MA

Shaye Stalians, Grade 7
Glen Edwards Middle School, CA

Sarah Taylor, Grade 8
Our Lady of the Pillar School, MO

All Top Ten Poems can be read at www.poeticpower.com

Note: The Top Ten poems were finalized through an online voting system. Creative Communication's judges first picked out the top poems. These poems were then posted online. The final step involved thousands of students and teachers who registered as the online judges and voted for the Top Ten poems. We hope you enjoy these selections.

Back When

As I sit here on this bench,
Watching these corporations and everyday disasters,
I think of a simpler time.

Back when people didn't care where you were from,
Back when gas was a dollar fifty,
Back when cigarettes were fifty-four cents a pack,
Back when soda was a quarter,
Those were the days.

It's a harder time now,
The economy is in ruins,
Life is based off of what you can make,
But it seems the more you make, the less you make.

So I sit here on this bench,
Thinking of the simpler times…
The simpler times back when.

Nicholas Brobst, Grade 9
Wicomico High School, MD

Fast Break Madness

In the fantastic sport of basketball
there is no better moment or feeling,
it's like king-size candies, not very small
ripe for the picking, though some say it's stealing.
Three-on-one is easy some players say,
but it must be correct with no fail.
Just like the Phoenix Suns do every day,
failure brings sentence to basketball jail.
It starts with a stop and ends with a dunk
players zoom down the court like big freight-trains
the ending dunk certainly, comes with spunk
it's like the players are lifted by cranes.
For what is this called, you ask it ain't fake.
It's the king of kings, the mighty fast break!

Neel Hosamane, Grade 7
Kilmer Middle School, VA

My Wish

I wish all the beggars had money,
but they don't.
I wish the world would get rid of all its weapons,
but it won't.
I wish food would rain from the sky for the poor and the hungry,
but it doesn't work that way.
I wish the greenhouse gases would disappear, vanish, go away,
but they aren't leaving.
I wish that my wishes would come true,
but they won't.
I wish the world was a better place,
but it isn't.
I wish I could change it all with one wish,
but I can't. I wish.

Molly Magoffin, Grade 7
Blue Ridge Middle School, VA

Ode to the Rain

Pitter Patter
Drip Drop
The rain comes crashing down
As if it were weightless boulders
Waiting to cleanse the Earth.
Cleansing, soaking cleaning away the imperfections.
Whether it is day
Or night,
Rain doesn't care.
We don't know where the rain starts,
We don't know when it will end — if it will end.
But for now, on every rainy day,
I'll think about the impulse of
Every crash of lightning,
Every roll of thunder,
And each and every raindrop
Falling, crashing down.

Olivia Ross, Grade 8
Mount St Charles Academy, RI

To Achieve Your Dreams

A dream is like a star.
When you follow it, aspirations stretch far.
When you catch it, hold on, never let it go.
Rejoice in it, your heart will glow.

You'll burst with laughter,
because it seemed so far ahead.
Maybe you'll cry overjoyed, words left unsaid.

Whatever the dream may be,
don't let the happiness die inside.
When you achieve it, be sure that you keep it alive.

When you have a gift,
let it be known.
If it's what you love to do,
then it should be shown!

Catherine Benetti, Grade 9
St Mary Academy-Bay View, RI

My House Is So Scary

The block on the wall calls me over.
The invisible voice starts to talk.
Where does it come from?

I walk into the water room.
I go to the smaller room inside and turn the handle.
The water attacks me!

I walk down the hall and get stopped by the invisible wall.
There is someone on the other side that can't get through either.
He does everything I do.
I take a step away, and he disappears.

Jacob Haddad, Grade 8
Mount St Charles Academy, RI

High Merit Poems – Grades 7, 8, and 9

A New Beginning

I thought about it day and night.
Suddenly I saw a light.
It looked as though there was a path.
I did my best to do the math.
My list it got compared.
I told my heart to be prepared.
Trying to figure out my feelings was hard.
My heart will always be scarred.
My brain, too also had a voice.
Although I feel I made the right choice.
My choice was him.
Now let my new life begin.
Amber Riley, Grade 8
Parkside Middle School, VA

Some Dreams

Some dreams show
What you may become.
Some dreams beat and,
Some dreams strum.
Some dreams are sweet and,
Some dreams are scary.
Some dreams are silent.
Some dreams sing like a canary.
Some dreams jump and,
Some dreams roll,
But dreams all are windows,
Into your soul.
Susannah Martin, Grade 9
Homeschool Plus, VA

John Lennon

You "Imagine" a world full of peace,
But it seems that war will never cease.
"Strawberry Fields" is a dream,
Topped with cookies and cream.
A dream so simple it would seem,
How can someone be so mean?
You left a legacy that was great,
You want the world to be rid of hate.
"Come Together" the world is your friend,
Peace and love should never end.
Your message was clear to me…
That "Love Is All You Need."
Daniel DiCocco, Grade 8
St Clement Mary Hofbauer School, MD

Autumn

It is like a dream
Of death and cold, righteous night
The leaves are falling
Joyous and bright, in it goes
Void of all life, out it comes
Lauren Pettit, Grade 7
E Russell Hicks Middle School, MD

A New Beginning

I wake up each morning, feeling as miserable as I did the day before.
I look at the same plain face in the mirror each day,
wishing to look like those girls who paint their faces with makeup.
Every day, fishing for compliments left to right, through the hallways.
I search for a difference in the crowds,
to stand up and remind me that it's all right to be different;
that I don't need to have the latest outfit to get a person's attention.
I search for trust among my peers,
as they stab each other in the back at this very moment.
Feeling more alone than ever through my generation,
feeling disappointment, that I never know when I'm being told the truth;
due to the lack of respect and courage spreading through my peers.
My insecurities start to overwhelm me as high school begins to come around the corner,
Knowing that I'll have not one friend on my first day,
I think scares me the most.
I'll have not a clue of how to open up to each person I begin to call my friend at first,
considering I rarely give out my trust these days.
The thought though, of being unknown,
the thought of no one knowing my story,
makes me curious and keeps me open minded the more I think about it.
I won't have any expectations, because I want this chapter of my life to stay unimaginable.
Kayla Lally, Grade 8
St Columba School, MD

In the Dark

With the cold air blowing in the middle of the night,
I wake up with a gasp, a shiver, and a fright,
It came back around again to get me,
But it's too dark, "Where are you, I can't see, please don't hurt me,"
As I pull the covers over my eye's,
I feel it twirling, and playing with my pink hair ties,
I scream when my eye's release a tear,
My parents come in saying, "Honey it's okay we are here,"
As they speak in a calming, soothing tone,
I look around the room…and we are not alone,
It is watching, waiting for them to go,
As they try to leave I shout, "Please, please, no,"
They hold my hand until I fall back under,
It comes back around and interrupts my slumber
I tell people, but they don't believe,
So I lay alone with tears running down my sleeve,
Wondering if it will appear again,
And most importantly if so…when,
It wants me to suffer, it wants me to fear, it makes me want to get out of here,
I tell the family, they tell me "Nothing is there," it has disappeared…but where,
I wonder why it only wants me to see, is it real…or is it…me?
Katelynn Kelly, Grade 7
Western Heights Middle School, MD

September Eleventh

Whoooosh! The planes are going fast through the sky.
Crash! One of the plane hits one building.
Kaboom! Ahhhhh! The buildings fall to the ground with the people falling through the air.
Snap crackle pop! The fire is sparkling.
Alexis Davis, Grade 7
E Russell Hicks Middle School, MD

Hammock

Lie in a hammock and sway,
Sway into space
A pitch black sky
the glowing stars, you touch just barely

Then sway into a peaceful beach
The glittery water soothing your mind
Flowing side by side
Looking down you see the clear water staring right back at you

Sway into a world all about you!
Everyone you are enemies with will adore you
You never have to pick up a finger
And you never leave your gold throne

You next sway into a quiet rain forest
Where the gentle rain falls
All the animals swing tree to tree on vines
Then the rain falls (pitter patter)

No matter where you are
Outer space, a peaceful beach
In a world about you or in a quiet rain forest
You can always have a chilled glass of lemonade
Right next to you!

Natalie Cheung, Grade 7
Wicomico Middle School, MD

Forever and Always Love

F orgetting is the worst thing you can do
O r never letting go
R emember always and for
E ver to never forget the
V rooming airplanes
E xploding on the Twin Towers
R emember

A gain and again to
N ever let go of the past
D o what is right

A lways
L end a helping hand
W hen a needing hand is extended
A nd every September Eleventh
Y ell and hold your fist high and be
S low to let it fall because

L etting it fall means to let terror win
O h say can you see
V ying for our troops in
E very way possible
   Never forget, all gave some, but some gave all.

Christian Keller, Grade 8
Norfolk Collegiate Middle/Upper School, VA

Summer Mornings

The sun raises its sleepy head,
Pale gold and cool from the night,
Honeyed fingers reach through trees,
Casting shadows and light.

Birds flute and trill
Warming up for the daily choir.
Flowers open their petaled curtains
To display their delicate attire.

A gentle breeze dances through grass,
making the dewdrops quiver,
Like fairies preparing for flight,
With their wings all a-shimmer.

The mellow smell of summer mornings,
Refreshing and calm before the sweltering heat,
Floats through the air and up into the sky,
Leaving the new day fresh and sweet.

Alison Lindsay, Grade 9
St Anne's Belfield School, VA

Cease Fire

From the horizon, the sun doth advance,
Upon the darkened, red, once barren field.
Men's eyes lay open as if in a trance,
Wet blood filled wounds ne'er again to be healed.

Bullets fired in agony ne'er cease.
Bayonets charging in futility.
No lessons learned from all those men deceased.
Just further fighting and hostility.

Their war forces their own world to divide,
All men keep fighting in this war, ne'er quit.
They won't be forgot, by their families cried.
At the end of the light, all must forfeit.

To the horizon, the sun doth retreat,
Both armies recede and accept defeat.

Andrew Cowen, Grade 7
Kilmer Middle School, VA

Rest in Peace "Eye-Eye"*

When Eye-Eye died
Everybody started to look at the sky
Saying I thought he was going to be
The only one to survive
Eye-Eye was a funny person,
He always thought he would be high in the sky
With his lazy eye on the moon
Hoping God won't take him soon.

Ahmal McGainey, Grade 7
Emery Education Campus, DC
*Dedicated to my cousin.

Close My Eyes

Sometimes I close my eyes
And start to dream.
When I dream, I'm in charge
Of what happens
And it can be anything.
When I dream, I'm one of the
Lucky ones.
The ones who have everything
Life has to offer
And they can smile effortlessly
Without having to try.
Then I open my eyes
And reality hits me like a slap on the face.
In reality
No one smiles
Because here, smiles
Are nothing but myths.
Reality hurts
But sometimes…
Sometimes I close my eyes.
Pooja Devarakonda, Grade 7
Carson Middle School, VA

I Am the Sun

I rise every morning
To make your day bright
I give warmth
To the earth below
I am a fun time
If you don't get close to me
Because if you get close to me
I will burn you up
People bask in my light
It makes them happy
When I make them tan
I bask in their happiness
The moon makes me mad
So sometimes I have bad days
When I have bad days
I hide behind the clouds feeling blue
At the end of the day
I go to the west
It is time for me to leave
And for the evil moon to return
Ben Barrett, Grade 8
Norfolk Collegiate Middle/Upper School, VA

I Am

I am tall, strong, blooming
I am powerful and peaceful
I am unique
I am playful to some,
 helpful to many
I am the tree in your front yard
Ashley Wenz, Grade 8
Norfolk Christian Middle School, VA

On Turning 13

The whole idea of it makes me feel,
happy and joyful for some reason.
Something better than 12, or the butterflies I get from singing.
A kind of laughter of the spirit, a change of the soul.

You tell me it's too nice that I'm turning thirteen,
But that is because she is still twelve like me but I turn thirteen before her.
The perfect day the perfect party, and the beautiful day June 29 comes.
But I can lie on my bed and think of the years to come.
At fourteen I will be a person who cares about the things I never did before.
I could make myself anything I want by dressing up in my own way.
At fifteen I will get my learner's permit.

But now I am mostly on Facebook watching TV in the late afternoon.
Back then it was fun playing games like Monopoly, and Clue, Life,
and my bike was ridden every day as my life gets better today,
All my time is fun watching movies.

This is the beginning of happiness I say to myself,
As I walk in my house saying, "School was boring."
It is time to say hi to my new friends, time to turn the teenage numbers.

It seems only yesterday I used to believe
That I thought I was still a little kid. If you cut me you could see a little kid.
But now when I fall upon the sidewalks I cry, I skin my knees, I bleed.
Maranda West, Grade 7
E Russell Hicks Middle School, MD

Ode to the Evergreen

The Evergreen with your white and blue sails
You brought joy to me.
And to my grandfather who owned you.

Even though your motor sometimes didn't start.
We kept trying to get you to work, Rrrrr Rrrrr Rrrrr.
When we got you going we stayed out of hours until our fingers turned blue.

When we saw dolphins
Grandfather cut the motor,
We took many pictures of them.
Once my family even slept on you.

We would go New Year's day, we would eat oysters
And go for a ride in that boat.
Then we would come in and eat hot dogs grilled over the fire.

We all had great times.
I am glad I could go in that boat.
Yet I was the last person to drive the boat.
Before grandfather sold it to a man who said that he would take care of it.
I loved that boat and I am glad he had it.
Devyn Murray, Grade 7
St John Neumann Academy, VA

Searching

Have I not satisfied your every need?
Is there something missing that I can't see?
I searched for what it is you want,
I just can't seem to find it.

I looked beyond every mountain
And searched in the deepest depth of every sea.
Without this little item,
Can you not just be happy with me?

I look for it every day.
Dream of where it could be at night.
I even searched in my past,
To find if I could bring it back.

Nowhere is it to be found.
Should I just give up looking now?
Can I stop searching?
Can you stop asking?
For my heart was lost, but never found.

Cashae Butler, Grade 8
Dundalk Middle School, MD

Striking

There is something beautiful
about the way a lightning bolt flashes
clean and strong
through a dark sky
crisp and commanding
it demands attention, grabs your eyes,
and dares you to look away
entrancing
how bright and vibrant
strikes the sky, contrasting from dark and cloudy
thunder booms like a distant drum roll
building suspense for the lightning
as it rips through the canvas of night
powerful and mighty
then gone
just like that.

Becky Reid, Grade 9
Grafton High School, VA

The New Year

It's a new year
Still winter, but spring's almost here
I sit at the window and see the leaves on the ground
I see the trees' empty branches and frown
January, the first month of the year
A time to make new resolutions
In the new year
I plan to achieve a lot
Get good grades and do my work
I know that will happen in the new year

Christian Budd, Grade 8
George E Peters Adventist School, MD

I Believe in Love

I believe in love,
How can you not?
There's proof all around,
From the park where old people walk hand and hand,
To the gut-wrenching sobs that you hear through the walls,
As you remember what's gone,
That feeling that leaves you weak and vulnerable around them.
I believe in love,
How can you not?
Only love can truly lead to hate,
To their fighting and bickering,
To their shunning tones,
And to the glares that penetrate the heart.
I believe in love,
How can you not?
Love though, runs out for some,
It's wrenched from other's grasps,
Or for the lucky ones it stays in a trembling line never to be crossed.
I believe in love,
How can you not?

Demi Kappen, Grade 9
Forest Park High School, VA

Ars Poetica

A sigh of relief,
Breathe in, breathe out,
A thought oh so brief,

A memory or regret,
Past, present, or future,
An event you can't forget,

A pen and some paper,
Forget and forgive,
And try to be greater,

A poem of young, true love,
Being happy or sad,
Write something you can't speak of.

ErinLiz Coluna, Grade 7
The Academy of International Studies at Rosemont, VA

Me!

Liam
Brown hair, happy, funny, the best
Lover of food
Lover of fried chicken, Subway, and Gatorade
Who feels grass, land, and water
Who needs help in science
Who fears nothing at all
Who gives money to the poor
Who would like to see a million dollars in my hand
Resident of Grasonville
Callaghan

Liam Callaghan, Grade 8
Stevensville Middle School, MD

Midnight Sky

The midnight sky
so gloomy and dim,
dark and meaningless to many men.
But me, I look beyond that side,
for me it's filled with glistening pride.
The Milky Way from end to end,
looks as if it's going to bend,
around the buildings down the road,
all the time, it constantly glows.
Right up to me the Milky Way came,
filled with truth and not with shame,
it passes as if there's nothing to fear,
nothing at all, so bright and so clear.
Shimmering stars in the gloomy, dark night,
opening eyes to see the new sites.
So next time you see someone looking up high,
show them much more than the midnight sky.

Scotti Johnson, Grade 8
Norfolk Christian Middle School, VA

Passionate

Relationships are like car crashes
But to keep it on the right track it takes more than looks
It takes trust
Honesty
and LOVE!

With all that together we can rise over all of the above
We just need a little push and shove
1,
2,
3,
4,
If we don't love each other our relationship can hit the floor
But we stay together night and day
And when those gray skies and clouds fade away
We are still together to say
I love you!

Courtney Hatton, Grade 8
Kenmore Middle School, VA

Life Is Musical

As the notes rise high above the clouds,
I yearn to remember how it began.
It might have been a simple word,
Or a deep crescendo, but it was simply
Magnificent.
When I attempt to play it,
I tried to do it perfectly,
But that is not how we are supposed to learn it.
Why is it not coming together,
Like his or hers?
Maybe I have to write my own piece,
And perform it the way I want to.

Baldeep Kaur, Grade 8
Rachel Carson Middle School, VA

Winter

She comes joyfully and happily
Like a little toddler playing in the water

But if you make her mad it's like
Thousands of volcanoes erupting
All at the same time!

White glitter, cold days
She whispers in the air
Letting the kids
To finally come back out

She wishes she could stay
But her family was born that way:
Cold, bitter, in a beautiful kind of way
And sometimes with nobody knowing
She slowly slips away...
With a little hope sunshine coming their way!

Sidra Sharieff, Grade 7
Carson Middle School, VA

Urbanality

The absolute opposite of tranquility
Infinite opportunity and ability
Buildings abrading the clouds
Subways screaming rather loud

Trees are bricks providing shade
Corner bodegas; turkey heroes being made
Summer; sunshine season, beaches overpopulated
Bright lights in the city just keep you motivated

Sirens betraying that of a nagging mother
Urban originality like no other
Home of late Biggie, home of the brave
Big city lights with a style you will crave

Donté Ringer, Grade 9
Franklin Military School, VA

Fading Slowly

Spring Again
    The meadow shines with flowers of all designs
A crumbling Wall
    Reminiscent of an age so long ago
When Heroes died
    For to save the Wall which they fought
Long and Hard
    Waging war on a grim enemy
Laying siege
    To a place where now even the fawns cross freely
They Died for
    What seems petty today
But was all the world to them
They now lie in this Cemetery

Sean Anderson, Grade 7
Kilmer Middle School, VA

Night Sky

I like to look at the stars
I like to look at the moon
I love everything about the night sky
It is a different place
When I look into the sky I lose myself
I just sit there and stare in the darkness
Every little sound around me is gone
Every annoying prep is gone
I just lie there in my bed
I think about what goes on
What is wrong with me?
But when it fades away
I just completely zone out
I got lost in the stars
After I have lost myself I try to come back
When I notice I am in my room I fall asleep
I dream of what I want to happen
Whenever the stars are gone I dream them
This is my therapy
This is my luxury
This is my time alone

Tori Dowling, Grade 9
Delaware Military Academy, DE

Dark

Dark
I am dark
My mother is the moon
My father is the shadows
I was born on the dark side of the force
I live on the moon
My best friend is night
Because we like to make shadows
My enemy is light
Because he is my opposite
I fear lightning
Because it is my weakness
I love my mother
Because she gave birth to me
I dream I will rule the world one day

Eric Hill, Grade 7
Clear Spring Middle School, MD

Japan

so many died
so many cried
what a day for shame
and no one to blame
we try to help as much as we can
to help that poor land
I pray for little kids to be safe
and that they are not waif
I hope they are okay
so let's pray

Xena Barreto, Grade 7
Thomas Harrison Middle School, VA

The Sound of Rain

When a rain shower comes, I close my eyes
I listen for the splats and cries
The rain drops falling from above
The sweet smell of replenished earth that I so dearly love
I reach out my hand to feel a drop
It splats on my palm with a wet-sounding plop
I inhale the sweet wet sidewalk smell
The drops still sound like a wet tinkering bell
I suddenly no longer feel drenched
For the rain has subsided, the gray clouds have slowly inched
To reveal the shy sun slowly peeking out
To dry up the earth and begin a hot drought
I walk home with a sigh, for I do love the rain
I gaze up at the sky expecting it to be depressing and plain
I am surprised and delighted to see what I was hoping the sky would show:
A wonderful, gorgeous, multicolored rainbow!

Abbie Wolf, Grade 8
St Jude Catholic School, MD

I'm Short and Proud of It

Just because I am short
I have to sit in the back seat
I can't do anything the right way
Doesn't mean I can't reach anything
Doesn't mean I need a ladder
Just because I am FIVE feet tall
Shouldn't mean I am treated differently
Just because I am short
Doesn't mean I'm different
From people who are tall
Doesn't mean I am helpless
Just because you are taller than me
Do you think of me differently?
Do you treat me differently than everyone else?
Am I still a real person?
JUST BECAUSE I'M SHORT DOESN'T MEAN I'M DIFFERENT THAN YOU!

Lex Selig, Grade 8
Norfolk Collegiate Middle/Upper School, VA

Proud to Be What I Am

I am the ocean
                I am the land
Humans cannot live without my natural resources
                Humans cannot live without my natural resources
My waves roll or crash
                My soil moistens or cracks
Ships go over me
                Cars go over me
People can swim in me
                People can run on me
I am a part of nature
                I am a part of nature
I am proud to be what I am
                I am proud to be what I am

Mahnoor Asad, Grade 7
Carson Middle School, VA

High Merit Poems – Grades 7, 8, and 9

Bay Love

The Chesapeake Bay
What a wonderful place.
A resource to its residents
A home to what lies beneath

Crabs have returned in abundance
A specialty to Maryland
A livelihood for its citizens

Unimaginable critters, grass shrimp to channeled whelk
And even a sea horse found in the grasses
The stench of detritus rising from the marsh

The Chesapeake Bay
The jewel of Maryland
Why are you always in crisis?
Conservation efforts
Oh, so important.
Let's all SAVE THE BAY!

Lauren Freeny, Grade 8
Washington Episcopal School, MD

Fishing with a Friend

The lake
Shimmers beautifully like a new glass window
The fish swim lazily with the morning breeze
The water tempting you to splash your way in
Your friend opens up your fishing box
And strings a worm through the sharp, pointy hook
You take the rod and cast it out
Just to ruin the pristine lake
Now we wait
For the tug of a clueless fish
And wait for the sight of a lovely bass swimming by
The tug finally comes
All the waiting has paid off
You reel in your rod as fast as you can
To find…
Nothing
But a shiny hook
Good as new

Eric Totten, Grade 7
Carson Middle School, VA

Baby Bird

Miniature wings flap and tiny feet lift,
eyes are bright with excitement,
jumping up high and way down low,
flipping here and there,
leaving mother all alone,
body shaking violently,
suddenly falling down.
Plop!
And yet the bird gets up for another try.

Meryl Menezes, Grade 7
Longfellow Middle School, VA

Standing Up

As time is slowly flowing,
and bursts of wind are blowing,
the blood in my veins coursing,
the process of life strikes me then.

What had I been missing my friend?
A heart with feeling that flows?
A thorough mind that always knows?

Yet try as I may I had no courage to say,
after so many times I failed,
conclusions to no avail.

Though this time it was change,
that came to save the day,
no longer would I quit,
no longer would I sit.

I must save the world,
for the beauty of its truth,
that everything breathing or not holds,

do not fear to speak,
do not say you're being meek,
for the world is just as bad,
if you never had.

Aric Justice, Grade 8
Norfolk Christian Middle School, VA

Seasons

Spring is like a wake-up call
Flowers blooming
Leaves are coming
Everything's turning green
Life is coming back again

Summer is like a perfect paradise
Warm weather
The warm, blue water
Is like a mirror
Reflecting the perfect blue sky above

Fall is like a painter's palette
Colors everywhere
Leaves are changing
Animals hibernating
Winter's coming soon

Winter is like a snowy wonderland
The trees are like long, bony fingers
Waiting to be awakened
And to bloom again
For leaves to inhabit every branch
Waiting for spring to come again

Caitlin Hopkins, Grade 8
Norfolk Collegiate Middle/Upper School, VA

Smile

Smile,
If you want to see the sun shine,
Smile,
If you want to see the birds fly,
Smile,
If you want to see the flowers bloom,
Grass grow,
By the light of the moon,
Smile,
If you want to change the world,
And make it new,
Smile,
It's the least you can do.

Mary Reis, Grade 8
Exeter-West Greenwich Jr High School, RI

Disgust

Disgust is a heavy fog
coating everything
in a layer of mist.
misleading
you, making things seem
dark.
It leads you
farther and farther
until you are
lost.
So lost that you
will never be able to find
the truth.

Jeffrey Xia, Grade 7
Carson Middle School, VA

The Perilous Journey

Leaving of the voices behind,
I slowly enter a new world.
Greeted by glints of sun
And shadows of clouds.
Floating higher and higher,
Into the unknown,
Not sure where I'm going.
Not ready to get there.
All I knew is I'm lost,
In a new world.
This is my new world.

Chase Barrand, Grade 7
Kilmer Middle School, VA

Babies

Bundle of joy
Adorable and cute
Barely started life
Yet they bring much joy to your life
Sleeping so cute

Makayla Herbert, Grade 7
John Poole Middle School, MD

On Turning 12

The whole idea of it makes me feel
Like I had been riding a roller coaster for twelve years and it just ended
And now I am on a more dangerous roller coaster with flips and tight turns
The seats have no leather, and the carts have no seat belts
And the only light I can see, Is the light at the end.
I can remember, The great times before
But I can't tell you every single one so I may just skip a few.
At one, everything was simple, as well as two, four, ah, the good old days
At six I was a super hero, eight a king, and at ten and eleven I was a famous soccer star.
But now I am mostly at the TV
Wasting my evenings away watching shows I have seen one hundred times.
There are good times that I have, but I mostly dislike middle school
The kids have never acted as they do today
The rudeness and hate they possess.
This will never end I think to myself, but it will
Because the light is not too far away
And it is in fact only two more ice cream cakes away
But for now I roam the 7th grade hallways
Waiting for the roller coaster to reach light trying my best to get through
Because on this roller coaster
If I let go. I fall.

Cole Mills, Grade 7
E. Russell Hicks Middle School, MD

What Paper Holds

Take a piece of paper, fresh from the package.
Blank and white,
An empty canvas,
Full of possibilities to what it will become of.
Hold onto it a little longer,
And it turns a bit more shriveled —
A couple of creases in it here or there;
Remnants of being stuck in a jacket;
Perhaps a binder;
Or a back pocket, casually hanging out.
After a while,
It becomes evident that it is no longer new.
Scribbles dangle on the edges —
Equations and to-do lists scribbled hastily down for future reference,
In case they slip from memory's grasp.
A splotch of water stains the corner,
Signs of tears desperately wanting to be hidden,
While a jagged piece of tape prominently binds the middle
In attempt to bind the two pieces back together.
The paper is thrown in the bottom of a bag into darkness,
Forever holding the mistakes of our once perfect lives.

Grace Chuang, Grade 9
Thomas Jefferson High School for Science and Technology, VA

Burdens
(Sijo)

He walks up the mountain with the burden on his back
He climbs slowly as it weighs him down, the peak within reach
He grasps at the edge, pulls himself up, and drops his burden off the top

Ian Armstrong, Grade 9
Forest Park High School, VA

How to Wait for You Too
Jumping on my toes, jumping!
I try to stay warm, anticipated
The man behind me sleeps on my back
Gosh, this line won't move!
Love stuck in one hand
Expectations propped in the other
No sir, you may not have my sandwich!
The line moved an inch! Hooray!
I've stayed here for days, weeks…
Wake up! The line is moving again! Get up man!
This is getting frustrating
It'll all be worth it soon
I'm next! I'm really next!
I step up to the booth
As perky as can be
When the ticket man looked at me
"Sold Out!"

Ashley Gray, Grade 9
Woodbridge Sr High School, VA

Peace Bye Hope
I wish I was more powerful
I wish my family would open their eyes
I wish we weren't waging war
I wish I could send away the detestation and hate

I hope I can influence others' lives
I hope my brothers and sisters would stop the bloodshed
I hope the anguish will pass
I hope I can help

I dream of immense change
I dream of a day of peace between each other
I dream it all away to a place not here
I dream I have the power

Graham Balog, Grade 8
Mount St Charles Academy, RI

To Be Free
To be free — can take a lifetime —
They say it just takes courage —
It's so close — yet so far away —
And out of the blue — it can be taken away for good —

A person can make a difference —
President Lincoln freed the blacks —
He fought for them and fought for them —
Until he got their freedom back —

The joyful — exciting — feeling —
In the country we call America —
Has buried the hate — to make room for the love —
For every human has the right to be free —

Zoe Lorusso, Grade 9
Mount St Charles Academy, RI

You're Not Like Anyone
You're not like anyone
When you say "Hi"
You're not like anyone
When you kiss me
You're not like anyone
When you look into my eyes
You're not like anyone
In your eyes I see no lies
You're not like anyone
Just say bye

You're not like anyone
You're the one I care about
You're not like anyone
You're the one I can't be without
You're not like anyone
You're my sun that lights up my day
You're not like anyone
You're the one that completes my heart
You're not like anyone

Horace Clark, Grade 9
New Directions Alternative Education Center, VA

Life Is Beautiful
Life is beautiful:
Summer nights under the bright moon,
Lying on the warm beach in June.
Smell of the ocean surrounding me,
Just live happy and carefree.
Watching the sun rise up and fall,
Being with family above all.
The wind that blows the flower petals away,
Watching the ocean waves sway.
Listening to Mac Miller with a smile on your face,
Watching the stars and wondering what is up there in space.
Taking pictures and making moments last,
Life is beautiful, but it goes by so fast.
You only have one time to live — make it your best!
I'm not lucky; I'm blessed.
Life is beautiful, and I never want it to end.

Maria Souranis, Grade 8
St Clement Mary Hofbauer School, MD

Secrets
Secrets, secrets,
So dark and deep,
My friend has told me for only my mind to keep,
Those dark secrets burn a deep, dark hole,
Into my once enlightened soul.
That dark secret will forever be in my soul,
Until my life takes its toll.
But until that day my soul will forever hold,
That very dark secret that my friend had once told.

Miyah Boyd, Grade 7
Paul L Dunbar Middle School for Innovation, VA

A Dim World
I look around me, and what do I see?
Everyone's trapped and no one is free.
I yell, "Give equal treatment to all."
They tell me that order's too tall.
I don't see freedom, not even joy;
Instead, the hurting of all girls and boys.
But what can I say when they don't hear?
What I try to explain we endure.
"Will someone help me please?" I cry,
But all I get are shameful lies
That everything's equal and everything's fair,
When what I see is awful despair.
I sit by myself and stay all alone,
Resisting to turn into a brainwashed clone.
For that's what they are, sadly it's true,
And I'm running out of things I can do.
But what should I do? Should I stay or go?
Run to my kind or stay with my foes?
Making this decision is the last thing I choose,
For when I pick one world, the other I lose.
Susan Donaldson, Grade 8
Cape Henry Collegiate School, VA

I Am
I am a creative boy with a hopeful future
I wonder what I'll be in the future
I hear my future calling for help
I see success everywhere but it's not mine
I want a perfect life with a family
I am a creative boy with a hopeful future

I pretend to have a big house
I feel happy about growing up
I touch my heart to guide me
I worry about failing in life
I cry about leaving my family when I'm older
I am a creative boy with a hopeful future

I understand I'm going to leave my home
I say work hard for success
I dream about helping animals
I try to be a good person
I hope to be a veterinarian and save animals
I am a creative boy with a hopeful future
Josh Sadler, Grade 8
Corkran Middle School, MD

Forgotten Homework
The soft saffron sun melting onto the emerald grass.
Amethyst and fuchsia asters,
the delicate cherry tree with olive-green leaves,
the kids playing hopscotch — boisterous laughter.

Radiant rays shining through
the ruby red bushes
and the sparkling, polished pane,
stopping on an algebra textbook
and a notebook,
homework halfway done,
slathered with smearing silver scribbles.

Resting on the rug
is a mechanical pencil;
the door slightly ajar.
Enxin (Mary) Wan, Grade 8
Carson Middle School, VA

Back Behind the School
Back behind the school,
Where the bugs duel,
You will find many things that,
You might say it's COOL!
A duck in the muck,
A fish in the water.
A flower on a bush,
A leaf on a log.
A bird hidden in a nook,
An ant in the grass.
These things are what entertain the class.
You might think this poem is eerie,
But really you're just leery,
Of the things you might find back behind the school,
Where the bugs duel.
Kendall Bohenek, Grade 8
Norfolk Christian Middle School, VA

Heads
They all look at me, but never see me
Blankly staring to the wall ahead
They scoff and chatter happily
Exchanging glances, gladly with content
Embracing their best friend
But no never me, you see
Not even a plastic heart can fathom the pain
Pinging, pattering, panging
Running from a shadow
My plastic heart will never feel actual pain as if it were broken
Jordan Haley, Grade 8
Norfolk Christian Middle School, VA

Spring Has Arrived
I take a hesitant step out the door,
And leave the warmth and safety of my house,
Ready for the rush of frigid, arctic winter winds to blow me away,
But to my surprise, I feel nothing,
Instead, I hear innocent birds,
Singing their melodious, beautiful spring songs,
A pleasant, gentle breeze wafts through the air,
A single flower has started to bloom,
Exposing a slight hint of color,
Into the dull, depressing winter setting,
Spring has arrived.
Lauren Brunner, Grade 8
Carson Middle School, VA

Eagle

A bird that you will always see
Is an eagle, soaring high and free
Only visible to see its chest
Chewing on its prey's breast
An eagle that is so proud and so gay
Hunting for food every day
An eagle which will always care
About a lovely eagle pair
An eagle soaring over train
Elegantly swooping down in rain
Nesting in a cliff or tree
An eagle is what I would like to be

Vishal Akula, Grade 7
Kilmer Middle School, VA

Emptiness

I was his grandchild.
I came to him every summer,
His wide smile spreading across his face.
Spending long hours on that wooden porch,
No cares at all.
His voice like a warm blanket,
Comforting every worry.
Now I sit on that old porch,
Empty except for me.
No more long days.
No more soft blanket.

Kevin Salassi, Grade 7
Kilmer Middle School, VA

Home

The warm glistening feeling,
A steady hold on my heart.
I was home.
We were meant to find a peace,
I was home.
I've never been a lover of nature,
Or warmth and what they call comfort.
Not even the heat.
To me, it was always suffocating.
But this was a kind of fire that I liked
I was home.

Emily Garzon, Grade 8
Norfolk Christian Middle School, VA

Hurricane

Hurricane
windy, powerful
crashing, swaying, breaking
the wind and waves break the dock
storm

Ryan Noell, Grade 7
Cape Henry Collegiate School, VA

Fairness

Fairness hides behind the words we say,
It creeps along the actions we display.

Fairness holds heavenly hope in its arms,
Yet, sometimes it is held back, as if it does harm.

Fairness is like the right to live.
Filling our lungs with precious air, no matter to the world what we give.

But every now and then, air doesn't reach the lungs, even if we have the right,
So is living a privilege, maybe…It just might.

Fairness is a decision made by one,
But we must all give fuel if we want it to run.

Fairness give us equality,
So give back what you've been given, but with better quality.

Oneib Khan, Grade 9
Mount St Charles Academy, RI

Late Night

Ugh, I'm so tired,
I want to go to bed.
Another late night, I think I need an aspirin for my head.
All those people coming in like a mob,
I'll be dead before I quit my part-time job.

Yes! only 200 dollars more,
For this month I can finish paying my college fee.
I would be overjoyed with glee,
If only I didn't have my homework to finish.
I need to have my homework diminished and my free time replenished.

Stupid college, it costs so much!
If only I had a scholarship, I missed it by a touch.
For you this life may look different, but to me,
This horrible life is…
Just another late night.

Sushma Reddy, Grade 8
Carson Middle School, VA

Left Unsaid

These words
That are buried beneath guilt and sorrow
Each a mixture of vowels and consonants
Spelling out the broken sentences that wish to flow like rivers from my mouth
But they are trapped in a jail
A jail that holds my truths and lies
Locked away like they committed the crime
When it was the keeper who committed the foul play
The words are rotting away, never to be said
Because the key that I hold but am too cautious to admit
Is being held bitterly in my bewildered thoughts
And my mind is not willing to let the key or the truths go

Ariana Miller, Grade 7
Rachel Carson Middle School, VA

Sorry
I was told the news at school.
"I'm sorry honey." They say.
What's that supposed to mean?
Sorry.
It doesn't help; if that's what they want.
I can't believe it though.
I think they're lying.
But then they say it again.
Sorry.
Then I know.
Tears spill from my eyes,
Like a waterfall on a stormy night.
"I'm so sorry sweetie." They say once more.
"STOP IT." I yell.
"Stop saying you're sorry."
Because sorry won't do a thing.
Sorry
Won't change the fact that he's dead
D — E — A — D.
Farheen Raparthi, Grade 7
Rachel Carson Middle School, VA

Future
I am really so confused
About what'll come to be
All the things the future holds
And has in store for me

I can try to guess and dream
About the things I really want
But God's the only one who knows
My life story or my story plot

So who knows what'll happen
What my job may be
Who I'll fall in love with
Or will decide to marry

What college I'll end up going to
Or where I'll settle down
Expect the unexpected
And my future is profound.
Alicia Rivera, Grade 9
Mount St. Charles Academy, RI

The Wonders of the Sun
The sun shines,
it's the brightest star at night,
and the light that
shines down from the heavens and beyond.
It keeps our bodies warm,
and gives our hearts joy.
I am a son.
Ryan Marlow, Grade 8
Connections Academy, MD

The Sparrow
As I look up
At the sky
I see a sparrow
Flying by

I look at its wings
Brown and white
As it flaps them
While in flight

If I could be
A sparrow
And fly both
Long and narrow

I could see
What it sees
And glide along
The gentle breeze
Mary Kate Greening, Grade 8
St Jane De Chantal School, MD

Ode to Friendship
See you feeling,
Hurt inside
See you screaming,
"Help me now!"
When you cry without an end…
I'll be there
See him yelling,
Every night
See you falling
Without a fight
When no one will lend their hand…
I'll be there
In moments when you feel alone
Forced to find your way back home
Look to me
And don't be scared
I won't tell
My friend, I'll be beside you
Until the end…
Taylor Harrell, Grade 8
Norfolk Collegiate Middle/Upper School, VA

The Beach
The ocean looks grand
When we walk through the sand.
My feet get hot
From standing in one spot.
The water feels cool
Just like the pool.
I could stay all day
And play, play, play!
Austin Stevens, Grade 8
St Jane De Chantal School, MD

Still in the Sky
It gives off an eerie glow,
From the sun around the globe,
Nothing like what we know,
The moon is still in the sky.

It gives off the brightest light,
With nothing to hinder it except night,
All day it glows so bright,
The sun is still in the sky.

It's the planet we all inhabit,
From big people to little rabbits,
With life that tries to stab it,
The earth is still in the sky.

The moon with its glow,
The sun with its light,
The earth with its life,
Are still in the sky.
Courtney Chmielewski, Grade 9
Spotsylvania High School, VA

The Night Sky
Stars in the night are oh so bright,
It's not enough to make it light.
But they will try so very hard
To wash away this dreary night.

The moon shines like a crystal shard,
It illuminates my backyard.
When it shines, it might hurt my eyes,
But it's worth it to see it far.

Sometimes it seems not worth a try,
Because the sun shines in that sky.
It may be brighter, that is true
But don't fade out stars, do not die.

The morning sky is very blue,
The green grass even has some dew.
The night sky comes back, don't be blue
The night sky comes back, don't be blue
Nicole Hudler, Grade 7
Trinity Lutheran School, MD

Stars
The stars began to burn
scintillating in the sky
slowly melting their strings to the clouds
falling, falling one by one
leaving trails in the night sky
every which way they shoot down to Earth
like confetti from the heavens
twinkling in the moonlight.
Alexa Mengenhauser, Grade 7
Joyce Kilmer Middle School, VA

Mythical Creatures
These mythical creatures
Stalk in the night
They have unique features
That give you a fright
They live in silence.
Their weapons pierce
They don't like violence
But can be fierce.
They're mean as a scorpion
Their weapons poised to strike
The gnarled faces.
The tremendous wings take flight
Light as a feather
Slicing through air
They might change weather
Face them if you dare…
Henry Frazier, Grade 8
Corkran Middle School, MD

Just Because It Makes Me Stronger
Just because I'm blonde
Doesn't mean I am stupid
Doesn't mean I'm ditzy
And doesn't mean I'm a Barbie
Just because I'm bad at poetry
Doesn't mean I can't be an English teacher
Doesn't mean I know nothing
And doesn't mean I won't get far in life
Just because I fight with my friends a lot
Doesn't mean I hate them
Doesn't mean we're not friends anymore
Doesn't mean we can't stand each other
So what if I'm blonde?
What if I am bad at poetry?
What if I fight with my friends?
It just makes me stronger.
Helena Banks, Grade 8
Norfolk Collegiate Middle/Upper School, VA

Spring!
Spring has sprung
Fragrant flowers fill the air
Bright butterflies fly
There's a good mood as flowers bloom

Children play
On a warm sunny day
The bright spring sun
Makes the day fun

Creepy creatures crawl around
Birds chirp all day
Bees fly around flowers and trees
I'm so glad spring came!
KeiAsia Coates, Grade 8
Stevensville Middle School, MD

As Told by a Military Brat
Sometimes at night
When its very quiet
I hear my mother cry
Soft sobs in the twilight
I look out my window
See her sitting by our creek
She looks at the stars
Looking for my dad
He must be in Heaven
That's why she's so sad
The stars shine bright
Over all the roofs
But my mother's tears are dry
Back in the house she goes
To fake a smile
Fake strength
Fake that she's
Happy.
Amber Lowery, Grade 9
Woodbridge Sr High School, VA

Summer Days
The days fly by.
Every day is one less
until the sun will be shining high.

No need for jeans and sneakers,
jackets or mittens:
It's time for
swimming, dancing, partying,
flip flops, and shorts.

I just can't wait.
Every day is one less
until I can kick back and relax:
Just chill
and rest.

Where are you summer?
Emily Hudenburg, Grade 7
Rachel Carson Middle School, VA

Rainbow
Beautiful rainbow up in the sky.
I saw it when I drove by.
So colorful and fun to look at
Everyone just stopped and stared and sat.

They looked at this rainbow all day.
In hopes that it would always stay.
When the rainbow started to disappear
Every person was filled with fear.
Stephanie Sarza, Grade 8
Mount St Charles Academy, RI

Baseball
The warm, shady dugout…
the other team takes the field,
our first batter strikes out,
the second refuses to yield.
He hits a double and slides to second.

It's my turn to bat;
I twist my left foot for stance.
I tap the home plate mat;
the pitcher shoots his coach a glance.
The ball comes, and fast.

I whack the ball
over the right fielder's head;
our man on second goes for all.
He makes it home and puts us in the lead.
The crowd cheers and shouts.

The fielder lobs the ball to second base
and then second to third.
I barely make a triple,
But that's more than the rest.
Sam Brown, Grade 9
Norfolk Collegiate Middle/Upper School, VA

The Bird
I will get back up
I yelled once
And couldn't get back up
I tried to stand
But my wing needed help
I tried to wobble and shake off the pain
But my wing needed help
So I yelled once again
I tried to stand and yell
But couldn't so instead
I stayed still
And pecked and my wing
For a couple of minutes
And wondered if I should try again
All of the sudden a child
Came and said please get back up
Once I stood and
Wondered if I was going to fall
But I stood with encouragement
And told myself
I will get back up
Savannah Ricks, Grade 9
Menchville High School, VA

Geese Hunting
See the flock lock up
Caller says, "Get ready boys"
Then watch the geese drop
Richard Ringgold, Grade 8
Stevensville Middle School, MD

The Way I Wish I Was
I am a unicorn that leaps.
I wonder what's over the rainbow.
I hear leprechauns talking.
I see people flying on clouds.
I want my mane braided.
I am a unicorn that leaps.

I pretend I'm perfect
I feel loved.
I touch golden geese.
I worry about what tomorrow brings.
I cry about what people say about me.
I am a unicorn that leaps.

I understand that life isn't always perfect.
I say it'll be.
I dream about flying M&M's.
I try to make my life the way I want it to be.
I hope it'll all be ok.
I am a unicorn that leaps.
Makayla Emrick, Grade 8
Corkran Middle School, MD

Path
My life is full of paths
always turning left to right
like different types of math
but God keeps me tight
even when I'm loose and falling apart
God ties the strings and pulls me together

When I have no where to go
God shows me the map
When the path seems dark
God shows me the light
When the path is rocky
God gives me might
When I get off the path
God leads me back
When I need a shoulder to cry on
God is there
No matter what happens
God's path is my way
God's written my story — always
Taylor Hobson, Grade 8
Norfolk Christian Middle School, VA

The Enemy
The silence does not go unnoticed,
it has become the enemy.
It wears a disguise,
hiding quietly in the darkness,
waiting for the innocent heart.
Invisible.
Jan Lyon, Grade 8
Norfolk Christian Middle School, VA

For Life Is About People
Love at first sight is all I remember
When I think of that day back in December,
Those black glitter heels seated on the display,
Causing my hands to search for my money.

Those heels sparkled like the midnight sky
As for then I realized I could never say bye!
Envy I had when to my dismay,
My money was gone like a needle in hay.

For then I was angry and whispered to my friend,
"I need those heels for I now depend!"
Truthful response she said quite frank
"No item shall ever you need, for life is about people, not money in the bank."
Kristen Rodrigues, Grade 9
Mount St Charles Academy, RI

Worlds Away
Thousands of miles to get here, still thousands more to go
But I had found the one place where time is gently slowed.
The land they call Australia, the park's name Kakadu;
Where I had sat in silence, and suddenly I knew.

On a boat cruise with my family, as the crocs were swimming by;
As sunrise met horizon, and horizon awestruck eyes.
'Twas then the birds sprang into song and banished midnight's strife;
'Twas then the sun had come awake, and the outback brimmed with life.

For as I sat and watched the world, my brothers watching too;
For as I went the many miles and came back to tell you.
Often do I find myself dreaming in that place,
Often do I yearn to share in it's grace.
Neil Pfizenmaier, Grade 9
Mount St Charles Academy, RI

The Fall of Icarus
It's sad to see what Icarus went through,
But if you ask those who were near they'd say, "Icarus who?"
Many people saw what happened that day,
But nobody would go out of their way,
They heard the screams, they heard the splash,
Most pretended it was a wind starting to pass,
The situation wasn't nonchalant for Icarus, he was drowning before their eyes,
Nobody wanted to aid Icarus as he fell to his demise.
I guess it's his fault for not heeding the warning from his dad,
Such a horrible fate for a boy that wasn't that bad.
Taylor Davis, Grade 7
The Academy of International Studies at Rosemont, VA

Summer Nights

Summer nights,
there is nothing like,
laying in a bed of fireflies,
yellow as the lilies,
that bloom,
in grass as green,
as your eyes,
looking at me,
like I am the only person,
you could ever see.
The night as black,
as a zebra's stripes,
light from the moon,
as bright as your smile,
as comforting as your touch.
Even when the fireflies,
fly away,
even when there is no light,
when the grass is no longer green,
and the earth is like a barren desert,
you will be there.

Meredith Perrine, Grade 8
Norfolk Collegiate Middle/Upper School, VA

Thunder

I hear a loud crash outside
And rush out in the rain
To find what has happened
And find a fallen tree.
Later I hear it again
Followed by a loud thump
I peer out the window
And see a new fallen maple.
Rain clatters against the windows
I try to drown it out
But to no avail.
I hear more loud claps
And a far of thump
Again I look
And see a third tree fall.

Daniel Heller, Grade 7
Phoenix Center Annapolis, MD

Now It Is Yours

One day you finally knew,
the secret was exposed,
no longer could it be kept,
and now it is yours.
The burden of this secret,
might overtake you,
consuming, and tearing you apart,
so from now, 'til forever,
keep it in your heart,
and never let it go.

Taylor Marsengill, Grade 7
Kilmer Middle School, VA

What I Love

I love to watch a brilliant butterfly floating through the sky
Timidly and delicately playing with the breezes

I love to hear the soft crackle of a campfire
Underneath the silent, starlit sky

I love to hear owls in the calm night
Hooting away while gliding across the still air

I love to hear the word congratulations after you have done something glorious
Such as receiving an award, winning a race, or conquering a goal

I love to taste a cold, fresh glass of sweet lemonade
On a sizzling, sun-drenched summer day

I love to taste hand-picked blueberries off the vine
Some sweet, some sour, but all making my taste buds wild

I love to touch the surface of calm water
Sending ripples throughout it with just the slightest contact

I love to touch someone's heart even when they might not need it
Just to let them know they will always have someone beside them

I love the way your best friend is always there
Watching your back and comforting you at any needed time

I love the way each and every snowflake is unique
Like the way every human is with their own characteristics

Teri Adelhardt, Grade 8
Most Blessed Sacrament Catholic School, MD

The Royal Thief

I gasp, absorbing the breathtaking image.
Magnificent webs of jewels linked together by threads of silver upon her head.
Vibrant gemstones adorn the Princess' royal tiara.

All of a sudden,
I snap out of this enchantment,
And I hurriedly snatch the crown from its perfectly styled hair.

And I run.

I hear the guards barking behind me,
The rain pouring down on me like sand in an hourglass,
My feet splashing in the mud with every step I take.

In the distance I see the bronze fence,
I gain speed with every sprint now,
For the more momentum I have, the better chances I have of escaping.

I hurdle over the fence and plummet into the woods.
I no longer hear the guards at my tail, but as soon as I gain my stability again,
I notice I have trespassed onto the Forest of the Lost Prisoners.

Stephany Rivero Anez, Grade 7
Kilmer Middle School, VA

Reading and Writing
Reading is like an adventure,
That begins when you turn the page.
Writing is like creating your own adventure,
That can be anything you can imagine.

Reading is like entering a different world,
Where things may or may not be real.
Writing is a way to express yourself,
Or maybe even create your own world.

Reading is a way to pass time,
While learning and having fun as well.
Writing is a way to be creative,
And share your knowledge with others.
Rachel Brodsky, Grade 8
Norfolk Collegiate Middle/Upper School, VA

Freedom Hearts
My heart is full of broken dreams
My soul is full of tears
To wait and pray for
freedom all these years
Freedom from hunger
Freedom from love
Freedom from the big man
up above
What is wanted is happiness
Time with you, love
and live in freedom
live in happiness
for one and
for all.
Cheyenne Hudgins, Grade 8
Independence Secondary School, VA

Right or Left?
Stick a knife
In my life,
It splits in two.

A fork in the road
Brings a heavy load.
Where to move.

Right or left?
Where to step,
I have no clue.

I guess,
I'll make my own path.
Maxwell Schlott, Grade 8
Mount St Charles Academy, RI

Dreamer
I am a dreamer, a wisher
I wonder sometimes what the sea would say
I hear the whispers in the wind
I see the trees dance
I want, I wish to see the world

I pretend I can move mountains
I feel a longing for adventure and for magic
I touch the Earth and its wonders
I worry sometimes about the future
I cry for what I've lost

I understand some call me crazy
I say to them they're only partly right
I dream that I will grow, that I will change
Though I try to stay myself
I hope that I have made a difference
I am a dreamer, a wisher
Willow Windrum, Grade 8
Corkran Middle School, MD

What Is Love?
Love is holding me through a thunderstorm
Telling me every thing's all right
Even though we both know they aren't,
Maybe just for tonight

Love is trust
Trusting in everything I do
Laying down at night,
Hoping you trust me too.

Love is pain
Something that cuts deep
It hurts so much
That I cry myself to sleep

I'm so scarred up that I hurt you
Maybe you should leave me alone
Before you get scarred too.
Alexis Herbert, Grade 7
St Columba School, MD

Seasons
The fall and winter are wicked cold,
But I have lots of fun.
Lacing up my skates for hockey,
Even though outside there's no sun.

In the spring and in the summer,
I go outside and throw and hit a ball.
Until the days get shorter and shorter,
And again here comes the fall.
Kevin Valentine, Grade 8
Mount St Charles Academy, RI

Writer's Block
In the imperfect light
In hope of rhyme or pattern
I think to myself
And now I have a case of writer's block
Bewildering words under
The common title

Today the title
Hides in the dark light
"If I could under —"
Stand how to make this a pattern
Now I have writer's block
But then I think to myself.

What could I write about myself?
Although first, what could be my title?
And again I have writer's block.
So I think, and I stare into the light.
Ben Higgins, Grade 7
E Russell Hicks Middle School, MD

When I Saw a Beggar
When I saw a beggar,
I looked into his face.
I looked into his eyes
And saw a look of grace.

When I saw a beggar,
I looked at his feet.
I looked at his clothes
And saw something incomplete.

When I saw a beggar,
I took a closer step
And saw that he was without a foot.

When I saw a beggar,
I handed him a rupee
And he cried with ecstasy.
And I left a better man.
Mohit Chandi, Grade 9
Norfolk Collegiate Middle/Upper School, VA

A Sunset
A sunset,
warm and true,
hugs the earth when its do,
colorfully unimaginable,
beautiful as nature should be,
brings us peace in times of worry,
beautiful is the sun set.
Erin McDaniel, Grade 8
Chickahominy Middle School, VA

Life, Love and Justice

Life is a matter of survival,
It comes with a package of three things,
It includes a heart, a body and a mind,
The heart keeps you breathing,
The body keeps you moving,
And the mind keeps you thinking,
Each life depends on how the organism acts,
If the organism treats it poorly,
It will soon go to the stars,
Life's best friend is love,
Love is within life,
There is one limit to life and love,
That is justice,
If justice prevails,
So does life and love,
So take care of these three,
Like they are three Gods,
Three jewels,
And three connections,
Then one day, you will become,
Life, Love or Justice.

Neswanth Keepudi, Grade 7
Carson Middle School, VA

Beneath the Veils

Burns, bruises, scars —
Emotional and physical.
This is what they must deal with
Day in and day out.
All of it hidden behind their veils.
Many say that the veils are to keep things out —
But I believe that they are also to keep things in.
To hide the pain from the world
Shielding the bruises and the burns, the battered bodies.
The fire that once burned beneath those veils,
Brutally smothered.
Their spirits fade,
Just as the dazzling light of day fades
Into the bitter frost of night.
So, too, their freedom has been wrenched from their grasp
It began so very long ago.
Most have abandoned the thought of ever gaining it back.
But some fight,
The flames beneath their veils blazing brighter than ever.
Those few women give hope, because they have hope.
Because of them, the flames are growing higher.

Casey Kelahan, Grade 8
Loudoun Country Day School, VA

The Eagle

Fierce majestic ruler of the skies
Whose wings soar beyond where the desert sun lies
Over valleys fertile and mountains wide
As mortals watch her fly

Elizabeth Larson, Grade 7
Parkside Middle School, VA

The Ocean

Day and night the oceans screech,
Crashing down onto the beach.

The ocean has a chilly breeze,
To families it is sure to please.

Surf the big waves or fly a kite,
And you'll want to stay every night.

See the crabs walking on the sand,
Watch out — they might pinch at your hand!

Ride on a jet ski or a boat,
You'll have a real fun time afloat!

Be careful of a hurricane,
It might be crazy and insane!

I know you'll miss the beach much, though,
Pack all your bags, it's time to go!

Steve Bishop, Grade 7
Carson Middle School, VA

Glass Half Full

Life is like a cloud
Sometimes it is cold, wet, and gray
It makes you hate
Makes your insides cold
Churning like a boat at sea in the storm
When the lighthouse's beam cannot reach you
The feelings that life gives you
Are horrible and isolated
But it never seems to last
Before you know it
Life has turned into
Something white, fluffy, and soft
It fills you with warmth and optimism
Makes you breathe deeply
Smell the remnants of the rain
Feel the sun's warmth
Share it with the ones you love
Always cherish this life, otherwise
You might end up with a rain cloud
In place of your life.

Samantha McCulloch, Grade 8
Stone Hill Middle School, VA

Why?

You always told me,
Peace, love and smiles make the world go round,
So why is the world in war?
Why do people hate each other?
Why is your face caressed in frowns?
War, hate and frowns is what you should say.

Cheyanne Smith, Grade 7
Western Heights Middle School, MD

A Swimmer's Thoughts

By the end of this poem you will see
How I have changed from land to sea.

By the end of this poem you will know
Just how fast my body can go.

By the end of this poem you will have asked
"Wow how could he go that fast?"

I trained all year, trying not to miss a day
I knew this would be the price I'd have to pay.

Each meet that went by I met goal times,
Trying to set the bar higher, and higher I did climb.

They say you get out of life what you put in to it,
goals, the ones you make, the ones you don't hit.

It's the end of the poem, hours of training I didn't shirk,
Success this week will be from all that hard work.

Neal McElhattan, Grade 7
Kilmer Middle School, VA

The Sea

The sea moves and crashes,
Crashes against the rocks,
Rocks that turn into pieces,
Pieces that turn to sand,
Sand that's on the beach.
The beach where there are people,
People who love the sea,
The sea that's turquoise and blue,
Blue and crystal, beautiful.
Beautiful like the fish,
Fish that are colorful,
Colorful like the shells,
Shells that cover the ocean floor.
The ocean floor covered in life,
Life that lives under the sea,
Under the sea there are animals.
Animals that are colorful,
Colorful like the seaweed,
Seaweed that sways under the sea,
Under the sea life emerges and it lives eternal.

Sophia Papelis, Grade 8
Norfolk Collegiate Middle/Upper School, VA

Karate Belts

White, yellow, orange, green, blue, purple, red, brown,
Brown senior, black
The smell the taste
The sight of the belt
It is not the glory of the belts
But it is the honor that makes us feel proud.

Cole Thomas, Grade 7
Clear Spring Middle School, MD

My Family

Sweet tangy melodies fill the room;
A mother enters,
Bright and sunny with a slight sad tune;
Her smile
Is like the sky's brightest star.

A deep bluesy tune enters the room,
Bringing with it a sense of gloom;
Father doesn't smile much,
But, with music's light touch,
That can change.

Strung up tight, a hard chord is strummed,
The clash of a drum set in on electric key;
Sister's nighttime symphony comes in, too.

Things turn brighter as I walk in,
Latest and greatest;
The beat marched infectiously, danceable heat;
My tempo is last, but not least.

Madelyn Gordon, Grade 7
Cape Henry Collegiate School, VA

Winter

I love the season winter,
I can make a warm fire.
Fire crackling in the dark night.
Sometimes, when it snows,
You can see snow falling and whooshing,
Before it hits the ground.
When you go out at night,
The wind is howling.
While it hisses,
You can feel the cold air crashing on your skin.
When Christmas comes,
Everything is decorated,
Bells on the tree are jingling,
All the while your skin is tingling.

Austin Kramer, Grade 7
Cape Henry Collegiate School, VA

The Sand

The sand at the beach
The sand at the beach is
Calm, smooth, soft, or hard
The sand at the beach has a mind of its own
It can be agitated at the slight gust of wind
Or be as calm as the glassy sea
It can be swallowed by water
And be still, hard, and breathless
The sand at the beach is so nice
On a hot day it can boil with excitement
Or lay hard, cold, and breathless
The full-of-life sand.

Alan Herbertson, Grade 7
Cape Henry Collegiate School, VA

I Can Do It

The cold, crisp feel of mountain air. The blur of snow beneath my skis.
The whistle of wind above me. The crunch of snow below me. I can do it

Racing towards the threshold of the point of no return.
Hoping my body follows, what my mind envisions. I can do it.

Only focusing on what's about to happen, and what intangible feats I can accomplish,
Calm and collected, like a golfer lining up his shot, yet adrenaline surges through my body, like a lion on the hunt. I can do it.

What bizarre gyrations can I do this time, before gravity forces me to come down from my domain high above the slopes,
Where time seems frozen, and each second lasts an eternity. I can do it.

I stay steady on my approach, trying to build up the speed I will need to go higher and higher than before.
I rush towards the seemingly innocent orange line that marks the tip of the jump,
But I know this orange line is there to mock me, to dare me, for me to conquer it. I can do it.

Whoosh. I sail past the lip of the jump, and for a second forget what I cam here for.
And then I remember. I start to twist and spin, and attempt to accomplish everything my mind tells me to do. I can do it.

But now for the landing. I steady myself out a couple feet above the white, tilted wall that rises up to meet me.
For the first time I am scared. I come down hard, but my knees absorb the impact. I did it.

Andrew Van Winter, Grade 9
Mount St Charles Academy, RI

Perfection

Perfection is an impossible task to achieve;
No human is made to be perfect.
Trying to achieve perfection too much will make you fail even more.
I myself am a perfectionist;
At everything I do I want to be the greatest at it.
Sometimes trying to become great at something you're just not good at can be stressful.
In that case, I would just back away from it and try something else.
A person once told me being a perfectionist is a great trait to have as a human,
But it could also be a bad one.
Some people would say that perfect means excellent or complete beyond practical or theoretical improvement.
To perfection means being the greatest at whatever you're doing
People say I try too hard;
Some say I am too serious or too focused,
But to me all I'm doing is trying to be perfect.

Theodore C. Rich, Grade 9
Norfolk Collegiate Middle/Upper School, VA

Sudden Realization

Look deep, deep, far beyond,
Beyond the universe and open skies,
Past the planets and the stars,
Further then your mind's reach.
Realize that there is so little time, very little to live in.
Open your eyes to the world around you and see the things that are nor commonly recognized.
There is much more to the world than what meets the eye, more than the ground you walk on and the air you breathe.
More than the clothes you wear, who you hang out with, the life you live. There is more, so much more.
Go out and find it and gain newly opened eyes.
Go out and find that sudden realization.

Abigail Roberson, Grade 8
Post Oak Middle School, VA

Routine after routine, door closed
CD player turned up
And attempting to meditate myself into a world of
Peace, Thursdays with Gramma, and Little Shirley Beans
But quickly and surely those 2 nagging voices crept back into my brain
And, as always, considered it a nice place to stay for the night
Stay for the month, stay for who knows (or even cares) how long
So I'd huddle in my sweater and soak up what little comfort it had to spare
Eventually those nagging voices stopped, and it was nice; but they never started back, and when I saw her luggage
I realized it really wasn't that nice at all
If Jon + Kate = 8, What does Jon - Kate = ?
And I'd listen to that ol' man sit up all night
Playing his records he bought back in Yesteryear
Playing that Johnny Cash song "I Walk the Line"
o v e r and o v e r and o v e r and o v e r
Sitting there with his cold wings and warm drink
That he wouldn't couldn't even touch
And that ol' man, he didn't walk the line
He crossed it.

Jessica Hinton, Grade 9
Tunstall High School, VA

My First Day in a New Land

Today,
I can hear, the people around me chattering, like clucking geese, they can understand each other but I can't understand them.
I hear something different, the reassuring words of my mother. I can hear my family's laughter when we were all together.
Today,
I can smell, people's perfume mixing, like the melting pot America is claimed to be.
The swirls of Chanel, Gucci, Hugo Boss and Prada all together with some other flair.
All the scents make me think of a place like Paris or Rome, with many new tourists and many more residents.
Today,
I can feel my shoes a bit too tight, like a burden I must carry. I feel too small to take these large steps.
My shoes pinching me are the pain of the place I left behind.
They are there hanging over me like a cloud of emotion darkening even the brightest days.
Today,
I can see the eyes boring into us, like we are a different species.
I see the people as lions looking at zebras, not believing what their eyes are seeing.
I am scared feeling so tiny with no friendly faces near.
Today,
Inside, I feel, curious, like a puppy walking for the first time.
I am excited for the new places I will go but also afraid to leave the safety of my home.
But once I take these risks I can discover amazing things and dream beyond the horizons of this new country.

Jacqueline Kolhof, Grade 7
Carson Middle School, VA

Missing You

Missing you is the hardest part
Hardest part of living without you
Missing you is like having no air to breathe
Missing you really hurts and the worst part is that you don't care
Missing you is worse when I have to see you
Missing you and telling myself that you're not worth it hurts worse
Missing you is something I thought wouldn't happen
Missing you is harder than I thought

Sara Thornten, Grade 8
Independence Secondary School, VA

If I Could Fly

I want to have the superpower to be able to fly.
I would fly to my favorite place, and maybe go to outer space.
I would fly until the sun goes down, and then fly back to town.
I would never have to walk; I would just fly right over the block.
I would have so much fun, and hate for each day to be done.
I would fly here and there, and take my friends anywhere.
I think it would be so cool to fly.
I would fly until the day I die.

Jake Yeager, Grade 9
Delaware Military Academy, DE

Balloons

the balloon
  floating higher in the sky
can it be touched?
  can someone stop it?
it must come
  down
its shining red color
glistening in the light

we hope it comes down
  but it just goes UP
    it climbs on the clouds
      and dances with the birds
     it soars with the wind
    until one day
   when it returns
  where will it fall
will it be back here?
there are so many questions
  but it races the wind
    never to be seen again

Christopher Lepine, Grade 8
Mount St Charles Academy, RI

After the Storm

A hot rain,
Pouring down from the sky.
Thunder and lightning,
The smell of wet grass and fire.
Tapping on the roof, splashing on the street,
Lasting for hours and hours on end.
When finally the roaring ceases
The flashes stop.
The tapping comes to a halt.
Look out into the sky, a brilliant blue.
And sweeping across,
As if it was painted there casually,
Brilliant colors;
The rainbow after the storm.

Tiana D'Acchioli, Grade 8
St Rocco School, RI

Untitled

Tear the nails off your finger tips
And smear the blood across your lips
Trying to disguise the lies
But they hide in your eyes
Just not tonight
It's not worth the fight
Lay down next to me,
We will search,
Find and see
It's pointless to put a lock on love
When we have they key

Angelica Bonnie Van Pelt, Grade 7
Western Heights Middle School, MD

I Will Never Forget

It is difficult to see you cry,
It is difficult to signify how much I love you,
There is nothing louder than the words that we never said,
Such chaos to look for your heart because there are thousand of them.
I will find your body, but how can I love without you?
I ask God many questions, but maybe He made this for us to learn,
I will never forget those faces,
Those places and never ever forget the tears of my family,
Now there is nowhere to go,
Now there is nothing to do in this wild world,
Maybe I don't know what I am saying,
It is just because of my anger,
Maybe there is someone who is waiting to me for help,
But I don't hear anything; I don't hear noises, only my heart saying
Never give up,
I think about all the difficulties
opportunities that all those people had, but there is always the devil
Extending his hands so he can make us do things that we don't want to do,
I will never forget you, my love,
I found your body; I'm touching it softly with my tears,
The tears that never gave up till I found you, I will never forget.

Maria Clara Gonzalez Lopez, Grade 8
Most Blessed Sacrament Catholic School, MD

Ode to Tennis

A peaceful sport, yes it is,
Unlike football, no one is caused much harm,
Maybe a leg injury, maybe an ankle sprain,
But never a concussion.
Six million more viewers than football,
Almost as popular as soccer,
Maybe not that big in the U.S., but never forgotten in Europe.
Wilson, Babolat, and Head are the best,
No one supports the sport like them,
The best at what they do, these companies are at the top,
Not a team sport, but not an individual too,
You may not have a team, but you have a crew,
Confidence, is big in the game,
Most of the people who win, are as tough as a nail,
But the best part of the sport, is not just the win,
It is in fact, what leads up to the win,
The pressure is starting to creep up on you, how to complete the win,
The complexity of the sport, never ceases,
To satisfy my energy, exercise my mind,
And especially, allow me to have a great time.

Narain Rijhwani, Grade 8
Norfolk Collegiate Middle/Upper School, VA

Art Is Poetry

Poems should be free, not locked in a bottle.
Wind is free, it flows anywhere it wants to go.
Let your heart pour out words onto the paper like a waterfall.
Poems should be quiet, yet exciting, full of love, but yet full of hatred.
Passion is like another word for poetry because it takes passion to make art, and art is poetry.

Taylor LaBarge, Grade 7
The Academy of International Studies at Rosemont, VA

Fire

Fire fire burning bright
A red orange demon flame you cause in the darkened night
Your flames captivate my house
You killed everything I had, sister, brother and a mouse

But most important of all you took Mom and Dad
And now I am lying on the ground feeling more than sad
Crying in the night
Feeling no hope, and no light

For everything I know, knew, that made me happy
Mom's strawberry pancakes in the morning
Dad teaching me to be a better me in the evening
Older sister's peaceful music in the afternoon
And brother helping me with math homework at night.
They're all gone!

And now here I am alone, crying, wondering why Dad risked himself and Mom for me.
Why? Why me? I'm a no one. No more memories to share. Nothing to do. Nothing to say.
At my new foster home they say it will be all right. But what do they know?
Do they know that I run away outside when I see the fireplace on?
Do they know how all the kids light matches and I just think of my parents trying to escape?
All they can see is: A pale white skinny boy with long brown hair who has just survived a house fire.

But what I am is scarred for life.

Adrian Gavrila, Grade 7
Rachel Carson Middle School, VA

Havoc and Pandemonium

Why does everything have to be so complicated?
'Cause every time I hear the news I only hear about more and more possession being confiscated.
We live in a world of sorrow, hatred, and remorse.
So why do we simply just brace ourselves for the worst, when it can be restored?

Remorse, regret, this is what people get.
Not any help, this is the one thing to fret.
Do you know what causes people to sweat?
And no it's not that exhausting exercise set —
It's the little factors called threats.

We're upset because we tend to forget,
About the exasperating little crises named debts.
If we'd stop acting like our crazy pets,
Then maybe we wouldn't be so desperate — not just yet.

Why do we have wars?
When all that's present is gore on the floor?
When it's the very things that our families deplore?
What else do I need to say more?

All I can see is the crying rain that pours,
That is currently soaking into our pores.
To remind us about the wonderful and precious things in life that we stand for
And like beggars on the streets, so desperately implore for.

Fiona Do, Grade 7
Longfellow Middle School, VA

As a Fish

We're a simple creature,
A beautiful creature,
A delicious creature?
We are small,
We're large,
We're dangerous
We come in all shapes, sizes and colors
I swim bravely
Across the ocean
Or rather that,
Your aquarium!
You might love us,
You might hate us,
But you have to admit that we have this sense of calm
And serenity to us,
And sometimes you wish you could own that quality
Because in your very, very, stressful human life,
You wish you could just keep on swimming,
As a fish.

Jackson Spickler, Grade 7
E Russell Hicks Middle School, MD

Dirty House

With four people living in a house
It's never quiet as a mouse
Dishes are piling up
High as a mountain
Clothes to be washed are overflowing
Like a broken dam
No control
The cobwebs have made a maze
And it has my dad's anger ablaze
Me and my mom are the ultimate duo
We tell dad and bro to stay back
Because we're about to attack
The work is long, hard and dirty too
But someone has to do it and it won't be those two

Paige Wellington, Grade 8
Corkran Middle School, MD

Story of My Life

In life the unexpected happens
Lose friends make friends
People change when you stay the same
Relationships break down and crumble
While others come out of the rubble
Your heart gets broken for the first time,
Once you realize all the lies
A family's dynamic changes,
Some for the best, others hate it.
You find new hobbies or things to do
After the one thing you love is taken from you
But in the end, one thing never changes
My love for you, never tainted

Kelly Burns, Grade 8
Norfolk Christian Middle School, VA

Things Unseen

What can I say?
One can only watch in dismay:
Too much one's emotions become,
And life becomes tiresome.

But, suddenly, far away,
A light comes into display
When darkness threatens to overcome
You on a time that is loathsome.

Emotions that can be felt,
Emotions that are heartfelt
Come into display,
When that bright light comes to help and play.

Positive feelings and negative feelings,
A part of our yearnings,
Including not only cruelty, despair, and darkness,
But also love, happiness, and kindness.

An empty shell one would be,
Emptiness in the eye,
With no feelings and no mind.

Anne-Marie L. Radiguet-Correa, Grade 9
Norfolk Collegiate Middle/Upper School, VA

Dream

They say you're supposed to dream while you sleep.
But my dreams are what keep me awake at night
And going the next day.
They drive me to work for the intangible,
Like a flower hungry for sun.
I long for my dreams to one day become a reality.

But people like to tell me
My dreams are impossible.
Yet they're what make me try,
Try until I have failed.
So I will continue to dream big.
Until I reach my goal.

But if I love only to reach my dream,
What happens when it is over?

Georgia Drinkwalter, Grade 9
Norfolk Collegiate Middle/Upper School, VA

My Reflection

I look down from the bridge.
I look at my reflection and try to find myself.
I try to see my future and what God has planned for me.
Suddenly I start fading and just see the sky and sun
and nowhere to be found is me.
Is this a sign? Am I not supposed to be here?
Oh, I wish this pond would make all my dreams come true!

Kayla Vanik, Grade 9
Menchville High School, VA

Cheetah

I'm stuck in a cage
Getting full of rage
I can run faster than a car
But I'm consider a cat
I eat meat
So that makes me a carnivore
I want to be free
People expect me to run
But I don't want to sometimes
I rather be in a warm climate
When I woke up one day I was in a zoo
I miss my family
If they let me go I will run as fast as I could
To a place I can call home
They give me food and a place to sleep
But I rather be home
I remember those days when I could run far away
I will be with my kind and you will see it as the wild
But I call it home
When I return I will say,
Home sweet home

Eletria Herbert, Grade 7
E Russell Hicks School, MD

Drums

Playing video games, surfing, and chilling out
Always makes me happy
But not as much as the drums do
When I play the drums
I feel like there is nothing else that needs to be done
Like there is nothing bothering
As if I had no problems
And was happy once again
This is one of the only things that
Makes me feel this way
The drums to me are like another friend in my life
But a friend who understands what I want
And that sometimes I just need to be left alone
It's as if they can read my thoughts
They are the only things that can make me feel this way
And I will never quit playing them.

Matt Santos, Grade 8
Norfolk Collegiate Middle/Upper School, VA

Cavorting

Being out at slumber parties,
Going to the mall,
Playing in the park, hanging out at the pool,
Texting on the phone with my buds,
Meeting with my friends,
Having lunch with my pals,
Going horseback riding,
Playing video games with the family,
Is what I do to cavort.

Leslie Cabral, Grade 7
Marshall Middle School, VA

Daffodil

Oh, daffodil, why do you rise so early?

Each and every spring, the daffodil will bloom
With even the faintest glimmer of hope –
It rises like the sun at dawn
And awakens us from
The yearly hibernation of our dreams
The symbol of optimism

But, daffodil?
Why do you rise so early?
Is it to make us feel less alone?
To make us smile?
To make us appreciate life
Just a little more?

But when it turns to summer, you stop warming us
And emitting your rays of sun
And you set, leaving us in the dark again.

Oh, daffodil, why do you rise so early?

Carolyn Klein, Grade 7
Kilmer Middle School, VA

I'm Up Here

I'm up here.
You're down there.
The only thing between us is a current of air!

I'm soaring.
You're walking.
And nothing is between us, just a current of air!

I look upon you with attentive eyes.
You look for me with unseeing eyes.
And the only thing between us is a current of air!

I glide to my treetop sanctuary where hungry mouths await.
You cruise to your two-story colonial where dinner is on the plate.
And still the only thing between us is a current of air!

Tommy Miller, Grade 7
Kilmer Middle School, VA

Live

Live for the moment.
Don't ever let anyone hold you back.
Dream big.
And fight for it.
Find yourself.
Never forget who you are.
Trust your instinct.
Because sometimes that's all you have.
And challenge yourself.
Because you never know when someone will challenge you.

Katie Heinold, Grade 8
Everett Meredith Middle School, DE

On the Move

My heart pounds
When I'm on my mark
As we all stand around
For the race to start.
I look to the gunner.
He lets us go.
Soon all the runners
Find their flow.
Almost done, I get a cramp,
But this is fun.
I wanna stop but know I can't.
It's the final lap,
And there I go.
I lengthen the gap,
Only to show.
I do what I love
And will never say no.
Because when I race,
I'm gonna prove
I can earn first place
When I'm on the move.

Steven Turack, Grade 9
Norfolk Collegiate Middle/Upper School, VA

Move On...

Never forget the ones
Who shot you down
You're not worthy of those tears
And for the people who shot you down
Never forget the ones who are on your side
And who aren't

Don't look back at the past
Seeing the ones who made you cry
Move on you are better than them

Although, I'll always be here for you
Because you are a true friend
Who will always be in my heart
And nobody can change that.

Emily Compton, Grade 7
Ridgely Middle School, MD

You

When I see you
Your face lights up.
It's like an angel has touched my heart.
And once I look at you I can't look back,
And if I choose to look back,
Everything I've had or ever was
Will *vanish*
But when you say "I love you Mariah"
My heart *stops*
And starts all over again.

Mariah Orr, Grade 7
Western Heights Middle School, MD

Friendship

When I was younger, I had lots of friends who all loved me,
Then one day my mom came to me and said, "We'll have to leave."
Everything was different, from the setting to the school.
I just wanted to make some friends, just wanted to be cool.
But no one would acknowledge me, or even just say, "Hey,"
Until this girl came up to me and said, "I'm Taylor Kay."
This friendship lasted days, then weeks, then months, and later years,
Then Mom came in my room, and what she said left me in tears:
"Your father has been laid off, so we're moving to New York.
There I'll find a nice place and your father will find work."
I thought my life was ruined, and I thought I was no more,
Until I realized all the things that New York had in store.
Dad found work, I found some friends, Mom found a place to stay,
And I've lived here, in New York, until this very day.
But right now, I'm not in New York, I'm miles and miles away.
I am at the funeral of old friend Taylor Kay.
She came back from a party with her boyfriend driving high,
And everyone knows how this ends…well, Taylor said goodbye.
Keep all your friends close, for there is something I must say:
After years in New York I'd forgotten Taylor Kay.

Hailey McNelis, Grade 8
St Anne's Episcopal School, DE

Fathers Return

Gone and home again, used to him being gone
All of a sudden it was real, growing up with one parent
Seeing other people have a dad and not appreciate it
My mom worked harder stressed more, wondering if he was ok
Years went by nothing changed, didn't want to move
Better opportunities near family, did we have to move?
Moving day comes, having to make new friends
Doors opened, joined sports teams, met new people
People reaching out to me, did they really care, why do they care?
Do they want to know me, the real me?
Mom worked more, had to provide, always trying to provide all she could for us.
Days without a father are coming to an end
Received the news, wondering what would it be like
Has he changed? Will he ever do it again?
Went to see him, excited, questioning, hopeful
He is coming home, now he is here
More fun, family is complete
Mom is less stressed, Dad is keeping us on our feet
Holding us accountable, making sure we don't make mistakes
Willing to talk to us when we need him, a father that is home again.

Kinnicko Robinson, Grade 8
Norfolk Christian Middle School, VA

Miss Judgmental

It's funny how much you know just from what you've heard
Hilarious how you know everything about me yet we've never spoke a single word
It's real cute how quick you are to judge when you've never walked a mile in my shoes
Or seen the tears I've cried, the life I've lived
If you don't like me, there's nothing I can do
Because Dear Miss Judgmental, if you don't like me why should I live to please you?

Cameron Broughton, Grade 7
Monelison Middle School, VA

Perspective

I thought I was having a bad day,
I said: "Anything but this!"
I had five tests I didn't study for, my homework remained at home.
Then I stopped, and the world flipped upside down.
I woke up in bed, with a spider on my head.
I was getting ready for school; my lunch was rats and gruel.
I got onto the bus, stomach churning, and headed off to school.
As the bus began to spin, out of control, I thought: "Maybe school wouldn't be so bad after all."
The last thing I remembered before blacking out was waking up in a hospital bed.
I woke up, propped against my locker.
I grinned, full of enthusiasm, and went and took my tests.
I failed them all. It was still great.

Daniel Rees, Grade 7
Kilmer Middle School, VA

To My Doorknob

Oh doorknob, who lets me enter,
I praise thee and your inventor.

Without you I'd be stuck outside,
Like road kill, I would have died.

You're my entrance to my humble home,
Without you, where would I roam?

Letting me in and locking others out,
You're super spectacular without a doubt.

If broken you can be repaired,
You are the coolest creation, I have declared!

Large, small, fancy, or meager,
I'll always be your confidential keeper.

The thrill of wondering what lies behind you
It's like wondering what lies in my stew.

My Noni gets you covered in chocolate
The aroma of candy in my nostrils, the smell of a nut.

Your supernatural sheen is very complex
To me, you surpass all other objects.

Doorknob, oh doorknob, you have always been my friend
Please don't turn against me and have the good times end

Jimmy Brannon, Grade 7
Most Blessed Sacrament Catholic School, MD

Ode to the Spider

O creepy crawly, so ugly and scary
With 6 bulging eyes and 8 legs so hairy

You hang in the corner and patiently wait to jump
You land on my head and then bite my rump

I feel your stares while I snuggle all up inside my bed
You dangle in front of my face on one single thread

You plot your revenge while you dismantle a fly
Your evil piercing eyes make me want to break down and cry

You never bother my sister not even my mother
You scare me half to death but you love my big brother

You're on my laptop or inside my book
When I turn around, your everywhere I look

You have a baby black body with fangs O so long
You frighten and mock me, why can't we just get along

I'm sorry I killed your mother, it was all by mistake
She was perched there relaxing right on my pate.

Ahhhhhhhhh! is all you want me to scream
The way you are always out of reach is part of your spiteful scheme

If you find me tied up in web or perhaps even poisoned
By then you realized the spider always wins in the end

Grace Riley, Grade 8
Most Blessed Sacrament Catholic School, MD

Spring Fling

There I look at the window.
Seeing grass sprout and flowers dance in the wind.
Before my eyes lay the blanket of spring on my front yard.
Robins sing warm, bees buzz, people go bird-watching
Now isn't that a sight to see on the very first day of spring?

Ythrip Karar, Grade 7
Glasgow Middle School, VA

NCIS

NCIS is the best.
The mysterious element keeps me on my toes.
Always something new, to ponder.
Never-ending clues.
Naval Criminal Investigative Services.

Rachael Posch, Grade 8
Norfolk Christian Middle School, VA

First Day

Mommy I went to school today
We worked on colors and got to play
I met a new friend named Mike
And my teacher Ms. May I really do like
I learned to add one plus one
We had a math competition and Lily won
Lily has red hair and lots of freckles
She's really pretty and always tickles
Then there was lunch, I had a bunch
Brownies, chips, and red fruit punch
At recess we played tag and played in sand
They buried me including my hands
We did shapes after that
Then we made paper hats
We read *The Three Little Pigs*
Then made pigs out of figs
I cannot wait to go back tomorrow
I wonder what Lily is wearing too
But everything we did today
I didn't understand, had no clue

Kyndall Nicholas, Grade 8
Corkran Middle School, MD

Why

Why do they look at me like that?
Why do they judge me?
Why do they assume who I am?
They don't know me
They don't understand me
They don't care about me

I'm not weird
I'm not insane
I'm not what they think
I'm unique
I'm perfectly fine
I'm happy

Why do they have to be mean?
Why do they make fun of me?
Why do they laugh?
It's not funny, it hurts
Why do they do that?
Why

Hunter Rowland, Grade 7
Forest Middle School, VA

Blessing

May the sun shine before you
May it give everlasting rays
May it guide you on your way
May it fill your heart with joy
And when the sun sets,
May it come another day.

Josie Brown, Grade 7
Marshall Middle School, VA

Before Your Very Eyes

As you look before your very eyes,
The world in its shell corrupting,
So prepare for the new upcoming arising,
The force has blended the delusional,
As coerce as the concoction penetrates through the hearts and souls of our human race.

Bound to disperse from the gates of heaven,
Unveil your wrath over the riches of ultimate power,
While to pursue with dedication for a driving ambition,
Is like $E=MC^2$ over the lava encrusted mountains.

But in the logical mind,
Brains and statistics perplex them quick,
Become discombobulated by the temptation,
Commemorated like a golden sensation,
Sadly portrayed by total annihilation,
As the world is corrupting in its shell…

Right before your very eyes.

Chioma Aneke, Grade 8
West Education Campus, DC

Being a Child

Every day we hear those words,
Playing constantly in our head,
We try to shake them out,
But nothing seems to work
We already have to look on to our future,
Not taking a single breath.
Thinking about college when it's five years away,
But it still worries us with all of the expectations to keep up.
We want to scream, and then everyone would look at us to hear what we need to say.
Then we remember being a child;
We wanted to grow up so fast; we now regret that.
We miss green eggs and ham,
We miss going to school with everything to look forward to,
We miss having a new playmate every day,
We miss pajama day,
We miss having free time all of the time,
And we miss screaming with joy during recess.
Now we have entered 7th grade;
It's time to stop being a child.

Rumika Imdad, Grade 7
Kilmer Middle School, VA

Hurt Me with All of Your Love

My heart has fallen hard in love with you.
I look to forever and I see your face and feel your love.
I want to be by your side and help you when you hurt.
I want my thoughts to crawl to your ear and whisper words of comfort.
When we feel bad because of a fight; don't run away. If you need me, I am here.
Everything will be better when we hug and promise forever.
All I ask is, you "Hurt Me With All Of Your Love."

Angelo Archibald, Grade 8
Stevensville Middle School, MD

Beauty

Beauty in a water droplet,
Pretty on the tip of a butterfly's wing,
Delight on a velvety flower petal,
Charm in a spring breeze.
Beauty in a water droplet,
Divinity in a melody's swell and dip,
Wonder caught in a sparkling rain fall,
Brilliance impressed on a sun-kissed lip.
Beauty in a water droplet,
Grace in a song's lilting tone,
Loveliness on a drip of dew,
Artistry in a coyote's lonely moan.
Beauty in a water droplet,
Majesty in the light of the moon,
Splendor in a sunset,
Harmony trapped by an evening in June.
Beauty in a water droplet,
Allure bewitched by a glance,
Elegance in a snow flake's gentle descent,
Class contained in a dance.

Jennifer Roach, Grade 8
Sandusky Middle School, VA

Never Forgetting

Never forgetting
cool water
flowing between my toes,
sand and shells
swiveling around.
The orange
of an autumn leaf
filling the sky
slowly
melting
into a deep red.
Stars
crowding
the imperfect
moon,
lighting up
the dark blue
and luscious purple
sky.
Never forgetting.

Jessica Manning, Grade 7
Kilmer Middle School, VA

Perseverance

We rise
We fall
But through it all
We stand tall
Proud of what we've done
Because we've just begun

Kenny Love, Grade 8
Norfolk Christian Middle School, VA

Blown Away in Dreams

The green light will never be there when you are in a hurry
The red never there when you need to stop
The cake always finishes one turn before you
And you are never at the top

Dreams and wishes pull you in
Not thinking in terms of logic
Something is always out there to reach for
Not realizing it might be toxic

And when you grab hold, swearing you'll never let go
Now that your dreams and prayers have been answered
Not knowing you're heading yourself for disaster

The chemicals start to surround you, enclosing you in a very tight space
And then your past you once hated seems like a very nice place

The past a dream
As you proceed
Now seems quite heavenly

One choice, one dream blew you away
Into the darkness
Gone astray
The air might clear, the sun will come shine
So give life a chance, give it time

Madeeha Lughmani, Grade 9
Glenelg High School, MD

What I Love

Chromatic sunsets over the crisp horizon in the relaxing summer months
Mellow waves crashing peacefully on the never ending seashore
Gleaming, white snow twirling steadily from the heavens above

Freshly clipped flowers from our ample garden
Newly trimmed grass after a hot and humid day
A flaming fire during a frigid winter night

The echoing ring of church bells beckoning you to come
The rhythmic melody of Beethoven's Fuer Elise
The placid chirps from birds announcing that spring is near

Moist blueberry muffins right out of the oven
A ripe succulent strawberry when I pluck it from its vine
A scrumptious coconut key lime pie for my special birthday celebration

Smooth, silky sand flowing through my toes as I walk down the peaceful beach
The intricate designs imbedded into angelic seashells
The ivory keys on my grand piano and hearing their divine sound

I've become generous, helpful, and loving towards those in need
I've developed a passion for baking mouth watering desserts
I live so close to the breathtaking beach so I can play in the sun all day long

Michelle Curtis, Grade 8
Most Blessed Sacrament Catholic School, MD

The King

I'm the king
I'm not very humble
I never mumble,
Because I'm the king

I have the biggest roar,
And when I eat
I want more
I eat up the jungle
Because I'm the king

I'm the meanest of the meanest,
And I'm not the neatest,
But when I'm ready to run
It's not going to be fun
For the others,
Because I'm the king

When the day is over
I lay where the sun is going to set,
And yawn where the sun and horizon met

Mitchell Wilson, Grade 7
E Russell Hicks Middle School, MD

Birthday

Birthday, oh, birthday,
It's my favorite day of the year.
Yummy chocolate cake,
The singing chorus of the birthday song,
It's all in melody.
Bright wicked candles,
It's time to make a wish!
The smell of black smoke,
It fills the room.
The scent of cake
Overpowers it.
Beautifully wrapped presents
Make you anxious.
The ripping sound of paper,
It's like murdering such delicates.

Sofia Gutierrez Cuadra, Grade 7
Cape Henry Collegiate School, VA

A Lawn Once Treaded

Her eyes are green like the grass.
Like a lawn once treaded,
I've been this way before.
I could go back across,
but the flowers are long dead
and I will not use my tears
to water them this time.
So I guess they might stay dead.
And when I look back across the yard,
I will laugh to myself and walk on.

Jack McLain, Grade 9
Woodbridge Sr High School, VA

A Letter to a Muse

As night envelops my room, I find that I cannot sleep,
So I slide off my bed and cross my room in a silent, steady creep.
I sit down and open my laptop; the glow illuminates the room,
And as my hands brush the keyboard, I find I'm sitting next to you.
You know I cannot see you; there's nothing to say that you are here,
But you are, like every other sleepless night; at least that much is clear.
You're my Muse, my Inspiration, my friend when only I'm awake,
My Guide through flaws, annoyance, stupidity; every mistake I make.
I write without thinking; your hands direct me as your words become mine;
It's the first relief of the day, sitting in my dark room as our ideas combine.
The room is silent save for the sweet, insistent tapping of the keys,
And the computer with the continuous murmuring buzz just like one lazy bee.
The screen's harsh glare is pleasing, memories of nights together past,
And the bitter reminder that, because of morning, this contentment cannot last.
Suddenly, I can't remember my words; you're gone and my work is done,
So I glance at my clock, numbers grinning, jumping, and dancing: four-oh-one.
A scant two hours remains as I stumble through sudden darkness to bed,
Perfectly imperfect memories filling me, running through my head.
I welcome the awaited wordless silence, letting nothingness run through my head.

Lauren White, Grade 9
Mount St Charles Academy, RI

Our Mother the Sky

The sky is like a blanket over the Earth,
Protecting us like a mother protecting her child.
But the sky seems to grow older,
She grows weak like an aging woman.

The beautiful blue is bright in the day like an ocean in the sky,
As the day passes the blue falls into a dark black, revealing the stars above.
For this we must be grateful,
And help our mother like she has protected her child.

The pollution fills the air like trash in a garbage truck,
If we do not save her soon we will put another hole in her heart.
Maybe we can make her whole again like sewing a patch on a blanket,
So our beautiful sky may shine bright and blue for many years to come.

Alexandra Cook, Grade 8
Norfolk Collegiate Middle/Upper School, VA

Brilliant Works

Nature is so beautiful.
The peaceful sounds of the birds,
and the wind moving the tree branches side to side.
See the bees buzz around the enchanting garden,
filled with Roses, Lilies, Tulips, and Daisies.
Look at the birds soaring free!
The graceful Dandelions moving with the wind again.
The twilight lit sky and the white frosted mountains in the background.
The big bright moon and the stars,
soon to paint the night sky.
Admiring the beautiful creations our creator creates.
He is the painter of our scenery.
How brilliant His works are.

Janie Poore, Grade 8
Norfolk Christian Middle School, VA

Behind a Velvet Curtain
Sweaty palms
Hands curling into balls and then relaxing

Pacing back and forth behind the heavy red velvet curtain
Hearing the heels of my dressy shoes
Clacking against the cold wooden floor
Stopping to adjust my costume

Hearing the heels of my dressy shoes
Clacking against the cold wooden floor
Hearing the lines being said by the actors on stage
Rising unsteadily

Walking to the curtain
Taking three deep breaths
One…Two…Three

I stuck my head out from behind the curtain
A huge Cheshire cat smile spreading across my face

My braces gleaming in the stage lights
I smiled and hissed at the actors
I let the curtain envelop me
Enjoying the feeling of it caressing me

Peace and calm coursed through my veins
I had done it
Hannah Foster, Grade 8
Cape Henry Collegiate School, VA

Camaraderie Sweet as Summer
When the canvas of Heaven is painted blue
And the sun smiles longer to embrace the azure hue,
When the heat accompanies the blazing light
And scarlet sunsets display such a lovely sight,
Approaches a humid, but oh so glorious time
When all the world changes her clime,
Known as summer vacation.

For all, a time so splendid and so sweet,
To savor nature's splendid treat.
Reclining on a hammock of linen white,
I dreamed of many a fascinating sight.
Of places so rich and so diverse, my only vain glory —
Was that I could not reach them; they were but a story.
Though this could never have been more mistaken.

For from the heart of a dear good friend,
Came truth so genuine — it would never bend.
I discovered and was all the more content,
No vast ocean did ever spread wider than that of Kindness's extent.
No towering pyramid reached closer to the sky than kind Fidelity.
No vintage plaza ever was more abundant than that of Generosity,
And, above all, I found that Love was the most prosperous mansion.
Theresé Sengpraseuth, Grade 9
Mount St. Charles Academy, RI

Rainstorm
The pitter, patter,
The soothing rhythm of the rain,
Softly landing on the roof,
And the wind, barely above a whisper
Is enough to lull me asleep

I wake from my deep slumber,
To the loud, heavy, bangs of the rain and roof
Arguing with each other

I walk outside.
BOOM!
The roaring sound of the thunder,
Far in the sky is deafening.

ZAP!
The intensity and brightness of the lightning
Out in the distance is blinding.

WHOOSH!
The coldness and speed of the wind all around me
Is enough to knock me down and send me inside shivering.

The soft, gentle raindrops,
Have turned into
A deadly, terrifying Rainstorm
Stephane Mohr, Grade 7
E Russell Hicks Middle School, MD

The Forsaken Road
Slowly I travel up the forsaken road
Forgotten by many, yet missed by those
Dreams and memories, littered on the floor
Because I missed the opportunity to open the door

My childhood's past, full of innocence and virtue
When my petty wishes could still come true
Like roses' leaves before they fall
Before the thorns stand all straight and tall

I couldn't wait to move out
To leave my parents and finally grow up
Never appreciating my delicate youth
When my life was still perfectly smooth

So please, I beg of you, to never let go of the past
Try hard to be young, until your breath is the last
Because we know that everything we love
Will someday disappear, and go above

Slowly I travel up the forsaken road
Forgotten by many, yet missed by those
Now I know my big mistake
And I know which path I shall now retake
Virginia Sun, Grade 7
Kilmer Middle School, VA

Who Knows

Who knows if we're not dead right now?
And this life is a second chance
To say what we didn't say, to do what we wanted to
Or to change a twist of fate

Who's to say that white is white, and black is black
Maybe there's a difference in our eyes
Who's to say there's someone to blame
When you're more alike than different
To the person you swore you hate

Who knows if we're not dead right now?
And this life is to change our minds
To know that your problem is tiny
Through the eyes of an unlucky guy
To make you realize that bad things happen to good people
To give you the life, you should of, could have deserved

Who knows if we're not dead right now?
And tomorrow will never end
If we'll live and relive, until we almost get it right
Until we have no regrets, and our worries are gone
Who knows if we'll fly into the sky like birds?
Perch on a tree branch, and tweet a happy song

Emma DePanise, Grade 8
Stevensville Middle School, MD

The Migration

Flying swiftly through the sky,
Flying together side by side,
But then came the storm
That smacked the little bird to the ground;

Flying slowly now, injured from the fall,
Flying alone without any friends at all,
He cried out for his flock
But when unanswered, he continued alone;

Flying over the frozen land,
Flying over the desserts of sand,
Over the plains of green
He entered the skies where the winds are cold and mean;

Flying through gusts and gales,
Flying into storms and past bursts of light,
The winds like the breath of gods
He flew on and escaped the storm;

Once he was out of the mighty gale,
Begins the end of his remarkable tale,
For he heard soft and familiar melodies,
The welcoming songs from his long lost family.

Jonathan Dow, Grade 9
Mount St Charles Academy, RI

Sunny Days

Sunny days are happy days,
When the sun is shining bright.
Birds are chirping, children playing,
And pretty flowers are in sight.

Sunny days mean sunshine,
And nice warm weather, too.
Not a single cloud is in the sky,
Just that plain, beautiful blue.

Sunny days mean rainbows,
When the rain has come to an end,
When we hear God softly saying,
"I love you, my friend!"

Sunny days mean picnics,
With family or with friends,
Those days when you have the time of your life,
And wish for it to never end.

We thank God for our sunny days,
When we can see His face,
And see the beauty all around,
And reflect on His saving grace.

Maria James, Grade 8
George E Peters Adventist School, MD

Bingo Night

Here's an ode to a woman I adore,
Someone I couldn't ever love any more.

Who saw me grow until I was eleven,
Though I'm sure she's still watching me from Heaven.

We had lots of fun together.
Fun that I'm sure I will remember forever.

It's been almost three years now,
With new neighbors who come and go, in and out,
Of the old house that used to be my usual route.

In the summer, what I miss the most,
Is sitting on the porch becoming engrossed,
In her amazing stories that she used to tell,
In the lands where she used to dwell.

Playing bingo until late in the evening,
Laughing and laughing until I wasn't breathing.

Being called back home was never much fun,
Because I don't think I ever had as much fun with anyone.

Danielle Caulk, Grade 8
St Clement Mary Hofbauer School, MD

I Used to

I used to involuntarily ignore the simplest strain with a whine or wail,
But now I worry and wonder why the formidable fates make fulfill or fail.

I used to leisurely and lightly linger into a soothing sleep from mystical music whispering,
But now I meander mindlessly in my thoughts until slumber salvages me, ever recurring.

I used to carelessly and clumsily cruise and crawl around
But now I swiftly spring into a spring to any imaginable place in this common ground.

I used to snicker as I scampered under our towering countertop table,
But now I look down upon that little low table, now unable.

I used to cherish the compendious hours repeating and reminiscing the ABC's,
But now I experience the extensive, impenetrable struggles of middle school on my hands and knees.

I used to fathom my feet with plentiful pride as I kicked my soccer ball,
But now I exhilaratingly arise from achieving a swim race during a close call.

I used to think I perpetually had everything precisely perfect,
But now I regretfully realize that it was once an impactful improvement, but now a wrecked reject.

I used to think that I distinctly discovered what I was on this extensive Earth,
But now I ponder the thought, that I am a puzzle piece that needs to find its worth.

Molly Wooten, Grade 8
Most Blessed Sacrament Catholic School, MD

Not Looking Back

What is she doing, doesn't she know she's hurting people?
Not only herself, her family and friends, the people who love her the most
I feel like she's a completely different person not someone I've known for
years and years.
I go talk to her and what's her excuse? "But everyone is doing it!"
She hands me one and I say "No!" I start to walk away.
She calls me a loser and I stop in my tracks, I turn around and say:
"I'm not the loser that you think I am look in the mirror it's you, you're
throwing your life away with the rest of the people that are degrading their lives day by day"
She looks at me as if I slapped her across the face, her face looks so shocked
But then she says "You're right" two simple words that somehow seems to amaze me
She throws it on the ground and smashes it with her feet, she gets up and walks away
She says "As of now I'm never looking back, I'm going back to the person I was."
I grab her hand and walk away as if she's the person who never made this bad choice.
We walk down the road and get into the car,
And we both smash our fists against the rear-view mirror because starting today we're both never looking back.

Sashini Passela, Grade 7
Carson Middle School, VA

The Glass and the Mirror

The glass takes the easy way out for you, not showing what you know is there but why do people edge on what is forgotten? The mirror shows all that you don't want to see an unspeakable truth, a copy cat image of your true self, yet for some they use a cover up tool to bring false hope but to hear the bell ring at that moment your imagination that you selfishly set yourself in falls like glass onto the dirty bathroom floor, and so it is written in the broken mirror "When I looked in the mirror I wish I saw someone else."

Alexis Thomas, Grade 8
Midlothian Middle School, VA

The Poem Poem
Poetry can be anything from a
SONG
to a moving piece of literature,
to the movements of one's body.
Can you poem something?
Though it may not be
PROVEN
it's up to you.
When you read poetry, can you
FEEL
the emotions?
Poetry can be anything from a
SONG
to a moving piece of literature,
to the movements of one's body.
You don't have to be a
GENIUS
To be a poet.
Just listen to what is
INSIDE
of you.

Alexis Williams, Grade 7
E Russell Hicks Middle School, MD

The Madness
People dying
In the streets
Who can stop the madness?
More people die
"Who can find us jobs?"
The ruler will help
Who can stop the madness?
People dying
In the streets
At the hands
Of the Iraqi police
They bash them with nightsticks
Who can stop the madness?
Iraq has oil!
They all complain
We have no jobs
Is what they say
As people cry in the streets
Holding up banners
Making the president feel worse
Who can stop the madness?

Sean Kelley, Grade 8
Norfolk Collegiate Middle/Upper School, VA

Waves
Waves come crashing hard
Pushing up the sand on shore
Treasures from the sea

Kyle Tompkins, Grade 7
Cape Henry Collegiate School, VA

Fire Burns Through the Skies
Stars light the dark, cold skies
Through a blanket of gray clouds
I can see light traveling through a hole in the clouds
I always wonder deep in my mind, how can this wonderful image be created?
How can something this beautiful be happening in this dangerous world?
But yet again how can anything great happen since nothing really stays
Since nothing beautiful can last forever
Even the mighty oak tree one day has to fall
Just as the great rulers who once roamed the earth
But with the bad times
Good things and wonderful things happen at times
Now I see that the once beautiful stars
Are slowly losing their beautiful light
Now I can tell that it is dark but that soon
This dark night will be changed into a radiant sunlight
Just like fire burning through the skies

Alejandro Nobre, Grade 7
Kilmer Middle School, VA

Remorse
Begins with a craven knife in the back,
flat, plastic, dull, but still and undoubtedly there.
Of a raw misconception, delusion, transgression.
They say it is a fight for justice, for hope, and for mankind.
How can it be for mankind, when the man is losing? When he is dying?
But pushing the truth away, the lie is far more appealing;
and they veil themselves with them and the cue to continue.
Once they reach the finish, past the twirls and dips of the ride,
staring down at the bloodless corpses infested with rats in front of them,
they all realize that they were fighting for a step away from nothing.
And they think, was it more than a quarrel between a child and a teacher?
Between mother and a father? Between a friend and a friend…?
And conclude, it was for a chance of independence, a chance to fight their own battle.
But some of those words were better off not spoken.
Some of those sparks were better off not ignited.
And some wars would have been better off not fought.

Deepika Gudavalli, Grade 7
Rachel Carson Middle School, VA

Cornfield
The sun begins to rise, bringing with it the moist dawn air.
Nothing: the only sound, a mouse skittering across the brown, dry dust.
One could be amazed by the beauties of a cornfield.
That rattlesnake darting after its prey.
The crow picking on a dry corn kernel.
The beauty of the sweet smelling air of the corn.
You can almost taste it.
But then is a cornfields foe, fall
The air is cold and wet
Leaves rustling to the ground
The second world has come to an end
the wonderful glory, now a wasteland
The only smell there is, are the wet, dead leaves,
Lying on top of the cut-corn stalk.

Nick Farr, Grade 8
Kenmore Middle School, VA

What I Have Learned

I lace up my shoes
And look out at the city.
To some people it's a beast that can't be tamed.

But not me!
To me it's a challenge,
And I run in headfirst and don't look back.

Not knowing what obstacles lie ahead,
I soon learn that it's not as easy as I had thought,
But there is no turning back.

I learn that there are no dead ends,
That there will always be another wall waiting,
And I must get over it.

I learn that decisions not only have to be made
But also carried through to the end,
And some may be harder than others.

I learned that when I fall, I must get up,
That bumps and bruises will heal with time
And make me a stronger person.

It won't be easy,
And I may get hurt,
But if I try my hardest, then in the end I will have succeeded.

Mitchell Addison, Grade 9
Norfolk Collegiate Middle/Upper School, VA

Break Up to Make Up

The love I have for you
Just won't go away
No matter what I do
Or what I say

I don't know why I can't escape
Why won't you let me go away
Let me be free
I wanna break away

But I just can't
I love you too much
So please don't break my heart
Because I'll be devastated if we break apart

To tell you the truth
I don't know what I want
I wanna be with you
And the more we make up
the more I love you than the start

Let's just stop this break up to make up stuff...
because I love you

Promyce D'eja Miller, Grade 7
St Columba School, MD

Why?

Why do I miss you?
Why do I cry?
I see you every day
When we pass in the hallway.
Wishing I could hold you close.
I hold back my tears.

Why am I incomplete?
Why do I remember every word you said?
You're always in my mind and I never forget your smile.

My head soars for miles and miles,
When I lay down at night
I'm haunted with sweet memories of you

As time goes by I learn to hold back my tears
And accept that we are no longer together
And as I say goodbye I feel the river of tears run out of my eyes.

Angelina Traversari, Grade 8
Stevensville Middle School, MD

Midnight in a Perfect World

At this time, everything seems to stop:
Everything so tranquil, so quiet, so calm.
At this time, we think of everything off of the top;
You wish that the world was in the grasp of your palm.

At this time, the street lamps are off:
Everything so dark, so mysterious, the time for doing wrong.
At this time, the world is like the ocean though;
Some people try to prepare for their swan song.

At this time, we ponder on life as we know it;
What should we do? Why am I alive?
At this time, we think about how we should acquit.
Maybe we plan, think, contrive.

This is the time that we figure:
That it is midnight in a perfect world.

Jack Markey, Grade 9
Norfolk Collegiate Middle/Upper School, VA

Home

Somewhere in the world,
There's a place that you can go,
To solve all your problems,
And when your spirits seem low,
That place is called home.

Somewhere in the world,
There's a person you can confide in,
Someone who will listen,
Someone who will know you from beginning to end,
That is a person you can call a friend.

Madison Marsh, Grade 7
Emmanuel Christian School, VA

Broken Then Loved

My heart you broke,
I cried so hard, till my eyes turned red.
My troubles were worsened.
The pain began to hurt,
I felt lonely with out you.
Now I see you here in front of me.
It seems as though you hold your hand to me.
Am I seeing things? Is this real?
Do you really love me, or is this another joke?
I don't know, am I still asleep?
Did my pain become too much to handle?
I feel your smile. I can feel your body heat in this cold place.
My heart tells me to take your hand, my senses agree.
My mind tells me to run and never turn back.
My gut won't answer to my troublesome decision.
I hesitate before I look you in your eyes.
I feel loved after a painful fracture of the heart.
I feel safe, secure. You touch me and I feel real.
I feel as though this time you do love me, I feel loved.
I do take your trembling hand though very cautiously.
I feel your love flow through me at the touch.

Victoria Gormley, Grade 8
Northside Middle School, VA

The Moon

It stands there shining so bright,
looking astonishing with its gleaming light.
It gazes down at the earth,
wondering companionless,
along with other stars of a different birth.
It looks so tired, it looks so pale,
gently fiddling within its misty veil.
It scales the sky from east to west
Does it ever take a rest?
Before the coming of night,
it seems to show a misty white.
Before the dawning of the day,
it simply fades away.
I stare up at it,
and it stares back at me.
Sooner or later it puts me to sleep.
If it weren't for the moon,
I'd be counting sheep.
The moon wakes up the owls, and all the chinchillas and things,
And that's why we should be grateful,
for all that the moon brings.

Kristen Leighton, Grade 7
St Francis International School – St Camillus Campus, MD

Mountains

As I walk down this road we call life
It's mostly flat with some small hills in the way
But in the distance I can see mountains
So I try to not to walk too fast

Peter Soucy, Grade 8
Mount St Charles Academy, RI

Remedies

Is it really worth it? Does it mean that much to us?
Ripping up Earth's skin
Just to kill ourselves in the end
People should understand
That hurt on the outside always reaches the core
There are voices shouting across the globe,
Longing for a remedy
But no one simply listens.
We rely on Earth to give us food, water
Nature wants to protects us
We are her children
But where is the respect for her?
Then there are the animals,
Our sisters and brothers.
Just how many have lost their lives to our greed?
We have slowly shattered their world,
And consumed what they call home.
Every time we tear up the World's skin,
And destroy nature's houses,
We lose our home.
One tiny step at a time.

Virginia Sanford, Grade 8
Norfolk Collegiate Middle/Upper School, VA

Battlefield

All the roses are dying out
You can hear the birds scream and shout
They are trying to tell us something
That love isn't just anything
You can take it just as a living
But that's not what it really means

And I, can care more of myself
If I can care more of others
And you, wouldn't care more of yourself
I wouldn't be so self-centered

It's not about starting war
It's about what we came here for
I was never meant to fight this battle
But I would care more, than not being helpful

It's nothing like you think
It's nothing you can see
A thousand times you blink
And the person you see standing is me

Destiny Massenberg, Grade 7
Fairfield Middle School, VA

A Ghost He Can See

When I see his gorgeous face,
His perfect smile, his stunning teeth, his beautiful eyes
I always wonder, does he even know I'm there?
I guess I am just a ghost he can see.

Amanda Andruzzi, Grade 9
Delaware Military Academy, DE

Boundless Mysteries

Have you ever looked into the sky or across the shining sea?
Have you ever wondered where the end could be?
Have you ever looked upon a leaf, falling from the sky?
Have you ever wondered what it has passed by?
Have you ever looked upon an eagle in its nest?
Have you ever wondered when it came to rest?

These are things we humans try to know,
But how far should our knowledge go?
Should some things be left alone?
Or should we pick them to the bone?
Should we search for every trace?
Or give the world some breathing space?

While it's good to explore and ascertain,
Shouldn't the mysteries of nature remain?
Our hands have grasped too great a berth,
Let's leave space for others on this Earth.

Spencer Weiss, Grade 7
Kilmer Middle School, VA

The Decision

The stars glisten above me in the clear night sky.
I have one choice and these stars seem to encourage me.
I will only be able to take one path.
It is not yet clear which one I should take.
My whole family is depending on me.
Whatever I pick may change the world.
I could become a great leader.
This could be the biggest decision of my life, yet, I sit and wait.
What am I waiting for?
I'm not sure.
My mom comes out of the house to sit next to me.
We sit in silence for a while.
Then she looks at me and says,
"So, will it be cheese or pepperoni?"

Carolyn Fusca, Grade 7
Kilmer Middle School, VA

My Hero

My hero writes songs,
He writes songs to makes those laugh, and others cry.
Some apply to those having trouble.
His songs make you realize the reality
Of others you can't see through.
Therapy makes you see troubles
That many relate to.
Lullabies makes you see the hardship,
Of losing a loved one;
Someone you want back.
My hero can relate to those who struggle.
He can see through fakes.
My hero knows how I feel.
My hero is amazing.

Erin Pontz, Grade 8
Norfolk Christian Middle School, VA

New York Fall

Dry leaves chitter softly over rough sidewalk
Swirl in small tornados here and there
Shuffle through the park
Newspapers abandoned clip neatly in precise teeth
Of skittered squirrels packing
Tangled nests; bare branches

Come a month ago, those papers: still new
Sheltered a desperate hobo
On that old bench

On the basketball court, jump ropes lie
Like sinuous, two-headed serpents
Writhe across fading hopscotch squares
Clatter against broken ends
Of yellow blackboard chalk

Net swishes back and forth
On the creaking hoop
Slam dunk, rebound echo

Empty spray cans hiss breathlessly against fresh paint
Of unfinished graffiti, rolling, clink softly against
Cold tenement brick

New York fall

Jennifer Coleman, Grade 9
Atholton Adventist Academy, MD

Grandma*

I miss you I need you
Where are you?

It's been a while but I still think about it
Why was it you

You were nice, no one understood me like you
Why did you have to go?

I know you're there inside my heart
I will never forget you

I hope you're happy up there in the blue sky
Oh, Grandma, I love you

I know you love me, too I'll see you soon
I just can't wait to see you

But I have to live my life
I must be set free

Have a good time, hope you can wait
Because I've got my life ahead of me

Hanna Holland, Grade 7
Wicomico Middle School, MD
*Dedicated to Grandma

The Word Artist

A Blank Canvas
A Ready Artist
The words flutter through your mind
A blistering wind caught in your hand
You're mind ready to be painted upon
The Words are pressed against the canvas
You try to say them, but they say themselves
Poetry is not an it, but a word artist, it is someone
A creator of things, Metaphors, Similes, Alliteration, Personification
Painting upon your canvas, You
The word describe themselves
About anything, can be anything
Poetry is words
Poetry is Poetry
The artist ready as ever to write a masterpiece
A written canvas
A tired Artist
Poetry sits down
Waiting to create another masterpiece
Another Canvas hung on the wall to dry
Another Canvas blank ready to be written

Shelby Resh, Grade 7
E Russell Hicks Middle School, MD

Ending as We Know It

It started back in the fifth grade.
I was new to the school.
Scared, nervous,
Then she walked on the bus,
And sat next to me.
She looked like someone you would see on
Americas Next Top Model.
Tall, short hair, welcoming eyes.
And she smelled like she had poured half a bottle
Of perfume on her clothes.
Her name is Irene Reid.
We became instant friends.
From that day on we did everything together.
We were like sisters
Until the day she moved.
I cried until there were no more tears left.
She told me it would be okay,
And that we could still hangout.
But now we barely talk,
And all that's left are the memories we shared
Together back in the fifth grade.

Kayla Corum, Grade 7
Blue Ridge Middle School, VA

Harmonies Grace

For whom shalt tell thy soul of another
and know their grace. For thy own heart
knows no bound to true harmony,
yet cannot tell others what tis true but only dream.

Jett Zopp, Grade 8
Riverfront Christian School, VA

Crossroads of Destiny

The world is your oyster,
That's what I hear people say
But to tell the truth to me it's all just a game.
Everything in the world is a treasure to claim,

But one must be quick;
There are other players in this game with antics;
Players like pirates or like new friends
They'll be deciding how things are played.

There are times to be wined and times to lose
There is time to grief and time to relief
Each path is a future, every crossroad is destiny
Each direction different; where left or right matters by choice,

With a toss of the dice I walk towards the horizon
Coming towards cross roads making decisions
The world is your game of life,
That's what they hear me say.

Geoffrey McCoy, Grade 9
Annandale High School, VA

Fishing

I cast my rod into the ocean floor
Hoping for a big fish to bite the bait
I got a hit it's a big one, I've scored
Can I reel it in lets find out, we wait
I got it, the bait I used was some squid
I think I caught a gigantic striper
What a huge fish for just a little kid
I should get this I am plenty hyper
Boy! What a fish, this will be real tasty
We should net it and get it in quickly
If I'm not careful I will be hasty
We got it, the scales are quite prickly
    Now we go home and cook the nice big fish
    It is time to eat a really good dish

Michael Walsh, Grade 9
Delaware Military Academy, DE

Michael Lawson

Michael,
Small, funny, strong, redneck,
Son of god,
Lover of bears, pandas, and call of duty,
Who feels that war is awesome,
there should be no school except Mrs. Sells class,
people should be joyful at Christmas,
Who needs an iPod, kinect, music,
Who fears spiders, snakes, and alligators,
Who gives candy at Christmas time,
Who would like to see space,
Resident of Stevensville,
Lawson

Michael Lawson Jr., Grade 8
Stevensville Middle School, MD

My Savior

For me He died
For my selfishness
My pride

When all was lost
Chains held me down
He came for me and paid the cost

For that I am thankful every day
Down on my knees I begin to pray
And give Him glory in my own little way

My God
My Savior
Change me and my behavior

Help me to become like You
And honor You in all I do
Amen
Carley Schanck, Grade 8
Norfolk Christian Middle School, VA

Spring's Thunderstorm

The gray clouds moving into the sky,
The pounding rain is on standby,
A distant rumble of thunder,
The lightning hears and replies.

Animals going to slumber,
The moon and stars go under,
People watching out their window,
Fabulous show of God's wonders.

The wet ground in the green meadow,
Lightning looks like an angel's halo,
The big thunderstorm is severe,
Just as fast it came it then goes.

Clouds that surround skies disappear,
Beautiful moon and stars appear,
Now they are gone there is no fear,
Now they are gone there is no fear.
Sydney Kirwan, Grade 7
Trinity Lutheran School, MD

What Does a Sister Know?

What does a sister know?
She knows guys her sister loves,
And her sister's ticklish areas.
She knows how to joke and
How to have fun.
She knows her own fashion and mine.
She knows how to bug me,
But I love her anyway!
Christina Martin, Grade 7
Homeschool Plus, VA

Hi My Name Is William Carr

Hi, my name is William Carr
I will become someone like a big star
A singer and dancer like James Brown
Or become a tap dancer like Gregory Hines
Light on my feet I could become a boxer
But that is just not me.

Hi, my name is William Carr the singer
I sing a lot and hit every singing line dot
It's what I do and I am good too
I sing tenor and soprano and the blues

Hi, my name is William Carr the dancer
I dance for God and I move for Him
I twirl and leap and do splits low and deep
As I lift my leg high up in the air
There, there, there is my flair
Now my leg turns flexible like hair
So precise it looks because I am a dancer
William Carr, Grade 7
Thomas Pullen School, MD

Thinking of You

I'm sitting alone
Thinking of you
You made my heart soar
But now I've turned blue

The skies were sunny
But now they've turned gray
My heart is in pieces
Hoping you would stay

My heart would soar
Or even start racing
When you walked by
I just couldn't stop pacing

I loved you then
And I love you now
I just couldn't stop looking
'Cause you made my heart pound.
Morenike Akintoba, Grade 7
St Columba School, MD

March of Waves

Crashing hard on a carpet of tan
Where white foam slinks like a thief
With golden promise and master plan
Back and forth, side to side under the reef
The army of waves exert their might
Where swimmers and creatures play.
A relentless march — as if a tidal flight
Took wings, and goes on its way.
Tess McKee, Grade 9
Mount St Charles Academy, RI

Never Say Never

When things go wrong
Maybe play some Ping Pong
Maybe even sing a song
And NEVER Say Never

When people go behind your back
And say all that crap
Just know how to act
And NEVER Say Never

Don't fret and frown
You 'gotta' cool down
Don't make that whining sound
And NEVER Say Never
Andrea Cheek, Grade 7
Emery Education Campus, DC

Bullies

So I am right and you are wrong
The tyrants start to sing their song
With tainted tongues
And judging eyes
I feel the sense I don't belong

Rebellion starts to spark and grow
For I won't be belittled so
Each trick they play
Expands my gain
I'll block the punches that they throw

Resist their power with all my might
For you are wrong and I am right
Elizabeth Monroe, Grade 9
Mount St Charles Academy, RI

Colors Are Alive

Like a drum, rain hits the roof,
Splash we walk in a puddle and poof

When I see the showers
I know the blooming flowers,

Are on their way,
Day after day

The unfrozen streams,
Are still cold it seems

We play in the meadow,
And gather flowers of yellow.
Victoria Dill, Grade 8
Mount St Charles Academy, RI

High Merit Poems – Grades 7, 8, and 9

A Freckled Flower

As white as a ghost
with a tint of sunshine,
and freckled like someone
who's been out in the sun.
Shines like a star,
but not the kind you see in space,
it tastes like bananas,
and moves like waves.
Dances in the wind,
and glitters in the rain.
It glows,
and I know,
it inspires.

Madison DiLenge, Grade 7
Kilmer Middle School, VA

How Do I Love Thee?*

How do I love thee? Let me count the ways.
I love the sun on me as I stretch,
When I put my goggles on my face.
Waiting to hear the gun,
Listening to the crowd yell my name,
And I dive into the water,
Feeling my arms lift up automatically,
Moving me forward.
One more lap!
I hit the wall and jump out,
Winning once again!
Swimming, I love thee.

Chloe Bialozynski, Grade 7
St Clement Mary Hofbauer School, MD
*Inspired by Elizabeth Barrett Browning

Summer Breeze

I take a step outside,
the warm summer air hitting my face.
The way the grass feels between my toes,
the way the flowers stand up tall,
the way the clouds form different shapes,
everything is perfect.
A cool wind blows,
giving the warm air a little kick
and reassuring me that the next 3 months
will be, well,
perfect.

Amanda Figueroa, Grade 7
Kilmer Middle School, VA

Untitled

Dreaming of all the memories
that are slowly turning into
nightmares that I wake up to
screaming; all alone in a dark room
terrified.

Ruby Corbit, Grade 9
Independence Secondary School, VA

What I Love

I love to watch brawny branches dance with the sounds that the wind makes.
I love to watch the soft, delightful snow falling delicately tot he hard ground.

I love the smell of the fresh cut grass in summer.
I love the smell of the strong, smooth, creamy coffee when I first wake up.

I love to hear the beautiful sparrow birds singing in the early morning hours.
I love to hear the severe waves crashing themselves onto the rocky shores.

I love to taste the hot delicious chocolate fondue running into my mouth.
I love to taste the juicy and sticky caramel apple.

I love to touch the fragile, delicate rose petals.
I love to touch the rain coming down from the fluffy clouds and the dark sky.

I love the way God created us, allowing us to control this whole world,
But He is always there with us.

I love the way we laugh until we cry.

Paula Andrea Gonzalez Lopez, Grade 7
Most Blessed Sacrament Catholic School, MD

Untitled

My weary eyes scanned the beautiful meadow
With them, I saw every little detail
From the tiniest working ant
To the largest and oldest pine tree

The symphony Mother Nature conducted was absolutely marvelous
The sound of little crickets chirping in the nearby bush
And the splashing of a nearby stream
Woven together in a perfect melody

Then I heard the drops of rain hurling towards Earth
First as tiny droplets and then as large dewdrops
I listened intently to the silent beating of the rain
And my heart danced along to it

I watched as others put on their hoods and opened umbrellas
Every single time I heard any of them wish for the sun to come out
I wanted to reply that whoever thought sunshine produced happiness
Has never danced in the rain

Patricia Pablo, Grade 8
Saint Columba School, MD

The Violinist

The violin's vibrant sounds surround me
As I fall into a deep blue sea
I hear the cries from my finely haired bow
From the violin which I will someday outgrow
Hoping to find happiness from this simple piece of art
Not knowing what is going to fall apart or how it's going to break my heart
The music that I play every day gives my soul a feeling of pride
As my music will one day get played nationwide

Aundia MehrRostami, Grade 7
Kilmer Middle School, VA

My Baleeze (Baby Blankies)

I have had you, blankie, for a while
You seem to always make me smile

I was never able to call you baby blankies
When I called you "Baleeze" it kept me at ease

I snuggle with you at night
Be sure the bed bugs won't bite

I used to suck my thumb and hold you close
Sorry for drooling on you, that was awfully gross

I will never be too old for you
If you weren't there for me what would I do?

It is getting excessively late
I lie in bed and thank you for being great

Where are you? Where did you go?
WHEW! I found you, you were just down below

Now come on up here, it's time for bed
You love to mess with my impractical head

Good night my dear old friend
I'll always love you till the end

Rosa Celozzi, Grade 8
Most Blessed Sacrament Catholic School, MD

A Lonely Road

Upon a lonely road I walk
Through a misty shroud
Through which I can't see
Following a light, beckoning through the mist

I walk and walk
Not knowing where
Following a light, beckoning through the mist
So close yet so far

I stumble along this stony road
Tripping upon cold rocks in the blinding mist
My feet torn, my knees battered
On the ground I lay
Tired, I want to give up
But still I rise and walk and again
Following a light, beckoning through the mist

When I arrive, the mist is gone
A beautiful world surrounds me
But time has taken its toll
I am tired and want to sleep
But here I am just in time
To see the sunset's last glimmering of light, with a smile on my face

William Randolph, Grade 7
Kilmer Middle School, VA

Snow

Its face so stark and white,
Lit upon by the moon's light.
Kept cool and intact
Carefully laid and packed.
Wind's breath permeates through down coats and sweaters
As I stand and watch my breath escape.
A cardinal disrupts the bland, white canvas
And calls across the pin-drop silent air.
Snow blowers and shovels push and shove,
protecting what is theirs,
But the silvery fleece remains with its arctic fortitude.
The blazing ball on its string shall arise
And scathe the flawless porcelain.
By night again, those alive,
With the moon shall heal and thrive.
And the stark white face
As smooth as lace
Will lay and sleep tonight.

Lauren Ridlon, Grade 8
Trinity School, MD

Death Is Coming for You

You will never expect it
When it's finally your time
You'll be begging for help
And losing your mind

You can't figure out why it's for you
What you did to make this true
Why can't it be someone else
I can't believe it's time for me

I still don't know what I did
So let me just prepare
For the day it's time for me to go
I will be ready and not shout…Oohh

Taisha Roman, Grade 7
The Academy of International Studies at Rosemont, VA

Fireplace

Kindling, crackling bright rosy flames;
Proud and robust your grand presence proclaims.
Warm heart of house in brisk winter chill,
Steamy moist fog forms on glass window panes.

Blow breath of winter and snow all night.
Be stilled by the draping, sweet, pooling light.
Blankets of snow cloak our humble, quaint town
Waltzing and dancing to soft frozen ground.

Come shelter ye people, one and all
Feel warmth and love. Gather your shawl.
All cluster 'round; feel the glow on your face;
Share great merry stories by our fireplace.

Emily Sullivan, Grade 7
Kilmer Middle School, VA

Days Gone By

Fifteen years have gone by all too fast;
Their imaginary games quickly fade to the past.
He has stood by her in the worst of times,
And boosted her up during the toughest of climbs.

Her heart, filled with joy, watching him succeed;
But more time with him, is what she needs.
She knows his future is bright and sure,
These four years will be his of grandeur.

In her life he has been like a guitar,
Softly strumming her imagination to lands afar.
Through the years, memories have been made,
No distance could possibly make them fade.

As he packs up and leaves her alone,
The sunshine lets out a solemn groan.
Their love and friendship never to be torn apart,
But as he leaves, he takes half of her heart.

Amy Schmitt, Grade 9
Mount St Charles Academy, RI

A Sonnet for Springtime

When Old Man Winter's strength begins to ebb,
And rains of April wash away the cold,
The spiders start to come and spin their webs,
Then nature's young replace the weak and old.
The world turns green, as lush as fair Eden,
The dainty grass is damp with gentle dew.
Springtime is a lovely youthful maiden,
Or an infant, the earth reborn anew.
The young birds learn to take flight and to sing,
While flowers bloom and make the air smell sweet.
I take delight in joyful sounds of spring;
They make my worries become obsolete.
Yet don't forget about the stinging bees,
Nor the pollen, which causes me to sneeze.

Madeline Westrick, Grade 9
Stone Ridge School, MD

Princess Diana

Princess Diana is someone I admire,
Her acts of kindness should always inspire.
The princess of Wales had a good heart,
And to so many lives she became a part.
She visited hospitals and schools,
And as a princess she followed her own rules.
She comforted many people with AIDS or who were ill,
And these acts of kindness were truly a skill.
She treated everyone she met like a friend,
She always showed grace and dignity until the end.
She left this world in 1997,
And I'm sure she has a spot in heaven.

Kaitlin Blake, Grade 8
St Clement Mary Hofbauer School, MD

The Untamed Beast

The breeze like a touch of freezing glass
As strong as a bite of lion
You don't see it
As it blows by

When it picks up it howls as if alive
The pain it feels is unbearable
The scream makes your ears bleed
Then it slows the loud howl to a low whimper

When the breeze steadies
The boat stays upright
A large gust of wind
Flips the boat into the freezing water

The wild wind
Never to be tamed
As faithful as a dog
Pushes us along to the next adventure

Nick Petrillo, Grade 8
Norfolk Collegiate Middle/Upper School, VA

There Is Hope

The waves thunder on to the land,
Sweeping everything in their path,
Men, women, children, buildings —
All are lost.
Shocked looks of despair follow the faces of the Japanese,
But
All is not lost.
There is hope and healing and comfort that they can find
In Christ Jesus.
He has sent his disciples there,
To help the devastated people.
They fix their homes, provide food and water,
And give them the Bread of Life and the Living Water.
They are there to tell the Japanese that
God cares about them and their future.
After the waves recede to the ocean,
And the rains return to whence they came,
There will be a rainbow —
Smiling on the people of Japan.

Hannah Shearer, Grade 8
Homeschool Plus, VA

Life Lesson

Life is a journey.
   You could made mistaken choices.
But you could also made honorable choices.
   It is a journey you can do by yourself,
Or just with others.
   We are human.
We rise, but then sometimes we fall.

Haboon Osmond, Grade 7
Carson Middle School, VA

The Art of Music
A beautiful sound, a beautiful tune
That can describe many things in this beautiful world
Form soft sound tune, to a hard rock beat
From talking about love, to talking about life
It inspires many people, including me
To make this world sing
From the percussion to the strings and to the winds,
To the brass and to the vocals
All together they make a beautiful chorus,
That makes this world sing
From the many shapes and forms it's in,
It's still a beautiful sound
It never gets old, it's always in style
It plays every day and we don't even realize it
From the TV, to the radio
And from a computer to a cell phone
You'll always hear a sound
That makes this world sing
Dominique Palangdao, Grade 8
St Columba School, MD

The Game of Soccer
Soccer is a game of patience and skill,
It takes heart, teamwork, desire, and will.

The point is to maneuver the ball down the field,
While the other team tries to make you yield.

Once your opponent ends your run,
Then your attacking towards goal is done.

Now it is your turn to defend,
You must bring their momentum to an end.

The game cannot be won without a score,
Once you get that goal, the entire crowd will roar.

The match is over, the day is done,
Hopefully the next week will be just as fun.
Tyler Olmsted, Grade 8
St. Jane de Chantal School, MD

Fire
Fire explains to us humanity
It destroys so much
Yet without it the earth would be empty
It can be warm and welcoming
Yet evil and cruel
Fire can forge great empires
Yet it can strip the world bare
It is wicked
It is good
It can be ended in an instant
So we should always take care not to blow it out
Ethan Guevremont, Grade 8
Mount St Charles Academy, RI

A Crack
Everything starts with a crack,
Where the ice of winter begins to breathe its last breath,
Where the grass on the fields awaken,
Where creatures look out their den for the first time.

Streams flowing,
Flowers blooming,
Leaves whooshing,
Winter making its last stand.

Like a wildfire, spring takes off,
Eating up everything it sees.
The grass is greening,
And the clouds are parting.

Rejoice, rejoice, spring is coming!
The world has endured another winter!
Flowers are stretching,
Children are playing,

Icy ponds melting,
Animals appearing,
The world renewing.
An amazing metamorphosis,

And to think it all started with a crack…
Jake Cui, Grade 7
Kilmer Middle School, VA

Ode to Summer
Oh summer, with your warmth and sun
You make it scorching hot while we're having fun
We dream about you all year in school
Asleep on our desks as we drool

Lazy nights hanging out late on the beach
While new friends begin to meet
I learn new things
As the ocean wave crashes and sings

You are the time for summer love to begin
Surfers are out in your ocean chargin'
People all around dream of the first day
They swim freely in the ocean and the bay

You make our lives gracious for a while
But then we have to start preseason and run a mile
We make new friends that go to the same school
We pray and hope that we will be cool

Oh summer, with your warmth and sun
You make it scorching hot while we're having fun
We love you and forever will
We're already preparing for next year and our skill
Maggie Allison, Grade 8
Most Blessed Sacrament Catholic School, MD

The Shattered Plains

Above the newly shattered plains,
He has nothing at all to gain…
A rock of sorts that floats up there,
Forever floating in the air.
He looks around, left and right,
To see if there are rocks in sight.
When all is clear,
Nothing to fear,
He jumps into the shattered plains.
Falling slowly, like a feather,
He looks into the twisting nether.
Down below the world he knew
Is coming back to haunt him, too,
But the plains aren't there, not like before,
Or even back on the stormy shore.
He's almost there,
No time to stare,
He fins his way to the shattered plains.
Zachery Adam Miller, Grade 9
Norfolk Collegiate Middle/Upper School, VA

Seasons of the Year

The cold winter wind
Making people shiver shake
Throughout the cold town
The nice summer sun
Wanting kids to come outside
Ready for some fun
I think I might go swimming
Or maybe play some baseball
The sun
Is almost here
I can't wait 'til it's here
The weather will get warmer yay
It's here
The sun is going away
So I don't like today
Leaves are changing
Colors rearranging
I will have fun and go play
Landon Buzzerd, Grade 7
E Russell Hicks Middle School, MD

Outside the Book

He called her beautiful
But didn't know
That behind the eyes
That held his stare
Was pain
Pain from ignorance
Of love
DeAndre Sellars, Grade 7
Emery Education Campus, DC

Realizations

In the darkest corner
Shines the most radiant light

In the woe of death
There is a candle burning bright

In the murkiest of caves
You'll find a gem

When a girl loses all hope
She will find her him

These are all the realizations
That I have made

To keep hope, love and faith
And to never ever let it fade!
Zakiya Sidney, Grade 9
Leonardtown High School, MD

Nature's Song

Nature's beat
In the summer heat

The whistle of the trees
As the leaves rustle in the breeze

The thrum of energy
In every petal of rose and lily

The way the sky calls out to me
How it makes me feel truly free

Birds twitter and flit
While a ball thumps into a little boy's mitt

All these sounds resounding like a gong
For this is nature's song
Lauren Eberhardt, Grade 8
Mount St Charles Academy, RI

The Party

My mom is talking in the ball room
I am in the kid's room helping my sister
Now it is time to go
Out in the cool air we go
We are partying
Sipping warm apple cider
In the cool fall air
Snowing leaves
You can't see the ground
We and brown under tow
Red berries fall from bushes
All over the ground
Izzy Haddad, Grade 7
Cape Henry Collegiate School, VA

I Am

I am an unconfident and emotional girl
I wonder what people think of me
I hear a girl crying
I see kids laughing
I want to be noticed
I am an unconfident and emotional girl

I touch a mirror and do not like what I see
I worry that I'm not special
I cry for not being noticed
I am an unconfident and emotional girl

I understand I'm not fun to be around
I say anything is possible
I dream about being happy
I try to be perfect
I hope to be the best person there is
I am an unconfident and emotional girl
Amanda Bray, Grade 8
Corkran Middle School, MD

Escape

Walking.
Jogging.
Running.
Sprinting.
Trying to escape
the monster.
Then coming to
a sudden stop.
Because
you realize
there is no
escaping
reality.
But start again.
Face the monster.
Don't let it rule
the life
you chose to live.
Ally Brown, Grade 7
Kilmer Middle School, VA

One Heart

One heart for the soldier's pride,
One heart for the times we cry.
One heart, that will survive.
One heart for the city streets,
One heart for the hip hop beats.
One heart, oh, I do believe,
That one heart is all we need.
Caroline Maruca, Grade 7
Kilmer Middle School, VA

A Spark

I always searched for my own path
As I searched, I found wrath
I thought it could help me become a better person
But with wrath, I knew nothing could be done

I wished for once in life god had shown me the way
Yet nothing happened, and nothing will happen, I say
Without a spark in a life, there can be no spirit in it
Without a spark in your life, it will remind you about your mistakes bit by bit

Last night, I looked up in to the sky with a billion stars across it, like a spark,
A spark in a life, the life of the sky, which makes me take a deep breath
Without the stars the sky is filled with emptiness and darkness, a darkness which can haunt you to death
There is pain yesterday and today, but the only fact that my wonderment of the future keeps me alive
For just a moment I want to see a path with a spark of light, at least in a dream, a dream that I can drive

I am still waiting for that moment, and I can never stop waiting…
I will always will still will be waiting
Waiting for that moment
That heavenly moment…

Sai Singh, Grade 7
Carson Middle School, VA

Scattered Petals

One cold and dreary night, I was as happy as can be,
My Grandma and I were visiting Great-Grandma Anna's grave.
We always bring a flower, tonight it was a rose,
I was honored to carry that rose,
But I fell and knocked off all its beautiful petals.
I cried and cried, for I was only 6,
But Grandma had a solution,
She said, "Little one, don't cry, we shall make potpourri."
"Potpourri?" I asked,
"We'll put the petals into a bowl and watch them dry out, and they'll still have their beautiful fragrance."
"That my dear, is potpourri."
Then Grandma told me something I will never forget:
"Remember those who have perished with memories of their beautiful lives."
Years passed as I flashed forward, as I watch myself swirl those petals,
And feel their sweet fragrance surrounds me, like a protected blanket.
I woke up then, realizing it was only a dream,
But a dream I will never forget,
So thank you, thank you, Great-Grandma Anna.

Erica Haschert, Grade 8
Stevensville Middle School, MD

Diary

This is my little sanctuary of words; my peace of mind.
It's the world through my eyes, no one seems satisfied.
Everything I feel everything I see. How much I believe,
It's always changing. It's my way to escape just for a moment. A great way to hide my secrets from this world I see. They don't understand me. These pages are my best friend that will never die, lie, or judge me. The one that I can tell anything, that will never tell anybody. I know my secrets are safe and my identity is known. My memories will live on in the pages even after I'm long gone. The soul it holds is mine forever, I live through the memories of those pages. It holds my life in its binding; it will carry through life as I express myself by filling the pages with ink.

Catherin Caparaz, Grade 8
Lafayette Winona Middle School, VA

Promises

You were once a little boy
Who had love and a home
I didn't appreciate you while you were here
I would give anything for you to be near
You were strong and lean
You were also kind of mean
I loved you a lot
Mommy and daddy too
Remember Foxy, she loved you too
I know you want me to be strong
It's kind of hard 'cause you're gone
My heart is always a frown
I miss having you around
You did the stupidest things
And you made me laugh when you did
You were the cutest puppy with the funniest howl
You're in a new place now
And I will be there soon
Promise to not forget me
'Cause I promise I won't forget you
Let's keep our promises.

Ariana Barrett, Grade 8
Academy of International Studies, VA

Helping Friend

Sometimes I feel like
I am falling down
But I never touch the ground
Because of you
And when I am in pain
And need a friend
You're always there to lend a hand
You make my heartaches end in a flash
Always lending me your shoulder for a unpredicted rainstorm
You always give me that much needed embrace
You fill the dark empty spaces of my heart
You know me better than I know myself
You help me through my troubles
You treat them like they're your own
And you always use a comforting tone
So thank you

Mackenzie Turner, Grade 8
Time 4 Learning School, VA

A Cold Winter's Day

Winter is the best season of them all
It's so much better than the fall
You play outside on a cold winter's day
You have so much fun and the time fades away

But it's time to come inside now,
It's time to come in
As you sip on hot chocolate,
The day comes to an end.

Kailyn Huffaker, Grade 8
Stevensville Middle School, MD

March 11th 2011

Peaceful
Was how we lived
Upon our land
Without a doubt
Of doom nor death up rise

Disaster
Came with a wave
Struck our land
And swept away
All happiness or hope

Gone
Was everything
From our food
To people dear
Leaving nothing to spare

Hope
Replaced our fear
It was warn
It's all we have
To keep inside our souls

So here we wait for happiness, to regain it's formal name.

Kai Shapard, Grade 8
Carson Middle School, VA

The Ending of a Leaf

I can feel the rush of the cold wind making me rustle
On the dead grass I can see leaves, all fallen and dead
I see men, children, women, and animals taking the leaves away
Leaves which were once my family

I hope cold, windy days will not arrive
But I know the time will come
All around me are weak, red leaves waiting
Waiting for the end
To fall and get carried away with the wind
To crumble into dust

I can feel the wind gaining strength
I can feel it trying to take me down
I'm the last one left
I'll be the last to fall

My mind is fading
The world is blurry
I can see a man staring at me with a camera in his hands
He pushes a button and watches me; the last one to fall
And now I'm falling...

Falling
Falling to the ground

Reema Patel, Grade 7
Carson Middle School, VA

Life Is Like a Bird
Life is a bird.
It goes by quickly.
Sometimes it leaves nice, pretty memories.
Other times the memories are gooey and disgusting.

Sometimes, the beautiful bird is free.
It soars with its freedom.
The bird enjoys its time.
Making many companions along the way, this bird lives long.

Other times, the bird is stuck in a cage.
It is forced to do things it doesn't enjoy.
The bird isn't given much freedom, keeping its wings stiff.
This bird dies an untimely death.

Birds make the journey south, to escape the winter.
No matter how far they go,
Most come back in the spring, to go back to their regular lives.

Once the bird loses its life,
It slips into total darkness,
In an endless continuum, never coming back.
Raksha Pothapragada, Grade 7
Carson Middle School, VA

That Girl
You're not like anyone.
You have a smile brighter than the sun.
You're not like anyone.
It's like my love for you is all but done.
You're not like anyone.
You make me smile and you're extra fun.

You're not like anyone.
You give me a feeling of bliss.
You're not like anyone.
Your laugh and voice I oh so miss.
You're not like anyone.
I sit here and reminisce.
You're not like anyone.
All I can say is this.
You're not like anyone.
Deonte Kilson, Grade 9
New Directions Alternative Education Center, VA

Never Ending Laughter
Laughing, laughing, laughing
Will it ever end?
No one will ever know,
Will there be a day that the laughing stops?
Coming to school and seeing your faces,
It reminds me that I will never see the day when the laughing ends
Even though at the end of the year we will split,
I will always keep this laughter in my heart.
Emma Mugford, Grade 8
Summit School, MD

City Life
Walking along a crowded sidewalk,
Hands burrowed in my comfortable pockets,
Minding my own business.

Skyscrapers that tickle God's toes
Rise on either side of me.
Yellow beetles crawl along the roads
Taking passengers all across the city.
Horns and whistles go off like a synchronized symphony
That is performing in front of world-renowned judges.

I pass the occasional tree
That is daring enough to grow in the harsh city environment.
Street vendors boast their scrumptious food
By cooking pretzels and hot dogs fresh in front of me
And letting their enticing smell make its way into my nose.

As the smell of pretzels and hot dogs makes its way behind me,
A slight grin makes its way across my face,
And I continue at a brisk pace
Making my way through the crowded city,
Just minding my own business.
Connor Ganley, Grade 8
Trinity School, MD

What Happens in Class
We leave the best for last
Everyone's alive learning about the past
"No talking!" the teacher said
Half of the class is ready to go to bed
Glued to our seats
Can't wait 'til our food and mouth meet
Bottom is getting numb
Wishing that God will come
Passing notes back and forth
Waiting until the paper comes north
Hide the paper, she's coming our way
Feels like this class will take all day
Questions come every few minutes to avoid work
Everyone is about to smirk
"Ding!" there goes the bell
Throw all the papers away, "shhh," don't tell
Monet Watson, Grade 7
George E Peters Adventist School, MD

Dreams
Everyone has dreams.
Some are extreme, some are even like laser beams.
When you're little, you want to be president.
When you're older, you want to represent
for what you believe in and not what you don't.
You want to be here and there and not at home.
Dreams, they're everywhere.
So discover yours before it goes into thin air.
Victoria Phillips, Grade 8
Norfolk Christian Middle School, VA

I Wish

I wish I could hold you again,
Be only a heartbeat away.
I wish I could touch you again,
Be able to feel your heart again.
I wish I could kiss you again,
Be connected through a butterfly's kiss.
I wish I could still be with you,
Be the keeper of your heart.
I wish I could make my wishes come true,
Be able to have my love back.

I wish I could make my heart whole again,
Instead of it being broken beyond repair.
Amaya Robinson, Grade 9
C D Hylton Senior High School, VA

Autumn

Crunch, crunch
go the leaves
falling, crashing
always dashing
whoosh, whoosh
goes the breeze
flying, soaring
I'm adoring
ha, ha, ha
children playing in the leaves
and these are my wonderful reasons
autumn is my favorite season
Brandon Luke, Grade 7
Cape Henry Collegiate School, VA

Rain Drops

Tip top the rain drops,
From the stormy sky.
Tip top the rain drops,
On my window pane.
Tip top the rain drops,
As thunder rolls in.
Tip top the rain drops,
As the birds start to flee.
Tip top the rain drops,
As lightning flashes by.
Tip top the rain drops,
On my window pane.
Mokshyada Poudel, Grade 8
Lake Braddock Secondary School, VA

Hope

Hope, everything will be okay.
Hope, things will turn out best.
Hope, expectations are high.
Hope, always have to have it.
Hope, always gets you the farthest.
Elizabeth Ryan, Grade 8
St Paul's Lutheran School, MD

Night

I look out the open window;
I see a distant light.
I feel delight from the distant light
that will guide me through the night
to the faraway place I seek.

I look out the open window and I see a distant light.
At this time a breeze that breaks the quiet of the night
brushes my face with a sweet kiss good night.
Then I feel a sense of completeness from the ruffle of the breeze,
and I remember that there is always another night.

I look out the open window and I see a distant light.
The light rises and saves us from the sight.
No more night and no more thoughts of good night.
The idea that the night will always come again
is like the joy of knowing that the sun will always rise again.
This saves us from the dark days
and revives the idea that there will always be another chance to save a day from night.
David J. Baldwin, Grade 9
Norfolk Collegiate Upper School, VA

Flowers

It is a breathtaking sight of how a small seed,
transforms into a fabulous flower
just as flowers, people blossom too,
they are uncertain little seeds that don't know how or when they will blossom

Soon after they realize who they are
they become a beauty for everyone to admire,
these flowers are loved by everyone whenever they are roses or sunflowers
every flower will blossom and so will you

Little children are seeds with big dreams
they all dream to be something incredible,
like a doctor, dancer, writer, or whatever they choose
all will blossom and become something new.
Olivia Moore, Grade 8
Stevensville Middle School, MD

Croatia

Shining on us all was the sun
We'd sit next to the glistening water
The only feelings were of joy

Stretched across our faces were smiles of joy
Bright and merry, making the mood we had the sun
We swam in a turquoise clear puddle of water

Beautiful animals called it home, so free of pollution unlike our water
As well as us, the sea creatures felt joy
We'd all felt so refreshed by the sun

It was a paradise, tranquil water, cheerful sun, and warm joy spreading through
Sabrina Richards, Grade 8
Norfolk Collegiate Middle/Upper School, VA

Rain

You can smell the rain before it comes.
In the fog of the morning, the distinctive smell of rain breaks through the haze.
The smell of spring enters your nose and warms your being.
The rain is coming.

You see the first drop fall, then the next, each one coming faster than the one before.
And soon the pavement turns from a gray to a black, covered in the moisture of the falling water.
And at once, all the people and animals that were outside have disappeared into the safe havens of their homes.
The rain is here.

Rain brings new life to everything it touches.
To the brown grass it brings green growth.
To the wilted flowers it brings color and fragrance.
The rain is here.

And when the rain is done, all is back to normal.
The people are again walking on the side walks and the animals rustling the branches of the trees.
All that is left is the puddles on the ground, waiting to be jumped in by eager children,
And the occasional drip of water from the roof of a building.
The rain is gone.

Marissa Wharton, Grade 7
St John Neumann Academy, VA

Hershey K

Hershey K
    i
     s
      s-
   es are
  one of my
favorite candies.
They are sweet and
good to eat. They are es-
pecially good if you are hav-
ing a bad day and you need some-
thing nice to help cheer yourself up.

Hershey K
    i
     s
      s-
    es
  are little
treats that don't
have too much choco-
late to the point where you
could get sick to the stomach.
They are small and convenient.

On Holidays K
    i
     s
      s-
   es have
  different color
wrappers. The wrap-
per colors can range from
shiny red to golden. When I
was little I used to put them in
a rainbow order and count them.

Meagan Sturla, Grade 7
Trinity Lutheran School, MD

Stage Fright

S ound of your heart beating in your ears,
T rembling hands, sweat glistening upon your forehead.
A thousand eyes watching, waiting.
G lowing beams of light obstruct your vision.
E veryone's staring, piercing your soul.

F rozen like a deer, clouded with fear,
R egret seeping in through every corner of your mind.
I mpatient whispers sound your alarm,
G rowing louder and louder.
H undreds of dark spots creep up behind the corners of your eyes,
T ime slows down; your senses dull, going numb. Your knees crumble and darkness engulfs you.

Quinn Chu, Grade 7
Kilmer Middle School, VA

High Merit Poems – Grades 7, 8, and 9

Ode to Chocolate

Ode to chocolate
Dark and sweet
Smoothing our worst
Moments with its taste
Melting in our mouth
The delicious aroma filling the room
Making us long for more
Sweet, sumptuous
Melting in your mouth
A piece of heaven
A drop of happiness
A ray of sunlight in dark skies
Chocolate lifts the spirits
And brings people together
So whenever your day goes awry
And your skies are gloomy
Eat a piece of chocolate
And make it all depart
Whenever I feel blue
I reach for a piece of chocolate.
Would you?

Julie Duetsch, Grade 8
St John Neumann Academy, VA

Achievements

The wind is against your face,
the cold is whistling in your ears.
You keep going,
for you have only just begun.

The wind progressively blows
harder and harder against you,
but you continue moving forward.
You want to get to your destination.

Just when you feel like giving up
and succumbing to the wind,
you notice
the wind is dying down.

You soon find that the wind
is no longer going against you,
but pushing you forward.
So you glide on top of it
and fly higher…
and higher…

Abigail McShane, Grade 7
Kilmer Middle School, VA

Believe

If you believe…
reaching the stars will be easy
you'll never see the limits

Sarah Butler, Grade 8
Mount St Charles Academy, RI

A Picture of a Soldier

Pain can be within a smile,
Hundreds of feelings are entangled within a single image.
Unimaginable weapons unveiled, said to be progress, really
mistakes.
Mistakes that open our eyes to the havoc we, humanity, have
Created. And though we sometimes learn, why can't we see that we shouldn't
have
wars
at all.
Cracks in the lives of those who fight, cracks in the lives of those who see the
Horror from a distance that still seems so close.
You cannot fully describe a war. If this is good or bad I cannot say.
But now I understand, from 12 years of life, that a
picture
is
worth
a
thousand
words.

Gil Osofsky, Grade 7
Carson Middle School, VA

Winter Wonderland?

I stand out like a rainbow on a blank canvas.
I'm surrounded by colorless gloom that threatens to overtake me.
The cool air whips at my face, it enters my nose and mouth as I suck in.
I can feel the bitterness like what I get
When I try to eat the chocolate chips my mom uses for her cookies.
Where has the sweetness gone?
My hair flies out behind me.
A whirlwind of leaves left behind by Autumn's gales scurry past me trying to catch up.
I listen to the absence of the chirping birds.
I gaze up at the sky that isn't there,
Only the treetops dancing in the wind.
I pull my coat tighter around me and my hat down lower.
I wish someone was there to hold me tight
And tell me everything will be all right.
I exhale deeply and I can feel the life silently escaping through my mouth.
The fields are empty and the world is white.
I reach up slowly to cover my Rudolph nose.
The hand in front of me is bare and numb just like the world around me.

Dana Bachman, Grade 7
Carson Middle School, VA

City Night

The clouds watch me from above.
Fireflies glow in the distance; the sky blackens.
I squint my eyes and the street lights shimmer with a delicate glow.
Twittering birds gather along telephone lines
and abandoned benches.
Sprinkled gold dust sprays the city with happy faces and good deeds.
Slowly, each light flickers,
Then goes out.
Good night, world.

Bita Golshani, Grade 7
Kilmer Middle School, VA

Bubbles

Sunlight shines
On bubbles
And makes
Them sparkle
And dance in
The breeze
It shines through
The bubbles
Creating rainbows
In the air
Bubbles brush me
Tickle my arms
I spin around
Surrounded by
Bubbles
Rainbow orbs fly
Around me
I catch them in
My soapy hands
Like Christmas balls
Near the 4th of July

Lydia Kivrak, Grade 8
Home School, MD

Soldier's Wife

I need you by my side
So why do you have to go
I don't understand why
But this is the path you choose
Your life is a special thing
We hope you don't have to lose
In my eyes you are sacred
But in others may be hatred
'Cause, the time we share is always precious
Since you left, my nights have been restless
I know you're far away
But in my mind you'll always stay
So, please come home to me
For a children of 3
Will soon be…

Bailey Foust, Grade 8
Corkran Middle School, MD

A Piece of Pie

My life is like a piece of pie
Sweet, easy, but hard to eat
I try not to lie
But I can't keep on my feet
I think I have it hard
People tell me they have it worse
I dream of laying in my yard
Alone, trying not to burst
I don't like feeling this way
But just have to cope

Alexa Weatherwalks, Grade 7
Western Heights Middle School, MD

Shy

Why are you shy?
They asked me once
And asked again

My mom asked me,
Why is it that you always lock yourself in your bedroom
And never go out to play with some new friends?
She asked me today
And the next week too

My sister questioned my way of living
Why is it that you never come to any sleepovers with me
Or go shopping with me, like every other normal sister in the world?
I sat there quietly
As anger raged through my burning body, like an untamed tiger ready to get loose

I got tired of the same question
Why are you so…SHY?

I am not shy, maybe I am
I can talk, but not as much as my friends
I can dance and sing, but I choose not to do any of those things
I'm afraid that if I become too close to someone I love I will lose them
So yes, I am shy, but that's what makes me who I am
Unique

Tasnia Nokib, Grade 7
Farmwell Station Middle School, VA

On Turning Sixteen

The whole idea of it makes me feel, like I'm opening a new present,
The adrenaline you get when you tear open the paper,
A kind of energy drink for your blood, a type of coffee for your brain,
An electric shock for your body.

You tell me I can't act like I'm ten, to grow up and be a man,
But you have just forgotten,
The fun of being young, the friends you get to meet,
But I try to live my life,
As much as I can, before I have to wear a suit,
And go to meetings.

So now as I think about,
I have to use my time wisely, make sure it goes as planned,
As I look at my room,
I think of the crayon filled walls, the night light by the bed, illuminating the room.

This is the beginning of manhood,
With a side of child fun, as I walk out the door a new man,
It is time to get a job, get a life, but keep it fun.

It seems only last year I used to be, sitting in a small classroom,
happy as can be,
I could never get in trouble, but now as I walk down the street,
I have to be good. I have to make a future for myself.

Miguel DeCastro, Grade 7
E Russell Hicks Middle School, MD

A River's Life

I am a fast-flowing river,
careless and free.
I explore my region of the world
until the beavers stop me.
They build dams
that block my path.
I build up my water
and break through their walls.
I return to being
a divider of the land.
I am a fast-flowing river,
careless and free.
The children come
splashing here, there and everywhere.
But I am so used to it
that I really don't care.
When it gets dark
they leave me alone in my banks.
I am a fast-flowing river,
careless and free.

Carissa Smith, Grade 8
St Paul's Lutheran School, MD

I Sit with You

I miss you now
But I know it was time
I miss you now
As I sit alone

I know you're up there
Happy as can be
So please always keep
One eye out for me

As I go through life
I'll face many tests
And I'll look up to you
For the decision that's best

Please be safe
I know you will
And I will always pray
So when I sit alone
I sit with you

Jack Heaps, Grade 7
Kilmer Middle School, VA

Blessing

May your life be peaceful and happy
May the joyfulness come in
May laughter and joy fill your life
May cheerfulness make you laugh
And love with happiness
May love surround your family.

Madison Kerns, Grade 7
Marshall Middle School, VA

I Remember

I remember when I just wanted to have fun
I remember when I didn't care what I wore
I remember when I used to cry when I had to turn a card
I remember when I thought school field trips were the best
I remember when I thought that the Playstation 2 would be the best thing ever
I remember when school was easy
I remember when math wasn't so complicated
I remember when computers were big and bulky
I remember when I thought every wave at a beach was huge
I remember when nap time was my favorite part of the day
I remember when I didn't pay any attention to sports
I remember watching my sister spend hours on homework every night
I remember when the world was so much bigger
I remember when my parents would buy me toys
I remember when the Power Rangers was my favorite show
I remember when I used to wake up early on Saturday
This were certainly easier back then, but I'm ready to face life's upcoming challenges

Michael, Grade 8
St Columba School, MD

Childhood

The melancholy darts of ice rain down
Shadows of gray echo in your vision.
The shock of impact from your body
to the impenetrable pavement sends water bursting into the air.

The rush of a passing car
chills you to the bone
And the motley smell of exhaust and rain
works its way into your nose.
You're oblivious to the wetness,
feeling only a tickle as the drops maneuver their way down your face.

And as your rubbery coat
repels tiny beads of chill
you travel farther
into the world of childhood.

Amanda Johnson, Grade 9
Woodbridge Sr High School, VA

Guilt

Guilt is a dark, gray storm cloud
It hovers around you, it is a spaceship waiting to attack
Its thunder pounds harder than a herd of buffalo
Its lightning strikes are more powerful than an atom bomb
Nobody likes it, for it is an enemy of happiness
The people who love it are invisible
It is a puppy waiting to be fed
It will never go away unless you fix what you've done
Accept the storm cloud's demands, and you will live in pride and happiness
Decline them, and it will kill you, for it is a puppy waiting to feed
On your pain.

Ellen Gurung, Grade 7
Carson Middle School, VA

For Granted

Widely taken advantage of
more vast than any sky you see
whether it be blue or gray or green

Always never stopping
movement rules my life
but no matter how far I go, always,
there's something killing me

Whether I run or crash
or rest in bed
no matter where I'm going I'm taken from

You always see me
you never notice
I've always known you
I'm wherever you are

I'm half of you, but you don't care
and without me, you die
but all you've known me as,
is simply that stuff that falls from the sky

Alexis Brooks, Grade 8
Norfolk Christian Middle School, VA

Fragile Things of Air and Thought

The heavens rained down their sorrow,
As a single figure stood alone.
"Give me your wings,"
Was whispered to the angels.
"You at least owe me that."
So they did.
Fragile things of air and thought.
The falling rain had no effect
As the figure slowly rose up from
The dirt and grime.
Images below
Growing dimmer
And dimmer,
Until eyes finally closed
In relief.

Shirley Shields, Grade 9
Woodbridge Sr High School, VA

Jesus

Jesus
Awesome person
My Savior forever
He fulfilled His purpose
He died to save us
Born in a manger
Prince of Peace
Everlasting God
Jesus

Yanni Allen, Grade 8
Norfolk Christian Middle School, VA

Winter

I sit inside,
Anticipating, waiting,
For the moment when it comes.
And it comes, the silent blessing of the clouds.

The flower petals fall gently,
Swooping down to meet the lush grass like birds upon prey.
Soon, a blanket of white covers the ground that thickens with every moment.
Snow.

I walk out and look to the right.
The evergreen tree is dusted with snow,
Little white flowers, of a second spring,
That sprouted on the spiky green leaves.

To my left, the strangely silent pond,
Where the fish and turtles used to playfully zip through the water,
Glazed with ice and snow,
Like a glassy windowpane to the world beneath.

All around, fine white dust fills the space.
Everything, a picture of white.
And then I know in the deepest sense,
It has finally come to change the tide of the year.

Winter.

Kevin Lin, Grade 7
Kilmer Middle School, VA

So Tell Me, Yeti, Are You Real?

Oh Yeti, world-renowned be your illustrious name
Your pure white, wooly mane enshrouds your fortified height
In the snow-clad Himalayas, you are said to harbor
From the irritating presence of the glistening camera lights

Concealed always must you be, the cost of your fame
Back and forth, to and fro, they find your footprints
They seek to encounter you in your obscure habitat
But every time they come close, you break into a sprint

Do you live in the colorless wilderness of this planet Earth?
Or do you rest quietly in our hopeful imaginations?
Some claim they have seen you; they stared at you in awe
As you sought out refuge from them, teeth baring in frustration

Your cousin, Sasquatch, is very different from you indeed
Brown eyes, thick matted, dirt brown hair
He looks at the cameras with unsettling ease, or so it seems
Why don't you tend to do the same, allow your reputation to be exposed and bare

To this day, no one is certain about your whimsical existence
Skeptics are more critical of you than ever before
But always remember this, dear Yeti
Your far-famed legend will live on ever more

Tabby Hayes, Grade 8
Most Blessed Sacrament Catholic School, MD

High Merit Poems – Grades 7, 8, and 9

Love Is Like a Labyrinth
Love is like a labyrinth.
A complex system,
easy to get lost in.
never knowing when there's a dead end,
every so often you get lost,
and can't find your way out.

Both are complicated and twisting.
Sometimes you may think,
you are going the right way,
you think you have found your soul mate,
but end up at a dead end.

You just got to turn around,
keep hiking past all the obstacles.
Soon with the help,
of the compass of your heart,
you will find a way,
to be united with your true love.

There is only one path to love,
only one way out of the labyrinth,
follow your heart
or follow the light of the labyrinth.
Annie Abraham, Grade 7
Rachel Carson Middle School, VA

Still Burning
Still,
I can smell something sour
like a smelly sock
that got thrown behind the couch
and forgotten.

Still,
I can feel the prickly, thick smoke
that crackled the surrounding air,
like the hair-raising shock
I got from a rubbed balloon once.

Still,
I can see the fire spit out red-hot embers
and bellow ashes from its mouth,
like an angry dragon woken up
by the yellow-clad firefighters.

Still,
Inside, I feel like I am a powerless bug
trapped in an oven,
like I can do nothing but cry
as the fire laughs at me,
laughing still.
Alison Li, Grade 7
Rachel Carson Middle School, VA

Alone
I am new
To this school
All alone
Wandering the halls
I am lost
I need help
But I have nobody to help me
So I ask someone
They ignore me
It takes me days
Just to make a friend
I found one person
Who can't fit in
With others
Just like me
Just like me
Havisha Annamreddy, Grade 7
Rachel Carson Middle School, VA

America
Land of…
Glistening oceans,
Bountiful with vast trenches,
And endless coral reefs.
Damp, foggy forests,
Immense, snow covered mountains,
Rapid, rushing rivers,
Plains filled with dancing grasses,
Like beautiful gold ribbons.
America, Land of…
People who never gave up,
And will never give up.
People who are free,
As free as free can be.
God Bless America
Land of the free.
Angel Jones, Grade 8
Homespun Schoolhouse Of Agape, VA

I Dream
In the mist
Before dawn approaches
We live not with restriction
But with the freedom of our souls

I lay dormant
In the solitary absence of light
I live without restraint

I dance with the deer
I prowl with the lions
I soar with the eagles
I swim with the sharks
I dream
Nicholas Thomas, Grade 7
Kilmer Middle School, VA

I Am the Rainbow Lord
I am the rainbow lord.
I wonder if the rainbows bow down to me.
I hear red cry.
I see yellow dance.
I want them to be my friends.
I am the rainbow lord.
I pretend I am the rainbow lord.
I feel colorful.
I touch a pot of gold.
I worry that I will fade.
I cry at the color blue.
I am the rainbow lord.
I understand the rainbow colors.
I say "please don't cry."
I dream of a place with magical charms.
I try not to think of unhappy things.
I hope I will be happy.
I am the rainbow lord.
Brianna Hartlove, Grade 8
Corkran Middle School, MD

How Do I Love Thee?*
How do I love thee? Let me count the ways.
I love thee when I'm all bundled up,
About to hit the slopes.
I love thee when I'm in line,
Waiting to get on the lift.
I love thee on the top of the mountain,
Feeling the cold, crisp air.
I love thee when I take off,
Swerving side to side.
I love thee when snow is under my board,
Blowing in the wind as I go by.
I love thee by feeling free,
All under my control.
I love thee every time I'm out there,
Having the best time of my life.
I love thee just thinking about it,
Ah snowboarding!
Kayla Alvey, Grade 8
St Clement Mary Hofbauer School, MD
Inspired by Elizabeth Barrett Browning

Daylight Savings Time
Sun
Scorching, dangerous,
Blinding, radiating, dazzling
Fiery, golden, rough, silent
Soothing, peaceful, cooling
Lunar, romantic
Moon
Matthew Saviano, Grade 8
Mount St Charles Academy, RI

The Year's Journey

Going to the park,
She walks under the arc
And climbs onto the swing.

Swinging into autumn,
She is forced to succumb
To the cold approach that
Winter brings.

She begins to ponder
How much longer
She will be able to stand the cold.

Looking forlorn and deplorable,
She does something horrible:
She stays on the swing 'til the cold is
Too much to bear.

So…dismounting the swing,
She falls onto spring's pulchritudinous mien.
And then?
She starts all over again.

Sammi J. Rappaport, Grade 9
Norfolk Collegiate Middle/Upper School, VA

Why Don't They Remember?

The sight of blind men,
An ugly thing to witness
Not knowing how to use a pen,
Always having a moment of sickness,
They question their doings,
And move away from everything good
Do they understand what they are losing?
To a place less understood
A place less understood — a home for them,
Their position; they don't get
They see their den
Only here, not there — no fret
They cannot remember, they only forget,
The sun never rises in their souls,
The loss of salvation, they will always regret,
The sighted look down with sorrow upon the burning fools.

Noreen Malik, Grade 8
The Banner School, MD

Astrohippies

Meteors float in endless troops,
The universe sheltering them in its confusing coupes,
Aliens fly around and away,
Followed by the Astrohippies every day,
Saving the ecosystem by living in space,
The Astrohippies keep up the eco-race,
Life as we know it completely changed,
Astrohippies just saved the day.

Neil Chiruvella, Grade 7
Kilmer Middle School, VA

Secrets

The beauty of a secret no one knows.
It all starts with a slip of the tongue.
You can keep or break them.
You decide, tell or die?

They hold the answers to a thousands mysteries.
And, keep the peace in friendships.
You can't live with or without them.
Don't smile or you'll give it away.

They start off innocent, as little white lies.
Swear, nothing but the truth?
In a blink of an eye, you'll tell a lie.
You wouldn't dare break a secret.

Secrets are like a promise.
They can last forever, if no one tells.
Lips sealed, I cross my heart and pray to die.

Shama Nathan, Grade 8
ISSL, DC

The Future

No one really knows what the future will bring for me.
I believe a lot of it depends on fate,
But I guess I'll just have to wait
And see.

Maybe the future
Will be the same as the present,
Or maybe the future
Will be more like the past.

The future could be a time
When everyone gets along,
But who knows?
I could be wrong.

Hannah Cote, Grade 9
Mount St Charles Academy, RI

Wonderland

Have you ever wondered where it leads?
   Down the dark and winding abyss,
Hidden somewhere beneath the rotted weeds,
   The tunnel opening very easily missed.

Have you ever wondered about the Cheshire's smile?
   Teeth bright as stars, big and frightening.
His look of wry and mischief lingers awhile,
   And his sarcastic remarks strike like lightning.

Have you ever wondered why he is Mad?
   His talk is random and mostly jibber-ized,
His eyes are wild, but always sad.
   I like his Hatter style, and think he's crazy-wise.

Emily Farnum, Grade 9
Mount St Charles Academy, RI

Score
Kicking the ball down the field
Suddenly I come to a yield
To find a girl standing in front of me
Getting around her is my cup of tea
I fake her out
Left then right
This is so easy I could do it all night

I see the clock counting down
I zone on in and block out sound
I kick the ball off the ground
It flies in mid air and goes in the net
You tell me I can't do it again
I just smile and say, "Want to bet?"
Kelly Wojciechowski, Grade 8
Corkran Middle School, MD

Power Over Life and Death
We have so much power,
So much power over life,
But not over the thing we dread, death.

We all will pass through death,
When our power,
Will be done and we will have no life.

Life,
Is what we live through, death,
Is what is after we lose our earthly power.
We might not always have life
When we are passing through death,
But we will always have power.
Jacob Oliver, Grade 8
Norfolk Collegiate Middle/Upper School, VA

A Violin's Voice
Strings of silver
With pressure make the right sound
Bow of gold
With a push of confidence
A pull of fear
Up down, down up
Encourages you to speak
The sweet sound of slowly dripping honey
Or the powerful voice of fire and thunder
Changing moods as the sky
A rattle of your skeleton
A cloud of dust
Reminders of what you've spoken
Your reward is applause
Millicent Wise, Grade 8
Norfolk Collegiate Middle/Upper School, VA

Breathe
The water crushes
You're sinking, you're drowning
You feel like you can't ever
Breathe.

Friends turn and leave you
You're betrayed, you're crying
They turn though they know you can't
Breathe.

You feel like you are
So beaten, so broken
Not a shoulder to cry on
Can't breathe.

Surface above you,
With the father that loves you
But still you are afraid to
Breathe.

A ladder drops to you
But you are still scared to rise
Just climb it, I beg you
Just breathe.
Mark Rodriguez, Grade 8
Norfolk Christian Middle School, VA

The Little Girl
A little girl survives,
The ultimate attack
She never looked back.

The worst day of her life,
Was met with considerable strife.
The dreams that were dreamt
Were never kept.
So young, so innocent, so energetic
What happened to her was pathetic.

There was a mad dog on the loose.
That frightened the girl to her boots.
She tried to get away
But no one could save the day.

The attack dislocated her jaw.
And there was more, more, more.
The girl wished she could go back in time.
But, life had other ideas.
And offers us others who are dear.

So, now I am with Mrs. Theim
Sharing with her these few lines.
Jeannette White, Grade 8
St Jane De Chantal School, MD

4th of July
We feel excited all day
We hear the music of the marching band
and see the colors of red, white and blue
We taste the mouthwatering hotdogs
The ice cold drinks freeze our tongues

Sparklers look like tiny stars
We see explosions bright in the sky
We hear the screams from the crowd
It feels like we're on a battlefield
There's the small of black powder in the air
It looks like they're shooting rockets
across the sky

We feel proud
It's a great way to celebrate
America's Independence
Matt Megge, Grade 7
Cape Henry Collegiate School, VA

Things I See
Every day is an adventure
Stars in the air
The trees in the sky
A beauty in every smile
"Make music with your life"
A tune we can all swing to
A day is not worth living
Until you've seen the world
One day won't cut it either
You need a spaceship
A plane
A ship
Fly with no limits
It takes no pain
No worries
Every day is an adventure
Live it up until your time is up
Nicko Patron, Grade 8
Kenmore Middle School, VA

Butterfly
My appearance in the beginning
Is much different than in the end
I build a house
Where I can change
The wings I grow
Help me to fly
When the time is right
I show the world the new me
Now I am beautiful on the outside
But I am still the same me
My outer beauty
Now matches my inner beauty
Brooke Pilkington, Grade 7
Cape Henry Collegiate School, VA

Alone

Alone, again
My dust left me behind.
Stuck
In my own head.

My sobs
Suffocate.
My tears
Drown me.

Trying to reach out,
Touch the surface,
Grasp reality.
But I slip!

I fall! I'm lost.
I try harder,
So I fall…Harder.

Alone, again.
My dust left me behind.

Allie Apsley, Grade 8
Stevensville Middle School, MD

If Only

As we walked in the sand,
He was holding my hand.
Waves crashed all around,
No crowd to be found.

His eyes are like the bright blue sky.
He never makes me want to cry.
I never want to say goodbye,
If only I was lying…

Water crashes over my head,
I wish I just stayed in bed.
I thought he knew,
What I said was true.
If only I was lying…

Ruthie Vinson, Grade 8
Corkran Middle School, MD

Moonstruck

As I lay in the rustling grass,
Gazing at the full moon,
Such gentle light,
Burning with such passion
And such celestial beauty,
The bittersweet melody
Of luminous silver.
She is the essence of grace and elegance,
Queen of the night sky,
Shining amongst the stars.

Justin Ku, Grade 9
Richard Montgomery High School, MD

Corrin's Poem

As I sit here in my cell, I know the reason all too well,
For why I've cause you so much pain, you're standing there, wet from the rain,
The "friend-ship" sailing bravely, fell.

When I met you on that day, your eyes were dull, depressed and gray,
"I want to do just what you do, an alchemist, confident and true,"
The inner thoughts you dared to say.

I understood. I heard your plea. That's when I gave you my old key.
"True confidence it will unlock, you'll be the very best. You'll walk,
No, *run*, with me and alchemy."

You were my student for a while, I loved the way you'd always smile,
Yours were truthful, mine were lies, and soon we'd have to say goodbyes,
I'm cunning, fake, a poisoned vile.

Then I was caught for all my crime, and now I'm stuck with doing time,
Here's to the end of all my thieving, trust is gone, but you're forgiving,
Thus concludes my little rhyme.

Lily Bickford, Grade 9
Mount St Charles Academy, RI

Confirmation with God

Where you get to know God,
Is Confirmation,
A place to worship and make new friends.

You and your mentor become friends,
We meet in the house of God,
The five months we spend together is Confirmation.

We feel the presence of God,
With every step we take through Confirmation,
The more we learn, and share our experiences with friends.

With God watching over us, we spend time and learn with our friends,
Welcome to Confirmation of Virginia Beach United Methodist Church.

Hayley Tate, Grade 8
Norfolk Collegiate Middle/Upper School, VA

Tick, Tick, Tick…Caboom

I am a ticking time bomb.
I wonder if people see through my mask of being diffused.
I want to really be as ok as I seem and act.
I pretend to be walking on air at times.
I feel crazy enough to try it.
I worry that one day I will be out of time…
I cry when I am at my wit's end and ready to explode.
I am a ticking time bomb.
I understand why it will happen…I held it in and now it's time to face the wrath.
I say that nothing is wrong
I try to hold it in.
I hope that no one is in my path when the explosion comes.
I am a ticking time bomb.

Tamira Carr, Grade 8
Corkran Middle School, MD

My Twist of Happiness

In a rush this soda flows out,
It makes a big splash in an ice cold glass.
As it bubbles, my problems dissolve away.

I smell lemon-lime flavors, a crisp and clean taste,
Then open my mouth and swallow with haste.
Thirst is quenched, tongue is drenched.

Glancing in front of me,
sad to see the glass is now empty.
No more for me, what a tragedy.
I look up and fill with glee
A new bottle sits and mocks me.

Hours pass, ice cubes melt away.
My twist of happiness made it through the day.
In my heart this Sprite will stay.
On another thirst quenching day,
I will twist the cap,
pour in my glass, a refreshing drink.
My sip, my chug, my moment, my memory.
My twist of happiness.

Jennifer January, Grade 8
St Paul's Lutheran School, MD

Skate Until the End

One hard push, I stand straight and still
The world flies by me, it makes it a thrill
I bend my knees, I move my feet
I think of nothing, as I make the art neat
I try my best, I give it my all
I never quit, I stand straight and tall
I fall and get hurt and lose my heart and my control
But nothing can hurt the bond between you and my soul
Wherever I ride you're always there
Being my closest friend and the most for whom I care
As I'm in the air and I look down below
I don't lose faith because I know you will not go
As I land on you for the final turn
I feel happy to be great but there is always room to learn
When I ride with the feeling of being free
There's nothing else but the sky, my skateboard and me

David Dichoso, Grade 8
St Columba School, MD

The Howling Dog

My dog is a Wheaten terrier named Finnegan.
His fur is as soft as a blanket.
His bark sounds like the howl of a wolf.
He is playful and joyful with his family.
He is loyal and well-trained.
His eyes are brown like chestnuts.
His tail is always wagging wildly.
My dog is my pride and joy and he always will be.

Glenn Dixon, Grade 8
St Paul's Lutheran School, MD

2012

The new year that has yet to come,
It will be filled with memories for me.
A school year of utmost importance,
Cramming for the straight A's.
Shadowing at high schools,
Making a tough decision.
Saying bye to friends and teachers,
With a golden tassel and a gown of blue.
The future filled with promises
Of a high school called NDP.
Waving goodbye sadly to my sister,
As she is driven off to college.
Starting a new school with new classes and teachers,
Walking through the gates of NDP, to welcome the new students.
That will be the coming year!
Filled with sadness, happiness, and goodbyes
But this is not the end,
For I will be doing this again in another four years.

Daniele Nitkowski, Grade 7
St Clement Mary Hofbauer School, MD

Never Lost

Friendship is what bonds people together,
But when you lose that best friend
Hope is not lost,
And you may feel that sad feeling in your heart
But you know they climbed the mountain of life
To the top
Only to know
That's their end
But life continues,
It may seem
That you can't see them
But they see you
And when you
See them again
In the afterlife
That united bond
Starts again.

Jimmy McCaffrey, Grade 7
Summit School, MD

Take Me Away

Let me leave this place where the smoke blows black,
And the dark street winds and bends.
Take me where the sun shines bright,
And the people are like angels.
Let me leave the place where the cities are dead,
And the houses are burned.
Take me where the schools are clean,
And the grass is green.
Let me leave this place where the trees are dead,
And the yards are graveyards.
Take me away from the truth.

Akshay Kumar, Grade 7
Kilmer Middle School, VA

Fated*
Why this little boy, who was willing to try in life?
Why wasn't he showered with toys and things?
All day, he talked to no one at home, no one at school
With a Mom that hit and didn't care
Teachers at school worried but said nothing,
Why did he walk alone? Play alone? Eat alone?
Why did he come home to a house of chaos and fear?
Why not to a mother, who loved? Who cared?
Why him, why not the boy two houses down?
Why did no one hear the screams? Why did no one care?
Why did he try to please the malice he called mom,
When she never seemed to be satisfied with her perfect son
A child who longed for the life of the family,
Who had family game night and ate dinner together,
Why this little boy, the one who suffered a life of fear?
What had he done to deserve such a terrible childhood?

Valerie Papineau, Grade 9
Mount St Charles Academy, RI
**Imitating "Astonishment" by Wislawa Szymborska.*

No-Fly Zone
A country in turmoil.
Controlled by dictatorship.
A hated dictator stripping citizens of their rights.
Protests begin in the streets.
Hatred for the dictator rises as the protests continue.
Tanks roll in and soldiers armed with guns enter the streets.
Fights break out.
Guns are shot.
People are killed to fight for their rights.
A bomb is dropped.
The dictator bombs two major cities.
The citizens are furious at the event.
Militias form and the rebels are well armed.
50-cal guns pointed at the sky
Ready to shoot any military plane over head.
The rebels test their cannons,
To make sure the only thing dropping out of the sky is a fighter jet.

David Smith, Grade 8
Norfolk Collegiate Middle/Upper School, VA

Anticipation
I sit in my seat,
closely watching the clock.
The minutes go by,
slower than a single flake of snow falls to the earth.

I almost shake with anticipation,
as does everyone else,
counting down the last few seconds.

When the bell rings we jump for joy,
as a long year of school has finally ended,
and a wonderful summer is hardly beginning.

Erika St.Germain, Grade 8
Mount St Charles Academy, RI

Ten Ways to Look at the Sky
1. You give me rain when you are cloudy
and sunshine when you are clear.
2. You fill my days with laughter and
happiness when I go outside.
3. You let animals float in your presence
with their nice and joyful songs.
4. You provide a way of traveling to get
to places near but also very far.
5. When I look up you can make pictures
and shapes with the clouds you provide.
6. When your sun goes down, you show us what
beautiful colors you can make.
7. Long ago you made day and night for those who
roamed the earth night and day.
8. You give the ocean its color. When you are cloudy and gray
the ocean is the same and when you are sunny and bright
the ocean is the same.
9. For fun people dive out of planes and float
in your atmosphere until they reach the bottom.
10. When people pass they assume that
you take them up to their heavenly place.

Yalaina Dupre, Grade 8
Norfolk Collegiate Middle/Upper School, VA

Danger Is But a Bowl of Soup
Danger is but a bowl of soup,
A sea of uncertainty,
Filled to the brim
With many memories.
You can smell it from afar,
And you are lured to the exhilarating brew
But don't get too close,
Or the steam will cloud your vision.
The soup tastes different for everyone,
All diverse, unique recipes
Each adding their individual spices
To flavor their exquisite concoctions.
But make sure you know what you're dealing with,
Because you might just —
Burn yourself.

Sano Nagai, Grade 7
Rachel Carson Middle School, VA

Week of Prayer
Five school days on which we worship God,
responding to powerful statements with an "Amen" and a nod.
Singing hymns to Him who is glorious.
Thanking Him for all the things He has done for us.
Learning from the Word to grow closer to Him,
for we need its knowledge in the battle against sin.
We have seasonal prayer to talk to the King,
who made the Earth and everything.
A week to be able to accept Jesus as our Savior,
and grow with Him in favor.

Kyra Samuda, Grade 8
George E Peters Adventist School, MD

I Am a Book

I am a book.
I have information.
Anything you want to know
I have it.
The older you get
the more sophisticated I get.
I give advice to all
whenever you need it.
I can tell a pretty good story.
Once upon a time…
I tell you about the past.
I read you poems just like this one.
Recipes? I got them.
I can tell you how to make the best cuisine.
Some of the greatest words ever spoken came from me.
I can teach you all subjects.
I can define words for you as well.
You can laugh or cry to the things I say
I won't tell anyone
Because…
I am a book.

Martijn Goossens, Grade 8
Norfolk Collegiate Middle/Upper School, VA

Charisma

Charisma is a piano,
When you play certain keys,
Magic happens,
You have to spend hours and hours practicing,
It comes in different sizes,
Grand or mini,
You really just want to show it off.
It seems like all sophisticated people have one,
It really attracts other people's ears.
It can hurt when you drop it on people,
Its sound is not always as fine as it looks,
It's really hard to hide,
There are so many ways to play it,
And when you press one key wrong,
The piece collapses.

Andrew Huang, Grade 7
Rachel Carson Middle School, VA

Ricky Iannucci

Ricky
Nice, kind, trustworthy, and very responsible
Son of my dad
Lover of Taylor Swift, lacrosse, basketball, cats, dogs, and tigers
Who needs water, food, and shelter
Who fears hungry tigers, angry sharks, and the grudge
Who loves Taylor Swift music
Who would like to see Taylor Swift
Resident of Chester
Iannucci

Ricky Iannucci, Grade 8
Stevensville Middle School, MD

Love and Chaos

With all this stuff around me.
And chaos here and there.
I cannot help but wonder.
Do people really care?

I know that people love me.
I know that they have heart.
But there's too much devastation to really do their part.
I cannot help but wonder.
Do people really care?

With all this darkness and dread.
I'll just lay on my bed.
And wonder every night.
Do people really care?

I have found the answer.
People do care.
But there's too much devastation.
To really know they're there.

So cling to what you have.
And cherish every moment.
You'll never get your life back.
But good people will be there.

Charles Hummel, Grade 9
Delaware Military Academy, DE

The Ballad of Guinevere, the Wife of the King

The charming, desirable Queen Guinevere,
The second wife of the beloved king.
Arthur loved her with his whole heart,
But slowly a romance with Lancelot was growing.

Beauty radiated off her porcelain skin,
She illuminated even the darkest place.
Her face glowed like a star in the midnight sky,
She carried herself through the castle with grace.

She tried to ignore Sir Lancelot,
But soon she was under his spell.
He was a noble and magnificent man,
But she couldn't tell Arthur farewell.

Like a flower was their undeniable love,
Gradually blooming ever so slowly.
She coveted to be with Lancelot,
But was joined with Arthur in matrimony.

People became suspicious of Guinevere
She couldn't bear to hurt either man,
She couldn't listen to another awful story.
Guinevere needed to start her life anew,
So she entered the convent in Amesbury.

Amy Jackson, Grade 7
Most Blessed Sacrament Catholic School, MD

Memories

Thinking of the past
Gets me swept away in memories
All the times I've had
A fair amount of good and bad

The bad are like storm clouds
Evading a perfect sky of blue
Sometimes they pour down upon me
Reminding myself of times I which I'd never knew

But the good ones are to remember
They sum up my life in all
Times with family and friends
And when upon me I felt grace fall

But so surely do I know
That my memories, good and bad, have let me grow
That they have indeed made me
The person that I'm meant to be

Elizabeth Bose, Grade 8
Norfolk Christian Middle School, VA

The Mighty Fire

The fire which burns throughout the darkest night,
That shimmers and scintillates as it glows,
Shall quench the strong fear and still the great fright
And warm the tiniest of hands and toes.
Whenever the impressive fire burning
Begins to slowly quiver and die out,
Then sets in the most powerful yearning,
For fire to return and remove the doubt.
This great inferno of orange and red
That shineth on like a beacon so bright,
Doth flicker and flash as its shadow spreads,
Scaring away the blackness and the fright.
Yet when all is lost and our needs are dire,
Mankind can always depend upon fire.

Patrick Ryan, Grade 7
Kilmer Middle School, VA

Pray for Peace

Every night we to go to sleep for rest
Most of us sleep in
Our beds, praying for peace.

It is very difficult to make peace,
Especially with countries that don't get a rest
Because of their poverty and economy that they live in.

Everyone has a difficult time fitting in
Because this world does not create peace.
No one deserves to get a good night's rest.

Rest in peace, for the world will hopefully come to its senses.

Trey Ritter, Grade 8
Norfolk Collegiate Middle/Upper School, VA

Tick Tock

Sitting there, waiting for the bell to ring.
The kids with their hands clasped, just waiting to let loose.
The teacher's lectures just drag on,
And the clock's hand just moves slower.

Some students waiting to go on vacation,
Others just are waiting to get out of this place.
One thinking of her plans for the week,
Another just sitting there imagining sleep.

The clock seems to move slower and slower.
One minute will drag on and you'll think its over, but it's not.
The teacher will be still at the front,
And you will still be in the chair.

Tick tock the time continues,
As you think to yourself about the fun ahead.
The bell finally rings and you jump up,
Not realizing you will soon be back here.

Natalie Kanter, Grade 9
Norfolk Collegiate Middle/Upper School, VA

Lost Love

She was a golden girl, the only one for me
He was the perfect boy, only one I can see
I can still feel her hand walking along the shore
I wish he was here now…but he won't be anymore
Even though our sweet, sweet love was torn at sea
I will still never dream of letting go of thee
My warm heart will always be yours to hold
No matter what, even nature's freezing cold
The salty waves will come breaking down…come what may
Until the end of time, no matter how harsh the day
I will love you no matter what people say
Our love can only go stronger from here
And you know I will often shed a tear
Know I love you…and know I always will

Jayna Kirk, Grade 7
Kilmer Middle School, VA

If I Were in Charge of the World

If I were in charge of the world
I'd get rid of silent letters and reality television shows
And keep comedy shows
If I were in charge of the world
There'd be no irritating people
Including people who rush
And nag others
If I were in charge of the world
You wouldn't have to eat brussel sprouts
You wouldn't take medicines by needle
You wouldn't even have to cook
Or clean
If I were in charge of the world

Darius Elliott, Grade 8
Corkran Middle School, MD

A Number

A number given to you
To mark you
And to let you know of life
Children use it as a contest
Adults use it as an insult
But everyone uses it to judge
To say that they are too young to know
Or say that they are too old to understand
When underneath it all
The old may learn from the young
Just as the young are able to learn from the old
The old look at the young
Saying they do not understand
Or that they don't know anything and have much to learn
Some is true
But yet the old have much to learn as well
Some things they may have understood when they were young
Will never be thought of again
The number does not matter
For the mind and wisdom do

Sara Borowy, Grade 8
St Paul's Lutheran School, MD

The Shrinking Island

Behind the island's beauty,
The island is fading away.

Vivid lives once on this island,
Are now miserable lives on the mainland.

The animals that are most cherished,
Are now slowly dying off.

Fine marsh that made well for animal homes,
Is rapidly changing into a massive beach.

A well-known island,
By the name of Tangier,
Will in, 50 years,
Be just another particle of land.

Cameron Watson, Grade 8
Washington Episcopal School, MD

Poetry

How do I love thee? Let me count the ways.
I love thee when I have ideas in my mind,
Paper and a pen is what I find.
I love thee when I feel like expressing myself,
I grab the rhyming dictionary off the shelf,
I love thee in writing class,
Poetry is something I would never pass.
I love thee, Poetry, you are my life,
To me poetry seems larger than life.
I love thee, my dearest Poetry.

Ally Lanasa, Grade 7
St Clement Mary Hofbauer School, MD

Fire

To some it is a tool or a life saver
To others it is the devil's breath
A tool, a life saver, and the devil's breath
No matter what you think it is,
It's Fire
It is warmth and light
It is destruction and hurt
Warmth, light, destruction, and hurt
No matter what you use it for,
It's Fire
To campers it is fun to tell stories around
To the lost it is warmth and safety
Fun to tell stories around, warmth, and safety
No matter when you use it,
It's Fire
A fun and exciting family time
A family left with nothing
Family fun and excitement or left with nothing
No matter what is does to you,
It's Fire

Joshua Stroh, Grade 8
St Paul's Lutheran School, MD

No Sympathy for the Dead

The powerful wind shook my shivering spine
Blowing the lights out of my soul

Beating slowly *boom, boom*
And only in a matter of time, my heart turns sour
Sucked within the black hole
Bursting off shooting stars

Siphoning out the pure inside of me
Inside the darkness of my mind:
Lost forever in the circle of lies "Please, wake me up!"

Begging in vain for my sins, screaming at the devil,
He whispers back to me:
"I win."

Joseph Portillo, Grade 8
Kenmore Middle School, VA

Joy

Joy is a field of flowers.
Fuchsia, golden, teal,
It's a place where you can be happy, and have fun.
It blooms and it's
Beautiful,
And it makes your heart warm just seeing it.
Sometimes joy dies, but it can always come back and
Flourish.
Joy is a hard thing to hide, but what is the point of hiding it,
When there is enough for the world to
Share?

Madeline Miles, Grade 7
Carson Middle School, VA

Game Day

Game day! Game day! Game day is here!
It's chilly outside, but hot in here.
The quiet tension before the game,
The calm before the storm, or
The eye of a hurricane.

Many people in the hallway,
With hot dog in hand,
Can't wait to see their home team
Play and take the win away!

The crowd heats up,
After the National Anthem,
It's time for tip-off,
The beginning of the game!

Hoorah! Hoorah!
The home team is ahead,
A great game to watch,
But a better one to play.

Glenn Canfield, Grade 7
St John Neumann Academy, VA

Friendship

Friendship.
A ship.
A lifetime journey.
That will take you
Through waves
Big and small.
Friendship.
An adventure.
A venture
Through the world
Taking roads
Bumpy and smooth
Throughout your life.
Friendship.
A true friend
Stays with you
Through these waves and roads.
Friendship is the key to success.
Friendship is the key to life.
Friendship.

Molly Sullivan, Grade 7
Barrington Middle School, RI

Shadows

Shadows
Spooky, scary
Following, watching, waiting
Mimicking your every move
Darkness

Julia Martin, Grade 8
Mount St Charles Academy, RI

The Road

The road is dark and twisting
but at times it's sunny and clear
like a spring morning
but it can be hard
there's been lots of tears and blood on this road and I know there's more to come
but when I look back I know it's worth it
I'm still on the road
but I'll never give up
I'm still on the road
and I don't plan on leaving anytime soon…

Christine Teague, Grade 8
Norfolk Christian Middle School, VA

Ode to My Skates

Yesterday I got my brand new, newly sharpened skates
oh, how the blades reflect on the ice like calm waters,
and the white vapor symbol gives off a glow
like a full moon in a clear summer night.
My feet were invincible like titans of the ice,
as I power through my stride
they were two black barracudas swimming through the rough waters
oh how I wanted to bask in their glory but I had an important game,
and I needed their help to win.

Zachary Vanasse, Grade 8
Mount St Charles Academy, RI

Moth

My wings beat soundlessly
Toward the flickering light
Moonlight reflects my silk wings
And stars shimmer in the distance
The light grows steadily closer
As heat warms me
Intricate dances weave
In and out of the light
And a heat current
Lifts me up toward the sky
And I ride it
Spinning twirling and dancing
Above the piercing light
Smoke swirls all around me
As a splash echoes in the darkness nearby
The light dies from sparkling rubies
To blackness
Plunging the world into
Darkness once again

Shannon Rommel, Grade 8
Stevensville Middle School, MD

Your Family Is Your Best Friend

Family is love
They are always there for you
They stick up for you
And do anything to help you

Your parents are your guardians
They yell at you
They torture you
All for your benefit

Siblings are your friends
They give you advice
They make fun of you
But they will always love you

Through thick and thin
Through love and hate
With you every step of the way
Your family loves you

Evelien Steendam, Grade 8
Norfolk Collegiate Middle/Upper School, VA

On Turning 16

The whole idea of it makes me feel
Like I'm finally able to go where I want,
To places my parents don't want to take me, or not being a little freshman —
Or a small sophomore, even an old senior, but an awesome junior

They tell me it's too early to be looking back,
But you know I kind of miss being little,
The tantrums I used to throw when things got too hard and the simplicity of being in preschool
But I can remember every age; at five when all I wanted were new toys
I would get what I wanted, by saying in a sweet voice 'please'

But now I am enjoying everything, getting my license and driving places I want to go
Back then it was just so easy, against the back of my fort
And my toys never collected dust
As they do today, all the color drained from them
This is the beginning of something new, as I walk through the halls a junior
It's time for me to get my license, time to have the big party

It seems only yesterday I was in diapers
There was nothing I had to worry about, you could boss me around
But now it's different, I'm turning 16.

Natalie Stevens, Grade 7
E Russell Hicks Middle School, MD

The Light

Hallways dark and dull
Nothing moving
The faint hum of air conditioning can be heard throughout the corridors of the empty school
The darkness is impenetrable
Only the artwork of students on the walls give off faint glows
Suddenly there is a light
Then another
Then more and more
The hallways are lit in a brilliant display
The darkness is torn away by a barrage of light
The light of students' ideas
The light plows through the hallways
Yet the light does not last
Soon, all the light has gone away
No sound
Nothing but darkness
And the faint hum of air conditioning and the clicks of a distant clock

Tyler Griffith, Grade 7
Lake Ridge Middle School, VA

Beauty of a Tree

A tree reaches its peak of prettiness in the fall.
Then, its beauty literally drops from its branches, as winter approaches with a deadly cold lurking behind it.
Just as everything seems to go wrong, spring comes with its beautiful flowers and its swaying vines to right the world once more.
As summer comes along with its sad weeping willows, it revives the areas where life does not yet exist.
Fall, yet, once again, comes.
The beautifying trees realize that winter is to come again,
But the trees see this as a blessing,
For winter say good bye to the old life and hello to the new life.

Morsal Mohamad, Grade 7
Stone Hill Middle School, VA

But Time Marches On

In 1996 I was born, with two parents, two dogs
and a brother who was scared of me when I was born.
But time marches on.

Two years later I was practicing my karate kick,
"Hi-ya!" I yelled with attitude.
But time marches on.

1999 was the year I moved.
What a sad time for me and my family,
we packed up and left for Virginia.
But time marches on.

Three years later was when
I was a "panda bear" in kindergarten,
I was so happy to go to school.
But time marches on.

I have so many memories, good and bad
and more are still to come,
But time marches on.

Gabriella Vaccaro, Grade 8
St John Neumann Academy, VA

I Am

I am a dreamer and a believer
I wonder if people really do think good things of me
I hear whispers underneath my bed at night
I see a two-headed dog in my backyard
I want to know the truth
I am a dreamer and a believer

I pretend to be in a different world
I touch the clouds underneath my feet
I worry that I'll lose everything someday
I cry when people don't listen to me
I am a dreamer and a believer

I understand that people are different from me
I dream about my future
I am a dreamer and a believer

Kayla Pleasant, Grade 8
Corkran Middle School, MD

You Make My Day!

You're my hero because you make my day
Every time I'm sad or lonely you make my day
Whenever we talk you make my day
When somebody gets on my nerves you make my day
When I'm having a bad day you make my day
When nobody wants to talk to me you make my day
When people are making fun of me you make my day
So I wrote this poem and I want you to know that you will
Always you make my day!

Isaiah Cromer, Grade 7
St Columba School, MD

Ode to Clouds

Lying down and looking up
I see the clouds pass by
Gently, softly, so very swiftly
Swaying through the sky
Cumulus, cirrus, altostratus
Floating and shading the sun
Even the cumulonimbus
Are lovely when the rain is done
There are clouds that sway with grace
And clouds that tremble with might
But my favorites are those that move slowly
Enjoying their peaceful scenic flight
Without clouds sunny days would get boring
It's easy to grow tired of blue
But with the clouds ever-changing
There's always something new
I'd love to say thank you up to a cloud
I know exactly what I'd say:
Thank you for being and staying so lovely
Each and every day.

Olivia Meehan, Grade 8
St John Neumann Academy, VA

Jesse James

Jesse Woodson James was born on September 5, 1847,
One of the best robbers of all time,
Little, young, Jesse didn't know it yet
That his life would soon lead to endless crime.

Jesse formed a small dangerous gang of thieves,
These members helped him with his dirty work,
Most of the gang members didn't realize
That Jesse was a mean, nasty jerk.

One night they robbed a bank in Northfield, Minnesota,
James had an important, precise plot,
Some of his members were seen creeping around,
And those that were seen were soon shot.

Gang member Robert Ford was secretly against James,
And he wanted a reward for the well known James's head,
So Ford pulled out his firearm and shot him
And James fell to the floor bloody and dead.

Nick Curtis, Grade 7
Most Blessed Sacrament Catholic School, MD

Memory of Haiti

Only one year past from mass destruction.
A cruel senseless act from Mother Nature.
Some think hope is lost but others still hope.
Many dreams and lives crushed.
Only one year past from victims hurt, injured and crying.
Many people crushed by falling rubble, bricks and rocks.
Only few survived.

Baldwin Williams, Grade 7
George E Peters Adventist School, MD

Travel Wonders

Across the globe, in Kyoto
You hear the call of a Japanese tree sparrow
The sakura trees burst with blossoms pink
As the stork dipped down for a refreshing drink
The purple lotus shyly gaze
At the sun's shining rays
Ireland's castle turrets tell the tales of yesteryear
Each stone unfolds a different story you can almost hear
What royalty must have resided in those noble castles
With all of the embellishments and tassels
The lush green meadows, blanketing the hills
The quaint towns giving you thrills
Every place is enchanting
This world is a perfect painting
Painted by a fine brush a flitter
The brush of detail and beauty, held by the dreamer
The dreamer who dreams of glorious places
Whose dreams are the earth full of different faces
This magical planet is the world in which we live
Full of travels that may seem fictive
Travel opens your eyes to true beauty

Katrina Uher, Grade 8
Kilmer Middle School, VA

Los Angeles Lakers

The team with purple and gold
Is the team I want to see
Over 10 million tickets sold
LA is where I want to be
Last year's championship team
Under the coaching of Phil Jackson
Playing the game of basketball is my career dream
Lakers are playing get ready for some NBA action
The guards are Kobe Bryant and Derek Fisher
Dish it off to Pau Gasol
Or pull up for the open swisher
Now that's how you play basketball
Shannon Brown with the amazing dunk
Ron Artest with the steal
Your winning steak has just sunk
LA Lakers are a big deal

Justen Whitsitt, Grade 8
St Columba School, MD

Big Beautiful Ocean Sea

The wind blows while the sand is still
And the waves crash into the hills
The ocean smell is so strong
That's when I know this is where I belong
The gentle breeze is inspiring to me
When I look around and see
The big beautiful ocean sea
Now it's time for me to go I had lots of fun though
I'll come again and when I do I'll see you then

Anna Parris, Grade 8
Norfolk Christian Middle School, VA

I Am Unique

I am unique.
I am a 13-year-old artist.
I wonder what surprises my future holds.
I hear gossip and chatter around me.
I see life and death rise and fall before me.
I want to be free.
I am alone and curious.
I pretend not to feel sadness around me.
I feel like I need to cry.
I touch the past.
I worry my memories will fade.
I cry about the ones I love.
I am strong and reminiscent.
I understand the past cannot be brought back.
I say memories are just dreams.
I dream about the things I miss.
I try not to think about them.
I hope one day I can visit my past.
I am ever-dreaming and extraordinary.

Jacquelyn Wilson, Grade 8
Corkran Middle School, MD

My Dog

When I was a little girl,
You ran so fast it made me twirl.

When I would get upset or mad,
You always knew just what to do to make me glad.

Always happy no matter what,
Kissing and licking my every cut.

Celena, you were a faithful friend,
You loved me 'til the very end.

Life is so sad without you now,
You were my first and closest pal.

I tell you together in heaven we will be,
Untied together again, just wait and see.

That is the way life is meant to be.

Candace Casale, Grade 7
St Clement Mary Hofbauer School, MD

Youth

Life is hard,
I wish it was easier.
Life is short,
I wish I was younger.
Life is unfair,
I wish I was taller.
But when life is all said and done,
All the best parts happened when you were young.

Teddy Fenton, Grade 8
Mount St Charles Academy, RI

Blessed Gale

It was going to break,
Had broken before...
Rained down on calloused faces
Hard with the earth's mud.
All the world seemed to wait this
Morning for a simple shatter
And even the birds predicted its coming.
Now the tears patter down,
Silver kisses from heaven that ride the
Wings of answering angels.
Of cotton their voices cried,
Water soaking skin bruised by sun, anthems
Rise from the very souls of the trees,
From the very hearts of the scorched harvest grains.
Pools have collected
In desert-stricken places.
The misery they once portrayed now
Low in the ground.
Spots licked by perspiration, its sweet beads
On the rims of ebony skin,
The storm offers sanctuary on the molten highway of life.

Brittany Crow, Grade 9
Woodbridge Sr High School, VA

My Life

Some days I'm sunshine yellow.
Full of kindness and love.
Overcoming fear with my calm spirit.
Spreading happiness,
Relieving somber,
And coloring the world around me

But other days I'm ocean blue.
Bubbly, bouncy, and bounding about.
I'm an Energizer Bunny full of creative ides.
I'm like a wave as it crashes down on the sand,
Surprising everyone

You never know which one I will be,
Blue or yellow
It's up to me.

Peyton Green, Grade 7
Carson Middle School, VA

What Makes You Laugh?

Love is love
Pain is pain
When I'm with you
All pain disappears
Simple love
Makes me fall deeper
Hope this makes you laugh
If not
I will still remember all the precious moments

Jaime Gomez, Grade 9
New Directions Alternative Education Center, VA

White Sandy Beaches

White sandy beaches and teal blue water
Sitting by the fire at night listening to stories
No stress
No holding back
Around the ones you love
Paradise and happiness
What more could you ask for?
You can only imagine great things from within
Great palm trees and blue skies
This is the paradise I want to be
The paradise I want to be
Great palm trees and blue skies
You can only imagine great things from within
What more could you ask for?
Paradise and happiness
Around the ones you love
No holding back
No stress
Sitting by the fire at night listening to stories
White sandy beaches and teal blue water

Charlie Doyle, Grade 8
Norfolk Collegiate Middle/Upper School, VA

Kite

The ball sails smoothly like a flurry of white
My movements, so swift and free, like a kite
I grin widely with joy
Like a two-year-old with a toy
I dodge out of the way of the other team
Grinning with glee
I reach my target
Determined not to be thwarted
A still second passes in anticipation
The crowd holds their breath, waiting
I move like I'm in a trance
Then take a chance
I kick it
Thump, swish
Our last chance, last kick of the game
Suddenly the referee yells
"Goal!"
My heart leaps inside my soul
I run back to cheer with my team
Like a kite, I am free

Katelyn Gartner, Grade 8
Corkran Middle School, MD

My Family Flower

My mom is the stem and is the support,
My dad is the roots and gives us strength,
My sister is the pistil and is the center of attention,
My brother is the leaves and is the brains of the family.
I am the petals and bring beauty to the flower.
And that's my family flower.

Samantha Jenkins, Grade 7
Western Heights Middle School, MD

Hard Times

Hard Times have visited me;
In the darkest times
Of my life.

They have stayed
There on the sidelines; waiting
For a chance to come again.

Haunting me —
Like a grim reaper,
Come to steal the joy from my life.

Hard Times have visited me —
Have leeched the light from my eyes,
And the colors of my soul.

They will stay on the sidelines,
As they always have.
But this time —

I will fight

Brittainy Sechler, Grade 7
West Frederick Middle School, MD

The Internet

The internet is like a family,
It's made of different sites.
Some are good and some are bad,
And pop-ups are bright like a light.
Google is like the mother,
She knows everything.
And Bing is like the father,
Who is really the king.
Facebook is like the uncle,
Everyone loves him.
And MySpace so lost,
Like a long lost cousin.
Youtube is like the aunt,
She always entertains you.
You can listen to artists sing,
And also comment too.
The internet is like a whole different world,
Where you can always be free.
You can hear and see anything,
Without it, I don't think I'd be me.

Russhell Ford, Grade 8
Corkran Middle School, MD

The Moon

Shimmering all night,
In the dark and mystical sky,
Its magical glowing light,
Makes me want to fly,
Into the breathtaking sight.

Avanthika Singh, Grade 8
Carson Middle School, VA

Being a Christian

It is not easy to be a Christian
I am not going to lie
Sometimes your friends are doing something and you have to pass them by
That something might be wrong, they know it, too
But then they will turn and smile at you
To be a Christian you can't be of the world and in God, too
They just don't work together, no matter what you do.
There is a fine line that can be easily crossed
But, you have to remember Who's your boss
Who is He to you? Do you have a personal relationship with Him?
It might be hard, but sooner or later you'll have to answer; but then,
For me, I don't need worldly things, not even a friend
Because I know that Jesus can be all of that and more in the end.
He knows you better than all the people you know
Even your best friends you think you need, So
Let Him be your Friend, Comforter, Parent and anything else you need.
It is not easy to be a Christian 'tis true
But, it is definitely possible to do.

Moriah Gaskill, Grade 8
St Columba School, MD

What I Love

I love to watch: the rapid rain slowly slide down the window on a rainy day
The luminous sunrise from night to day
Pleasant people conversing in the café
I love to smell: the burning wood in the crispy air
The sweet aroma of coffee being prepared
The scent left over in my previous washed hair
I love to hear: the sounds of Taylor Swift's sweet singing
The silence in the graveyards of the wind lightly blowing
Your voice at night in the dead silence over the phone talking
I love to taste: dark chocolate melting in my mouth
Nachos freshly made from down South
Cookie dough when it sticks to my mouth
I love to touch: people's heart with sweet melodic noises
Sand, and let it slide through my fingers
Ocean water, it washes on shore and through the sand lingers
I love the way: he thinks about me when he sleeps
In fields children leap
I know where I have been and the friends and memories I will always keep

Cecily Sass, Grade 8
Most Blessed Sacrament Catholic School, MD

Live It Up

Live it up!
Because life is a big surprise, with something new around every corner.
Life brings beautiful, and sometimes terrible things.
But besides that, life is precious.
People have forgotten that.
But they shouldn't.
They should live their lives to the fullest, like there's no tomorrow!
Because if they don't, life may become boring, or unlivable.
Life basically means live it up and have fun doing it.
So live it up!

Cailin Jones, Grade 8
Tasker Middle School, MD

On Turning 12

The whole idea of it makes me feel
Like I'm going through a war
Like a million shots every day
Starting middle school
The drama attacks you
Problem by problem
You just try to fit in

You tell me not to remember
But it's hard to forget
The annoying sound of teachers
I can remember every problem
Losing friends and fitting in

The homework piles up, A new school
New teachers, new classmates, and new friends
Trying to figure out, how to open a locker, or work a lock
The schedule changing each marking period

Your true colors come out and you show who you really are
Who you want to be
But you just remember that you have friends
Who will get you through anything

Abby Giancola, Grade 7
E Russell Hicks Middle School, MD

A Special Someone

To show me his love,
God sent angels from above.
I feel the support that all you give,
To make my life a little easier to live

I thank you for the trust you share.
I don't worry about anything because You show me that you care.

I'd like to give you something back to you
To show you that I love you too

I wouldn't trade you for anything

I always see your warmth
And generosity
By how much time you spend
With me

I know it's not Valentine's Day
And you're probably wondering who I'm writing this to
And, your answer is…

A special person, who will come to me

Loretta Davis, Grade 7
St Columba School, MD

Behind My Mask

You may think you know me
But there are parts that you can't see
The fear and hate I hide away
The words and things I can never say
My fears are hidden in a pile
My hate hidden behind a smile
I pretend to be someone I'm not
But no one would like the real me a lot
If you knew me and not the person I planned
Maybe just maybe you would understand
That I can't be the person inside
Cause they will take you for a ride
Through all the pain and suffering I've endured
With a heart wide open with love out poured

Heather Conrad, Grade 9
St Mark's High School, DE

Dreams

We all have dreams
We just have to make them come true
We've all had our downfalls
We've all received our uplifting call
We've all had our unforgettable moments
But, it's all a part of making them come true
We've all had trials bigger than mountains
We all have dreams
We all experience crying
But, everything ends up okay
We hear people say that they aren't going to come true
But, little do they know…they have no clue

Kiarah Ford, Grade 8
Corkran Middle School, MD

Defense

I keep my eyes on the ball
No time to fall, we are like the great wall
Protect the goal, have to be alert
Even if we get hurt
We have to win, no time to waste
Clench the championship title for goodness sakes
Got to have amazing aim
Kick the ball like it's your last game
Whistles, penalties, and yellow cards are a part of the game
Short sprints, punts, throw-ins, and shots aim for the fame
The dirty jerseys, wet hair
Shoes muddy and our eyes glare

Heba Beshai, Grade 8
Corkran Middle School, MD

My Family Pizza

My dad is the crust he gives us power.
My mom is the sauce she gives us flavor.
My puppy is the cheese she gives us energy.
I am the topping that gives us spice.

Bethany Pruchniewski, Grade 7
Western Heights Middle School, MD

Just Dream

This poem is not about reality,
Or the problems we come to face.
But the dreams that suddenly come true,
And the ones we go to chase.

When you wish upon a falling star,
Your heart will lead you to your choice.
For every wish isn't meant to be the same,
But to be unique and different in every way.

The dreams and wishes that you have,
Are patiently waiting to be found.
If you seek them they'll be seen,
Usually somewhere over the rainbow.

The world is filled with many things,
Hopes, desires, and aspirations.
So fear not and dare,
Because sometimes all you really need is to just dream.

Elise Murillo, Grade 8
St Clement Mary Hofbauer School, MD

Senses of the Lake

The sweet scent of decaying pine
The sound of the wake crashing the shoreline
The senses of the lake

The wisp of the wind
Chimes sound like a thousand pin
The senses of the lake

The heat of the sun
Sound of the motorboat engines run
The senses of the lake

The rain suddenly began
All on the docks and in the boats ran
The senses of the lake

Even though the day was a bummer
There will always be another
The senses of the lake

Julia Sheehan, Grade 8
St Jane De Chantal School, MD

Change

I am a simple leaf
Floating and fluttering as the wind rustles my limbs
I admire a golden bird nearby
I wish for wings to fly
To carry me across the horizon
To places unknown
To see the world beyond my tree
To live a life in a different harmony

Sydney Applegate, Grade 8
Rachel Carson Middle School, VA

Ode to the Grass

The lush green stalks,
growing upright in the fertile soil of my backyard.

The golden gleam of the sun,
reflecting off the sparkling shoots.

The beauty of, the serene field
of emerald strands.

The wind's gentle blow,
on the flimsy tips of the vast meadow.

Walking through the enchanted estate,
my feet crushing the tranquil stems of the green pasture,
all the time my feet remain cool while being tickled by
the point of the soft, stem.

Laying on
the peaceful ground in the countryside,
I experience the bliss, of the grass,
for one last time.

Angela Dansereau, Grade 8
Mount St Charles Academy, RI

It Must Be Spring

It must be spring:
Dancing raindrops tap on my roof,
Waking me up to warm sunshine.
With birds chirping and waking the world,
A sense of warmth rests on my window.
Flowers will sprout for us to pick and smell:
Yellow daffodils, blue violets, and iridescent tulips.

Walking through green meadows,
With pinkish blossoming cherry trees,
Rainy and sunny days with rainbows,
Long walks in the park,
Butterflies dancing by,
Wishing you could, too:
Yes, it must be spring.

Andrina Kraettli, Grade 9
Norfolk Collegiate Upper School, VA

Flowers

Frozen in the winter ground,
Flowers are not seen
Spring thaws out the snow-covered grass
Everything turns green
Peeking out from the warming ground,
Flowers start to grow
Just a stem at first but then,
The petals start to open as the sunlight welcomes them
Bees and bugs swarm all around
And people gasp at the beauty of the flowers

Jennifer Lepine, Grade 8
Mount St Charles Academy, RI

Hero

I remember what he was like, but he
wasn't just another person, no. Rhode Island and Massachusetts with flags at half staff, honoring the fallen hero; the first roadside bomb on target as well as one of the last.
He was the older brother we never had, a
hero, a knight in shining armor. When I fell, he was there. He wasn't some far away uncle.
As her mouth, unintended for a deadly weapon, formed those searing words, they scorched, and
burned as they mercilessly slammed into me.
Someone viciously ripped my heart out with no sympathy and it just hurt, it hurt so badly.
We blankly heard what our minds couldn't comprehend, as if an ocean wave roared and enveloped our bodies, washing over us, leaving us dripping with the salty residue.
I wanted to come to the surface. I didn't want to drown.
Our lungs were flattened from gravity; all the oxygen unwillingly forced outward, and the pressure mounting and crushing our tiny bodies.
Grappling, gasping, fighting, struggling for the breath we so desperately needed. My limbs numb, and vision blurry, our body in a coma.
He was a hero. My hero. Our hero; dying to rescue a precious baby's
life. I still can't wrap my head around it. A baby, one of their kind, and yet the war continues.
This isn't supposed to happen to heroes, they aren't supposed
abandon us, leaving us to fend for ourselves like this, no.
How can small children ever believe the world is good when we were so harshly
denied a goodbye. My mind was spinning and my body in an unnatural fog, left with so many unanswered questions. I couldn't come to terms with the world, or myself. I wasn't ready to forgive.

Brianne Drury, Grade 9
Moses Brown School, RI

My First Dance Performance

Today
I can hear, the parents chatting loud and clear, like a teacher giving you directions when she is the only one in the room talking.

Today,
I can smell, new dresses, like your fresh clothes that just came out of the dryer and are ready to wear!

Today,
I can feel, the bells pressing against my feet, like a friend who will always stay with you no matter how much you hurt them.

Today,
I can see, the makeup on everybody's face, like a person standing in front of an endless number of mirrors that make you look pretty.

Today,
Inside, I feel, nervous, like a new baby chick that just learned how to fly and is taking off for a long journey.

Leela Ekambarapu, Grade 7
Carson Middle School, VA

The Holocaust

H itler's reign took over millions of Jews' Lives
O ut in concentration camps where not a person is able to survive
L iving under dominant pressure with soldiers guarding the place
O bserving and hiding their belongings in buttons or in a shoelace
C hecks are done to make sure all ghettos stay in order
A crumb of bread is definitely not allowed anywhere around the border
U sually, gas chambers make people's lives not long but shorter
S ome think the only way to get out of this mess is to get a supporter
T he people are finally liberated from the camps when Germany surrenders with wanting payback from their offenders

Nidhi Kumar, Grade 7
Moody Middle School, VA

The Roller Coaster

The roller coaster was high and tall
If you get on it…
You were sure to fall
You can try to stay on with all your might

And if you got scared
You could hold on tight
And close your eyes
So you can lose your sight

The radio attached to it
Would sure give off a great beat
It would go up through your ears
And down through your feet

You can move and wiggle
Your friend would sure start to giggle
It would kind of mess up your groove
So you stand up still…wouldn't budge or move

Now that you know the instructions ahead
Don't get tense or scared
Just sit back and have fun

In the meanwhile
My job here is done!

Erica Jones, Grade 7
Emery Educational Campus, DC

Wind

Though the wind pried, we walked on
to our freedom, to the life we never had.
We could see the faint outline of our destination
in the distance, longing to see more,
but the wind pried.

It pried at our skin, pulling it apart,
leaving stinging cuts. It pushed at our bodies,
maliciously whipping up dirt and sand
into our bloodshot eyes, never relenting.

And, it pried at our hearts and souls,
reaching out to whisk our hope and energy
right out of our backs, into the swirling air
so that we could see the tendrils of it
curling through the air behind us.

Each night we died.
Each morning we were reborn,
helpless in the cruel world.
We walked long and hard.
But, the wind pried.

And we never got there.

Sandy Ng, Grade 7
Kilmer Middle School, VA

Summer

It consists of six letters;
Long nights, late mornings,
Peacefulness

I forget my troubles, I forget my worries,
I live my life for the moment,
"For this moment is your life."

I work until this season,
The one that gives me a break,
It's my special retreat,
A secret escape.

It smells like ocean,
Wet towels, chlorine,
And smoothies.

It sounds like laughter,
splashing,
The flips of the flip-flops,
And the gulls of the seagulls.

It's my favorite time of year,
The time without the snow,
The time when having fun is all you can do,
Summer.

Sydney Anne Celestine Seerden, Grade 9
Norfolk Collegiate Middle/Upper School, VA

Food Fight

In a great land near Loch Mournn Lake
Lived two kingdoms that loved to cook and to bake
The kingdoms were named Qari and Asu
They loved to eat sweets because grass tastes like goo

Qari had the chocolate all sticky and sweet
If you were caught stealing they made you eat feet
Asu had the lollypops so nice, round and funny
They traded with Qari for a big chocolate bunny

Then Qari got mad and raised the price
Said, "give us more lollies or we'll make you eat rice"
Asu said no, they'd never give more
"If you don't stop this now it will mean candy war"

The Lollypop Towers fell to the ground
When the Qari's in corncobs shot it down with one round
The battle got messy when the food hit the floor
Cabbage and spinach made everyone sore

Alas the war had finally ended
Asu had won and the two kingdoms befriended
With fireworks and candy they began to have fun
So sad it's too late as they burned under the sun

Landon Courville, Grade 8
Linkhorne Middle School, VA

Pandas

I bask in the sun
And eat bamboo
I'm a walking menace
But they think I'm cute
I'm black and white
And loved all over
But I'll tear out their eyes
If they come any closer
I live in China
In the depths of jungles
Still they seek me
Either wanting to eat or pet me
But still I will hide
Eating bamboo and vines
Until I decide
They may find me.

Aislinn Cohen, Grade 7
E Russell Hicks Middle School, MD

Poppies

I see the poppies looking at me
Their vibrant colors shining with glee
Some see them as the enemy
I only see their beauty.
Some use them to do the devil's deeds
Others think of them only as weeds.

God made them sweet,
Their seeds for us to eat.
It is by man's hand that it has come
That the devil's deed is done.

Let us do what God has planned
And plant poppies across the land.
Their silky blossoms for us to enjoy
And not to be used as the devil's toy.

Justin Barnes, Grade 8
St Paul's Lutheran School, MD

A Necessity of Life

Hope is within
Me and You
Hope should be
In all of you
Hope sets us all together
Hope will get us
Through the stormiest of weather
Hope will make us see the light
Hope will make it seem oddly bright
Hope will lead us wide afar
Hope will take us past the stars
Hope will set us up all together
Hope will get us
Through the stormiest of weather

Peter Barrett, Grade 9
Wicomico High School, MD

Wind

Whirly, swirly wind
During the winter it's cold and harsh
It blow and blows and blows
Whips its tail making it cold
The whirly, swirly wind
During the summer it's nice and cool
Creating a breeze by the pool
All enjoying its kind gentleness
The whirly, swirly wind
During the spring it's quick and exciting
Reminding of the last snowing
The wind ruffles the flowers and leaves
Like a king shouting loud large decrees
Yes the whirly swirly wind
During the fall its dark and reminding
Knocking the leaves off the tree
It lets people know that winter is coming
Especially down by the sea
The whirly swirly wind.

Max Sacher, Grade 7
Carson Middle School, VA

Rainbow

A rainbow is a piece of art
Letting everyone see its beauty
A never-ending river
Of color

A rainbow is a bird
Flying across the sky
In search of a pot of gold
Never giving up

A rainbow is a waterfall
Flowing gracefully
With no care
Of who's watching

A rainbow is a shadow
You have to look carefully to find it
But when you do
"POOF" it's gone

Emily Fan, Grade 7
Rachel Carson Middle School, VA

Tree Swingers

Apes are so easily amused,
kept away from their family,
they would swing from trees happily, wildly,
yet, they are used,
for our entertainment they weep,
they would be happy,
if only they could find a jungle tree to sleep.

Samuel Beasley, Grade 8
Norfolk Christian Middle School, VA

Music Is Live

Music is live
Moving through your body
Making you feel like you are someone

Music is live
Welcoming your ears
And warming your soul

Music is live
Explaining your life like you never could
Relieving you of the pain

Music is live
You feel it
And your mood lightens

Move with me, move to the beat
'Cause you know
Music is live

Jazmine Jackson, Grade 8
Corkran Middle School, MD

My Brother

Not just any brother,
my brother,
who makes me angry,
irritates me.
I pick him out in a crowd
by his curly brown hair.
His chocolate eyes
stare me down.
The pimples on his face
distract me.
His arms are sticks,
but hurt when he hits me.
Embarrassing,
when he tries to show off
in front of my friends.
Thinks he is funny,
but no one laughs.
I like him,
but I won't tell him that.

Colbee Mattheiss, Grade 8
St. Paul's Lutheran School, MD

Pont Neuf

Sunrise over my pale skin
Hot and spicy
Silence
Exhausted
A big bag on my back
A crowded sidewalk
Sky blue like the ocean
Hot coffee on the corner

Natalia Gutierrez Ribera, Grade 9
Fairfax High School, VA

Why?

All alone,
No one here,
No one at home,
Someone please help me,
I can't do this on my own.
Why me,
What did I ever do to you?
Even though everything is going well for me,
Someone please help me.
I can't do this on my own.
Why look at me?
I may be different,
But on the inside I'm just like you,
Someone please help me,
I can't do this on my own.
Why me?
I don't get why you're mean.
At night I cry myself to sleep,
Someone please help me,
I can't do this on my own.

Kailee Mitten, Grade 8
Stevensville Middle School, MD

Fear Is War

Fear is war
In which many lives are lost
Blood shed
And even the bravest of all solders
Are left feeling cowardly
We cannot look ourselves in the eye
For we are living our lives
Behind a dark shadow
Because we are scared
Scared to look even at the faintest hint of truth
We are losing
There appears to be no option
In many cases
It seems to be the final choice
Fear is war

Madeline Doane, Grade 7
Carson Middle School, VA

My Hot Air Balloon

My balloon, big and bright
How beautiful and magnificent
Will you find your way at night?
I see the city not far below, gazing over the side
The buildings, how do they sustain their height?
My eye glimpses the fire in the center,
Can it win its fight?
Against the winds blowing hard
Fire, will it fade your light?
Sitting here, in my peaceful place, my thoughts begin to wonder
My balloon, how beautiful, will you stay in flight?

Katrina White, Grade 7
Kilmer Middle School, VA

The Wall

They were separated by a wall.
She could hear his voice, but it wasn't enough
He could imagine her hands
Pressed against the concrete
And longed to touch them but couldn't.
His heart ached to be with hers
And her eyes wanted to swallow him whole
3 ft thick concrete held them apart
For many, many years
Until it was knocked down
By people who couldn't stand it
Any longer
To be apart from loved ones and to see
Their country divided
They stayed alone
Until they finally met
28 years later,
She held him as tightly as she could
And he lifted her from the ground,
His love still as strong as
It had been when they were youths.

Pamela Dahl, Grade 9
Menchville High School, VA

The Musical Painter

The pianist is a painter,
Vivid-minded, meticulous, and creative.
Taking black ink blots on a page
and transforming them into a colorful picture,
an original, individual interpretation.
Painting portraits with sounds
using fingers as a paintbrush.
Putting thought into every note and sound,
painstakingly attentive to every detail.
Creating a scene depicting despair,
elation,
tranquility.
Transforming black and white keys
into a rainbow of colors and textures.
An artist who never runs out of ideas.

Evelyn Mo, Grade 7
Carson Middle School, VA

Captain Phil Harris

Captain Phil was a king of the sea,
A king whose throne was the Cornelia Marie.
When twilight sank beneath the bow, he would never fear,
The dark or stomp the danger here.
He loved his sons, he loved the seas,
He loved his life even in the deadliest freeze.
The man the world loved so much is gone,
But his spirit and memory will always live on.
In memory of my favorite captain — Phil Harris.
I will always remember you.

Emily Gruszczynski, Grade 8
St Clement Mary Hofbauer School, MD

Just Remember

It was always around the middle of the day,
when we had nothing to do but just play,
I had always stood in the sun and the oldest would say,
"Remember that we can't split up, okay?"
I could hear the buzzing in the air,
the wind blowing through my hair,
the days were always beautifully rare,
though at the time we didn't really care.
The days were full of our excited cheer,
no matter where we went the memory, held dear,
some places we had waited in fear,
while in others we couldn't wait to get near.
I think I just wanted to let you guys know,
that no matter where we come and go…
That no matter where our lives may take us,
or no matter if we're just feeling low…
That if our lives meet separate ends,
just remember,
that the four of us will always be the best of friends.

Shanell Fan, Grade 7
Kilmer Middle School, VA

My Wings of Freedom

I fly like an eagle
Through the clear blue Skies of Freedom
The wind howling over my mighty wings
I was once an eaglet
Wingless, feeling helpless
As others flew by my nest
Now I look up I see limitless possibilities
I look down
I see the wingless creatures below
Those who are eager to fly
I want to reach down
And lend a feather or two
So that they may break free
From the turmoil and harsh restraints of Earth
And soar with me in the free skies
Above who was once their master.

Thomas Johnston, Grade 9
Mount St Charles Academy, RI

Summer Fun

The best are those late nights,
The heat of the sun,
Beating down on my friends.
I love camp with all my best friends,
The 10 of us playing cards at night,
Then waking up from the bright orange sun.
The lake sparkling from the reflection of the sun,
While sailing with my friends,
After a long day I love just relaxing at night.
Summer is my favorite season I love seeing my best friends,
The warm summer sun high in the sky, and staying up all night.

Becca Schwartzman, Grade 8
Norfolk Collegiate Middle/Upper School, VA

What Is Poetry?

Poetry is expressing what you feel
And when you write what you think
Poetry is a message that comes from a writer
That readers read and might not figure out

Poetry can also be funny or silly and easy to understand
Written with picture to match
You can find it at your favorite library
And when you read it makes you laugh

Poetry is long or short with some sort of form
It can be structured, traditional or free verse
And it doesn't have to rhyme
And the poems personality depends on the speaker

Poetry writers use rhythm or rhyme
Repetition, Alliteration, Metaphors, Similes, and Imagery
You either love poetry or you hate it
Is this poetry?

Zenobia Charleus, Grade 7
E Russell Hicks Middle School, MD

A Leaf and a Flower

A leaf is like a day going by in the fall
A flower grows like a little girl growing up
A leaf is like chameleon always changing colors
A flower is like a beautiful painting by Leonardo Da Vinci

A leaf is as green as an apple
A flower is as small as one's hand
A leaf is as thin as a piece of paper
A flower is as delicate as china

The best time for them
Is the fall or spring
When the flowers and leaves are fully blossomed
And fill the streets and gardens

Demetra Protogyrou, Grade 8
Norfolk Collegiate Middle/Upper School, VA

The Park

The sky is light blue,
And the grass is covered in a morning dew.
The sun is amazingly bright,
Shining with all its might.
The red birds chirp, chirp, chirp
And a child eating ice-cream, burps.
You see the fluffy white clouds
And the children being loud.
You see a dazzling lily amongst the rich green grass
You stop to look while others just pass.
The man by the corner, selling lollipops and balloons
"Just another one of those perfect afternoons"
Go try it, go for a walk in the beautiful park.

Yashica Kaushal, Grade 8
Carson Middle School, VA

The Picture

I hold memories,
I watch you smile at me,
I sometimes sit in a frame,
Looking over everything,
Your friends laugh at the moments I hold.
You put me on your walls,
I'm so glossy,
So square,
You see me on your dresser,
Look at me, and smile.
I watch you with your friends,
You capture the moments,
I capture the laughs,
The cries,
The happy days.
I am a picture,
Holding the memories,
I make you remember,
All the times you had,
I am a picture worth a thousand words.
Rachel Klavan, Grade 8
Norfolk Collegiate Middle/Upper School, VA

Deep Forest

I am surrounded by them.
They listen quietly.
Wherever I go,
my disciples follow.
   Under the shadows,
   the ground is old and worn.
   My feet are one of many
   to walk among its paths.
I ponder my problems,
and sometimes
their solutions
are whispered.
   I hear the singing,
   the murmurs from above.
   They come from the living,
   for there are many.
I have no destination
other than forwards,
so that's the way I go,
forwards to my destiny.
Benjamin Stephens, Grade 8
St Paul's Lutheran School, MD

Wind

The wind, it carries a silent whisper.
Moving carelessly through time,
anything in its way is bound to be
whisked away by the harsh moving wind.
The flowers sway back and forth
as they ride the unpredictable wind.
Savannah Spriggs, Grade 8
Norfolk Christian Middle School, VA

On Turning Eighteen

The whole idea of it makes me feel, like a new man: an independent.
Someone who does whatever he pleases, without anyone else's consent.
A god of Olympus…a president of the world.
You tell me not to be so selfish, To worry about others.
That I'm not the most important person: The world doesn't revolve around me.
But I can sit down and explain about how I am the best right now,
And how all eyes are focused on me.
About how I run my world without a care.
I have dreams though: I've made plans.
And I intend to put them into action.
To be the best of the best, because I am the only one.
My training wheels have been thrown out, the back of my car.
This is the beginning of the rest of my life.
As I drive down the impossible road.
To be not only my own hero, but everyone else's.
It feels like just yesterday
I used to be a child: an immaturity.
I played and I didn't think ahead.
But now I'm alive and I'm ready.
Watch out world, because here I come.
John Strauss, Grade 7
E Russell Hicks Middle School, MD

Did You Make It

Life is just one hard lacrosse game
When you're so exhausted but you push yourself harder still
When the other team scores the first goal you feel slightly defeated, can you still make it?
The only thing that helps is that you know your friends will help you get back on top
You finally score a goal and make some progress
You feel a sense of pride in your ability to play
It's half time and you see your friends and family in the stands
Ready to catch you if you fall
You promise yourself you'll do better then you've ever done
You go on with a new power
Determination
There's almost no time left
It's all on you, You have the ball
This is your big chance
And…
You go for it
The ball has left your stick
It's flinging towards the goal…

Did You Make It?

Valerie Abbott, Grade 8
Stevensville Middle School, MD

Best Friends

We stick together, no matter the weather
Even though the time has come to go our separate ways.
I will always think of you. Though we might have moments we always will stay true.
It is not goodbye. It is I will see you later.
God has a plan for us and one of those plans was for us to become true friends.
Kennedy Blye, Grade 8
George E Peters Adventist School, MD

From Red to Blue to Gray

There are many parts of me,
From red to blue to gray.
Most of the time,
I'm rambunctious and reckless red.
Loud, energetic, and annoying like a commercial on TV.
Crazy and cuckoo; loud and lively,
Having the time of my life with all my friends.
Other times,
I'm bright and quiet blue.
Shy, silent, and still like a sea at low tide.
Modest and meek; peaceful and placid,
Wanting to do what is right.
Though very seldom,
I'm glum and gloomy gray.
Tired, drowsy, and dreary like a bear going into hibernation.
Sleepy and sluggish; lethargic and languid,
Wishing I could fall on a bed.
They are all very different,
But they all make up me.

Matthew Guo, Grade 7
Carson Middle School, VA

Nature's Balance

Through the overwhelming darkness is light
Through the blinding light is the hidden dark
The light seeps through the moonless, dreary night
But through the day, darkness might make its mark
With a dreadful death, there is hopeful life
With blissful life, there is horrid death
With wonderful joy, there is evil strife
With hideous sadness, there is joy's breath
With the glorious day are stars astray
With the superior strong are the meek
Like the ruthless predator and the prey
With the good honest one is the tricky sneak
There is a powerful balance in all
One will greatly rise, and one will greatly fall

Krishna Vemulapalli, Grade 7
Kilmer Middle School, VA

Friends

Friends can know you inside and out
You can never live without them
But what is a friend?
Two souls that live inside one body
Jokes and laughs, friends can care
A true friend picks you up when you fall down
They let you spread your wings
A real friend walks in when the world walks out
Friends, they are there, in your heart and soul
They are like angels from above
I'm so glad I have my friends
Friends, forever and always

Emma Nagy, Grade 8
Stevensville Middle School, MD

Surrender

Cracking her toes, licking her lips
Struggling to silence a frantic heart
With slow, deep breaths and hands on hips
A single question, tearing her apart

Recess lights and a linoleum floor
Clutching a cross in a sweaty palm
As a figure enters through the door
Attempting to appear calm

The figure, taking note of his clipboard,
Reveals the news apologetically
And within sounds a dark, resounding chord
As he takes his leave sympathetically

And of her cross, she lets go
A feeling empty and surreal
And of her tears, she lets go
Nothing more to conceal

Jennifer Flaherty, Grade 9
Mount St Charles Academy, RI

Life as We Know It

The sand, the waves, the clouds, the sky…
since when does this life fly by?
The wind, the flowers, the earth, the grass…
does this goodness ever pass?

Days pass by, then weeks, then years.
Have we really shed any tears?
The happiness we share, with people we love,
the only way to look is above.

The simplicity of life cannot compare
to the great times we seize to share.
We desire, we want, we have, we envy…
the only thing we don't want is a life that's empty.

Anna Newbold, Grade 9
Norfolk Collegiate Middle/Upper School, VA

The Victor Is Me

Right now you hurt,
Right now you cry,
But think of the day,
That it passes you by,
The day you can shout,
"I was there! That was me!
Look what I went through,
See the difference I see.
I struggled, I fought,
But I came out free,
No longer the victim but,
The winner, the victor, the champion is me!"

Sandra Webb, Grade 8
Poe Middle School, VA

The Shallow Pool
In the valleys it lays
In the dark and nights of thunders and rain
The shallow pool is alone
Nobody jumps or runs into its fun
Its cool waters lovely and still
Calming with beauty
In its amazing spot by the hill
The shallow pool never stirs
Or was hard to enjoy in the past summer sun
It has been a long time
Since I have gone to that pool
At the crack of dawn
We would play we would cheer
Now those times and memories
Have past just as the years
Each day I dream of the pool
Which I would enjoy with my friends
When the temperature was cool
Many times have I played
In that shallow pool but never gone to stay
Jabraughn R. Hill, Grade 8
St Jane De Chantal School, MD

If I Were in Charge of the World
If I were in charge of the world
I'd do what I want to do, go where I want to go,
Change the age for getting a license and permit,
Say what I want to say.

If I were in charge of the world
There'd be no rules, school, and homework

If I were in charge of the world
You wouldn't ever be bored
You wouldn't ever get into trouble
You wouldn't have homework
Or do any tests or quizzes

If I were in charge of the world.
Tiffany Wright, Grade 8
Corkran Middle School, MD

Crayon Box
Some short, used to the nub
Some long, more on the paper to rub
Some fat,
A big round cylinder of color.
Some vibrant and bright, while others are duller.
But all crayons, in the end make their mark
On the paper of the world, clean, white, and stark.
All different shapes,
Different colored marks they make,
But in the end they are all crayons
Let there be no mistake.
Swetha Ramesh, Grade 7
Kilmer Middle School, VA

My Little Sister
When I was in first grade
It was May of 2005
My family full of cheer
My new little sister finally arrived!
When my mom and dad brought her home
We had finally met
Even though she cried and it was loud
It was the best day, best day yet!
My family called her Sophia
I really liked that name
I wanted to play with her
And knew just the game!
She sat on my mom's lap
And I said, "Peek-a-boo"
Sophia started to laugh
And I did too!
Now Sophia is five, almost six
We fight but make up in the end
Even though she makes me mad
I couldn't have asked for a better little sister and friend!
Anna Mishoe, Grade 7
St John Neumann Academy, VA

Poetry for You
The definitions of poetry is too hard to understand
All of us don't believe in one
Not even by a show of hands
There are lots, you know is true
But here's my definition
Which I think is strong and true
A poem is strong, descriptive, and you
It can show how you feel
ON certain things, like YOU
It has imagery, onomatopoeia, metaphor, and simile
White as a cloud, a simile would say
From "Hey!" to "Boohoo!" is all you have to say
Just take a paper and think of something new
For you have a poem
This is right for YOU!
Justin Mitchell, Grade 7
E Russell Hicks Middle School, MD

Do You Remember?
Do you remember?
When it didn't matter what you looked like,
No one even cared about what you wore,
People thought that money was the least of their worries,
Popularity had no value,
All art had beauty,
Every creature was cared for,
It only mattered if you tried your hardest,
What if you could get things back to this way?
Would you try to change them?
Your actions can make a difference!
Nicole Bowman, Grade 8
St Rocco School, RI

Dark as the Night
As it all turns to blackness
Dark as the night
All of my fears seem to take flight
I walk by the house
Where you did that to me
A dark scary place
Where fear lives daily

When will I wake up from this nightmare?
As it all turns to blackness
I run away scared

As it all turns to blackness
My demons, my demise
As I wait for the crimson sun to rise
I'm up on the bridge now
Thinking of you
There is nothing anyone can do
Everyone's happy; I wish I could be too
As it all turns to blackness
Everything's about you

Brianna Lockard, Grade 8
Corkran Middle School, MD

Jesus
Jesus is the nicest person I know.
He is loving, caring, and gentle.
I can talk to Him through prayer.
It sounds like music to my ear.
I love the name Jesus
My Lord is patient.
My Lord is kind.
My Lord is loving all the time.
Jesus is a jewel to my eye.
He died on the cross to save my soul.
He is the one who makes me whole.
He is the Alpha and Omega.
The beginning and the end.
He is the true and only God.
He is my dearest friend.

Rhoderic Rubin, Grade 7
George E Peters Adventist School, MD

In the Best Sort of Way
In the lonely summer days
I walk down by the pond.
Gazing at cattails
And tossing stones
To pass the time.
Sitting on the bank,
Dipping my bare legs
Into the chilling water –
Wasting my time
In the best sort of way.

Garrett Brothers, Grade 7
Kilmer Middle School, VA

That Single Star
That single star above my bed shines a radiant light upon my head
As I pray for the sweet scent of the morning's dew.
It brings with it an army of hope, to fight the misfortune with which you and I cope,
And answers all of the many prayers that emanate from me and you.

That single star above my bed is the unlived future from which you and I fled.
It brings about the mystery that we wish not to know.
Our bodies turn away; scared for modification, too afraid to witness a big transformation.
But our souls hunger for change in this world, wishing for goodness to emerge and grow.

That single star above my bed is a symbol of peace looming from the dead.
It arises as swiftly as it goes, from the dark, black blanket that covers the earth.
It is the only star that stays in the sky watching over those who merely pass by
And don't stop to admire God's true beauty and have no knowing of it's true worth.

That single star above my head shines a radiant light upon my head
Holding the secrets I dare not say aloud and comprises the dreams of what I wish to be
For if there is magic in the air to act as a medicine for this world's deep despair
Then I will let my soul run free and thank that star for shining down on me.

Sarah Kennedy, Grade 9
Mount St Charles Academy, RI

Writer's Block #4534
"Brilliant"
"Just brilliant"
The accursed obstruction from progress "Writer's Block" strikes again.
A roadblock standing firm in front of the pathway of writing

It bars me from the roads of progress, so stalwart a barricade that I cannot
Slide it
Upturn it
Rotate it
Remove it in any way.

It forces me to careen, to swerve, to create excess that upsets the terseness,
the conciseness that I value, that I treasure so.
"Brilliant"
"Just brilliant"

Alexander R. Wallace, Grade 8
Kenmore Middle School, VA

What I Love
I love to watch my twin baby brothers gently tackle each other.
I love to watch playful puppies play together and fight for attention.
I love to smell the sweet smell of freshly baked chocolate chip cookies.
I love to smell a fresh coat of paint on the wet walls.
I love to hear the rushing and roaring of the ocean.
I love to hear my little sister laugh like a chipmunk when I tickle her!
I love the taste of descriptive words rolling off my tongue.
I love the taste of a cheesy ham and cheese omelet, yummy!
I love to touch a soft and fluffy yellow lab puppy.
I love to touch other people's hearts with my kindhearted words.
I love the way Ledo's makes their pizza in square slices.
I love the way my gray, turquoise, and purple Vans look on me.

Madelynn King, Grade 7
Most Blessed Sacrament Catholic School, MD

Me, the Best I Can Be

I am a rainbow
Coming and going
Sometimes I bring comfort to others,
Other times I am just there,
With no real purpose,
Just for after the rain
Just something in the distance, overlooking everything
Though I'm bright and colorful,
I am hidden
Behind clouds, clouds,
When they separate,
I will become the one
The rainbow standing out,
Showering, showering,
In a bright spectrum,
Showering others with my presence
The pink and purples, past and present
The teal and the turquoise, the black and the blue
And the green and the gray
Finally, finally standing out
For now, it is my time to shine.

Anika Sindhwani, Grade 7
Carson Middle School, VA

Shutdown

Like the flick of the switch
The noise droned out,
The unwanted process began.
The dreaded final moments when
You don't want to leave.
It faltered,
Slowly shutting down,
all images blurred.
It whitened out to such a hue
brilliant as the Antarctic landscape
flashed for about a millisecond, then
only a shrinking four-point star,
before finally blinking out.
"It's time to do your homework, son."
"But dad, can't I watch some more TV first?"

Brandon Castillo, Grade 7
Kilmer Middle School, VA

Kingdom of the Knight

Above the sleeping earth
Upon the soft clouds of the dreamlike night sky
Among the ocean of shadows lies a kingdom
Of infinite gems bearing the flickers of hope
For mankind and its uncertain future.
Beyond the reach of humanity
Along the fragile borders of eternity
Beneath the warrior of the light of darkness
Down on the world does the kingdom look
In hopes of a paradise.

Evan Laverdure, Grade 8
Mount St Charles Academy, RI

The Roaring Twenties

In the twenties there were
Gangsters, flappers, and beggars
Conmen, suffragettes, and bootleggers.
Speakeasies were the place to be,
But someone was always watching,
Almost no one was unseen.
But under it all, were the worst criminals of them all,
Al Capone, "Big Jim" Colosimo, and Bonnie and Clyde,
But they couldn't even hide.
Jazz music, the Harlem Renaissance,
Dance clubs, movies, and fashion
Would lay the foundation for generations to come.
The Olympics were founded,
Babe Ruth became famous and other sports stars were astounded
When he hit sixty home runs in a season.
The first solo flight across the Atlantic,
Things were going great, but not for long,
When the stock market crashed on Black Tuesday,
No one understood what kinds of despair that would prolong
Into the thirties. Greed, extortion, and depression
Brought an end to the Roaring Twenties.

Charlotte Leinbach, Grade 9
Norfolk Collegiate Middle/Upper School, VA

Friends

Friends are always there;
They always show they care,
Through good times and bad they always have your back.
They never judge who you are;
They just sit back and watch you soar.
They're someone you'll always need
To help you reach the stars.
When you're feeling down,
They'll help you turn your frown upside down.
They'll be there no matter what;
Even a fight can't break them up.
They'll make you laugh;
They'll make you cry.
In the end time will fly by.
They will never leave your side.

Katherine Alyssa Renesis, Grade 9
Norfolk Collegiate Middle/Upper School, VA

My Passion

MUSIC takes away all your fears
MUSIC can help you wipe your tears
   MUSIC enhances all your joys
   MUSIC pleases all girls and boys
SING when life's a parade
SING when you feel afraid
   SING when everything's going great
   SING when you have too much on your plate
Feel the song within your soul
In MUSIC it's okay to lose control

Shreya Bhatia, Grade 7
Kilmer Middle School, VA

Unseen Beauty
Through the glistening waves,
across the glittering sea,
down the dark depths of the ocean,
beyond where the eye can see.
Among the sparkling schools of fish,
past other colossal creatures too,
lay a lonely coral reef,
no bigger than me or you.
Within a little crack,
underneath dark and cold,
sits a single clam,
inside a story to be told.
The shell begins to open
a mystery no longer concealed,
inside a sparkling pearl,
its beauty now revealed.
Thomas Clark, Grade 8
Carson Middle School, VA

Friendship
The thing that keeps me going,
Helping me through the day,
Through thick and thin,
Good and bad,

It will always keep me pushing on,
Without it I am lost,
Clueless, confused, and cluttered,
Dazed and distracted,
Like a wandering dog,

But with it I am happy,
Which I can depend on,
Like a cub depends on its mother,
A friend,
Right by my side.
Riley Young, Grade 9
Mount St Charles Academy, RI

Fireworks
Bright light burst illuminates the sky
Sending pleasure to my eyes
Laughs and voices fill the air
People conversing everywhere

Fireworks light my heart
Making a beautiful New Year start
Sitting in the glistening grass
Sadly all of the fireworks have passed
Looking in the darkened sky
My little dog starts to cry

Past years, memories so bright
Ending our fire-lit night
Kalisa Fuller, Grade 7
Cape Henry Collegiate School, VA

A Game of Faith
Love is ERS,
it starts out simple,
slow and smooth.
The eyes wander around,
slapping 10 hearts down.

Hands begin to shake,
fingers begin to sweat.
The heart beats faster and faster,
nervous to make a statement.

Gathering pieces of 52 together,
but struggling to win the king of hearts.
Looking for a match,
one worth fighting for.
I stare at my goal,
waiting for the right moment.
Shashank Ojha, Grade 7
Carson Middle School, VA

What Is Love?
Love is a gum ball,
because as you start to chew,
you notice how hard it is
and you don't quite understand the flavor.
It becomes softer later on,
and juicier!

You taste the flavor.
It goes on for awhile regularly,
then slowly,
that flavor disappears.

You are sad,
but you know,
that someday,
you will find another twenty-five cents,
and chew an even better gum ball.
Jenna Colturi, Grade 7
Carson Middle School, VA

Who We Are
Every day a new door opens up
Giving us choices
Shaping who we are
Giving us individuality
Our traits are a puzzle
Fitting as one
That completed puzzle is us
All different shapes
And all different sizes
Everything completely different
We're different because of who we are
No one is the same
Marida Khan, Grade 8
Chickahominy Middle School, VA

Life Is Like a Bicycle
Life is like a bicycle
When you're learning to ride
You might fall off
But if you get back on and keep trying,
It will be rewarding later

Life is like a bicycle
It is made out of many parts
If one breaks, it won't function properly
But it can be fixed to continue your ride

Life is like a bicycle
It won't fall down, unless
You stop pedaling
So you must always put in effort

Life is like a bicycle
It might squeak sometimes,
But it then needs to be oiled,
So the rest of the ride can be smooth

Life is like a bicycle
You must work hard to get past a big hill,
But on the other side
You can enjoy a fun downhill ride.
Sashank Thupukari, Grade 7
Carson Middle School, VA

Dishes
Of all the chores in the world
Washing dishes is worst of all
I wait and wait and wait and wait
Until they are ten feet tall

Odd days are mine
Evens are my brother's
I got one done
Now I'm onto another

I can't stand dirty dishes
With the little bits of food
Sticking forcefully to the plate
Puts me in a terrible mood

I pick up a plate
And immediately let it fall
It felt like a slimy snail
I jump when it hits the sink's wall

It's been a long journey
But in the end
All the dishes shine bright
As the water descends
Ciara Johnson, Grade 8
Corkran Middle School, MD

Christmas

The sights to see on Christmas
are the best of them all.
It snows, it ices, and all such things.
Christmas is a time of giving and seeing others give.

The smells of Christmas are
loving smells of family members and friends.
It also smells like a Christmas tree and a burning fire.

The sounds of all the ringing bells,
and people singing "Glory to God!"
and "Merry Christmas!" they say.
They laugh, and sound happy and joyful.

The tastes of Christmas are great.
Cookies and hot chocolate, Yum!
Christmas is a time to spend together
and a joyful time of year.

Lots of giving and getting. Yay! Gifts!
Christmas is a great time of year!

Megan Cotellese, Grade 7
St John Neumann Academy, VA

Melo Comes Home

All over the news is Melo's return.
A text from ESPN is how I did learn.
The Knicks picked him up in a three team-trade,
The man the Orange of Syracuse made,
After being a Nugget his whole career.
He's coming home to New York.

He plays with no fear at all.
He's always loved to play ball.
He isn't in it for the fame.
He has such a love for the game.
With time winding down, you know he'll make it.
He will be welcomed to the Big Apple.

New Yorkers are happy, and throughout it is known.
With championship in mind, Melo's coming home.

Timothy Mark Howlett, Grade 9
Norfolk Collegiate Middle/Upper School, VA

Catch

Drops of sweat jogging down my face
All on me, the catch, the score, the fame
Now all I have to do is trace
Speed down the field and in return, the game

The ball is beamed, not as I thought
Flying fast like an eagle in the sky
I look in my hands, the ball I caught
With joy and love, I cry

Alexander Mina, Grade 8
Corkran Middle School, MD

The Wolf

The moonlight that bathes my fur and melts into me
Lights my path through the forest

The melody of howls, calling to me, reaching into my soul,
Revealing their anticipation
My paws, skimming across the loving Earth, are silent
As they race towards the song of my beloved
I reach them; my pack, My Pack, they welcome me
As I join their ranks once again
I run with them, through our homeland, following something
The scents, the beautiful scents
That drifts through my nose
They whisper to me, what my comrades already know
The prey we chase does not die — not in vain
This is just another routine instincts force upon us
The forest weeps as we sing our motive
To each other: I am chosen to go forth by my pack
I shoot forward, ahead of my comrades, and give chase to our goal
I leap onto my prey, and hold it down
While my beloved deal the finishing blow

Alicia Niles, Grade 7
E. Russell Hicks Middle School, MD

What Lies Beyond You

What lies far beyond your endless blackness?
I stare at your clouds reflecting in ponds
Your blazing yellows and azure calmness
Are only masks to shield what lies beyond.
Is it close? Or buried deep with the stars
Guarding like twinkling majestic sentries.
Is it behind planets? Jupiter? Mars?
How to solve this puzzle? Is it elementary?
If I move over there will I see it?
Your multicolored easel stares at me,
The sun's last rays strain and trees are lit
With the last burning light the eye can see.
I stay and watch the ripples left after
I throw a rock and break the reflective azure pond.

Penelope Mort Ranta, Grade 7
Kilmer Middle School, VA

Sound

Sound, everything has a sound.
Some sounds you can't hear,
Some sounds you can hear.

You might say what an awful sound that is,
Or that is the most beautiful sound I ever heard.
I love the sound the rain makes when it bounces off a windowpane.

The sound of a baby crying is what you wait for when it's born.
You can't wait for the sound of the bell on the last day of school.
Hearing the sound of the wind on a summer day.
Sound, what would we do without it?

Joy Floyd, Grade 7
Marshall Middle School, VA

Glass Dreams
Dreams are stories
Waiting to be written down.
Full of adventure, horror
And awestruck beauty.

Dreams are nightmares.
Endless black holes.
You are swept into the horror,
But there is no backing out.

Dreams are fantasies
Full of miracles.
Where everything you wish for,
Will always come true.

Dreams are memories.
Spread out in your mind like a spider's web.
Each one is precious,
But not always remembered.
Christie Xin, Grade 7
Carson Middle School, VA

A Thousand Miles
A thousand miles,
A thousand fears,
Upon thousands and thousands
Of cold shred tears

A thousand miles,
And what have we left?
Upon thousands and thousands
Of malicious heart thefts

A thousand miles,
Starts with a single step,
Upon thousands and thousands
Of nights we have crept

A thousand miles,
Of hearts they won't mend,
Upon thousands and thousands
Of help that we lend.
Kate Deng, Grade 7
Carson Middle School, VA

Martin Luther King Jr.
He said he had a dream,
That everyone should come together,
It doesn't matter what you look like,
This cannot last forever!
We will not forget those amazing words,
Because they were so powerful.
We will never forget him,
Because he was so wonderful!
Shantaya Thomas, Grade 8
St Clement Mary Hofbauer School, MD

If I Was in Charge
No one cares
About your personality,
They all care
About your clothes.
But if I was in charge,
I'd stop the wrongful judgment.

No one likes
Working for something.
They just like to get it.
But if I was in charge,
You would work for your payment.

Everyone wants to be
Big and tough.
If I was in charge,
People could get along.
They could stop
Casting out people.

But still,
That's if I was in charge.
Dante Barnes, Grade 7
Wicomico Middle School, MD

Bliss
Bliss
Underneath the tree
I lie
The wind is calm
The world is quiet
I uncurl and look at the sky
Clear blue sky
The tingles of a laugh rise
And I feel the thrum of my voice
I turn and stare at the dewy grass
The blades dancing in ways I can not
I close my eyes
The wind is calm
The world is quiet
All is bliss
Max Wang, Grade 7
Kilmer Middle School, VA

Tap Shoes
I am a tap shoe
Fast and slow
Loud and quiet
Tapping to the rhythm of the music
Difficult steps could be challenging
Taps moving to the beat
Metal clanking
Screws from the metal falling out
Tapping is easy
Meaghan Dubois, Grade 8
Mount St Charles Academy, RI

Winter Wonderland
The clouds in the winter sky,
Are as white as snow,
Like the snow on the ground,
That has fallen that winter.
Walking in the night,
Is like looking in a freezer,
Searching for something you want to eat.
The trees are sad,
They look like they are crying silently,
Because of the cold,
Their cry is like a newborn baby.
The wind is fierce,
Roars like a lion,
Like it's searching for its prey,
Its howls are heard,
Through everyone's windows.
The ice on the roads,
Glisten like glitter,
Looking like a winter wonderland.
Liesel Abraham, Grade 8
Norfolk Collegiate Middle/Upper School, VA

Come
The wind whispers softly
Like a mother to a child, gliding downward
"Come with me."
It cloaks around me, sending chills
Down my spine
And coos gently
"Come with me."
It roars wildly twisting and turning
Like an angry tornado
"Come with me."
Whistling, dancing gracefully through
The glowing white pines
"Come now."
And I do,
Falling back as I let go
Time stopping in its tracks.
For now I am free.
And at peace.
And the wind keeps going.
Valerie Cyphers, Grade 7
Kilmer Middle School, VA

Friends
Some are graceful,
Some are peaceful,
Some are pretty,
Some are jolly,
Some are sad,
Some are mad,
But they will always be there for you,
Because that's what friends do.
Guillemette Fialon, Grade 8
St Jane De Chantal School, MD

High Merit Poems – Grades 7, 8, and 9

Poetry Is…

Poetry is a way to speak.
A way to express feelings.
A way to entertain with words.

Poetry is made of many things.
Emotion is key.
Stanzas are almost always there.
Sometimes rhythms and rhymes are included.

Poetry can be odd at times.
For it consists of almost anything it desires.
No rules are set in stone.
All is possible.

Poetry is always around.
Though no one realizes it.
It surrounds us all the time.

Poetry is…life.

Savannah Martinez, Grade 7
E Russell Hicks Middle School, MD

A Minstrel

Back in the Middle Ages there was a minstrel
Who went wherever his instinct took him
He journeyed from town to city to castle
His future destinations had always been dim

Wherever he stopped, wherever he performed,
He could always entertain any bystander
But his utmost talent was well known to all
He was the most wonderful storyteller

With his words he could turn a mere tavern
Into the most mysterious world ever imagined
Or he could transform a simple house
Into a beautiful golden wheat field

He made an impact on everyone who heard him
And so he walked on his solitary road
I wish that I had been there to hear him
To hear some of the greatest stories ever told

Paul Quesnel, Grade 8
St Jane De Chantal School, MD

A Brush of Nature

A path made by horses trampling the undergrowth.
Delicate and dainty flowers blooming at the end of this road
are replaced by delicious colors of bright berries.
Blue jays painted with the sky's blue
cooled off in a crystal pond nearby.
A summer's frame
is now frozen forever.

Sara Zhu, Grade 7
Kilmer Middle School, VA

Lost Toys

They lie abandoned, gone.
The child will cry,
for just a few days,
relentlessly search for weeks,
months.

Then it will be forgotten.
Hidden in the back of the mind.
Forgotten.
Gone.

Then,
Every once and a while,
they will be remembered,
more sadness.

But maybe another child has found the abandoned toy,
and given it a new home,
and it will be loved again.

D. Scott Szpisjak, Grade 7
Rachel Carson Middle School, VA

Who Am I

I am a young girl,
who sometimes feels cold and alone.
Who feels down and gray
in a cell of metal bars like a trap.
With huge gray walls of darkness.
And no one around to sit by
or talk to.
Who also feels deserted
and abandoned by many people.
It's like a bright summer's day
quickly turning into a huge disaster.
With thunder and lightning bolts
striking down upon many poor and innocent people,
including me.
With horrible nightmares
and dark scary thoughts all around me with pure silence
that no one could ever break.

Marian Shenoda, Grade 8
Carson Middle School, VA

Reflection

I spy with my little eye something staring back at me,
it looks a little bit like me
I lift my hand and so does she
I turn around and start to think it must be me
But she's wearing pink, and I'm wearing black
She's who she wants to be and I'm not
She's the inside, I'm the out
She's the soul, and I'm the skin
So she's the reflection and I'm just…me

Meghan Settle, Grade 8
Floyd T Binns Middle School, VA

Home Is Where the Heart Is

Outside my window I see moving trucks closing their doors,
   It is time to leave.
I was told our new house would be better,
   but I want to stay where I am.
After what seems like forever of a drive,
   we pull into a driveway.
This house looks new and big,
   but also foreign and strange.
We march inside,
   it was empty and cold.
Clothes are unpacked,
   we are settled in.
I'm with my family.
   I'm safe and going to be okay.
Today, seven years later
   I still miss my old house, my old friends.
I've learned that home isn't where you are,
   home is where your heart is.

Madison Haas, Grade 8
St Paul's Lutheran School, MD

Time You Shouldn't Waste

Time, it's something that can quickly go by
without you stopping to think why

It goes on and on
it never stops
it's eternally long
as the clock ticks and tocks

It can't be felt, smelled, touched or seen
for time can only be described in one's dream

time can be taken and thrown away
people use it and abuse it still to this day

If you do stuff in such a haste
you will notice all the time you waste
So next time you do something way too fast
look back at the time you had enjoyed in your past

Ben Mekkes, Grade 8
Norfolk Christian Middle School, VA

Invisibility

I run my fingers through your hair,
But I know sometimes you are not there.
You tell me about your journey, as you rubbed upon my head
And how you made mistakes that were both good and bad.

I stood at the bus stop on a rainy day,
Listening to the pain in my head, waiting for it to go away.
I knew you'd be there waiting, cheerful and happy,
But when I saw you, you weren't what I expected.
I thought that maybe you could be affected
I ask you what's wrong, but you tell me you're fine.
I knew one day you would no longer be mine,

The person who read me stories and the one that cared for me,
The one who was always there for me, even when I was oblique
I don't want to think about it, but I know it's coming to an end,
But you'll be in my heart, and flowers I will always send.

Skylar Kissam, Grade 9
Norfolk Collegiate Upper School, VA

If I Were in Charge of the World

If I were in charge of the world
I'd make sure no kid would ever have to go to school again.
I'd make ice cream a main dish.
I'd make sure Ravens won every Super Bowl!!!

If I were in charge of the world
There'd be no books,
Lower gas prices,
BMX tracks everywhere.

If I were in charge of the world
You wouldn't have to wait till you're 16 to get your driver's license.
You wouldn't have to eat your vegetables.
You wouldn't have to take out the trash,
Or clean the scummy toilet. Someone else would

If I were in charge of the world.

Anthony Karn, Grade 8
Corkran Middle School, MD

What's Inside Not Out

There are good days and there are bad
Sometimes it makes me happy
Sometimes it makes me sad
At times I look in the mirror and notice flaws
Other times I notice beautiful features that strike out…

And then I realized it's not about what I see,
It's about what's inside of me
A golden heart and a loyal friend who will be with you to the end
So now when I look in the mirror I don't see a beautiful face,
But a beautiful person in its place

Bakhita Mukundi, Grade 9
Pencader Business & Finance Charter High School, DE

Here to Stay

Snowflakes rained down, as if god were sending sprinkles of salt
to fall from my sky.
I gazed longingly out the window,
waiting for the slightest ease in the harsh weather.
But it was cozy sitting there, for the house had certain warmth.
The fireplace crackled and popped
blending with the melancholy sound of the violin in the next room.
The smell of gingerbread drifted through the air
overwhelming my chilled nose with its piquant aroma.
The animals may have fallen asleep for the winter,
but the Christmas spirit is here to stay.

Anjali Khanna, Grade 7
Kilmer Middle School, VA

No Hate

I had a strange dream,
When I was a child,
That everyone was friends.
And there was no need for hate,
Nor violence,
Or war.
Life seemed peaceful and calm,
And with no need for hate,
It seemed like Heav'n on Earth.
But then I woke up,
And then I grew up.
And I found the dream false.
For it was just a dream,
A momentary glimpse,
Through the red-tinted windows of life.
For it was but a dream,
A momentary glimpse,
To the wonders that lie beyond.

Mary Korendyke, Grade 8
St Columba School, MD

Then We Said Goodbye

On this lovely day,
Strolling on the side walk,
Going our separate ways,
I went left,
You went right,
Of course we bump into each other,
I don't know which way to go,
We'll end up finding each other,
Either way,
We'll end up…finding each other,
I don't know which way to go!
Of course…we bump into each other,
You went right,
I went left,
Going our separate ways,
Strolling on the sidewalk,
On this lovely day,
Then we said goodbye.

Sarah Green, Grade 8
Norfolk Collegiate Middle/Upper School, VA

Light/Dark

Light
Illumination, luminescent
Glowing, shimmering, shining
White, day, night, obscure
Consuming, blackening, misleading
Lurking, ominous
Dark

Austin Clemmey, Grade 8
Mount St Charles Academy, RI

Love

Love is like a blinding light
but don't let it blind you
or you will get hurt
but remember there is more
to come for you

Anthony Tadeo, Grade 7
Western Heights Middle School, MD

Freedom Is a Bird

Freedom is a bird
Flying high above the skies
In search of where home is
Soaring above the mountains
Avoiding many obstacles on the way
The bird may be captured
Never to be seen again
The bird will fight its oppressor
Reclaim its freedom
Unfold its wings
And soar over the mountains again

Andrew Raj, Grade 7
Carson Middle School, VA

Snowboarding

Snowboarding
Cold, tough
Shredding, balancing, speeding
Wiping out down a mountain
Snowsurfing

Seth Stitik, Grade 7
Cape Henry Collegiate School, VA

Grades 4-5-6 Top Ten Winners

List of Top Ten Winners for Grades 4-6; listed alphabetically

Kate Bowling, Grade 5
Stilwell Elementary School, KS

Rachel Edwards, Grade 6
Heritage Preparatory School, GA

Jessica Hodge, Grade 6
Highland Elementary School, NY

Darby Holroyd, Grade 5
Indian Hills Elementary School, KS

Shaylee Jerabek, Grade 5
Traeger Elementary School, WI

Anne Elise Kopta, Grade 6
Hamilton International Middle School, WA

Victoria Martin, Grade 5
Mornington Central School, ON

Hannah Pincus, Grade 6
Kittredge Magnet School, GA

Rachel Roberts, Grade 6
Ode Maddox Elementary School, AR

Sophie Williams, Grade 4
W R Croman Elementary School, PA

All Top Ten Poems can be read at www.poeticpower.com

Note: The Top Ten poems were finalized through an online voting system. Creative Communication's judges first picked out the top poems. These poems were then posted online. The final step involved thousands of students and teachers who registered as the online judges and voted for the Top Ten poems. We hope you enjoy these selections.

Last Night I Dreamed of Dragons
Last night I dreamed of dragons,
there were dragons everywhere,
they were chewing on my sneakers,
they were sneezing in some pepper,
they were looking through my jackets,
they were burning down the door,
they were messing with the light switch,
as they flew about the floor.

They were dancing on chairs and tables,
they were puffing smoke everywhere,
they broke the bathroom mirror,
they were eating all the sweets,
there were dragons, dragons, dragons
for as far as I could see…
when I woke today, I noticed
their mere scales on top of me.
Birch Ambrose, Grade 5
Blacksburg New School, VA

Who I Am
Right now I am a little girl
turning into a strong woman

And I am adored
by my family and friends.

When my friends are upset
I always support them
Cause I love them
they are family to me.

I am picked on
and I try not to cry.

But I am a strong little girl
and nothing can stop me
and nothing will be in my way.
India Zhane' Thompson, Grade 4
Featherbed Lane Elementary School, MD

Civil War
The Civil War was fierce
People fighting one another
People dying for a cause
People crying
Why would people do this
For something they believe in
Battles here and there
Nothing but war
Families want to reunite
Not with this war by their side
People fighting, not because they want to
Because they have to
Eli Rhodes, Grade 5
St Christopher's School, VA

Windy Day
Wind blows through my hair
And blew upon my face
On the windy day

Clouds are forming
The day is transforming
On the windy day

The sky is dark
Rain drops falling
On the windy day

Clouds are parting
Beauty is starting
On the windy day

It feels much better
Take off your sweater
For now it's a sunny day!
Ben Rosenthal, Grade 5
Nottingham Elementary School, VA

Spring Has Begun
Spring oh spring,
the flowers are blooming,
the sound of children's laughter,
baby caterpillars hatching,
the sun shining upon us,

Acorns forming on trees,
squirrels seek upon joy,
as the sun goes down,
fireflies shimmer at twilight,
owls waking up from their slumber,
awaiting for the next day,
spring has begun,

The rooster awakes us,
warmth once again at my door,
starts again this morning,
till twilight,
spring has begun.
Sravya Pinnamaneni, Grade 6
Lakelands Park Middle School, MD

Smaller Than…
Smaller than a tiny seashell
Smaller than a piece of sawdust
Or a grain of desert sand
Smaller than a hair on my head
Smaller than a pencil tip
Or a dot on a ladybug
Smaller than an eraser on a pencil
That's how small an atom is
Alex Brown, Grade 4
St Christopher's School, VA

Green
Green is a sweet and sour apple
Green a hard, flat ground
Green is a round, small grape
Green is a big, slow turtle
Green is a small, dark closet
Green is a mean, scary dragon
Ryan Buck, Grade 4
Greenville Elementary School, VA

Fourth
F alling into a world of learning
O utstanding teachers
U nderstanding division
R eading groups end
T wo semesters
H ow did I learn all this stuff?
Henry Rodriguez, Grade 5
St Christopher's School, VA

Where Shall This Road Lead Me to Next
You're walking through a dusty road
Just walking then you see two roads,
Which one shall you take?
Are you confused, scared, lost?
But, no matter what road you shall take,
You will always find your way home.
Bria Covington, Grade 4
Courthouse Road Elementary School, VA

Easter
E ggs
A scension
S ongs
T ime of Joy
E aster break
R esurrection
Rita Rogers, Grade 4
Angelus Academy, VA

Your Gone
Me and you used to play and
you took my breath away
but now your gone
we can't bond
I'll see you soon
when the clock strikes noon
Dekel Johnson, Grade 4
Featherbed Lane Elementary School, MD

Desk
My desk is messy.
It keeps my books,
Holds smashed folders
And lost pencils.
Frank Royal, Grade 4
St Christopher's School, VA

Rain

Drip, Drop, Drip, Drop,
Pitter patter,
Drip drop,
The rain is like a pretty pattern,
Keeping a steady beat,
When it thunders you can hear it,
Even when it's weak,
It comes pouring,
Fast but still,
Like a beautiful butterfly!
When the rain falls,
It is cheerful,
Like a tasty chocolate pie.
When it lightnings in the nighttime,
The sky glows up bright,
From dark to light,
Second to second,
What a pretty sight!
The beauty of the rain falls down,
And then out of sight!
Drip Drop!

Peyton Kluger, Grade 5
Nottingham Elementary School, VA

Branches of a Tree

The branches reach out,
guiding me towards my tree,
lets me climb,
holds me tight,
doesn't let me fall.

The branches reach out,
sturdy,
lets me sit down to rest,
holds me tight against its bark,
doesn't let me stop believing.
Leaves fall, I don't mind though,
I love this tree.
The ground likes this tree,
welcomes its roots below me,
doesn't let them go.

The branches reach out,
like they are trying to hug,
lets me love
The branches of a tree.

Hannah Karlin, Grade 5
Glebe Elementary School, VA

Softball

Throwing, catching, running,
Hitting, sliding, waiting,
Having fun with my friends.
It's my pride and joy.

Haley Iannantuono, Grade 5
St Clement Mary Hofbauer School, MD

Wind and Sunshine

I am wind
I wonder how long I will last
I hear crying
I see sadness
I want happiness
I am sunshine
I pretend to dance
I feel alive and free
I touch gently on the faces of children
I worry that I might be to hot
I cry when I hurt people
I am everlasting sunshine
I understand I can be harmful
I say I will try not to be
I dream everyone will appreciate me
I try to be loving
I hope I don't get too hot
I am beauty

Cody Smith, Grade 6
Page Middle School, VA

Football

I am a football
I wonder if I will get thrown
I hear a whoosh when I go by
I see football players
I want to score a touchdown
I am a football
I pretend to score a touchdown
I feel the wind when I go by
I feel the hands of the football
I worry if I don't get caught
I cry if I don't score
I am a football
I understand if I don't score
I say "touchdown"
I dream to score
I try to get caught
I hope to score
I am a football

Austin Hogge, Grade 6
Page Middle School, VA

Maroon

When I see maroon
I think of the Redskins
And my mom's car
Bricks
Even some leaves
And the school bible and hymnal
The color of wood
And some mud
With a sunset
Maroon

Christopher Schroeder, Grade 4
St Christopher's School, VA

Garden

With rocks and with weeds
We have a garden to see
I can remember when the grass
Sprouts
The leaves turn green
When the flowers
Begin to grow
The garden is decorated
The rocks
From there to there
With children running
And stumbling on them
Bird houses
Yet to be filled
The loneliness
Of the garden
Spreads across it making it
Peaceful and quiet

Hope Parsons, Grade 5
Charles Barrett Elementary School, VA

Friend

I hear them singing in the morning,
I hear them singing in the afternoon,
So many of them sitting in the tree,
All singing to me.

I wonder what they're all saying,
All talking in a different language
That I don't know of,
I wonder if they see the world the
Same way,
But in a bird kind of way.

Spring is the best time of year,
I get to hear the singing birds that
Are near,
So many of them flying through the
Air,
Many of them flying without care.

Kelsey Kron, Grade 5
Charles Barrett Elementary School, VA

A Getaway

Where people talk and play,
To where we walk and sway.
Beautiful grains of white sand
On a majestic peace of land.
A dip in the waters is worth the burn.
When touch our skin or even turn.
Although we may have pain
We receive happiness on this great day.
Next time remember to say
"Slather on the sunscreen!!!"

Savannah Trail, Grade 5
Rocky Gap Elementary School, VA

Every Day Is the Same

Every day is the same
Every day a bird takes me to school
Every day the teacher gets hit on the head
Every day the bus falls apart
Every day mom makes hard rocks
But today was different
Today I walked to school
Today that teacher didn't get hit on the head
Today my mom made soup
Today was different
Yesterday everything was the same

Vilma Chicas, Grade 4
Courthouse Road Elementary School, VA

Spring

Spring is like a flower that blooms every year.
The blooming flower brings peace to the world,
Every year spring comes and goes.
In between that time the grass is greener and the sky is blue
When it rains we are still happy.
After rain comes and goes a glowing rainbow appears.
Its bright color brings happiness to people's souls.
Spring colors are different in many ways.
There are happy colors and sad colors.
Rain and sunshine like the petals of the flower.
That is why spring is like a flower.

Zachary Valverde, Grade 5
Rosemont Forest Elementary School, VA

Penguin Penguin

How do you fly? How do you fly high in the sky?
Do you live in the sky? Do you live in the sea?
Do you live on land just like me?

I cannot fly, but waddle and swim.
I live on the land up on the ice.
You may like seals…
but to me they're not nice.

Thurston Moore, Grade 5
St Christopher's School, VA

Green

Green tastes like a nice big green jelly bean.
Green smells like the grass that grows outside.
Green sounds like the leaves that blow outside.
Green feels like a green leather baseball.
Green looks like the Boston Celtics.
Green makes me think of the Celtics.
Green is the chalkboard in school.

Nickolas Reeder, Grade 5
St Mary School, RI

Prayer of the Discrete Swinging Monkey

In the forest with low, green vines and
Enormous dark brown branches
I must pray for my baby monkey, and for
Me, protection from swift panthers and
Pointy toothed wild dogs.

Asa Castleberry, Grade 4
St John Neumann Academy, VA

Rain

I hear the pitter patter of rain on the street
I smell the wet leather in my car
I walk outside and feel the cool rain on my face
I stick out my tongue, and drink some rain
It is like fresh water from a pool

Ryan Mark, Grade 5
Nottingham Elementary School, VA

The Goblin

Swinging on a bell
Swinging in a tree
The goblin is coming for you

Walking on the ground
Swimming in the river
The goblin is coming for you

Walking towards the town
Walking through the street
The goblin is coming for you

Walking towards your house
Walking through your door
The goblin is coming for you

Walking towards your room
Peering in your room
The goblin is coming for you

Walking towards your bed
Peering through the blankets
The goblin is coming for you

Reaching towards the blankets
Pulling them back
The goblin has got you

Jasper Davis, Grade 5
Nottingham Elementary School, VA

Forest/Nature

Forest
Fresh, beautiful
Running, enjoying, savoring
Everything has inner beauty
Nature.

Ryan Dobson, Grade 6
Immaculate Heart of Mary School, MD

The Big Game

That day it was pouring out soccer teams running about
The ref said it's our turn to play on such a cold gloomy day
The game has just begun but there is still no sign of the sun
My coach has put me in I'm not sure if this game we'll win
More spectators begin to leave that's when I begin to pull moves from up my sleeve
I dribble the ball up the field my chances of scoring are not sealed
I almost fall in the deep puddles the coach calls a time-out and we all huddle
The whistle blows; it's time to go back in the game our positions have stayed the same
The ball was now passed back to me an open shot is what I see
I kick the ball as hard as I can in the goal is where I should land
This goal I have now scored the game is over because it has poured
The parents have congratulated the team my mom then said she would treat me to ice cream!

Natalya Moody, Grade 6
Immaculate Heart of Mary School, MD

What Would You Do on the Last Day of Your Life?

What would you do on the last day of your life?
   Would you say goodbye to all you friends, or party without looking back? Don't think you'll die because God doesn't need you.
You've played an important role in my life, and it's not over yet.
   But all I want to know is what would you do on the last day of your life?
Just one thing and one thing only is what would you do on the last day of your life.
You started a hard life, but put it aside.
You live a great life now, with a caring family, and a child watching over you, saying you're doing a great job.
So tell me this now, it's all I'll ask from you!
   What would you do on the last day of your life?

Ethan Orozco, Grade 5
Monocacy Elementary School, MD

Blueberry Muffins

The rain hit the roof like marbles and echoed through the structure. With every passing impact another weight is on my shoulders, making me more bored. Trapped in my imagination, crammed by a squall of thoughts. Suddenly a scent drifts from afar, it makes me leave my door ajar. Slowly I turn step by step, inch by inch, before it pulls me in like a vortex. I think about batter, a strange, mysterious liquidy matter. Eggs, just so good they get me on my feet and move my legs. The blueberry, so plump, round, juicy and merry. They smell so good and taste so divine, so good in fact, they're gone before nine. The recipe's confidential. Even my access is denied. There is only one explanation; the whole thing's classified! It has won many contests. My grandmother's a genius, the recipe's creator. I want to know the secret, I'll find out sooner or later. Every judge has been surprised. Their faces are speechless; they can't believe their eyes. They know they have a winner, we're going to get first prize!

Connor Cuevo, Grade 5
Flint Hill Middle School, VA

My Sister's Awful Double Dare

I ate lots of ice cream from my sister's double dare. I turned into a popsicle and it messed up my hair. I went to the kitchen and ate some peanut butter, my mouth got stuck together, and I dropped some honey on the floor. I went to my room and got the straightener out and straightened my hair; it caught on fire; I have no hair. My mouth was stuck shut, my feet had honey on them and I'm a popsicle. I hate my sister's awful double dare.

Darla Rawls, Grade 4
Halls Cross Roads Elementary School, MD

Rain

Rain runs down the ripped red door, eventually it rains some more. Rain falls quickly out of the sky and goes back up as if it could fly. Flying fast to hit the ground and make that delightful plopping sound. Creating puddles so you can splash, be careful if you dare to dash. Some say rain, rain go away but I wish it was always here to stay.

Bennett Detweiler, Grade 5
Monocacy Elementary School, MD

Gymnastics

A...
Wrist wrecking,
Ankle twisting,
Hand ripping,
Bruise making,
Body breaking,
Blood bringing,
Sport
This is the best sport to me!

Madison Harris, Grade 5
Norfolk Collegiate Lower School, VA

Visionary Blue

Blue lightning strikes
As if seas and oceans were pouring
Out of the night sky
As if there was a flood in outer space
So much water in the moonlight
The heavy rain knocked down a tree
The water almost made a flood
High enough for me to swim
Blue lightning strikes

Seth Peterson, Grade 4
Greenville Elementary School, VA

Winter

Brrr!
It's so cold
Look at the snow!
It is like little men on parachutes
Floating down slowly.
Flying down on my sled
It feels as if I am going 50 mph.
Look at the snow on the ground
It is like a blanket that never ends.

Colton Zang, Grade 4
Boonsboro Elementary School, MD

Soldier

An old soldier
Sat
In the evening
On his porch
Just remembering

William Tappen, Grade 5
St. Christopher's School, VA

A Summer Day

Lying in the grass,
Flowers tickling my feet,
A breeze rustles my hair,
A cricket chirps beside me,
A bird flies overhead,
What a beautiful day.

Sara Pettyjohn, Grade 6
Monelison Middle School, VA

Goldfish Crackers

I am a goldfish cracker
I wonder if I can really swim
I hear crunch crunch
I see darkness
I want to see light
I am not alone
I pretend I'm a real fish
I feel the ocean
I touch shells
I worry if I will ever be real
I cry as if I'm a storm
I am a goldfish cracker
I understand that I may not be real
I say that I want to see the world
I dream of the day
I try to believe
I hope every day
I am the sad goldfish cracker

Myranda Ealey, Grade 6
Page Middle School, VA

The Saddest Day

I had just woken up and gleamed,
And ate my breakfast.
I heard sirens and worries
And not even happiness.

My dad comes back
Sad as can be.
And then
He cried with me all day long.
My neighbor had passed
And I wasn't happy.
I cried all day long.

I played old gloomy songs,
Trying to forget about him.
Nothing worked at all. After
Time I forgot,
That good old man.

Adam Hastings, Grade 6
Seaford Middle School, DE

You're Gone

I opened my eyes
you were gone
Right now I don't want to cry
but all I have to say is bye
you were all that mattered at that
point of time
in my heart you're still there
but when I see you
for that last time
I die!

Dominique King, Grade 4
Featherbed Lane Elementary School, MD

Christmas

Christmas
Presents under a Christmas tree
Gingerbread houses
Children laughing
Sweet gingerbread men
Ripped present wrapping
Christmas

Meade Hall, Grade 4
St Christopher's School, VA

Purple

Purple tastes like juicy grapes.
Purple smells like hydrangeas.
Purple sounds like a juicy plum.
Purple feels like my blanket.
Purple looks like Justin Bieber's high tops.
Purple makes me excited.
Purple is my favorite favorite color.

Sabrina Gambardelli, Grade 5
St Mary School, RI

Pink

Pink tastes like a new pack of gum.
Pink smells like a bunch of tulips.
Pink sounds like my little sister calling me.
Pink feels like a lovely new dress.
Pink looks like my favorite ice cream.
Pink makes me feel wonderful.
Pink is a nice color.

Meghan Clark, Grade 5
St Mary School, RI

Fitness

weakness
lazy, sugary,
sleeping, watching, boring,
tired, slow, fast, weighty,
lifting, walking, running,
strong, muscled,
strength

Teliza Bracey, Grade 5
Linwood Holton Elementary School, VA

Purple

Purple tastes like yummy grapes.
Purple smells like a lilac.
Purple sounds like the wind blowing.
Purple feels like the sun's rays.
Purple looks like a bird flying.
Purple makes me feel happy inside.
Purple is my favorite color.

Darien Cabral, Grade 5
St Mary School, RI

Love
Love is beautiful
Love is strong
Love makes me sing a song
The world is crazy I say
But when you everything will be okay
Love is like a rose
But no one knows when you love
Your spirit grows
DaNaisha Langston, Grade 4
Featherbed Lane Elementary School, MD

Fox
If I were a fox
I would eat pork chops
For breakfast,
Lunch,
And dinner.
And I would stay up late
Looking for food.
Pigs better look out!
Christian Butler, Grade 4
St Christophers School, VA

Gummy Bear
Teeming in a jar,
full of each other,
waiting for someone to open the lid,
planning an escape for freedom,
sticky body swaying back and forth,
squishing their faces against the jar,
the lid opens,
a rush of color bursts out.
Jennifer Lounsbury, Grade 5
Nottingham Elementary School, VA

Letters to My Friend
Dear Abby that's how I always begin
A note to my bestie, my sister, my friend
I think of you often, most every day
Wondering what's going on your way
I write my letters about everything I do
Hoping to get a response back from you
Love Meredith that's how I always end
Miss you, your pal, your friend
Meredith Beavers, Grade 6
Midlothian Middle School, VA

Angels
A s sweet as flowers
N ice and kind
G uardian
E xcellent
L oving
S ilent as night.
Julia Riordon, Grade 4
Angelus Academy, VA

Life Is Full of Choices
Life is full of choices
you can make a good one or a bad one

In life you can
live a happy life or a sad one

You can follow your dreams
or not follow them at all

Life is full of choices
so choose carefully
Mariam Hydara, Grade 4
Featherbed Lane Elementary School, MD

A Cheering of Chirps
I hear them chirping
Singing
One of their majestic songs
Once it's over there's a moment of
Silence
Then there are a burst of chirps!
Clapping, cheering
Begging for more
Yet he rejects, just turns away
Maybe he'll be back
Another day
Casey Hoag, Grade 5
Charles Barrett Elementary School, VA

Missing You
Missing you day and night,
Always want to hold you tight

Thinking of you makes me cry,
Even though I said bye bye

I can't get you off my mind,
Because your beauty always shines

Waking up from an awful dream,
Still hoping you were missing me
Perry Lawrence, Grade 6
Magnolia Elementary School, MD

That Diary
That diary
That diary
What is in that diary?
I need to find out, it holds the future.

I can see if that boy still likes me
I can see if that girl's just jealous

What is in that diary?
Rebecca Scott, Grade 4
Courthouse Road Elementary School, VA

Purple
Purple tastes like a juicy plum
Purple smells like a sweet smelling lavender
Purple sounds like a good time
Purple feels like excitement
Purple looks like happiness
Purple makes me very cheerful
Purple is my favorite color
Gia Bonaminio, Grade 5
St Mary School, RI

Wish Wish Wish!
When you throw a rock into a pond
It ripples
It sinks
Sometimes I wonder
Is that wish really going to come true?
I hope so
Do you?
Meigs Helms, Grade 4
St John Neumann Academy, VA

Foodie
cake
brown, tangy
cutting, slicing, fighting
yellow, soft, sweet, succulent
eating, biting, finishing
yummy, delicious
crumbs
Trey Fleming, Grade 5
Linwood Holton Elementary School, VA

Movie and Book
Movie
scenes, funny
sounds, listen, laugh
theater, home, school, car
read, understand, follow
chapters, good
Book
Austin Rodriguez, Grade 6
St John Neumann Academy, VA

Ice Cream
Ice cream is the best
Ice cream can be a big mess
Some kids think of ice cream is the best

Ice cream is so creamy
Ice cream is not very stringy
Ice cream is very tasty
Ryan Lough, Grade 4
Courthouse Road Elementary School, VA

Fire

Fire is neat, fire is cool,
It's not something you want in school

Fire is cool in the clear sky,
But look out, fire can go really high

Fire lasts all night,
Till the sun comes up and it's daylight.

Alex Anderson, Grade 4
Courthouse Road Elementary School, VA

God

God is strong
God is powerful
God made us
God made the world
God protects us
God is the reason we are alive
God may take people from us
but without God nobody would be here.

Pedro Vazquez, Grade 4
Featherbed Lane Elementary School, MD

Football

F antastic
O uch
O ver ouch
T ight End
B uccaneers
A wesome
L inebacker
L ooking good

Noah Morales, Grade 4
Angelus Academy, VA

Blue

Blue tastes like the juicy blueberries
Blue smells like the blue sea water
Blue sounds like the bluebirds chirping
Blue feels like my soft bedspread
Blue looks like the sky
Blue makes me happy
Blue is everywhere

David Pagliarini, Grade 5
St Mary School, RI

Easter Eggs

E legant eggs
A rtistically made
S miling excitedly
T enderly they lay
E ggs are colored
R ed, purple, green,
silver, and gray.

Riley Anne Redden, Grade 4
Angelus Academy, VA

I'm a Party Girl

I'm a party girl
I like to stay up at night
and sleep through the day

I'm a party girl
I like to go place to place
and not race
So everyone can see my face

I'm a party girl
if it's a party
you know I'm there
clean cute and fresh
uhmp
everyone wants to stare

I'm a party girl
yeah me
Camryn Briscoe
intelligent as can be
I'm a party girl

Camryn Briscoe, Grade 4
Featherbed Lane Elementary School, MD

I Will Never Crash

I am a military helicopter
I wonder when I will get destroyed
I hear the sound of bullets
I see missiles coming at me
I want to stay alive

I am as fast as lightning
I pretend I am human
I feel bullets bouncing off my tough metal
I touch the soft soil when I land
I worry that I will crash
I cry when I need to be repaired

I am a military helicopter
I understand that I will crash
I say we will never lose the war
I dream I never crash
I try to land but not crash
I hope the humans will treat me better

I am a military helicopter

Matthew Boyd, Grade 6
Page Middle School, VA

The Building

They are as still as a sloth
and as quite as mice,
but they are always
watching you.

Jason Lee, Grade 5
Nottingham Elementary School, VA

Summer

The shouts of kids having fun
The hot, warm, heavy air on your back
Splashes from the pools
Bikers biking,
Soccer players playing soccer,
Ice cream melting in their cones.
Smelling barbecues in people's backyards
These are the clues that summer has come
Saving kids from the school
Only wishing summer was longer
Wishing it was still here.

Dina Liacopoulos, Grade 5
Nottingham Elementary School, VA

The Bite

I have a mosquito bite on my nose,
it's so big I can't see my toes!
It's starting to itch I know I will scratch it,
I think I'll need a tennis racquet!
Now the bite is bigger than before,
it's red, plump and oh so sore!
I scratch, scratch and scratch some more,
oh how I hope it will go away.
Soon, I'll be scratching the whole day!
It's finally night and all is swell,
my first day at camp didn't go so well.

Lauren Bennett, Grade 6
Willow Springs Elementary School, VA

My New Kitten

I got a new kitten.
It is as small as a mitten.

When I first saw it, I cried tears
The little muffin will calm my fears.

It is an orphan — plump, warm and gray
One day, all we will do is play.

I'm not even sure if it is a girl or a boy
My kitten still brings me joy.

Rachel Galbreath, Grade 6
St Columba School, MD

Sledding in the Sky

Stand up, holding your sled
Run! Jump! Slide!
The "whoosh" of going down fast,
The hope that this moment will never end
The jump's coming up!
You feel yourself lift.
Up! Up! Up!
You wish you could stay in the sky forever
Sledding in the sky

Rachel Arruda, Grade 5
The Compass School, RI

The Time I Got My Dog, Molly

In 2005, after my cat passed away, we wanted a new pet.
We saw a dog named Molly at the rescue shelter,
And under the table she lay. I told my parents I wanted her.
They said we should look around first, since she was the first dog we saw.
I liked her because she was cute and had nice black fur.
Then the worker told us she was beaten, by her previous owners, and was shy.
I felt bad for her, but we kept moving, and walked into a room where everything was eaten.
We came to a very destructive, but sweet canine,
Who bit my mom's zipper. My parents and I looked around some more.
I said I liked Molly the best, and they said that was fine.
So we would visit her often. We bonded with her, and she began to trust us.
At this time she was a puppy, and not even close the age ten.
Finally we adopted Molly, and took her home.
The first thing she did was sit on the couch like a human.
That has been her spot ever since. At first around the house she would roam.
But eventually she knew that this was her residence.
She got comfortable around us, and we loved each other very much.
My family gave her confidence. We turned her into a sweet, loyal dog.
Molly is so loyal to us, she really gives back, for all of the things we give her.
When it comes to eating, she's a hog. Now she is a little pushy, especially during belly rubs,
And she may be a little lazy at times too. But even with her few flaws, you can't help but give Molly a hug.

Emily Pipkin, Grade 6
Immaculate Heart of Mary School, MD

Birthdays

I love birthdays
Birthdays, birthdays
It's an annual thing
Birthdays, birthdays
It does not matter what age I turn
I may turn nine but my birthday is always mine
Birthdays, birthdays
For a day I'm queen and eat divine
Birthdays, birthdays
The best part of all is when I make my cake with its rose design and its center filled lemon lime
Birthdays, birthdays
I just love that unique date of the year where all my family and friends are together it just couldn't get any better
Birthdays, birthdays
The scent of barbecue in the air and everyone laughing without a care
Birthdays, birthdays
Now it's time for me to blow out the candles and make a wish, I wish to eat my favorite dish
Birthdays, birthdays
Before you know it, it's time, it's now, it's the day to tell my mom and dad "Hey!"
It's my birthday, My birthday, birthday? Birthday! Hoora-a-a-ay!

Adilia Espinoza-Jones, Grade 6
Magnolia Elementary School, MD

Sometimes I Wish…

Sometimes I wish that there would be world peace. Sometimes I wish that we weren't in the Great Depression all over again. Sometimes I wish that life wouldn't be so hard. Sometimes I wish people would be nicer. Sometimes I wish that there would be no violence. Sometimes I wish that people would all live at peace. Sometimes I wish that we weren't at war. Sometimes I wish that everyone would be fair. But for right now I guess we will need to keep on wishing.

Ava Torres, Grade 6
Paul L Dunbar Middle School for Innovation, VA

Friends

The flowers that are next to you when you need them
The sun that shines down on you to make you blossom
The faces that make your heart swell with happiness
The chocolate that is so sweet
The people that love you with all their heart
They're really special
They're called friends.

Ellen Gulian, Grade 5
Cloverly Elementary School, MD

Deployed

I'm still there for you.
No matter what you do.
If there's an ocean that comes between us,
I'll send a message across the sea.
If you can't sleep tonight, knowing its all right.
I hope that you are listening to my words.
I miss you.

Laudina Gwira, Grade 6
Ansbach Elementary School, AE

The Ocean

Looks like waves crashing to the shore
Sounds like seagulls singing to God
Feels like cold salt water breeze spraying your face
Tastes like salty water getting in your mouth
Smells like fresh cool air

Kori Gregory, Grade 5
Church of the Redeemer Christian School, MD

Prayer

Smells like food from a provider
Tastes like provisions from the bread of life
Looks like faith in one God
Sounds like a heavenly choir
Feels like hope for another day

Luis Felipe Rubio, Grade 5
Church of the Redeemer Christian School, MD

The Cousins

My cousins and I fight just in the night.
We tumble and rumble with a fright.
But during the day,
We all just like to play,
Yet, we are always right to fight through the night.

James Price, Grade 5
St Clement Mary Hofbauer School, MD

The River Boating Trip

I see the lovely mansions on the banks.
I feel the refreshing, cool water on my body.
I hear the steady hum of motorboats speeding past.
I smell the sweet scented water underneath me.
I taste the delicacy of my mom's homemade brownies.

Julia Pettus, Grade 4
Crestwood Elementary School, VA

I Used to But Now I

I used to eat all kinds of mashed up foods
But now my choice is based upon my mood

I used to play golf in my backyard
But now I hit the ball unbelievably hard

I used to color outside my coloring book's lines
But now I draw my now pictures
while on a red leather chair I recline

I used to sleep in a wood furnished crib
But now I can eat without a baby blue bib

I used to be afraid of grotesque monsters in the dark
But now I can prance around them like I'm playing in the park

I used to sit in a bucket of salty water at the beach
But now I'm as free as a dog off its leash

I used to shoot baskets on a mini hoop
But now I zig and zag, crossover, dribble,
and sometimes pass for an alley-oop

I used to not want to go to sleep with my teddy bear
But now I sleep deeply because I really care

I used to make mistakes innocently
But now my conscience helps me choose diligently

Will Sass, Grade 6
Most Blessed Sacrament Catholic School, MD

A Dream

The sun is disappearing
The moon is shining
The stars are twinkling
High in the sky
Up above and blinking
And when they do I think,
How far does the world stretch?
What if there was somewhere else to live besides Earth?
What if I could hold the sun in my hand?
And then I dream
For an immense amount of time
About discovering the universe.

I stood on the sun
I slept on the moon
I touched a star
I scanned a meteor shower
I saw a black hole swallowing up a planet
Wow! I said
Vroom! I was pulled into the black hole
And then it was over
It was nothing but a dream.

Andy Chuang, Grade 4
Colvin Run Elementary School, VA

The Beach

At the beach, I see huge waves crashing
And lifeguards running.
There are hungry seagulls
Hovering around my head
As I eat my lunch on my towel by the water.
At the beach, I hear a lifeguard's whistle blow for help
As a man is screaming
"HELP!" in the twenty feet deep water.
There is the sound of children screaming and splashing.
I hear the sound of seagull
Calling to his friends
To join him to feast
On a bag of potato chips by my blanket.
At the beach, I feel the sand
Burning my toes
As I run for the booth
To get a cone of cold ice cream.
The chilly water
Feels refreshing on my body
As I enter the salty sea.
I love the beach.

Katelyn Martino, Grade 6
Wyman Elementary School, RI

What Becomes of a Seed?

A flower
Starts as a seed.
Shortly after,
It branches out
Planting its roots in the soil
Then bursting out
Of the cold, hard ground
To show its warm, soft beauty
As a flower.
It reminds me how
I was a seed.
Branching out into
Addition, subtraction, and long division.
Bursting into
Science fairs and algebra
With other bees and bugs supporting me
Along the way.
Guiding me to become
The strong, beautiful flower
I am
Today.

Olivia Simmons, Grade 6
Montessori International Children's House, MD

Ballet

To me, ballet is full of grace and drama
How it tells its own story through the interpretation of music
Sometimes happy, playful, exciting, and other times sad and dark
How I think of ballet is calm, beautiful, flowing movement

Jennani Jayaram, Grade 4
Blacksburg New School, VA

Magic

Magic is a mysterious thing.
Once I looked it up on Bing.
It gave me lots of confusing information.
No one had an explanation.

I then decided I was going to go to a magic school.
I thought it was going to be cool.
Unfortunately, it was very boring.
It made me feel like snoring.

So then I went home to take a nap.
Of course with my cat laying on my lap,
And I slowly drifted off into a dream.
At the beginning of the dream I was eating ice cream.

Eventually I couldn't figure out magic.
So I gave up, and it was tragic.
When I awoke, I realized that magic had died.
I decided I had to confide.

Victoria Hertenstein, Grade 5
Lightfoot Elementary School, VA

My Dog Jake

I have a dog and his name is Jake,
And Jake ate my birthday cake.
He is a Lab which makes me glad,
I always wanted a Lab which isn't a fad.

He's playful which makes me thankful,
To have a dog that isn't hateful.
He's always so extremely frisky,
He'll chase a truck which is really risky.

When he lifts his gigantic paw,
Sometimes he scratches me with his claw.
My dog's eyes are deep dark brown,
And sometimes it makes him look like a clown.

When I'm playing football and running,
He jumps up and down and is so cunning,
He'll run excitedly right under my legs,
And for a scrumptious treat he always begs.

Zachary Morgan, Grade 5
Lightfoot Elementary School, VA

Lacrosse

L eading your team to victory.
A ction at every turn.
C radling the ball in your net.
R unning up and down the field.
O pposing team has lost the fight.
S core, is the magic word!
S cores are racking up.
E ndurance is what you need.

Jaren Chester, Grade 5
Church of the Redeemer Christian School, MD

Sun and Moon

I am the sun as hot as fire
I wonder why I sometimes go away
I hear the sunset calling me
I see when the moon comes up
I want to be the cool dark moon
I am the moon in darkness
I pretend to shine
I feel great high in the sky
I touch the stars above
I worry that one day I will disappear
I cry when I go away
I am the sun in the blue sky
I understand that the moon wants me
I say I wish we could meet
I dream to be one another
I try to rise when the moon comes
I hope the stars splish, splash to our wishes
I am the sun and moon in the beautiful skies

Morgan Slavnik, Grade 6
Page Middle School, VA

A Flower

I am a flower blooming beneath the sun
I wonder where my life will begin
I hear bees buzzing by
I see other flowers just like me blooming by the minute
I want to see the world
I am a flower wanting to go places
I pretend I'm somewhere else even though I know it's not possible
I feel happy when I see new things happen here
I touch my beautiful petals that will wither away when I'm old
I worry what would happen to me if I let go of my roots
I cry at the thought of myself going away
I am a flower who won't stay where she is
I understand my future
I say my prayers
I dream of where I will end up
I try to pull at my roots
I hope I will make it through my journey
I am a flower who let go

Sydney Cook, Grade 6
Page Middle School, VA

That's Who I Am!

I am a bubbly person.
I am a person that likes to play with my relatives
and friends

I am a person that was born in the summer
I am a Christian
I am a talented person
And my talent is to dance

That's who I am!

Jordan Plater, Grade 6
Magnolia Elementary School, MD

Environmental Problems

Environmental problems happen everywhere
On every continent it happens, it is very sad
We must do something fast or it will stay here
If we don't do something it will turn out bad

Not too long ago the Gulf went black
It was bad, the plants and animals were in oil
We must do something or else the ducks won't quack
If we don't do something, everything will be soiled

The Earth is hotter, it is getting warm
The polar bears' need is dire
The caps are melting and taking a different form
We have a problem the water is getting higher

The world is sad, our future looks black
If we don't help some things will never come back

Chase Klemkowski, Grade 6
Immaculate Heart of Mary School, MD

My Mom

My mom is someone I admire very much
She knows what to say when things make me sad
But she never stops loving and hugging me and such
And I love her, too, because she makes me glad

My mom really looks out for me a lot
And she always knows what I want and need
I'm very glad she is the mom I got
She is always doing a nice, kind deed

I am fortunate to have a mother
My mom is so affectionate towards me
It's great that we really love each other
I am very fond of my mom you see

Because she is my mom I really love her
I am very glad she is my mother

Brittany Trees, Grade 6
Immaculate Heart of Mary School, MD

The First Thanksgiving

The colors of autumn are all around;
Wildlife and frolicking children abound.
The crackling flames of a campfire leap,
The wind whistles through corn that the Pilgrims will reap.
They all greet each other with joyful embraces,
Nothing could compare to the smiles on their faces!
The smell of cooking smoke hangs in the air,
Abundant food is everywhere!
Spicy sauces, juicy jam,
Flavorful fruits and fresh-roasted ham!
Pilgrims gather together to pray,
Thankful to God on Thanksgiving Day!

Emma Eyre, Grade 6
Homespun Schoolhouse Of Agape, VA

The Amazing Foul Shots

It was the last basketball game of the season we only have one game left to win
Our team could not lose another game
Or we would be put to shame

We started by winning the tip-off and we had a good plan going into the game
Our team played like a real team that night
We passed and shot baskets just right

All of my teammates were playing great the score was neck and neck
The other team put up a good fight
But we were playing with all of our might

The fourth quarter came and we switched our defense to press we were thirsty and tired but we couldn't give up
I know everybody's hearts were pumping as they run
But sadly the other team scored, and they were up by one

With fourteen seconds left the ball was passed to me someone on the other team fouled me
The ref gave me foul shots, but I missed
The ball bounced right back to me with a hiss

I got fouled again, and I got more foul shots with seven seconds left I shoot. SCORE!
With my heart pumping crazily I shoot. SCORE!
As time runs down the clock expires, we succeeded and more.

Frankie Tumminello, Grade 6
Immaculate Heart of Mary School, MD

The Empire of Love

Love is a funny thing you know. When you're in love you do silly things. You will sing as beautiful as the heavens for your lover. You will shrink as tiny as a mouse to get your lover what she wants. You will be a Cupid, shoot her with an arrow and she will forever be in love.

Fall in love with dignity and respect and your relationship will remain intact. Love is the empire of life. If you're in true love, it'll never end. Sometimes true love may even be found with your best friend. Never let the fear of striking out keep you out of the game. Love is the exact same thing.

Fall in love with dignity and trust. Love is the game of us. Falling in love can be lots of fun. If you fuss and fight I can assure you that they are the one. Once you've found the one you want to spend your life with, you will begin to build your Empire of Love.

Shianne Randolph, Grade 6
The Academy of International Studies, VA

What I Love

I love to watch – The colossal crashes of wonderful waves on the beautiful Ocean City beach
And the BOOM BANG A BANG of Star Trek voyages to distant worlds
I love to smell – The salty vinegar smell of delicious Thrashers french fries
And the smell of fresh blacktop, that's as strange as a three-eyed polar bear
I love to hear – The DING DONG DING of a computer I'm using
Mr. Record's voice saying, "No school today"
And the sound of the ice cream van bringing delicious flavorful ice cream and joy
I love to taste – A fresh juicy Billy's meatball sub, with the meatballs I helped to make
And the delicious fried heaven of a Fractured Prune donut
I love to touch – A soft Tempur-Pedic mattress cushioning my fall
And jumpy Jell-O cushioning my ravenous appetite
I love the way – I'm great with technology, solving any problem that so gallantly comes my way
I'm pretty smart, getting good grades and being happy

Jimmy Neely, Grade 6
Most Blessed Sacrament Catholic School, MD

Portrait of a Crab

My shell, my fortress, is smooth as glass.
Beware my jagged pincers, they'll snip you anywhere.
If you disturb us, we'll fight you in mass.
Our limbs are disposable; they're like the clothes you wear.
Who will guess our color? Maybe red, green, or blue.
Our lands are as diverse as our color, or shall I say hue.

We live all day, and all night
Defending our homes, or tying not to fight.
I scuttle around the ocean floor,
Or maybe explore the sandy shore.
All lobsters, all shrimp, inferior are thee,
For even a constellation have we.

Our meat is priceless, our shell valuable.
But do not take our skills to be dull.
Even though we're tiny, don't take us fools,
since we can use our claws as tools,
Ta ta, silly land walkers, we live another day!
So come fellow crabs, we'll scuttle away.

Luke Burger, Grade 5
Forcey Christian School, MD

Basketball

People proudly praise their teams.
Coaches continuously call out to the players.
Their teammates cheer them on.
How can we win this game?

Sweat runs down the players' faces.
Then the basket goes in — swish, swish
When one side gets so many fouls,
They can take two shots.

She attempts the first shot.
Everyone is silent…No point.
She takes the second shot.
The basket is good!

The crowd goes wild — whooh!
If we win the game that's great,
If we lose, that's great too.
At the end we always shake hot hands.
We are all wonderful winners!

Emily Small, Grade 6
Trinity School, MD

Beauties of Life

It was a late summer night, and we were so tired.
The moon was shining so bright we could see every thing.
One very bright flashing light appeared, it was a firefly.
We ran inside and got a jar, and caught it.
After we caught it more came out and we caught so many.
They were so beautiful I thought I would never let them go.

Delaney Hughes, Grade 5
Francis Asbury Elementary School, VA

Bill

There once was a man named Bill.
Bill lived next to the big old mill.
Next to the mill was an "empty" cave,
And a visit there, Bill began to crave.
He'd been there many times before,
But he dreamed to go there even more.
Bill though to himself: "It won't hurt to go in.
I've done it before, and just scraped my skin."
He entered the cave, and heard a low growl.
Then, a large bear began to prowl.
The bear started to run at Bill.
The very same that lived next to the mill.
Then, Bill fled.
He fled past the mill, past a shed.
Bill entered his house as fast as he could,
And this small dwelling made of wood,
Gave him a feeling of great safety.
He was happy that his actions were hasty.
Bill never again entered that cave, my friend,
And this poem has now come to an end.

Abbey Tharp, Grade 5
Lightfoot Elementary School, VA

The Striped Beast

The tiger prowls through the dark forest
On its own little quest.
The tiger tries all night,
Looking for a bite.
The tiger leaps —
Knowing the prey is his to keep.

The stripes of a tiger,
Are like the bars that strain a prisoner.
The tiger's legs are powerful and strong.
While its tail is long —
To balance its fall,
It's standing tall.

The call of the untamed,
With a roar that grants fame.
Snarling when there's danger,
To scare away the stranger.
From the mother to its cubs are moans of affection
At the end with love as a reaction.

Valerie Ho, Grade 5
Forcey Christian School, MD

The Mountain

The mountain is scary, stormy and old
as I climb the mountain it gets dark and cold
I'm cold I'm scared I wish I could be cozy
I want to go I want to flee oh I have so much fear in me
The spooks and critters scare me as I go
I just wish I could be at home.

Sylvan Moore, Grade 4
Blacksburg New School, VA

Soccer Ball
I am a new soccer ball.
I wonder when I'll get kicked.
I hear the dog barking.
I see people coming.
I want to be played with.
I am a shiny soccer ball.
I pretend to be on the pitch.
I feel the cleats kicking me.
I touch the wet grass.
I worry I'll get put away.
I cry because I might get lost.
I am a soccer ball.
I understand I might get replaced.
I say kick me around.
I dream to be shiny again.
I try not to cry.
I hope to be new.
I am an old soccer ball.
PJ LeBel, Grade 6
Page Middle School, VA

Laptops
I am a laptop,
I wonder who will type on me,
I hear the keys clicking,
I see my life,
I want to be free,
I am sick and tired of work,
I pretend to have a screen saver,
I feel fired and fried,
I touch that disk to make it run,
I worry I won't get used,
I cry when I'm not awake,
I am an old hard drive,
I understand I can crash,
I say I won't stop,
I dream I will get new software,
I try not to die from overload,
I hope to have a webcam,
I am a Macbook.
Ryan Chriscoe, Grade 6
Page Middle School, VA

Summer All Day
Summer is the time of year
That is hot and sweaty
And very sunny
You can swim and play
And laugh all day
Except for when it's a rainy day
You never read all day
Or write all day
You don't have to go to school all day
You can just sit back and relax all day
Taylor White, Grade 6
Seaford Middle School, DE

Hummingbird
It lands with a light touch
Then
She stops
She stares
She sees us
She's gone
Where'd she go
She flies so fast
    Faster than lightning
        Faster
        Slower
    Slower than anything
She flies so slow
NO
Her wings beat one hundred times
All in a second
She loves the wind
She loves it in her feathers
She is the hummingbird
Emma Carroll, Grade 5
Charles Barrett Elementary School, VA

Japan
Japan was nice
Japan was awesome
Until something happened
They had an earthquake
It was really bad
I was unhappy
I was really sad
It was devastating
People died
People were sick
People came to help
But it was hard to fix
They also had a tsunami
It messed up their origami
It ruined everything in its way
It messed up everybody's day
I hope they're ok
God will help them
Find a way
Aaron Budd, Grade 6
George E Peters Adventist School, MD

Spring!
Spring is here.
It's warm outside.

Spring break is near.
With fun filled days.

Spring is fun.
Fun on the front lawn.
Alexandra Saathoff, Grade 4
Courthouse Road Elementary School, VA

Marbles
One day a marble
Rolled along with its children.
"Okay" said the daddy marble
"Roll"

"Jessica?" "Here"
"Jacob?" "Here"
"Jeremy? Jimmy?"
"Jordan?"
All said here until…
"Jamal?" Silence
"Jamal?" Silence
Then Jessica rolled away,
So did the others
"ARRRR" "I'm losing my marbles"
Said the daddy marble.
Haley Gilday, Grade 4
Courthouse Road Elementary School, VA

Powered Up
Powering the first house with electricity
Flying the metal kite in the storm
Incinerating the key in the process
Watching the lightning strike
And travel down the string
Electricity had been invented
Seemed so rare
Powered up
Battery powering my wristwatch
Seems so normal
Hearing my radio playing
Turning on the lights
When I walk in the room
Powering the pencil sharpener
I use frequently
Seems so normal
Taylor Tucker, Grade 4
St Christopher's School, VA

Beauty of Spring
Flowers blooming with the
Clammy and broiling days
Birds chirping to the
Awakening of seed time
Bright green leaves
Growing upon trees
Ahh…don't you love spring!
No more cold bitter days,
Gloves, scarfs, and hats
All go away
Buzzing bees and bugs
All come around you to get some hugs
Everything's coming to life again in this
Cheerful season!
Fatima Kargbo, Grade 6
Magnolia Elementary School, MD

My Dad

He is kind.
He is considerate.
But the only thing wrong
Is that he is leaving.

He will be gone for a long time.
I will miss him very much.
He is going to Afghanistan.
I have fear that he might not come back.

He is also about 5'6" or 5'7"
He has black and grayish hair.
He also has a good heart.

Well after that there is only one thing to say
"That man is my Dad."

Tamara Masciola, Grade 6
St Columba School, MD

The Boat

The boat,
The coast guard of the sea
She tears through the clear blue water
Afraid of nothing
In her way
Her mast,
Clear as the sky,
Ruffling through the wind
Like a flag
The boat,
A conqueror of all waves,
Sailing
High above the wave
Making other sailors
Stop and look
At the beautiful boat

Fuller Wise, Grade 5
St Christopher's School, VA

Love Stinks

Love stinks if you just think,
it goes down a drain in the sink

People say love is gentle
like a white dove.

My heart is young and tender
my first love, I'll always remember

Love stinks and sinks till it's all
gone.

Love will always stink
just remember.

Ja'Qwaun R. Henderson, Grade 4
Featherbed Lane Elementary School, MD

Maryland

Spring, spring, spring is here!
Time for plants to grow is near.
Spring spring, lots of sun…
Spring will be a lot of fun.

Sun, rain, and love…
The main growth for our plants.
The plants get happy that we love them
So then they dance!
Raindrops pour near and far.
Take care of them…
Then they will shine like a star!

Spring, spring, spring is here,
Time for plants to grow is near!
Spring, spring, lots of rain…
This season is the main.

Hajah Conde, Grade 6
Western Heights Middle School, MD

Loneliness

It's lonely without her, I
can't stop thinking about her.

What should I do without
her? It's my Aunt I love

her to death. I'm so depressed
life is a mess. But I

realize it's okay because all
you have to do is pray. She's

in my heart and nothing
will keep us apart. She's

my one and only work of
art.

Arion Peterson, Grade 4
Featherbed Lane Elementary School, MD

Ice

Wraps around me as if holding me back,
from slipping and falling
on its slick path
I pull against its force
listening to the other children's laughter
Giggling and having a good time

I hear the scraping of the skates
against the brittle ice
And suddenly the frozen water loses its grip
and I fall through
as it cracks.

Rebecca Holsinger, Grade 5
Nottingham Elementary School, VA

Snowflake's Life

I am a snowflake
I wonder what the ground is like
I hear people yelling
I see snowflakes following me
I want to get played with
I am a happy snowflake
I pretend to dance in the sky
I feel a soft mitten
I touch a silky jacket
I worry I'm going to stick
I cry when I hear the door shut
I am a sad snowflake
I understand that I will melt
I say "I'm doomed."
I dream to play all day
I try not to cry again
I hope I won't melt
I am a brave snowflake

Alexandra Woller, Grade 6
Page Middle School, VA

A Brand New Book

I am a brand new book
I wonder if somebody will take me home
I hear cars outside
I see a kid run in
I want the kid to buy me
I am ready to leave this shelf
I pretend I'm not excited
I feel the kid grab me
I touch his sleeve as he runs with me
I worry he'll be rough with me
I cry because all my friends are here
I am lonely
I understand I have to be bought
I say I'm ready to go
I dream I'll be read a lot
I try to stay calm
I hope I am treated well
I am a book that has been bought

Christopher Glenn, Grade 6
Page Middle School, VA

Now and Then

I used to be afraid of talking to a crowd,
But now I love to talk out loud.
I used to drink milk,
But now I drink water or soda.
I used to play with toy trucks,
But now I play X-Box.
I used to play soccer,
But now I love to play baseball.
I used to not be able to read,
But now I read chapter books.

Conor Crook, Grade 5
St Christopher's School, VA

High Merit Poems – Grades 4, 5, and 6

I Am a Football Glove

I am a football glove,
I wonder if I will rip,
I hear the sound of the fans,
I see people trying to catch the football,
I want to catch the ball and score,
I am a football glove,
I pretend to be a NFL football glove,
I feel the whoosh of the wind,
I touch the football,
I worry that we will lose,
I cry when we win,
I am a football glove,
I understand that I might drop the football,
I say I scored every time I catch the football,
I dream I will go to the Super Bowl,
I try to catch every ball,
I hope to win,
I am a football glove

Kyle Kilby, Grade 6
Page Middle School, VA

Fall Comes Back

Sitting by the sea one day
The sun, the wind, and the spray
Left on my face about fall

I was walking in the park one night
I looked and saw the light
I had no idea the sky was so clear
Or that stars could shine so bright

I happened to be looking for the swallows
who brought fall plants
I happened to be resting by the willows
when the sun went down, leaves started scattering
How I wanted to share the beauty
In the air, I wish they were there too
See, feel, share the world around us
Now listen to raindrops beating against the windowpane
Fall is back!

Ise-Oluwa Dagnon, Grade 6
Magnolia Elementary School, MD

Tippy, Tippy

Tippy, Tippy is my cat,
No, I didn't find her in a hat.
Tippy, Tippy! I found her in a pound,
And without her my heart would not make a sound.

Tippy, Tippy knows when I am sick,
She tries to make me better with her sandpaper lick.
Tippy, Tippy sleeps in my bed,
Right on my pillow above my head.

Tyler Hurst, Grade 5
Lightfoot Elementary School, VA

Your Last Breath

Many hugs you are given
rushed out the door
children's tearing faces tear even more
the house dark with sadness
you don't know why
rushed into the car
Not knowing you will soon take your last breath

A car ride, oh yay
off you go
having fun until you see where you are headed
Not knowing you will soon take your last breath

No, not to the dreaded vet's
into a room with a nice comfy bed
1 shot
2 shots, fast asleep
people crying and weeping all the while as a 3rd shot is given
slowly you drift off into a never ending dream of black
never to come back
Never realizing you have already taken your last breath

Helen Laster, Grade 5
Claymont Elementary School, DE

New York City

As I walk through the transparent door
of my sister's apartment building,
sounds start shouting at me
like a fire drill at my school.
The horribly loud music and traffic
start popping my eardrums
as my Mom softly whispers in my ear.
As I feel the sand pebbles
rub against my shoes,
my Mom grasps my hand
because of heavy traffic.
The brick walls of the building
are as coarse as sandpaper
as they touch my smooth hand.
As I walk through the city,
swarms of people are moving in every direction
as I push my way through.
The Empire State Building's point looks
as sharp as the tip of my pencil.
Even though I can't see more,
I know I will return to New York City.

Joseph Tocco, Grade 6
Wyman Elementary School, RI

Waves

Waves are like a glistening wall coming over the water.
They inspire us and enable you to be greater.
As a world full of worries tears it away.

Ransom Castleberry, Grade 6
St John Neumann Academy, VA

Soldiers
Soldiers
Brave, courageous
Protecting, striving, assisting
Duel for our freedom
Heroes
Thomas Palmer, Grade 4
St John Neumann Academy, VA

Twins
Twins
two, identical
crying, annoying, loving
They are equally loved
Boys
Dalonte Lightfoot, Grade 6
Floyd T Binns Middle School, VA

Just Me
I see myself walking around this world
Seeing new things with lots of new dreams
Dancing on TV, reaching for stars
In my world I'm on top
Being the best I can be.
Karima Christine Magruder, Grade 6
Magnolia Elementary School, MD

Kinect
Kinect
Fun to play on
Dance Central is so fun
I feel very tired after that
X-Box
Elijah Ford, Grade 4
Waller Mill Fine Arts Magnet School, VA

Horses
horse
huge, smooth
riding, feeding, brushing
Horses are fun to be around
Stallion
Paige Hamilton, Grade 6
Floyd T Binns Middle School, VA

Birds
Birds
Colorful, nice
flying, stunning, cunning
They fly at fast as a race car
Cardinal
Tristan Huseby, Grade 6
Floyd T Binns Middle School, VA

Be Clean, Go Green
Our fish and crabs want to stay alive
Don't throw your waste in the bay.
Keep our water fresh
Learn to throw your trash away.

Let's all recycle
There would be less trash around.
Collect all your paper, plastic, and tin
So we don't have to put it in the ground.

Exhaust from cars, smoke from people
The world should really care.
Quit smoking and take a walk
Stop polluting our air!

Let's all pitch in
Keep the world clean.
Do your part,
Let's all go green!
Kendel Dorsey, Grade 4
St Clement Mary Hofbauer School, MD

Nature Knows
Nature can here you
all around it listens
when you first step
it sees you

The wind's its guide
to listen with you
to listen with me
listen to the wind

The trees they laugh
you can't hear them
but open your mind
and it's all clear

They tell a joke
and everyone smiles
you are so happy
because nature knows
Cassidy Pruitt, Grade 4
Courthouse Road Elementary School, VA

Football
Football is so much fun
Sometimes it gets really crazy
Then the refs call penalties for no reason
It will make you really mad
When they score, they are happy
It is sad when you lose
When you win you are happy
Well I only have a one game bye.
Jacob Perkins, Grade 4
Courthouse Road Elementary School, VA

Baseball
I like playing first.
There are two teams in baseball.
I like the Red Sox.
You use bats to hit a ball.
I like Alex Rodriguez.
Brett Bowden, Grade 4
Battlefield Elementary School, VA

Cousin Andy
I have a cousin named Andy.
He really loves to eat candy.
He turns on the light,
Then he starts a fight,
With his little sister named Sandy.
James Luong, Grade 5
St Clement Mary Hofbauer School, MD

Molly
I have a pet dog named Molly,
She is a lovely gold Collie.
She loves bowls of food,
When she's in the mood,
She jumps and is always jolly.
Jillian Toomey, Grade 4
St. Clement Mary Hofbauer School, MD

My Mom and Dad
Although, I love my mom and dad.
They always make me mad and sad.
We fight in the night,
We scream with our might,
We argue until we are glad.
Kaitlyn Heddinger, Grade 5
St Clement Mary Hofbauer School, MD

Brother Angelo
My dear weird brother Angelo,
He's tall and loves red Jell-O.
He gets mad at me,
When I charge him a fee,
Just to say goodbye and hello.
Elizabeth Gepilano, Grade 5
St Clement Mary Hofbauer School, MD

Little Brother
I have a brother named Tommy,
He always runs to Mommy.
He thinks he is cool,
I punch him in the pool.
He wrecks the house like a tsunami.
Charlie Pietruszka, Grade 5
St Clement Mary Hofbauer School, MD

Portrait of an Ermine

The ermine is pure.
Like snow it is white.
It scurries out
In both day and night.

With thirty-three teeth
And a long black-tipped tail,
It catches the lemming
Before it can wail.

It must hide in the Arctic
Every day.
To the snowy owl,
The ermine is prey

The ermine is inquisitive
Poking its nose in cracks.
Although it is short lived,
There is nothing it lacks.

It is winter.
The ermine is up and around.
Except for the shuffling of feet,
It makes no sound.
Michelle Lui, Grade 5
Forcey Christian School, MD

Hand to Hand

Hand to hand we give a stand
holding our flag to join the band
with black and white together as one
we are a family to man income

As for we are today we pray
in God's name we praise
we step it up for the heat
so we may get the beat

To make a change in history
to make a wave in the story
in our memories back in our time
to have us remember in our mind

In a club named boys and girls club
that helps hand to hand
so let's give a cheer to the band
then make a bow for you

To all good day to all good night
we have a bond we share
but you can change to make a wave
hand to hand we make a change
Nyah K. Courtney, Grade 4
Featherbed Lane Elementary School, MD

Summer Time

The cool breeze runs through
my face giving me time to think

I watch the flowers and trees
move very slow and calm

I stay relaxed and calm by a tree
thinking about no school

The melody of the ice cream truck
calms me down with a cool feeling

I feel so warm inside with a warm
summer day feeling
Favour Maduka, Grade 4
Featherbed Lane Elementary School, MD

Dragon Ball Z

Dragon Ball Z is my favorite show
I also can blast people in a row.

As characters are fighting
My fist is tightening.

And I can almost feel the flow
As the fighters go and go.

The Saiyans and Genus use their powers
But the girls don't pick any flowers.

They fight too and beat the boys
And they beat them with lots of joy.
Daesani Ali White-El, Grade 4
Featherbed Lane Elementary School, MD

The Great Game Soccer

The soccer ball had a great run
Even though it was not that fun
The ball was faster than light
It put up quite a fight

Soccer is a game that is as good as gold
It made the net fold
Swish goes the ball in the net
Like the goalie was its pet

The midfields ran down the side
Like they were on a never ending slide
They fight for the ball
And they make the other people fall
Alejandro Reed, Grade 6
Academy of International Studies, VA

A Brick

Brown with grass on top,
Maybe it's a crown,
Ants to drop,
Spiders down below,
Decaying a little more,
Getting low,
Low,
Lower until it's gone,
A rock on my back,
Now falling to sleep,
Just by looking at a brick,
No more time on the clock,
One two three,
Bye bye brick,
You're gone now,
So far away,
Deep in,
The ground.
Briana Little, Grade 5
Charles Barrett Elementary School, VA

The Fish I Knew

You are gone
I wish you were here

He swam my fish tank
I cleaned it up all the time
He ate a lot of fish food
I fed it to him
He has small fins
I have large hands
His name is Flip
My name is Joseph
I will always know him
He will always know me
He was my fish
I was his owner

You are gone
I wish you were here
Joseph Lindsay, Grade 5
Claymont Elementary School, DE

Tag

Running, hiding
Dipping, diving.
Dodge the trees
Skin my knees.
I hear footsteps
Crunching leaves
Snapping branches,
Through the grass.
I feel warm, sweaty hands touch my arm.
I turn around and run after her
Lucy Mangum, Grade 4
Immersion School, VA

Rain

The rain is wonderful
As it gently falls
All over this big earth

Spring rain is warm and soft
And to flowers and trees
Gives a brand new birth

Rain comes down in
A million little drops
Like a huge watering pot
I love rain and even the smell
I hope we get a lot.

Hannah Perkins, Grade 4
Mary Walter Elementary School, VA

Help Me

The hushed voice of the wind
blew through me

As my shadow disappears
my thoughts flash before my eyes

I try to pick the blossoms
but they fall through my hand

I am as clear as a window

I am a…
ghost

Savannah Davis, Grade 5
Francis Asbury Elementary School, VA

Paddleboats

I jump into a wet slippery paddle boat
And almost fall into the cold water,
But catch myself on the pedal
And pull myself up.
I sit down and start to pedal
I immediately take off.
The other paddle boats move
Like snakes in the jungle.
All of a sudden I lurch to a stop.
I look back and see a hook
Attached to two paddle boats.
I unhook it, paddle to shore, and dock.
I say to myself, "Till next time,"

Hunter Maxwell, Grade 6
Wyman Elementary School, RI

Spring

Animals come out
All flowers will start blooming
What beauty spring brings

Eleni Kataxenou, Grade 4
St Joseph School-Fullerton, MD

Racing

If I don't win, I ran a good race!
If I don't lose, it's because of my pace.
But I don't have any
Trouble to
Believe
That a boy
Like
Me
Could
Take
The
LEAD!

Jarred Barr, Grade 4
Barr Family Home School, VA

Feeling Blue

Sadness isn't a great feeling
The greatest sadness you could feel
Is when you lose someone
I lost a few loved ones
My dog Max
May have been just a dog
But I loved him

I lost my uncle when I was little
He and I were very close
But all I can say is that…
I MISS YOU!!

Cekiya McIver, Grade 6
St Columba School, MD

Friends

Friends are there when you need to talk
They show you the right way
When you are feeling down
They help you day by day.

Follow your mind and heart as one
And when your day is over
You will find you've just begun.

When you go to the mall with your friends
They help you find what to wear
And when you go home you will share.

Jadyn Whitsitt, Grade 6
St Columba School, MD

Middle School

Small red lockers, bigger kids,
longer classes including gym.
Louder bells and even stairs,
more drama ever before.
How could this year get any worse…
braces, isn't there a base to keep me safe.

Kristi Wyland, Grade 6
Monelison Middle School, VA

The Purple-White Bike*

So much depends
upon
The purple-white
bike
With a tire
flat
Speeding down the
sidewalk

Adia Davenport, Grade 5
Linwood Holton Elementary School, VA
*Patterned after William Carlos Williams

Fire Burns

Fire is evil and kind
Fire can be my enemy
Or my partner
Fire helped during World War I and II

Fire is hot
It lights our way to freedom
It is fiery and fast like a snake
Fire, why're you so mean?

Isaiah Ford, Grade 6
Magnolia Elementary School, MD

March's Events

March is a beautiful time of the year
Snow drifts off
Flowers start growing into colorful shapes.
Winter grows into spring.

March has beautiful things like
Flowers of all kinds
Sprout from the ground
And it's finally spring.

Alyssa Aldridge, Grade 6
Warwick Neck School, RI

Baseball

Baseball
Fun, exciting
Hitting, running, cheering
The ball is everywhere
Sport

Kenneth Tremper, Jr., Grade 5
St Joseph School-Fullerton, MD

Mexico

I see yellow and red casas,
And feel the gritty, white sand.
I hear the maracas shaking,
And smell the arros con pollo cooking.
I taste them with my mouth,
And they taste so bueno.

Lizeth Carreon, Grade 4
Crestwood Elementary School, VA

The Red Jacket

My favorite is the Red Jacket.
The refreshing splash explodes in your face
when you come to the end of
one of the giant water slides.
I hear the fun-filled screams of kids
going down the giant water slides.
I see them getting drenched
by the giant tipping bucket.
The hot tub tickles my body with warmth.
As I climb the spiral staircase,
leading up to the Crow's Nest,
I feel the humidity rising right before me.
Finally I reach the part
where I can see the whole hotel.
Now I'm ready for a delicious buffet
of pancakes, waffles, scrambled eggs,
and sausages.
The smell of these foods puts a smile on my face.
Oh, how I love the Red Jacket!

Shawn McMillan, Grade 6
Wyman Elementary School, RI

What I Love

I love to watch babies giggling gracefully,
And babies trying to talk triumphantly.

I love to smell the newly bloomed flowers,
And that smell of just blossoming flowers.

I love to hear a newborn baby's giggle
This sweet sound makes me feel
happiness, humor, and excitement.

I love to taste the juicy watermelon
Wash wonderfully down my throat
Swish, Gulp! Ahh!

I love to touch the silky hot sand between my toes,
Just like a hot bubble bath on a cold winter's night.

I love the way horses gallop along the horizon,
And how I fly gracefully on horseback in the wind on the beach.

Callahan CB Weber, Grade 6
Most Blessed Sacrament Catholic School, MD

As the Wind Blows

As the wind blows it gives me a kiss on my cheek
As the wind blows it whispers a song in my ear
As the wing blows it makes me feel like I'm walking on air
I can feel the wind blow through my hair
I am flying with the wind as it blows
Making me believe I'm anything, everything
The wind is always with you
As the wind blows.

Mary Schauf, Grade 5
Nottingham Elementary School, VA

Where Is the West?

One of many, yet alone
Patient, steadfast, strong
Sown by one who dreamed big dreams,
Of open lands, wild horizons, freedom.
Watered by untamed rivers,
Nurtured at the hand of the golden prairie sun
Sank its roots into red clay, just a seed
But still growing, into a fresh green sprout.
Unchanging, still they came, their dreams shining gold,
Sieving in the wild rivers,
Resting on the shore.
The giant brown beasts
Shaggy manes flying, forced to the ground
New arrival, sadness on the wind
Feathered heads walk, a trail of tears
Bent low like prairie grass on a windy day.
Crying for the buffalo, crying, for their home
The tree stood tall, looking upon the land,
Once as free as the Mississippi on a windy day, destroyed.
Gone.
Gone away with the West.

Victoria Peace, Grade 5
Charles Barrett Elementary School, VA

The Cry from the Midnight Forest

The sun has fallen, night has come
And it is time for the cries from the midnight forest
The lake starts to flow and the wind, it blows
The frogs chirp from the creek
The moon is bright the raccoons come out for night,
And the opossum hang on the tree
The whoos from the owl echo through the forest
Then they all start their scary chorus
And the bats fly high in the midnight sky
Through the tall grass the mice scurry
They all are in a hurry
To scamper away from the wolves
But the wolves, they stop
Their standing on their howling rock
Realizing that night is done
They tilt their heads back
Posture they lack
But let out a great AHOOOO!
Night is done
The sun has come
And morning has silenced them all

Macy Calder, Grade 6
Page Middle School, VA

The Chasing

A small girl runs through the woods on a misty Winter day
Pine needles scratch her tiny face like fire
Barefoot and dressed in rags she freezes slowly
Risking her life, she runs from something but doesn't know what

Kamryn Conner, Grade 5
Francis Asbury Elementary School, VA

Dark Goodness

I am delicious
I wonder if I will be eaten
I hear that I can be made into Reese's
I see kids wanting to buy me but their parents say no
I want to be eaten so much
I am dark
I feel like someone is watching me
I touch things around me
I worry that I will be in the trash half eaten
I cry when people walk past me and just look at me
I am creamy goodness
I understand that I will not be a Reese's
I say what a lovely day it is being bought or not
I dream to be eaten
I try to be perfect
I hope that someone knows I am here to be eaten
I am dark chocolate

Kayla Tobin, Grade 6
Page Middle School, VA

I Am a Ballet Shoe

I am a ballet shoe dancing around the stage,
I wonder if I ever stop dancing anyway,
I hear a thud thud as I run across the floor,
I see the ground as I leap through the air,
I want to be like a mouse tip toeing about,
I am posing for the picture,
I feel old, worn out, and used,
I touch the cold floor as I begin to dance,
I worry that the person will always step on my strings,
I cry as they pull on my strap,
I am a ballet shoe,
I understand what I do,
I say "ok let's do this thing,"
I dream of dancing all day and night,
I try so hard to dance my best,
I hope I do good in the ballet recital,
I am a ballet shoe dancing around the stage.

Olivia Jones, Grade 6
Page Middle School, VA

Perfect to Different

I am a beautiful stallion running in the fields,
I wonder if the eagles fly as fast as I run?
I hear the birds chirping,
I see the river running,
I want to swim with the fish.
I am the stallion that stays in the shadows,
I pretend I am invisible,
I feel as though I'm nothing.
I touch the hard ground,
I worry that I'm the only one here,
I cry at night because I am alone.
I am as black as the dark night,
I understand that I am different.
I dream that I am in the fields.
I try to find my way to the fields but fail.
I hope to be understood,
I am different.

Taylor Fletcher, Grade 6
Page Middle School, VA

Forest on a Winter Night

The night is still,
Forest is holding her breath.
The silver rays of moon so fair,
Stream through the delicate spindly branches
Unto the glittering crystals of snow.

Above the smooth sheer surface,
Of a glowing frozen pond
There looms the black silhouette of
A mighty olden tree.

From that great old oak,
A winged figure silently glides
Across the pale white moon
With black wings outstretched
And its lonely, shivering call
Whispers softly through the moonlit woods.

Helen Zhao, Grade 6
Robert Frost Middle School, MD

The Hockey Rink

I wake up at 6:00 in the morning to get to practice,
And my hands get a chill
From the cold metal doors. I tie my skates as other players arrive.
When I get on the ice,
I feel it under my skates.
I feel the splintering stick in my hand.
As I skate down the ice for a practice shot,
The puck gracefully comes off my stick
And goes in the net.
After practice, I can see myself in a game,
Going down for a shot and scoring,
But only until I return to the hockey rink.

Ty Morgan, Grade 6
Wyman Elementary School, RI

What I Love

I love to watch: a fun-filled football game,
you know, that one professional refs can't tame
I love to smell: the church's colorful candles,
but sometimes the fire cannot be handled
I love to hear: my cousin's hysterical jokes
and the comical laughter of senile folks
I love to taste: the soury sensation of a clementine
and the always-holy altar wine
I love to touch: the beach's soft, white sand
and the exotic silly bands
I love the way: my friends care for me
and how I get fabulous grades in school WHOOPEE!

Kexxer Camarco, Grade 6
Most Blessed Sacrament Catholic School, MD

Nature

A bird sings a song
Never getting a note wrong.

A river runs nearby
Trees reach up to the sky.

The sky holds up a bright blue
While displaying a sight I never knew.

The clouds float high in the air
The wind whips and turns in my hair.

Living life everywhere
Moving around from here to there.

I climb a tree so that I can see
All of the beautiful things the world can be.
Madeline Brown, Grade 6
St John Neumann Academy, VA

My Sports

I like to play baseball
I like to play basketball
I like to play football

I like to throw the ball
I like to shoot the ball
I like to run the ball

I want to go to the MLB
I want to go to the NBA
I want to go to the NFL

I like to watch baseball
I like to watch basketball
I like to watch football

I love sports
Drew Halsey, Grade 6
St Columba School, MD

Family Vacation

Oh boy it's here
My vacation's today
All I can say is
Hip, Hip, Hooray!

I'm going to the beach
And taking a big, good peach
A nice treat

My family is in the car
It's kinda dark at night
I saw a star

It was raining
I was really upset
This family vacation
Is a family situation!
Angeline Gaitan, Grade 4
Courthouse Road Elementary School, VA

An Ode to a Softball

Oh, softball
With your bright red lace

How you come
Dashing to my face

With you coming
Very fast

I try to make
The moment last

Even though
You're leather smelling,

The urge to hit you
Is still compelling
Catherine Henkel, Grade 4
Greenville Elementary School, VA

Alex!

Words cannot tell you why Alex is so cool.
Alex is a fast and focused runner.
Alex does not seem to me as a fool.
He is an awesome shooting game gunner.

He is a fan of the orange color.
He seems to hate a tabby sort of cat.
To me his tastes in things are no duller.
Never has he touched a baseball bat.

Alex seems to have a very loud shout.
He is like me, and loves playing outside.
In kickball, Alex always gets an out.
For Alex, school is a very fast ride.

Alex is an awesome and very good friend.
He'll always be there to give or lend.
Manish Singh, Grade 5
Monocacy Elementary School, MD

How to Get Ready for School

Go get dressed
With what you want
To wear,
Then skip to the bathroom
To fix your
Hair,
Go get your
Lunch box and put it in your
Sack,
Then go get your
Jacket from the closet rack,
Run to school
Or you'll be late,
Then sit in your chair
You've arrived at eight
So you're not late
For school.
Abigail Pereira, Grade 4
American International School, VA

Summertime

The summertime is a time to go and play,
It is also filled with nice warm days.
You can go play with a friend,
Plus swim over and over again.
Summer is hot and nice,
You might just need some extra ice.
Ice tea is delightful too,
Because you don't have to chew.
Birthday shoes and clues.
And a lot of time to snooze.
But when summer comes to an end.
Fall starts all over again!!!
Juatonia Waters, Grade 5
Lightfoot Elementary School, VA

Unicorn

I am a unicorn
All pink and white
I sit on a shelf.
I am shiny and bright.
Surrounding me
Are books and a toy,
And pretty rainbows
That bring me joy.
I am a unicorn
All pink and white
I sit on a shelf.
I am shiny and bright.
Rania Sakhi, Grade 4
Crestwood Elementary School, VA

I Am a Dog

I am a dog
All tall and white.
I'm good with kids
So I never fight.
All around me
Are brothers and sisters
What a big world
With Mrs. and Misters.
I am a dog
All tall and white
I'm good with kids
So I never fight.
Landon Moore, Grade 4
Crestwood Elementary School, VA

Winter

The blistering Christmas lights
On the days and beautiful nights
The Christmas trees and presents
Look oh so pleasant
The jingle bells ringing and everyone is singing
Everyone is full of delight and feeling all right
The glistening sheet of snow you never want to go away
Children blowing snowflakes
and roller skating on frozen lakes
Then the snow goes away
Because it's time for spring!

Jonathan Ebubedike, Grade 6
Magnolia Elementary School, MD

My Grandma

My grandma died when I was age 9.
I felt so sad like I had no mind.
I feel so sad and no I'm not glad.
But I feel better now
because she's an angel and now
my mom is so sad
it's like nobody's glad.
But now that she's in a happy place
she will be in my heart for love in faith.
She was brave, lovable, sweet, and smart
she was also beautiful and had a good heart.

Chyna Breshay Leggette, Grade 4
Featherbed Lane Elementary School, MD

Precious God

Precious God
Perfect in every way most loving, caring, forgiving.
He is our Kinsman-Redeemer
Without His only Son our life could have never begun.
This is why every song should be sung to show praise and gratitude.
Before His Son we all had attitude.
Now we can rejoice and holler.
As we begin to grow, we get taller and reach His majesty.
We must remember forgiveness cannot be bought with a dollar
because it is priceless.
Come to know this wonderful, precious God whom I serve.

Alejandra Calvache, Grade 5
Church of the Redeemer Christian School, MD

Writer's Block

not a single word
mind not clear for every thought
blank white screen staring you in the face, expressionless
cursor blinking on and off, not moving at all
no more words from me
now my cursor blinking on and off, not moving at all
way too many thoughts
because of that darned Writer's Block.

James Jones, Grade 5
Charles Barrett Elementary School, VA

Bleacher Creatures

Walking up the shallow stairs,
Headed towards section two hundred thirty-nine:
Destination, the famous stadium chairs,
Where the moment will be all mine.

The first pitch is thrown out,
The famous hitter cracks his bat;
All the fans scream and shout,
I will remember this moment from where I sat.

This stadium where all the greats
Took their place among the fates,
From Babe Ruth to Derek Jeter,
No other players could make it sweeter.

This is baseball at its finest,
Yankee Stadium —
In all its glory.

Griffin Clark, Grade 6
Cape Henry Collegiate School, VA

The Pit

Walking out onto the field
Is a great feeling.
As my feet sink into the dirt
It is easy to feel it in my cleats.
Diving into the outfield grass
Tickles my face.
As I grip the leather strips
Nervously on my way up to bat.
I swing at the strike
And then a wild pitch.
It hits me right in the leg.
It feels as if my brother's punching me.
When I hear the crack of the bat,
Everyone listens for the "Safe" or "Out."
The players then start hitting the fence with their hands.
I jog to base.
I see my coach give me the steal sign.
The pit is a magical place.

Garrison Potter, Grade 6
Wyman Elementary School, RI

Birthdays

A birthday is when you get a year older
Time for fun and a birthday cake
Maybe a party invite some friends over
This day is most certainly not a fake

Play with your present
Or watch a movie or play a game
Now don't go to bed right now
We most certainly don't want this day to be lame

Bethany Sechler, Grade 5
Whittier Elementary School, MD

Blue Oceans

The beautiful blue water glistens in the sun,
All the little children having so much fun.
The brown and yellow sand all on the ground,
All the people on the boardwalk walking around.

The perfect blue sky,
All the adults saying "Oh my."
The big white seagulls coming down for food,
Everybody's in a peaceful mood.

People playing in the water with colorful beach balls,
A drop of rain is about to fall.
It is night, all you see is stars,
It is so quiet, you can't even hear a car.

I love the ocean,
And all its beautiful motions.
This is a moment I want to keep,
Now I am laying in my chair fast asleep.

Baylee Jones, Grade 5
Rosemont Forest Elementary School, VA

My Teacher Is Missing

My teacher is missing I don't know what to do
I looked under her desk
I looked in the closet
I looked in the bathroom

I looked under the table
I looked in my backpack
I looked in the copier room
I even looked in a bowl of soup

I asked Mrs. Belako
But she was missing too
Everyone was missing
And I was the only one in school

I don't know what to do
I came to school and there was
Nothing to do
And to think it was really Saturday

Mia Shepherd, Grade 4
Courthouse Road Elementary School, VA

Sports

Sports are fun to play.
I practice so I can win games I play.

There are different sports I can play.
Easy sports or hard sports.

When I play I have a great time playing sports.
I wish I can play them every day.

Trevor Ferares, Grade 4
Courthouse Road Elementary School, VA

The Story of the Boy

There once was a boy
Who was really a toy.
Then one day he was very sad;
Because it was the worst day he had.
Then he looked up in the sky,
That was so very high.
There was a pot of gold at the clover field,
He went to the field and a pot of gold he did wield.
This story which his parents once told,
A boy who held a pot of gold.
The little boy used his gold for buying things that were very expensive,
But one of the shopkeepers was very tense.
He didn't mind him,
But the keeper tried to find him.
He escaped from the keeper,
That was the creeper.
That was the story of the boy,
Who was a toy.

Brandon Johnson, Grade 5
Lightfoot Elementary School, VA

The King of the Swamp

Here comes the alligator very green,
Shh! You don't want to be seen!
Here comes the alligator ready to attack.
Hide! Sprint! You don't want to be his snack.

The alligator's back is as sharp as a nail,
The alligator's jaws will never fail.
The alligator is as green as swampy water,
He's always hunting animals like a turtle or an otter.

The alligator's quickness is as quick as a flash,
You'll have to get a head start because he'll be there in a dash.
And when you've seen the alligator's claw,
You'll never tell anyone of what you saw.

The alligator can disguise himself as a log,
Gliding so silently across the bog.
Day and night, hunting and eating,
Let's see which animal the alligator's meeting.

Sam Bowlds, Grade 5
Forcey Christian School, MD

Remember Me!

Remember me as me,
not what you wanted me to be.
Remember me like the wind,
a happy version of hope, peace and joy within.
Remember my smile, my walk, my hips
My laughter like the sunshine on the tip of my lips
When I am gone
Remember all the happiness you gave to me

Rashonna Payne, Grade 6
Magnolia Elementary School, MD

The Snow

I open my eyes and crawl out of the cramped den
To my dismay, the ground is covered with a soft blanket of snow
The gray clouds above me swirl around and around
Suggesting more

My friends and neighbors are celebrating
But I know that with this comes lack of prey
Huddling in that ever-cramped den with mother, father and my 27 siblings

The days draw longer
Sounds of the wild cease as the snow is built up by storm after storm

I feel as if I am trapped in a box of ice never to escape this horrible silence, bone numbing cold, and loneliness.

At last the sun peaks out from the horizon as if checking for enemies that were never there and rises high in the sky realizing that it is safe to spread its warmth without the presence of those horrible deep gray clouds

I rejoice as I know that my fur will be warmed by the sun's friendly rays, until the cycle starts again.

Matt Hall, Grade 5
Nottingham Elementary School, VA

What I Love

I love to watch: Barbaric waves bubble as they beat the sandy shore of Ocean City
    Glamorous movie start strut down the red carpet in dazzling dresses

I love to smell: Roses as the morning dew drizzles off the soft scarlet petals
    The fresh, honeysuckle filled humid summer air

I love to hear: The joyous triumphs of laughter from all ages
    The early dawn birds chirp as if celebrating their very own song

I love to taste: The salty summer air at the State Line Beach
    The first juicy crimson red watermelon of the summer

I love to touch: The chilly pool water on a summer's humid day
    The crisp pages of a new unused book from Barnes and Noble

I love the way: Children laugh, run and play without care on the gigantic Ocean Pines playground
    A rainy day beseeches you to leisurely spend your day

Clare Riley, Grade 6
Most Blessed Sacrament Catholic School, MD

Fall

Leaves falling
    Falling
        Falling
Leaves turning pink and yellow
  To brown, red and orange.
Days getting shorter as we speak, getting darker colder like a cloud staying over the sun forever
Decorating pumpkins, scary and funny all of the costumes and faint yells for candy
The pools closing forever
The best of all seeing the hot summer go away

Sophie Bracy, Grade 5
Nottingham Elementary School, VA

When Winter Will Come

I am a leaf and
I wonder when winter will come
I hear the wind coming so I know winter is near
I see the other leaves changing colors
I want to be as pretty as them
I am scared so
I pretend that I don't, but
I feel the crisp air
I touch the ground as the wind softens and
I worry if insects are close
I cry because when winter comes, I will die
I am staying strong because
I understand that winter is coming and
I say to myself, "It'll be okay" and
I dream of living forever
I try to not look at all the negative things
I hope that I stay strong because
I am a leaf

Maddie Manalac, Grade 6
Page Middle School, VA

I Am a Tank

I am a tank,
I wonder if I will get blown up?
I hear the clank, clank of my treads.
I see explosions and craters all over the ground,
I want to be a car; nice and safe,
I am a tank,
I pretend that I am not on the battlefield,
I feel the rough ground,
I touch mud and dirt,
I worry that I might get pummeled by artillery,
I cry rounds of bullets,
I am a tank.
I understand that the enemy fears me,
I say to myself I will survive,
I dream that someday there will be peace,
I try not to think about it,
I hope to live through this war,
I am a tank.

Benjamin Gibbs, Grade 6
Page Middle School, VA

Daddy, Come Home

She fell asleep on a cold winter night,
Excited for the very next morning to soon arrive,
For her father would come back home
From spending over a year working in Rome.

When she awoke, her father was standing atop her bed
With waffles, and pancakes, and cinnamon bread.
She leaped up, screaming with joy.
She said, "Daddy, I missed you!"
He said, "I missed you more!"

Nicole Krykanov, Grade 6
Cape Henry Collegiate School, VA

June

The flowers swaying in the breeze,
The ripples of water as I sneeze.
The birds chirping in the trees,
That's the month of June.

The water splashing on my feet,
The grass that feels like the sun's heat.
The blooming flowers by the street,
That's the month of June.

The wind blowing through my hair,
The natural smell of the air.
The trees growing without a care,
That's the month of June.

My birthday cake with icing on top,
The smell of vanilla I wish wouldn't stop.
A piece of cake landing in my mouth with a plop,
That's my favorite month of June.

Simran Rijhwani, Grade 5
Norfolk Collegiate Lower School, VA

Polex the Cat*

I am a cat.
I wonder when I will get my food.
I hear the sounds of children playing in the yard.
I see my master pet me.
I want attention.
I am a cat.
I pretend to be bad.
I feel very small.
I touch the scratching post.
I worry about my master.
I cry when I don't get what I want.
I am a cat.
I understand my master.
I say meow like a machine.
I dream about a cloud bumping into a mountain.
I try to be cute.
I hope that he does not leave me alone.
I am Polex the cat.

Joseph Howell, Grade 6
Page Middle School, VA
*Dedicated to my cat

Puppy

Puppy cuddles in my warm hands
Sleeping in the warm soft sofa
With a deep understanding
That I like sleeping in my owner's lap
The smell of the popcorn
Makes me want to eat the warm food
But I know that I can't have that buttery popcorn
Instead I will go and get my own food.

Delilah Morritz, Grade 5
Charles Barrett Elementary School, VA

I Am
I am the next generation
I wonder does the world have a place for me
I hear opportunities on my path
I see the future awaiting for me
I want an education
I am the next generation

I pretend that I have no flaws
I feel magical
I touch my future
I worry about the world
I cry because I feel saddened
I am the next generation

I understand that I'm not perfect
I say that education is the key
I dream of a better world
I try to take part in the world
I am the next generation
Tatyana Dowell, Grade 6
Ruffner Middle School, VA

Dr. D's Dilemma
Wanting to help this kid,
but knowing I can't.
I walk the hallway with
that musty smell that punches
me in the face every time
I take a breath.
It's hard to focus, as I feel
The carpet under my feet
cradling my every step.
Chris speaks up out of his
Rundown jaw.
I appreciate his effort, but
I can almost feel the money
In my hands, the soft paper
rubbing on my tender palms.
My mouth starts watering, like
I have not eaten in a week,
and I imagine ordering up from
Shin Hoo's on the top floor.
Hart Mankin, Grade 5
Flint Hill School, VA

The Flower
A flower with petals
Glistening
In light
Drip drip water falls
Stem soaks soil water
Children walk past flower
While it stands in ground
With stems
Isabella Fogg, Grade 5
Charles Barrett Elementary School, VA

Colors of Spring
I watched out the window,
Drinking everything in,
The colors of spring.

I saw everything,
I became it,
Part of the colors of spring.

I knew the flowers,
The animals coming out,
Adding to the colors of spring.

I couldn't miss it,
Not for anything,
The natural beauty of the colors of spring.

I recognized the beauty,
That wouldn't last for long,
The colors of spring.

I will know it forever,
In my heart,
Always appreciating the colors of spring.
Alexandrea Pouliot, Grade 6
Warwick Neck School, RI

Memories
Memories are times
that are fun
that are sad
that are loving
some are bad.

Memories are sometimes the best
others are not
some are hard
others are not

Memories are times that you remember
family, friends,
good times, bad times,
funny times, strong times.

Memories can be
sad, good
odd, frustrating
but memories are memories

but you can't change memories
they are a part of you
Marcus Johnson, Grade 4
Featherbed Lane Elementary School, MD

Monkeys
Monkeys
Exciting, mischievous
Jumping, climbing, eating
Crazy wild banana eaters
Mammals
Dominique Green, Grade 4
Hebbville Elementary School, MD

Horses
Horses
Big, brown
Challenging, daring, neighing
Trot silently in pastures
Four-legged
Hannah Jackson, Grade 4
Hebbville Elementary School, MD

City Coast
There was a place called City Coast,
There lived a boy who liked to boast.
It's by the river,
People would shiver,
But he had a house made of toast.
Nicholas Bosi, Grade 4
St Clement Mary Hofbauer School, MD

Hockey
Gretzky is awesome.
Sydney Crosby's amazing.
Capitals are great.
Tim Thomas is a goalie.
The Verizon Center's big.
Jeremy Kleczkowski, Grade 4
Battlefield Elementary School, VA

Dog
Dog
Fluffy fur
They drink water
They run and play
Puppy
Katelyn Waddell, Grade 4
Battlefield Elementary School, VA

Winter
Snow is on the ground.
It is cold and bright outside.
The town is silent.
Hot chocolate every day.
Winter's extraordinary.
Connor Dunlop, Grade 4
Blacksburg New School, VA

High Merit Poems – Grades 4, 5, and 6

Tiger
Waiting in the brush
A tiger ready to pounce
His heart a-thumping
Christian Banks, Grade 6
Page Middle School, VA

Critics
Critics' words are like weapons
If they were to make an army
They would win every war.
Maxx Polk, Grade 6
Page Middle School, VA

Gummy Bear
Melting, squishing, popping
Sticking, dancing, singing
I like the gummy bear song!
Anthony Comegna, Grade 5
St Clement Mary Hofbauer School, MD

Beaches
Sand so hot and dry
Then I play in the cold sea
Water is splashing
Hannah Fleenor, Grade 4
St John Neumann Academy, VA

Shark Food
I splash at the beach
A fin floats leisurely by
The shark looks hungry
Colin O'Brien, Grade 6
St John Neumann Academy, VA

Brackish Water
Brackish water, yuk!
Don't you drink it! You'll be sick!
Brackish water, yuk!
Aliyah Kubli, Grade 4
Waller Mill Fine Arts Magnet School, VA

The Pond
They lay in the pond
They want you for their breakfast
You had better run!
Ayreanna Smith, Grade 6
Monelison Middle School, VA

About Snow
The cold white rain falls
Touching to the ground gently
It's softly snowing
Christopher Milligan, Grade 6
Monelison Middle School, VA

Where Poetry Hides for Me
Where poetry hides for me,
In the slow soft melody of my piano,
In the gooeyness of a slice of pizza,
In the sirens wailing softly in the night,
In the awe of the crowd as you defy gravity with a one-legged tornado kick.

Poetry hides for me,
In the slow hum of the radio,
In the low scritch of my pillow,
In the darkness under my bed.

Poetry hides for me,
In the crack of the bat as you hit a softball,
In the security of knowing there is a bat next to the couch,
In the soft breeze on a crisp, fall day,

That is where poetry hides for me!
Emma Santee, Grade 6
The Compass School, RI

Where Is God?
A Japanese man crying rivers for his lost wife says, "Where is God?"
But God is there.
An orphan who has no one to love him says, "Where is God?"
But God is there.
A weak, sickly woman lies in a hospital bed and says, "Where is God?"
But God is there.
A weary, dusty soldier missing his family at Christmas says, "Where is God?"
But God is there.

Where is God?
God is in the luxurious light of the stars.
Where is God?
God is in the horse's fast, powerful run.
Where is God?
God is in the giant, crashing waves beating against the sand.
Where is God?
God is with us all in our hearts.
Kathryn Irene Amar, Grade 5
Church of the Redeemer Christian School, MD

Ode to the Earth
Ode to the earth that keeps us cool in the summer and keeps us warm in the winter.
Ode to the earth that provides water and food from its rich soil.
Ode to the earth for giving us wind to fly kites in the spring.
Ode to the earth that gives us joy within.
Ode to the earth that makes snow for us to make snowmen.

Ode to the earth that gives us warm sunshine.
Ode to the earth that gives us green grass.
Ode to the earth that provides rain when there is drought.
Ode to the earth that lets us put our belongings on it.
Thank you, earth, for everything!
Christina Collins, Grade 6
Homeschool Plus, VA

Bacon

Bacon, bacon, I'm in love with bacon.
By the sound of my voice you know I'm not faking.
I eat bacon every night and day.
I even eat bacon while laying in the hay.
I got to school with my bacon in my hand;
My friend asked for a piece and I panicked and ran.
I came back later and she said, "Where's your bacon?"
I said sorry girl, "It's already been taken."

Bacon, bacon so good to eat.
To me bacon is a yummy treat.
Bacon, bacon how can this be.
My refrigerator is empty so I went and sat in a tree.

Monique Ferguson, Grade 5
Lightfoot Elementary School, VA

The Beach

As I take my first step onto the never-ending sea
Of the warm, sun-burnt sand,
It grabs my toes.
I hear the seagulls' disturbing cries for food.
I run for the monstrous waves,
The size of the Empire State Building,
Crashing fiercely along the coast.
I walk in,
And the little ripples from the waves
Trickle up my legs.
As I get deeper,
My curls disappear into long, wet strands of hair.
I love going to the beach in California!

Elizabeth Blanchette, Grade 6
Wyman Elementary School, RI

Green

Green tastes like fresh green apples
Green smells like ripe green grapes
Green sounds like green leaves rustling in the wind
Green feels like the soft grass on my feet in the summer
Green looks like a four leaf clover
Green makes me glad
Green is my favorite color

Jared Mazzulla, Grade 5
St Mary School, RI

Snowflakes

The snowflakes fall and float
Just like they are on the water in a sailboat
It's like they are saying hi
As they softly float by

They float down on your face to feel like a kiss
Something I would never want to miss
I wonder what it would feel like to be snowflakes
To fall softly on the ponds and lakes

Courtney Haynes, Grade 6
Corkran Middle School, MD

Egypt's Freedom

On February 11, 2011
Hosni Mubarak resigned from power.
The people protested for him to go down,
Over his people he would no longer tower.

As buildings burned and people shouted,
Several men tried to protect
The museum that held ancient artifacts,
Each one of these things a precious object.

Mubarak intended to transfer his power
But no one agreed, and on went the flame.
He then decided to release his control,
And now Egypt's ruling will not be the same.

Millions rejoiced as Mubarak stepped down.
They danced and they sang and they beat on their drum.
A new Egypt's coming
A great future has come!

Claire Morris, Grade 6
St John Neumann Academy, VA

She

She used to have a light in her eyes
Until she found out that he was all lies
She has been caused a great amount of pain
Even though she looks happy, she will never be the same
She had a smile that could light up an entire room
It doesn't seem like she will be happy anytime soon
She used to wake up every morning loving life
Now she occasionally wonders what if she took that knife
She was so in love with an immature boy
Who didn't love her only thought of her as a toy
She made him her entire world
Now she asks, why Lord?
She is beautiful with an amazing heart
It's a shame that one boy tore all of that apart
She is slowly picking up the pieces
Even though it is him that she misses

She will one day be herself again
And her sun will shine after all this rain.

Nahela Castro, Grade 6
Corkran Middle School, MD

Culturefest

My friends join me as I walk to the fire
In the foggy mist of the night. As I walk
back to the dining hall I listen to the lone cello
player, with few audience surrounding. I get to the
dining hall and find two police men sitting drinking
coffee. I sit looking out the rainy window. As I sit I listen
to a guitar being played by an old man. I lay down on an old stained
couch, close my eyes, and fall asleep.

Eli Nachlas, Grade 4
Blacksburg New School, VA

High Merit Poems – Grades 4, 5, and 6

In the Wind

I see, I see…her face in the light fog
I try to reach for her face but then a slight gust comes,
she's gone then after awhile she's back,
then she says, "this"
then I reach for her face
and the wind washes her away
and then I gave up hope on getting to her and
then she's back, she says, "poem" and she's
in the wind…and then I hear her voice in the distance
I heard her say, "is," then I run for her deeper into the fog
and then I'm as good as lost.
then I heard her telling me to, "come to her"
so I do.
I see her face in the fog and she says
"awesome," that confused me, then I found her,
I said you're trying to tell me something
then I said this…poem…is…awesome and that's all that
she said, then I hugged my mom that was in the wind.

Dale Whorley, Grade 6
Monelison Middle School, VA

My Mother and I

My mother is a garden right in the middle of bloom
I am a trouble maker sent to my room

She is always joking
I am always fake-choking

Her smile is as bright as gold
I never do what I am told
Always laughing, I hear from her room
I will love until I am laid in a tomb

She is my wonderful mom
I am Rhys, a ticking bomb

Together
We are a team forever
My mother

Rhys Newcombe, Grade 5
Claymont Elementary School, DE

Summer

How I love when summer begins,
When I feel like I want to give a huge grin.
When there's a freedom in every day.
When nobody tells you what to do or say.
When you can stay up and sleep in as late as you want
and you can go and take a nice peaceful jaunt.
Being away as long as it takes you,
not caring about who says what, about what you do
Feeling that you always want to sing
Facing no dilemma(s)
In the peaceful, and fun times of summer.

Celena Gallardo, Grade 6
St Columba School, MD

Dakota

Dakota is not a state
It is not a place at all
I always laugh when I see him,
running down the hall
He's a big beggar
Waiting for it to fall
watching our every move
listening for the slightest call
His type is a rotty
Then add a little bit of lab
Now you've got the combo
to make any family glad
His colossal head
just flinging everywhere
as he flops into your lap
he makes sure you know he's there
This dog I love today
I know when you meet him
No matter what he does
you will love him anyway

Sydney Courville, Grade 6
Paul L Dunbar Middle School for Innovation, VA

I Am a Little Plane

I am a little plane
I wonder if I will ever take off
I hear other planes rumbling
I see people coming
I want to take off
I am a little plane

I pretend I am in the air saying "Hello" to the sun
I feel my engines roaring
I touch the baggage cart
I worry I will never take off
I cry that people are waiting for me
I am a little plane

I understand I have to wait
I say please don't fret to my passengers
I dream I can feel the clouds
I try to push from the gate
I hope I will leave soon
I am a little plane

Michael Weinstein, Grade 4
Seventh District Elementary School, MD

Spring

S now cones with colors of red, blue and purple
P eople lined up in front of the ice cream truck
R odeos and BBQ with food and entertainment
I ndigo, fuchsia, red, blue, pink and yellow flowers bloom
N ew clothes like t-shirts and shorts
G reat time to have fun with friends!

Gabrielle Sorresso, Grade 5
Nottingham Elementary School, VA

The Kid Who Had Big Ears

There was a kid who had big ears,
He was as small as a twinkle walking on a pier.
The mother always called him a very rude name.
It made him sometimes feel ashamed.
He always hears with his ears,
While others think they're the three musketeers.
While they were bullying him,
He kept thinking about kicking them,
He knows he is the smallest one of all,
But it does not hurt him at all.
When he shows he will fit in with everyone else,
Everybody will be happy with themselves.
But not everyone will be happy,
Some will even be extremely sappy.
After a couple of days,
People will be pleased in their own ways.

Bryce Matthews, Grade 5
Lightfoot Elementary School, VA

Baseball

When you play a sensational game of baseball,
It helps to be very athletic and tall.
When the ball is plummeting for our face,
You must move in extremely fast pace.

When you complain when the game is not fair,
It makes you want to pull out your hair.
When you're running toward the third base,
You want to slide into home and put dirt in their face.

When you are up at bat,
Make sure that fast ball doesn't go splat.
I hope the ball flies by me and hits the catcher,
So they don't carry me out on the stretcher.
The most exciting part of the game,
Is hitting a home run because you won't be the same.

Korey Spicer, Grade 5
Lightfoot Elementary School, VA

Sheet of Glass

The pond is a sheet of glass
It reflects the sun, clouds, birds and anything above it
The sheet of glass is silent
As you watch it you will hear a trickle
You follow your ears until you see a babbling brook
You see the water dancing upon the rocks and pebbles
The reflection of the sun almost blinds you
As you observe it, the night sky unfolds
It is dark
You look up and see a black canvas splattered with diamonds
Spotted with one crystal
And as you walk away
You notice in the sheet of glass
The light of the crystal and your reflections of the day

Ashley E. Hurd, Grade 6
John Bassett Moore School, DE

The Beach

I hear the water splashing against the soggy wet sand.
I also hear the seagulls crying as if they haven't eaten in days.
I hear the fish jumping in and out of the salty sea
Like they were playing a game of tag.
As the waves come over to me,
I accidentally swallow a gulp of salty water.
As soon as I get out of the overwhelming waves,
I go to my colorful towel
And grab a handful of Doritos that taste so cheesy.
I finally get the salt water out of my taste buds.
When I walk back to the water,
I can smell the greasy lotion all over people's bodies.
I can also smell the tiny spectacles of salt in the big blue ocean.
Oh, how I can't wait to go back to the
Ocean with its overwhelming waves and giant sunshine
Beaming on me!

Amanda Messier, Grade 6
Wyman Elementary School, RI

Flying

Feeling free,
As still winds arose,
Feeling as if I have flown.

I let the still winds of time start up as I fly,
Hooves flash beneath me as the sky of our world passes,
I think as if in a dream,
Time stands still and for that one moment,
That single moment,
I feel as if I can fly.

The beauty of the horse is released,
The freedom of riding spreads,
As I fly,
On the majestic horse.

Claire Robertson, Grade 6
The Langley School, VA

Bunny Rabbit

I have a bunny rabbit named Fluffy
I named him that because he is soft, and puffy
I also have a cow named Bess
She never makes a mess
Me, Fluffy, and Bess live on a farm
And we play on the tractor, but do not get harmed.
One day Fluffy ran away. Our town searched for him day, after day.
I found Fluffy in a town nearby
And I wondered why?
Why would Fluffy be over there?
Did he get attacked by a bear?
So, I brought Fluffy back to the house
Where everything was quiet, even the mouse
Fluffy, and I then lay down in my bed
All cozy, and on pillows we lay our heads

Alexis Lashbaugh, Grade 5
Cresaptown Elementary School, MD

Ode to My Kitten

Oh Pepper, with silken fur so black,
I'll rub your tummy when you roll on your back.

Feral yellow eyes, wild secrets you keep,
Except for the 22 hours you sleep.

So high you fly, how are you able?
It's kind of funny when you miss the kitchen table.

Dangerous carnivore, who loves to eat meats,
It's cute how you always beg for treats.

Retractable claws — one touch makes me scream OUCH!
Mom will have you de-clawed if you scratch the couch.

Fierce predator, dreaming of creatures to bite,
You're adorable asleep on my pillow tonight.

Angie Aleman, Grade 6
Most Blessed Sacrament Catholic School, MD

The Drawing

Scribble, scribble, scribble. I finished the head.
When that was done, I went to bed.
Then I woke up to hear the drawing say,
"I'm so lonely…I need something to play."
So I drew the body and drifted back to sleep.

But wake again to hear the drawing moan,
"I don't have a home and I'm all alone."
I think and think of what to draw.
I draw a park with a huge seesaw.
But surprisingly don't drift back to sleep.

I draw another person running,
like a cheetah with lots of speed, gunning,
and went back to sleep so happily.
Wondering who the drawings could be?
They were my brother and me.

Dorian L'Etoile, Grade 6
Burrillville Middle School, RI

Rolex

Rolex the horse —
handsome, black, elegant
trots around the ring,
water dripping from his wet nostrils
as he chomps at the bit in his mouth.

His tall, sleek and shining body is beautiful to behold
when his hooves tick and tock,
prancing around the ring.
His body shines like a gold Rolex watch.

After his lesson and rub-down,
peppermint and leather smells strike me
as I walk down the isle towards his stall.
He whinnies and kicks his door
in anticipation of the minty treats
he knows that I am bringing for him.

Parrisa Anvari, Grade 6
Trinity School, MD

My Grandmother's Tree

My grandmother had a cherry tree,
She was as proud of it as she was of me.
The tree was towering, tough, and tall,
Beside it, I looked very small.

The tree was a champion, the biggest in the county,
In the spring, it yielded a pure white bounty.
The beautiful, blooming blossoms were one gigantic cloud,
It whispered in the wind, always quiet, never loud.

The blossoms came and went, like her time on earth passed by,
Both lives were too short, and I wondered why.
The sweet aroma and petals, velvety as a fawn,
Gave a glimpse of life before it was gone.

The last time I saw the blossoms drop, I wept,
At the thought of my grandmother and her memory I kept.

Noah Adams, Grade 6
Trinity School, MD

Poor

Looking in the garbage can for food.
Thinking about the restaurants you use to go to.
Listening when people laugh.
You look at the families walk by.
Remembering where your family was.
Sitting on the street with an empty cup asking people for money.
Knocking on people's doors asking for food.
You remember the times you played with your friends.
You all grow up but you are the only one that is poor.
You pray every night for someone to help you.
But you realize…
You are not the only poor person.

Valeria Schwartz, Grade 5
London Towne Elementary School, VA

Water Wiz

As I run from my car,
I wonder what today will bring.
As I get closer to the entrance,
I notice the long, curvy line
Which looks like a snake making its turn.
I see a huge curly slide,
And I hear the wind whistling in my ear.
As I start to walk in,
Kids are shoving me from one place to the other.
It's that time.
I have to leave
From the best place in the world.

Destiny Barcelos, Grade 6
Wyman Elementary School, RI

Looking Out the Window
I watch the wind blow,
Making the trees sway side to side.
Some of the leaves shimmer
And try to stay attached to the tree
As if they were riding a roller coaster
And were hanging on for dear life
Others fall one by one
Like old Halloween decorations
That slowly disappear
For it is no longer October 31.

The jack-o-lantern's smile is now wrinkling,
Like an old man's face
Aging faster than it should.

Spider webs shiver cold in the brisk fall wind.

I wait and wonder
When Thanksgiving will finally arrive.
Ian Chalk, Grade 6
Trinity School, MD

Saving Today's Environment
Problems that we have all created
We need to stop littering and making waste.
For many it is surely not appreciated
As one day it will hit us all in the face.

If we all pull together and take some action
As we all know the air is thick with ugly smog.
There could be no better satisfaction
Everyone should pitch in and get your head out of the fog.

Now is the time to read and try all resources
We the humans must try to keep our natural wealth.
Or in the end there will be hard courses
Or by God it will eventually affect our health.

We all need to work hard and do our bit
Don't pollute, dispose of waste properly and all will be fair.
As one day we will all realize we are killing it
In hopes that one day, all will work together and really care.
Joey Kulikowski, Grade 4
St Clement Mary Hofbauer School, MD

Blue
Blue tastes like bleu cheese.
Blue smells like my favorite slushy.
Blue sounds like a blue jay chirping high in the sky.

Blue feels like a splash of water on a hot day.
Blue looks like a clear sky on a sunny day.
Blue makes me feel happy.
Blue is my favorite color.
Nicholas Sloat, Grade 5
St Mary School, RI

Waiting for the Bus That Will Never Come
I sit down on the stone cold bench,
Waiting for the bus.
In the rain or in the snow, I never do forget to go,
Waiting for the bus.
Some days I just sit there and weep, other days I jump and leap,
Waiting for the bus.
Sometimes I think the bus has forgotten this lonely little stop,
While I'm waiting for the bus.
I hope one day it will remember me,
Waiting for the bus.
I guess I am too ignorant to see that the bus will never come,
Even though I still wait for the bus.
The driver seems to steer the bus away from me,
I still wait for the bus.
I keep my faith and wait and see, if the bus remembers me.
I'll just keep on waiting for the bus that will never come.
Mary Claire Hollinger, Grade 6
Ravensworth Elementary School, VA

The Lion
The lion is as calm as the new fallen snow.

The lion is very large
    with hair all over.
    His mane is as red as rubies.
He is sitting in a forest
    with mud and grass all around.

His paws are huge
    with talons as sharp as knives.
He has a long tail
    and beautiful tan fur.
His fur coat is as dirty
    as a pig sty.

He sits there like he is on a throne as a king of the jungle.
Lucas Keighton, Grade 5
Blacksburg New School, VA

Ways of Life
This is not a poem about love
Or giving a description of a dove.

Instead this poem is about a certain way to live
Which is being able to forgive.

One way is to follow the Ten Commandments.
That is what gives Christians guidance.

Another way is to understand the bad and the good.
Everyone would do it, if they could.

Even though you can't do it perfectly,
You can try if you're pure enmity.
James Georgieff, Grade 6
St Clement Mary Hofbauer School, MD

My Dog Buster
My dog's name is Buster
He is very kind and sweet
When I look at him, my eyes have a luster
He loves to eat, treat after treat
One time he had an allergic reaction
I was heart broken and afraid
A midnight vet run was the action
That solved the problem, my fear allayed
Now he is better, he plays with his toys
He is happy and wags his tail
He loves to sit inside with the boys
But if first outside, he often leaves a trail
Sometimes he is a little bad
That's why I love him like mad
Ben Papa, Grade 6
Immaculate Heart of Mary School, MD

Dreams
When I am warm in bed,
I close my eyes and dream,
I fly and touch the clouds,
And see the shooting stars,
I fly and fly some more,
Until I find the cities of jewels,
Past the amethyst villages,
Past the pearl cities,
I find that the sky is silk,
As I find the soft cloud beds,
I feel much comfort,
And as I wake up, I think,
I love to dream
Molly Vaughan, Grade 6
Page Middle School, VA

Where Peace Flows
Peace flows through the breeze
And more follows down the river
But where peace flows, is not a mystery
I know we need the peace
To settle our ever moody hearts
Jessica Connelly, Grade 6
Monelison Middle School, VA

Green
Green tastes like Granny Smith apples.
Green smells like freshly cut grass.
Green sounds like the crunch of
mint chocolate ice cream.

Green feels like winning the lottery.
Green looks like a four leaf clover.
Green makes me feel good.
Green is great.
Peter Remka, Grade 5
St Mary School, RI

The Beauty of the Earth
From the shining sun
to the gentle hum
of the leaves' rustle in the wind.
From the silver moonlight
to a star-filled midnight
and places light has never been.

From the glowing fish
at the bottom of the sea
to the colorful birds
at the highest of trees.
And even the strangest of creatures
with ugly, horrid features
and even the flightless of birds…

…This unusual sight
brings joyous delight!
Oh, this is the beauty of Earth!
Alexa Castro, Grade 6
St Columba School, MD

The Torch
I am a lighted Torch
I wonder why people light me
I hear the crackling of the fire
I see the dark caves and light the way
I want to be free as a bird
I am a flaming Torch
I pretend to be the light to lead
I feel like I am burning blue
I touch the soft hand of a humans
I worry I will be put out
I cry when I die down
I am a dimming Torch
I understand I will die
I say please light me again
I dream I will be light again
I try to last long
I hope to be lit again
I am a dead Torch
Nathan Schultz, Grade 6
Page Middle School, VA

Spring
Spring is here and
It's as if a blanket of all things
Wonderful is wrapped
Around you and making you feel safe.

Time to plant
As the sap of a maple
Drips down the bark and
Lands on a new born flower
Spring is here; rejoice
Ann Wajda, Grade 6
Warwick Neck School, RI

Spring!!!
Birds chirping
Children playing
Picking flowers
These are some things that make spring
Looking for…
Easter eggs
And four leaf
Clovers and flowers

Find an egg
Pick it up
Open it up
And lock it up

Find a four leaf clover
Pick it up
Now you
Will have good
Luck!!!
Find a flower
Pick it up
Smell it and think spring is here!!!
Michelle Gold, Grade 6
Warwick Neck School, RI

The Pie and the Mouth
I am a pie
I wonder who will eat me
I hear the human
I see the mouth
I want to be free

I am a pie
I pretend to be rotten
I feel the tongue
I touch the throat
I worry about my life
I cry since I'm about to die

I am a pie in a horrible state
I understand that there is no hope
I say my prayers
I dream of a better place
I try to die fast
I hope to live another day

I was a pie
Joe Riva, Grade 6
Page Middle School, VA

Easter
Easter eggs hiding
bright colors in the green grass
fill your basket up
Jonathan Ellis, Grade 4
St Joseph School-Fullerton, MD

Sunset Beach, NJ

I watch the waves splash,
And smell the ocean breeze.
The sand slithers through my feet,
And seagulls flop their wings high in the sky,
Scavengers on a quest.

I watch the sunset and the half sunken ship,
The Cape May ferry,
Walk across the water,
And everywhere I look,
I can tell it is sunset.

Grace Bentivenga, Grade 6
Trinity School, MD

Raindrop

From the clouds,
they come playfully prancing in pockets of happiness,
silver as beauty never too far away.
A beautiful drop of water,
falling hard, to patter against the evil ground.
The snow isn't like it,
It finds itself pretty,
I know that the raindrop has beauty in its own way.
When the time is right,
you just may see,
rain falling down beautifully.

Kristin Ipock, Grade 6
Page Middle School, VA

Nature, Nature, Nature

Nature is when the cool breeze blows
And beautiful flowers fill my nose

Nature is when that woman noise
She's kind with long hair and an echoing voice

Nature is where the sun will shine
Where lovely trees grow over the pines

Nature is tragic, nature is peace
Nature is life and nature is me

Alexa Livingstone, Grade 4
Featherbed Lane Elementary School, MD

The Loving Dream

In the hazy dawn of every morning,
within my thoughts comes a new light
of loving memories and visions of the
the years before me. The happiest
wonders are in my thoughts when I sleep
away from the tragedy and internal war of life
and hope. As I lie awake at night, I know now
that there is no way to get away from it all except
in the dreams of a loving soul.

Maya Elliott, Grade 6
Paul L Dunbar Middle School for Innovation, VA

Book

I am a book
I wonder who will read me
I hear soft voices from inside of me
I see words written all over me
I want to be loved and appreciated
I am a form of adventure
I pretend not to know that I'm heavy with words
I feel fingers turning my pages
I touch people's hearts
I worry about my pages being ripped
I cry because my spine will break
I am a beautiful creation
I understand that my time will come
I say things that touch people's hearts
I dream of getting awards
I try to take people places they have never been
I hope that somebody will embrace me
I am a book

Autumn Farmer, Grade 6
Page Middle School, VA

The Hungry Bear

I am a bear
I wonder when is winter
I hear my tummy growling
I see my empty cavern
I want some food
I am the hungry bear
I pretend I am not skinny
I feel as if I have not eaten in years
I touch my flat tummy
I worry the end is near
I cry at night
I am the hungry lonely bear
I understand I will probably not survive this winter
I say do not worry
I dream of myself surviving this winter
I try my very best to get fatter
I hope the end is not near
I am the lonely hungry bear

Ryan Petty, Grade 6
Page Middle School, VA

Candy World

There's a place far away
Where no one really knows what to say
There's cotton candy clouds so high
The gummy bears taste so good I could die
This place is just like a wonderful dream
There's tons of chocolates, cakes, and cream
There's a caramel fountain that's really tasty
And the creamy peanut butter's kind of pasty
This place is certainly delicious
But you might want to know it's not so nutritious

Crystal Dye, Grade 5
Rocky Gap Elementary School, VA

Books

Books are a new world,
opened up to me,
and their pages, the open sea.
The words are my crew,
that I can see,
I can have one or two or three.
All of this seems so real,
though it's all in my head,
it's so vivid, it's not read.
It has no reason,
but with my greed,
I must proceed.

Shay Ladd, Grade 5
Blacksburg New School, VA

The Orange Old Basketball*

So much depends
upon

The orange old
basketball

Bouncing on the
ground

Going up and
down

Nadine Pope, Grade 5
Linwood Holton Elementary School, VA
*Inspired by William Carlos Williams

The Glum-Glum

I used to have a Glum-Glum,
I made it for myself,
First I took some bubblegum
And put it on the shelf.
Then I used some soap,
To make it clean and have a shine.
And then a big surprise!
I knew that it was mine.
I added DNA,
Then it was alive.
I knew that it was going to play,
So, of course, I made five!

Katya Mikhailova, Grade 4
Waller Mill Fine Arts Magnet School, VA

Mother

M y mentor that is
O n top of things
T erribly caring that anyone would
H ope to be like her
E asy to love with her
R ight intentions

Caroline Anderson, Grade 5
St John Neumann Academy, VA

Dequante and Antoine

Survive and believe
So you can achieve your dream

You should never hate
Just be great
And appreciate

If you survive
You will be alive
And receive the ultimate prize
Fight all the way through
And you won't be blue
But you will always be true

Antoine Booker, Grade 5
Linwood Holton Elementary School, VA

I Want Curls

Hey, hair, I am tired of you.
You never want to curl.
You never want to be straight.
I have asked for your opinion
But no you want to ignore me.
I'm not taking this anymore,
So you can forget trying to pull
The wool over my eyes.
Please, nothing can get past me
The bottom line is you're mine,
And I can do whatever
I want with you.

Kaniya Rogers, Grade 6
Trinity School, MD

What Am I?

I walk on reptilian, scaly feet
Slowly and sure-footed
My toes grasping a tree branch
With scaly vigilance I wait
Until an insect comes buzzing by
Thwap! It's gone in a second
And I walk on
Blending into
The forests
Of Madagascar

Answer: Chameleon

Kien Powell, Grade 4
American International School, VA

Dogs

Dogs
Lovable, Cute
Running, Barking, Eating
Fun To Be With
Pets

Hali Bourne, Grade 4
Hebbville Elementary School, MD

Pat, the Fat Cat

The fat cat's name is Pat.
Pat is a very fat cat.
Pat is a very lazy cat,
She met a pig named Matt.

Pat held a bat. Pat's hands are fat,
So she could not hold the bat.
Matt called Pat a very lazy cat,
So Pat wore a giant hat.

Joshua Butler, Grade 4
Courthouse Road Elementary School, VA

The World

The world is like a huge ball
But it does not fall
It is my planet
So I take care of it

People on my planet are smart
My planet does not fall apart
It is really cool
It sits on an invisible stool

Matthew KuKanich, Grade 4
Courthouse Road Elementary School, VA

The School

The school is like a kingdom,
only not ruled over by a prince
or a king but as a principal.
The staff are as the servants
teaching students to behave,
and if they're being bad
they take you to the king
like castle guards taking a
prisoner.

Jonie Phillips, Grade 6
Page Middle School, VA

Max

Max
Funny, goofy
Guarding, protecting, loving
He's a good dog
Sheepdog

Dylan Long, Grade 5
St Joseph School-Fullerton, MD

Lion

Majestic, proud
Roaring, snarling, prowling
Loud, large, small, quiet
Baaing, leaping, grazing
Meek, gentle
Lamb

Samuel Williard, Grade 6
St John Neumann Academy, VA

My Wonderful Cat
My cat, my cat
He is so very fat
My cat, my cat
We call him an acrobat

My cat, my cat
He is so furry
My cat, my cat
He always sounds so purry

My cat, my cat
He is so nice
My cat, my cat
He likes to chase mice

My cat, my cat
He is healthy
My cat, my cat
He is also stealthy

My cat, my cat
He is so smart
My cat, my cat
I love him with all my heart
Sarah E. Smith, Grade 5
Norfolk Collegiate Lower School, VA

April Showers
During April the Earth
Cries its tears of happiness
And joy that spring is here

As the night becomes
Dawn the frost bite
Fades away from the
Ice covered earth that
We call home

Birds come back to
Sing their songs
And the rabbits come
Out to frolic along
The bears come out
To have their first feed
For they're as hungry as
Any bear could be

As the spring is
Beginning it's just
Ending when April and
Its tears come along to play!
Angelina Olivieri, Grade 6
Warwick Neck School, RI

School/Prison
School
Boring, long
Learning, working, writing
A long learning year
Prison
Ian Whalen, Grade 6
Immaculate Heart of Mary School, MD

The Mall
At the mall, people are elephants,
walking around slowly and in groups.
At the mall, prices are skyscrapers,
very high.
But it's the mall, and we love it.
Amanda Davis, Grade 6
Page Middle School, VA

Friends
Friends
Kind, true
Loving, caring, exciting
Friends are very sincere
Companions
Anna Zittle, Grade 5
St Joseph School-Fullerton, MD

Red Fox
Fox
Red, furry
Running, hunting, hiding
A four-legged animal
Mammal
Brooke Menikheim, Grade 5
St Joseph School-Fullerton, MD

Fall
Fun, active
Jumping, playing, changing
Getting colder, leaves
Thanksgiving
Autumn
Eric Jurkiewicz, Grade 5
St Joseph School-Fullerton, MD

Nature
Wind is rushing by the trees.
I listen to the birds and bees.
The wind is blowing,
the water is flowing,
and it's happening around me.
Julia Cash, Grade 6
Monelison Middle School, VA

My Busy Life
I am so busy
What am I going to do?
I hope it's the end of my misery,
But I have a whole day to go!
11:00 — Clean my shed
12:30 — Take my dog to the vet
1:26 — Make some bread
4:00 — Take a ride in a jet
4:50 — Replace the lights
6:15 — Meet at the skating rink
8:30 — Go out and look at the moonlight!
Oops! I forgot to blink!
Bethany Mizelle, Grade 5
Mary Walter Elementary School, VA

Emotions of a Field Hockey Stick
I am a shiny field hockey stick
I wonder when I'll be used
I hear cleats squishing in the muddy grass
I see the balls, and people who use me
I want to be loved and used
I am the used field hockey stick
I pretend not to care
I feel the ball clashing against me
I touch the wet muddy ground
I worry they won't use me
I cry when I'm thrown away
I hope I get used again someday
Ashley Sprouse, Grade 6
Page Middle School, VA

Go Down Yonder
"Go down yonder,
The river pleaded to me."
"Go down yonder,
So I may touch the sea."
"Go down yonder,
The blue fish asked of me."
"Go down yonder,
So that I'll soon be free."
Standing on that riverside
I felt first touch of snow,
So I answered their pleas of me,
Now I yonder go.
Heather Parkin, Grade 4
Woodlin Elementary School, MD

Sky
The sky is a big soft blue blanket
with birds filling its space.
The clouds are big polka dots
trying not to catch a cold.
The night sky such a beautiful sight
as its stars light up.
Grace Small, Grade 4
Greenville Elementary School, VA

High Merit Poems – Grades 4, 5, and 6

My Hair
I really love my hair
I would play with it anywhere
It is really curly and black
It falls right down my back
Diamond Davis, Grade 4
Hebbville Elementary School, MD

Spring Day
I like the days of spring
I like to hear the birds sing
I would like to play
But sometimes I have to work all day
Christopher Medrano, Grade 4
Hebbville Elementary School, MD

Flowers
Flowers, flowers, flowers
Smell them during a shower
Watch out for bugs
There may be a bee!
D'Asia Wilson, Grade 4
Hebbville Elementary School, MD

The Night
The night
with whispering trees
and the whistling wind
it makes for a beautiful night
Mary Beth Beach, Grade 6
Page Middle School, VA

Soft as Silk
Rain as soft as silk
kissing your cheeks in the silent night air
as they dance down like you and I
rain soft as silk.
Megan Olson, Grade 6
Page Middle School, VA

A Morning at the Park
A peaceful morning at the park.
Kids of all ages laughing, playing
Until we hear "OUCH!"
A bee stung a little girl.
Brilee Leber, Grade 6
Page Middle School, VA

Spring
Flowers blooming now
Lots of butterflies fly by
Spring is everywhere
Catherine Valentine, Grade 4
St Joseph School-Fullerton, MD

Dreaming
I close my eyes…
I wake to see a cloudless sky.
I look forward to a glassy ocean.
No boats, no cars, no rude, clueless people
Behind me I see towering mountains dusted with green fading to purple.
Is this real? Perhaps I'm dreaming….
My question is answered, as the aqua colored tides sweep me back to reality.
Yes, I was dreaming.
Maria Navolio, Grade 6
Paul L Dunbar Middle School for Innovation, VA

I'm Talking Fat!
I'm talking fat!
I'm talking stout!
I'm talking obese, corpulent, fleshy!
I'm talking potbellied, beefy, brawny, plumply!
I'm talking burly, bulky, plump, heavy, chunky!
I'm talking large, gigantic, oversized, massive, chubby, big!
I'm talking big boned, husky, enormous, hulking, fullness, hefty, thick!
I'm talking fat!
Emma Poff, Grade 5
Blacksburg New School, VA

Lunch Time
Smells like baked potatoes, pizza, crème brûlée,
Taste like exotic flavors dancing on my taste buds like rosemary, and cinnamon,
Sounds like the chewing of 400,000,000 kids at several tables,
Looks like a room filled with exotic foods and beverages,
Feels like a feast with the nation.
Britney Black, Grade 5
Church of the Redeemer Christian School, MD

Candy Land
My happy place is Candy Land where everything is free
And the birds sing with glee.
People are peacefully roaming the streets.
It rains chocolate, it is your dream, and candy will be all you will eat.
No pollution is here. It is a dreamland indeed.
Franklin Hartley, Grade 5
Rocky Gap Elementary School, VA

Kings Dominion
I take sight of the huge, daring roller coasters and exceptionally large Eiffel Tower.
I feel blasts of wind whipping my face as I take the epic plunge.
I can smell the shockingly amazing food enchanting guests with their odor.
The fresh, buttery popcorn and sweet, frozen lemonade taste like heaven in my mouth.
Bailey Clark, Grade 4
Crestwood Elementary School, VA

The Eagle
The eagle soars through the sky
You can see the wildness in his eye
The hawk drops at a great speed
While very quietly taking heed.
Dillon Green, Grade 4
Waller Mill Fine Arts Magnet School, VA

Water
Activity filled water
gives pleasurable days
to the vast world
at any given time of year.
Jack Hanline, Grade 4
St John Neumann Academy, VA

Softball

Softball is like a drug
Once you start it you can't stop
Once you hit the ball you feel on top
The crack of the bat is very loud
Once you catch it so is the crowd

Your team becomes your family
They'll always keep you company
When you catch the ball they'll cheer you on
When you hit it they tell you to run, run, run

As you can see softball is the best sport to play
It usually stops at the end of the May
So don't waste any time
Go sign up for softball and have a good time

Kayla Buchanan, Grade 6
Academy of International Studies, VA

Ode to My New Nike Pursuit 7075 Lacrosse Stick

Bold colors of red, yellow, and black,
This new piece of equipment is so whack,
This is my new Nike Pursuit 7075 Lacrosse stick.

Can I maintain the skills that I had before?
I was hoping so when I brought it home from the store
This is my new Nike Pursuit 7075 Lacrosse stick.

Will I be able to perform and control?
I hope it will bring me luck to score goals.
This is my new Nike Pursuit 7075 Lacrosse stick.

If I practice extra hard and put in extra time
Reward will come and I think I may find
I'm going to love my new Nike Pursuit 7075 Lacrosse stick!

Tyler Springfield, Grade 6
Most Blessed Sacrament Catholic School, MD

I Wonder

I wonder if there is a kingdom,
Where the kids were successful,
I ponder if there was a majestic place,
Where the kids could make a difference

I speculate if there is a paradise,
Where we did not have anxiousness about the economy,
Because the children grew up to work for the government,
And repaired the economy,

I no longer wonder because the place,
Will come soon enough,
Because the children
of the world will grow up and make,
the world a better place.

Aly Dabo, Grade 6
Magnolia Elementary School, MD

The Hockey Game

The hockey game was at Hershey
The Bears were playing the Senators
The game was during the afternoon
It was held at Giant Center

During the first period
There was a great fight
Even two goals for the Bears
But the chance of the Senators winning was slight

During the second period
There were two fights which the Bears won
The Bears scored three goals
This time the Senators scored one

During the final period
There was one last fight
The Bears scored one goal
Again the Senators scored none and still had no might

The game was finished at night
And the bears won
The MVP was Kyle Greentree
The final score was six to one

Drew Barker, Grade 6
Immaculate Heart of Mary School, MD

Dolphin Song

Through the water they swim so gracefully,
Splishing and splashing through the waves.
Up and down they jump around,
Here and there you see them flare.

Romping through night and day,
Having fun in the waves,
Swimming in a pod,
Clicking and clacking through the darkness.

Down to the coral,
Up to the sky,
Minding their business every time,
Gray and blue like a stormy night.

The sun goes down.
A sunset appears.
They jump to touch the sun,
Spilling with color.

The moon comes up.
Their beaks long and thin,
They swim down to sleep tight.
Goodnight and sleep tight.

Rita Cordero, Grade 5
Forcey Christian School, MD

High Merit Poems – Grades 4, 5, and 6

Mom and Dad
This is my mom and my dad.
They can sometimes make me feel glad.
They're a pain to me,
But I can still see,
That they aren't really so bad.
Stella Nikolaou, Grade 5
St Clement Mary Hofbauer School, MD

Pencil
Pencil
Used for writing
Hits the piece of paper
I am glad it's here to write with
Use lead
Christopher Kurtz, Grade 4
Waller Mill Fine Arts Magnet School, VA

Sisters
Friends
Kind, sweet
Caring, inspiring, loving
Friends are always there
Sisters
Rachael Price, Grade 5
St Clement Mary Hofbauer School, MD

My Weird Grandparents
My two grandparents, Charlotte and Wayne.
Sometimes they can be a great pain.
They like to make punch,
And drink it with their lunch,
But sometimes they drive you insane.
Bethany Poplovski, Grade 5
St Clement Mary Hofbauer School, MD

Scooby Doo
Scooby Doo
Brown, black
Eating, solving mysteries, playing
One of the gang
Dog
Grant Howe, Grade 4
Crossfield Elementary School, VA

My Mom and Dad
Although, I love my mom and dad.
Sometimes they make me real mad.
They work and they clean,
'Til sunrise it seems.
They will put me in my room if I'm bad.
Kayla Asbury, Grade 5
St Clement Mary Hofbauer School, MD

Love
I love my mom, she loves me too
but when I make her angry she
wants to throw a shoe.

I love my family, they love me too
but when we play they don't want to
so I leave them alone until
the next day.

I love my friends in a type of way
they make me laugh every day

This poem is over I have to bail,
but until then see you next time y'all.
Jata A. Nolan, Grade 4
Featherbed Lane Elementary School, MD

Snow Glory
What is this white stuff
Falling from the sky?
It's so full of fluff,
And so pleasant to the eye!

What are these white things
Falling out of nowhere?
What are these white things,
Coming out of thin air?

This is truly snow,
Of which I heard many stories.
This is truly snow
In all its glory.
Abigail Eskinder, Grade 6
Banner Christian School, VA

Falling
Falling
down
into nothingness
the black
the white
is all that passes you by
you can't tell the ground from the sky
you don't know which way to fly
but you touch down safely
into
the colorful world
that
you
recognize
Shelby Johnson, Grade 4
Prospect Mill Elementary School, MD

Spring Is Here
Spring is here
fall is gone
the bees are buzzing
in my ear
flowers are blooming
here and there
springtime is everywhere
Danyelle Harrison, Grade 5
Rosemont Forest Elementary School, VA

Weather
Rain
Liquid, clear
Draining, moving, falling
Dangerous, weather, cold, storm
Melting, sticking, freezing
Thick, white
Snow
Vraj Patel, Grade 5
Linwood Holton Elementary School, VA

Food
Breakfast
Warm, sweet
Eating, drinking, yawning
Syrup, pancakes, steak, pork chops
Cutting, chewing, swallowing
Tasty, flavorful
Dinner
Miles Housley, Grade 4
Greenville Elementary School, VA

Spring and Summer
Spring
Windy, wet
Studying, working, cleaning
Leaves, school, vacation, friends
Running, hiking, biking
Warm, relaxed
Summer
Zachary Kidwell, Grade 4
Greenville Elementary School, VA

Socks
Oh misunderstood
so fluffy
and kind,
But we all make you stinky
from time to time,
And yet, shoe still says,
"Back to the grind."
Victoria Patacsil, Grade 5
Charles Barrett Elementary School, VA

Pets

Some are large; some are small,
But no matter what, we love them all.
Some have feathers, others have scales,
And most of them have cute little tails.
Some can fit your lap, but many don't try,
For they may be so big, that could make you cry!
You can enter them in shows, and hope to win,
Or put them in your car, and take them for a spin.
You can pet them, or walk, or even just look,
As they curl up and nap in their own special nook.
The silly things they do, and the sounds that they make,
Are all what put the icing on the cake.
It's hard when you lose such a wonderful friend,
But no matter what, they'll be in your heart until the very end.

Caneel Cravotta, Grade 6
Cape Henry Collegiate School, VA

My Dog Luke

I have an enormous dog and his name is Luke,
His favorite dish is the flat fish called fluke.
He loves to frolic in the snow,
But he hates it when I mow.
Luke loves to pursue the ball,
And sometimes he makes me fall.
He hates when motorbikes cross the road,
Which makes him angrier than a devil toad.
If you meet Luke in the night,
You will be in for a huge fright.
He is really funny and nice,
And I sure hope he doesn't have lice.
Luke sometimes makes me mad,
But he is the best dog I have ever had.

Will Lawson, Grade 5
Lightfoot Elementary School, VA

Too Special to Lose

This is not a poem about messing around,
Or taking a walk down the street or to town.

Instead it's about being kind and learning to share,
And keeping moments to love and to care.

Like being with family and greeting each other,
And spending time with one another.

Helping with groceries and such,
Or to set the table for lunch.

Moments are too special to lose,
So keep them with you no matter what you do.

Maegan Krystkiewicz, Grade 6
St Clement Mary Hofbauer School, MD

Aberdeen Ironbirds Game

The game was going on
As I was sitting in the seats
The batter was left handed
I watched the ball until it landed

Many other uncontrolled balls had gone into the stands
I knew this one was different from the second it was already sent

We were going in slow motion
It spun round and round
Turning and quickly flipping
On the seats around me people were leaning and gripping

No one caught it, 'cause it resisted their hands
It landed on my chair all I could do was stare

After rolling off my seat
It hit the ground hard
I reached down to get it
As the child next to me had a fit

I was so joyful, my first fly ball at a baseball game
I couldn't wait for my parents to see they would be so proud of me

Leah Wieczorek, Grade 6
Immaculate Heart of Mary School, MD

I Used to, But Now I

I used to have a lot of friends
But now I hope for a Mercedes Benz

I used to strive to catch a mouse
But now I hang around the firehouse

I used to have a dog named Buddy
But now I look at pictures of him very muddy

I used to want a plane so I could travel far
But now I hope I get a car

I used to watch a lot of TV
But now I go fishing with my uncle Stevie

I used to show off my moped on the boardwalk
But now I model my way down the catwalk

I used to be a big pain
But now I'm like a hurricane

I used to complain about carrying my mom's shopping bags
But now I say, "It beats wearing rags."

Michael Knowles, Grade 6
Most Blessed Sacrament Catholic School, MD

A Dreamer

Is a dreamer, me?
Do my dreams, matter?
Are they substantial?
A dreamer is me

A dreamer isn't afraid to achieve success in life
A dreamer can accomplish goals without a problem
A dreamer is me.

Is a dreamer, me?
A dreamer defines me because I'm fearless
I'm ready to achieve my goals
A dreamer is me

Kennedy Blow, Grade 6
Magnolia Elementary School, MD

The Beautiful Earth

Sky, guide the clouds through the sky.
Moon, dance up to the sky as the sun goes down.
Night, remember to hold the moon up in the sky.
Mountain, remind all the trees to stand up straight.
Sea, tell the waves to be a little bit faster.
Sun, teach the stars to shine really bright.
Stars, listen to the sun very carefully.
Stone, show the waves where to go.
Morning, bring the fog to the world.
Dawn, look at the sun and see if it is going down.
If you all listen to what I said,
You will be a beautiful earth.

Makenna Luzier, Grade 4
Boonsboro Elementary School, MD

Math Class

In class with math, oh my
Not fair, not fair, why, why, why?
School never ends, what a flop
Being with my teacher, hop, hop, hop

Math is so boring, don't know, which way to go!
Some people like it, no, no, no!
A teacher with a smile
Haven't seen it in a while
Math is so boring
It makes me feel like roaring.

Jenna Taylor, Grade 4
Courthouse Road Elementary School, VA

Heaven

Looks like God sitting on His throne
Sounds like angels singing to the Almighty One
Tastes like eternal feasts
Smells like the great things of this new world
Feels like his love enduring in me forever!

Caleb Fernandez, Grade 5
Church of the Redeemer Christian School, MD

Poetry

Poetry is cool to me
It's boring to others
It expresses my feelings
And what I feel now
My teacher wants to get it across
That poetry is a wonderful thing
Feelings, emotions, a bundle of words
Can all go in a poem
Some of us want a princess
Make it come alive in poetry
Some girls have crushes
They express it with poetry
It comes your friend's birthday
You tell them happy birthday
With a poem from her to him
Poetry is cool to me
It's boring to others
I love poetry

Zachary Young, Grade 6
Paul L Dunbar Middle School for Innovation, VA

Friendship

Friendship,
Friendship is *lovely*.
Friends are people you can rely on.
Someone who never leaves your side.

Someone without a friend is like
A butterfly with no color,
A cat with no meow,
A dog with no bark,
But more importantly it is like me without you.

Everyone has their best friend.
Someone who is always there,
Right by your side.
But that is not friendship.

Friendship is being friends with someone,
Who has none.

Grace Powell, Grade 6
Warwick Neck Elementary School, RI

Spring

Tulips begin to blossom beautifully
Soccer players hustle on the green fields
Trees regain bright green leaves
Creeks flow smoothly through the whistling woods
Birds chirp their relaxing songs
Wind chimes clang as the new winds arrive
Butterflies dancing around tree blossoms
Bees buzzing and pollinating the vibrant flowers
Oh, the wonderful appearance of spring

Hunter Anderson, Grade 4
Mary Walter Elementary School, VA

Peace*
When there is despair, hope is found.
There is no more despair all around.

When there is hatred, let me sow love.
Pure and clean like a white dove.

When there is darkness, light we see.
The children of God we ought to be.

For it is in giving that we receive.
Loving others is what we should achieve.
Beatrice Reyes, Grade 6
St Clement Mary Hofbauer School, MD
*Inspired by Saint Francis

Pen*
So much depends
upon

A black and silver
pen

Glazed with
imagination

Waiting for
me at home
Dequante Thrower, Grade 5
Linwood Holton Elementary School, VA
*Inspired by William Carlos Williams

Baseball
Oh, baseball,
You're so important and fun
You make me fast,
Happy, and smart
You don't have many fans,
But I still really like you,
Baseball players in history
Changed the sport forever
I'd like to be one too,
You're so fun
You'll go down in history…
I hope!
Robbie Platt, Grade 4
Greenville Elementary School, VA

Blue
Blue is in the ocean,
Blue is in the sky,
Blue is on a cup,
I just don't know why.
Blue is on everything,
Even on stars!
Drayce Sears, Grade 4
Waller Mill Fine Arts Magnet School, VA

August Night
August night,
moon is bright
fireflies begin their flight.
When morning comes,
arises the sun.
Spreading across the land
like butter on bread.
Then comes noon
the land is parched
the plants plead for water.
Animals scavenge for water.
As day turns to night,
fireflies begin their flight.
Jacob Levy, Grade 5
Nottingham Elementary School, VA

Orangutans
The orangutans were in a forest.
The mom and the baby
had hair as red as the sun.
They were swinging
from tree to tree like gymnasts.
The baby was eating leaves
like a maniac.
Their arms were muscular snakes.
The mom's skin was faded leather.
Her hair was wild fire.
Their eyes were amber marbles.
They were happy
and free.
Cecelia Kominsky, Grade 4
Blacksburg New School, VA

May
Streams of water
Flow down the road
From all the rain so far
But soon to come
There will be more.
I watch as the bees buzz
And the birds chirp,
High in the trees.
Waiting to come out
I, a little girl, wait
To see
The world
And its beauties.
Meghan Hamby, Grade 5
Nottingham Elementary School, VA

March
March, my birthday month
brings double gifts for me
plus cake and ice cream.
Kearson Williams, Grade 4
St Joseph School-Fullerton, MD

Summer Time
Summer is when
I go to the pool.
Summer is when it's
no school.

Summer means no
teachers in parts of
June, July and August.
I love summer.

I go to summer camp
with my friends and
we always go to
the snowball stand.
Aysia Ferguson, Grade 4
Featherbed Lane Elementary School, MD

Summer
Summer is my favorite season.
Listen and I'll tell the reason.
Blue skies and lots of sun.
No school time for fun.
Idle days of relaxation.
How I adore summer vacation.
Excursions to see the sights.
New things and old delights.
Time with family and friends.
Days you wish would never end.
BBQ's and drinks so cool.
Splashing in the swimming pool.
Now I've told you all the reasons.
Why summer is my favorite season.
Carly Gatto, Grade 5
Lightfoot Elementary School, VA

Spring Tale
The light spring breeze
Whispers in my ear

As it takes its daily stroll
Through the park.

The bees are starting to come,
That means summer is near.

Pools will open,
Kids will cheer.

Sit back and relax,
Have no fear.
Ryan Allison, Grade 6
Trinity School, MD

What Am I?
I am small, I am silly,
I am soft, I am sweet,
I'm probably someone
you'd like to meet.
I like to chew on a shoe, and
to this family I am new.
I am gold,
I am not very old, and
I try to do as I'm told…
What am I?

A Golden Retriever Puppy!
Sophie Cleland, Grade 5
The Compass School, RI

Poetry Is
Poetry is silent music
It is a rhythm and a beat
The words are the melody
And your voice is the harmony

Poems show how you're feeling
And all you've got to do
Is follow your heart
And let it out
Let your heart guide your words
And let your soul bounce with the rhythm
Of poetry
Shaina Brown, Grade 5
Taylor Elementary School, VA

The Sailing Ships*
So much
depends upon

The rapidly
sailing ships

Sailing through
the wind and sea

And flowing through
the stream
Jaden Barton, Grade 5
Linwood Holton Elementary School, VA
*Inspired by William Carlos Williams

Books
I love to read all day
Every day I get lost in my books
I don't listen to anything
I can't help if I go
Without trying, I disappear
Then I come home confused.
Megan LeBlanc, Grade 4
Courthouse Road Elementary School, VA

Thinking of You
I thought of you today,
and of all the fun we had.
Just the thought of losing you,
makes me very, very sad.

I thought of you today,
when dreams filled my head
Of the good memories
and the love we shared.

I thought of you today,
and the games we used to play
The things we used to do,
and the sweet things you used to say.

Now that you have left me,
and I cannot see your face
I'm hoping and praying
You are resting peacefully okay.
Daja Pickett, Grade 6
St Columba School, MD

Love Yourself; You're No One Else!
People may think you're crazy,
Some might say curious.
Others may think you are lazy,
And that might make them furious.

It doesn't matter —
Girl or boy,
Don't let them treat you like a toy.
You shouldn't let anyone ruin your day,
With every little thing they say.

You know you're one of a kind,
So don't let them leave you behind.
Life is like a living game.
You're no one else!
You are not the same!

Love yourself,
And be inspired.
Jenalyse Edejer, Grade 6
St Columba School, MD

Your Face
Figures form a fabulous face
Your eyes are like spheres
Your teeth are like cubes
Each day something new appears
New dimples brighten your smile
Seven freckles sit upon your face
Your pupils shine like blue diamonds
Your face is a joy to mankind
Tyreek Davis, Grade 6
Magnolia Elementary School, MD

Parents
mom
short, pretty
cleaning, shopping, talking
long hair, smart, strong, trustworthy
working, driving, talking
tall, hairy
dad
Basheer Oumhand, Grade 5
Linwood Holton Elementary School, VA

Tree
acorn
small, hat-like
hiding, sprouting, growing
hard, cute, rough, brown
falling, swaying, moving
leafy, tall
oak
Alyssa Wiles, Grade 5
Linwood Holton Elementary School, VA

Metamorphosis
caterpillar
small, green
crawling, eating, growing
slow, sluggish, plump, fuzzy
fluttering, sunning, drinking
colorful, swift
butterfly
Owen Peck, Grade 5
Linwood Holton Elementary School, VA

Amphibian
tadpole
green, gills
swimming, jumping, changing
small, no bones, large, four legs
eating, sunning, croaking
long tongue, jumpy
frog
Tim Huth-Scruggs, Grade 5
Linwood Holton Elementary School, VA

Pink
pink tastes like pink lemonade.
pink smells like yummy bubble gum.
pink sounds like flapping butterfly wings.
pink feels like the ocean at sunset
pink looks like a family of flamingos.
pink makes me feel like a girly girl.
pink is pretty
Alessia Celseti, Grade 5
St Mary School, RI

The Class Kleenex Box

I am the class Kleenex box
I wonder how to run away
I hear the ACHOO! of the children when they sneeze
I see the darkness of the inside of me
I want to be alive
I am the class Kleenex box
I pretend to not hear the children and their noise
I feel the soft Kleenex inside of me
I touch the table in the corner of the classroom
I worry that I will be empty soon
I cry BOO HOO! at the thought of death
I am the class Kleenex box
I understand my time is coming
I say please don't put that dirty Kleenex in me!
I dream to be anything but a Kleenex box
I try to go away from the class forever
I hope to one day be free
I am the class Kleenex box

Jack Lagonegro, Grade 6
Page Middle School, VA

The Rain

I am the rain
I wonder if rain is better than fire.
I hear the sound of the thunder boom-crack!
I see the fire,
I want to defeat the fire.
I am rain!
I pretend that fire will beat me,
I feel the fire
I touch the fire
I worry that I will burn
I cry like the rain
I am the rain
I understand fire will burn
I say "Will fire beat me?"
I dream about the fiery, flaming, flowers
I try the fire
I hope that fire won't beat me
I am rain!

Daquan Paige, Grade 6
Page Middle School, VA

Who Is Linda?

Who Is Linda?
   Linda is where beautiful strikes creative
   Linda…Can't just isn't in her vocabulary
   She is a stone skimming across the water,
   Always busy, always moving
   Never has she given up on something hard,
   Never has she failed
   Linda is my life.
   Linda…is my mom.
   That is Linda.

Eliza Stowe, Grade 5
Margaret Beeks Elementary School, VA

Yellow Pillow

I am a yellow pillow
I wonder if I could change color
I hear the loud snoring of my person
I see her crazy hair in the morning
I want to be able to dance

I am a yellow pillow
I pretend to be fluffy
I feel very tired
I touch rough sheets
I worry about pillow fights
I cry when she is away

I am a yellow pillow
I understand my person when she talks in her sleep
I say that yellow is a pretty color
I dream about sleep
I try to ignore the pressure of my person's head
I hope she will wake up in the morning
I am Olivia's yellow pillow

Olivia Pohorence, Grade 6
Page Middle School, VA

Camp Lanakila

Camp Lanakila is my favorite place to be.
The sights get me filled with delight.
Each unit is filled with campers.
At archery, arrows sail through the sunlit air.
Campers can swim, canoe, and kayak through Lake Morey.
I see the silent castle resting in the meadow.
At the barn I gaze at the Viking shields.
I feel I'm traveling back in time.
What I hear is a different story.
When we hear the bugle, it sings louder than a choir.
We know what's happening.
We all run in a food frenzy.
I hear the stomping of the charge to the main house.
Then the creek bubbles and trickles along.
As campers walk to and from activities.
I can hear the wind whisper past me.
I can feel the creek pull my feet into a watery bath.
The lake showers me with a refreshing splash.
Finally, at night I climb into a warm comfortable bed.
Oh, how I wish to be back at Camp Lanakila right now!

Steven Kavanagh, Grade 6
Wyman Elementary School, RI

High School

When you go to high school…
You hear the rattles of freshman being stuffed in lockers
You feel dried gum stuck under the lunch table
You smell the stench of your lunch being burnt
You see the school colors
You taste the bitterness of the next four years of you life.

Olivia Branch, Grade 4
Waller Mill Fine Arts Magnet School, VA

Little River State Park

I wake up in the morning and find my brothers fast asleep.
My mom is slowly sipping her steaming hot coffee
as she scours the paper for exciting news.
My dad is now coming back from the general store
and brings us something warm and tasty for breakfast.
He soothingly wakes up my brothers
and tells us good news.
We are going to the lake!

I feel the slightly warm sand tickling my feet
as I tiptoe into the fresh clean water.
It creeps up my ankles and then my knees,
like quicksand in a jungle.
When I go under,
I feel the water brushing my hair out of my face
as it makes me feel like a mermaid
gliding through the ocean
and having a wonderful time.

I hear the crickets singing a melody
as the crackling fire pops in my ears.

I fall asleep dreaming
of the next year in Little River State Park.

Mary Mullane, Grade 6
Wyman Elementary School, RI

What I Love…

I love to watch the graceful Phillies
With their strong pitchers and powerful hitters

I love to smell Dunkin Donuts
With all its delicious wonders

I love to hear the
Cheering of the fans when the Phillies won the World Series
To hear the crack of their bats on a home run hit
And, at times, when they break like a stick

I love to taste sports
The way it's exciting when sports are tense
The taste of dirt or grass in your mouth
And the taste of a glorious victory

I love to touch animals
With their soft and smooth fur with fascinating patterns
And each animals different and beautiful colors

I love the way of people
Even when they think they are beaten, they get back up
When someone gets hurt there is always an angel for you
I love the way people say "I'm Sorry"

Matthew Torbert, Grade 6
Most Blessed Sacrament Catholic School, MD

Being Nocturnal for a Day

The guinea pig couldn't sleep a peep,
For his siblings snored selfishly noisily in their sleep.
Yesterday, except for breakfast, he had nothing to munch,
For his siblings greediness had left him no dinner or lunch!

It was eight o'clock in the morning that he last ate,
So sneaking to eat in the garden wasn't too late.
He maneuvered across the field without a squeak,
And upon entering the garden, didn't let the gate creak.

To the garden, he was so eager to race
And see if he could gulp down the whole place.
A warning to acknowledge in this case,
To make sure he did not see the gardener's face!

Carrots! Beets! Parsley! Goodies!
The guinea pig was so thrilled he danced a few boogies!
When his carefree time was eventually done,
He thought it was midnight, so he must run!

He had just left the carrot row when he heard the gardener yawn.
He finally noticed that it was actually dawn!
He was nearly freed from the net his leg was caught on,
When the gardener cried, "Who has demolished my whole lawn?"

Caitlyn Wong, Grade 5
Forcey Christian School, MD

Hershey Park Family Trip

In the car I was jumping up and down
Riding all through Hershey town
Ready to have lots of fun
A trip to Hershey is number one

When we got there my dad said he had a surprise
Though I was too focused on boardwalk fries
My dad got us a wonderful cabana
But it was still hot as a Savannah

We got a map to plan out our day
To see when and where we would play
I was a Jolly Rancher so I could ride all the rides
And once I got off them I would have much pride

My first loop-de-loop roller coaster was the Sidewinder
My mom did not go on so then we could not find her
I will never forget the feeling I got on the Stormrunner
The view I got was quite a stunner

When we left I was sad
Although the day was not bad
I was ready to lay my head
On my pillow in my nice warm bed

Gannon Conrad, Grade 6
Immaculate Heart of Mary School, MD

Half Moon Cay, Bahamas

It's quite a sight
To see two dogs playing in the surf.
The ocean calls out to me
Daring me to enter its 80-degree waters.
The quiet sounds of palm leaves swaying
Is really relaxing.
The pain of a sunburn on my back
Is soothed with aloe gel.
I love eating the peanut butter macadamia nut cookies
That you can only get there.
The unbearable pain
Of getting corn rows in my hair
Is worth it
When it's over.
I always find it funny
To see my mom carefully dipping her toes in the water
As if it's going to bite her.
The ocean is as blue as a husky puppy's eyes.
Half Moon Cay is the most relaxing place
I've ever visited.

Tamar Gershman, Grade 6
Wyman Elementary School, RI

I Am Who I Am!

I don't care if you call me uneducated, like a cave man
I don't even care if you call me ugly, like a clown
I am who I am — BEAUTIFUL

I love the way I talk, sing and dance
I don't care if you laugh
I also love the way I write and act beautifully
I am who I am — UNIQUE

Most people don't know me!

I have great grades
Friends and family to keep me company
I am who I am — LOVING

Yes I know I'm talkative as a gossip girl
Yes I know I'm loud like a police siren
I AM WHO I AM

I AM WHO I AM — ME!

Niyala Pritchett-Wilson, Grade 6
Magnolia Elementary School, MD

Blue Jay

Oh blue jay how do you fly?
I flap my wings and go high, high, high.
How do you know when to come back?
I come back at dark so I don't break my back.
Why do you like to fly?
Because the sky is where I stay.

Kendall Whitaker, Grade 4
St Christopher's School, VA

The Sky

The sky is blue
At night it is black
The sky always has friends
They are puffy and white

The sky has air
A blue sky with air
And puffy white clouds
But sometimes the sky turns black
But it's not night
Lightning strikes
Thunder roars
And then, it all goes back to that peaceful, blue sky.

Mason Eubank, Grade 4
Courthouse Road Elementary School, VA

The Change of Seasons

I sit on the cold bench as the breeze goes by
The cold whistle makes me shiver all down my spine.
I nervously await the ending of this harsh season.
Where everything in nature is dead from lack of things.
Cold and brittle I slowly notice a cloud move by.
The sun peeked out over the cloud bringing warmth out.
I look up at the sun with signs of joy.
The slowly growing leaves on trees go day by day
The flowers bloom with colors of the rainbow
I sensed the spring fever frolicking about
Birds were chirping and the heat made me warm.
My heavy coat I need no more until the next winter.
It may be the death of winter, but spring is reborn.

Kimberly Howard, Grade 5
Rosemont Forest Elementary School, VA

My Life in Fourth Grade

My life in fourth grade makes me go hooray!
I love it so much it feels like a rush.
It is the best!
I have lots of friends.

Like Trevor who is really clever.
Also Mia who always has an idea.
We are all good friends.
I hope it will stay that way.

My teacher Mrs. Nettles
She is a patriot and she shows it loud and proud.
That is why I love fourth grade!!!

Trinnity Sistrunk, Grade 4
Courthouse Road Elementary School, VA

Tulips

Tulips in the garden
Tulips in the park
But the tulips I like best are the tulips in dark

Pj Carter, Grade 5
Francis Asbury Elementary School, VA

Spring
Spring brings happy days
Flowers and trees are blooming
The birds are chirping
Sophia Edwards, Grade 4
St Joseph School-Fullerton, MD

Cherry Blossoms
Pink blankets on trees
Cherries in the summer time
A sweet treat to eat
Hailey Fink, Grade 5
St Joseph School-Fullerton, MD

Spring
Big, clear, cold raindrops
Colorful flowers blooming
Birds in trees chirping.
Zachary Mananghaya, Grade 4
St Joseph School-Fullerton, MD

Lions
They are very cool
They can very scary
They eat animals
Jason Gonzalez, Grade 4
Battlefield Elementary School, VA

Spring
Fresh, green, sturdy stems
popping here and popping there.
Spring is in full bloom.
Annemarie Bonner, Grade 4
St Joseph School-Fullerton, MD

Spring
Spring is coming soon
Showers and flowers are here
Bye bye to winter
Sarah Coffman, Grade 4
St Joseph School-Fullerton, MD

Dove and Fire
The dove and fire,
Yes, two very strong forces
In confirmation
Keegan Knox, Grade 5
St Joseph School-Fullerton, MD

Woodpecker
Annoying, pecks trees
Has a beak, eats bugs, unique
Is a bird, makes noise
Dalton Myers, Grade 6
Floyd T Binns Middle School, VA

My Day at the Aquarium
My dad, sister and I are going to the aquarium to see the dolphin show
When we arrived we were greeted with hellos
We went to the dolphin area to our reserved seats
We saw a dolphin swimming and hoped that would be one we'll get to meet
The dolphin show began and I was thrilled
But when they splashed us, I soon got the chills
I like watching the dolphins flip
At one point a trainer even took a dip
My sister and I were picked to help a trainer
The commands we did were a no brainer
By the end of the show we were soaking wet
But the best part of the day hadn't happened yet
My dad knew a trainer who showed us around
I learned that if you touch a dolphin on their head they make a funny sound
We met two dolphins name Chesapeake and Bailey
They were so cute, if only I could see them daily
We had to leave because the trainers had another show
I was happy that we got to go backstage though
In the car that's all we could talk about
I know we will go back soon, there's not doubt
Emily Finnessy, Grade 6
Immaculate Heart of Mary School, MD

Thanksgiving
The sight of the crispy brown turkey makes my stomach rumble,
Seeing family and friends coming one by one makes me feel warm inside,
The redness, hotness of the stovetop burns my face

The light of the chandelier making rainbows through the diamonds hanging on it,
The faint shine of the flickering through the window pane,
The light of the oven as the children watch the pies bake

When did they get up to cook all this?
Are more people coming next year?
Will they be gone to another house next year?

Happy all my family and friends are here,
Excited some might stay,
Hungry for some of that juicy turkey

People laughing giving hugs to one another,
The click clack of chairs as everyone sits,
The sweet silence of the saying of grace, wonderful
Cristian Davis, Grade 5
G W Carver Elementary School, VA

Black and White Sometimes
I am kicked around all the time as if I have an assigned bully.
I get some breaks when I cross white lines or land in a soft, white net.
In the old days I was black and white, but now I come in all sizes, styles and colors.
I always hear spectators cheering and the occasional grunts of players trying hard.
I am loved, hated, called names, and made fun of, but I always have to do my job.
I am a soccer ball.
Garrett Lusk, Grade 5
Nottingham Elementary School, VA

Bear Is Scared
Bear, Bear I'll be there don't
You worry about your scare
Don't be sad and don't be scared
I'll be there for you.
Amber Madison, Grade 4
Courthouse Road Elementary School, VA

Winter
Crawling, prowling in the night
Wolves are howling with strong might
The elegant beaming snow so nice
Like the wonderful color of rice
Lucas Piedmonte, Grade 5
Linwood Holton Elementary School, VA

Wish
I wish that there was a place
Quiet, peaceful, and safe
Where the harsh winds don't reach
On the vast plains of the world
Claire Spirtas-Hurst, Grade 5
Nottingham Elementary School, VA

Floyd T. Binns
Big, cool
Working, testing, learning
Floyd T. Binns is the best.
School
Brandon Hatcher, Grade 6
Floyd T Binns Middle School, VA

Microscope
Microscope
Magnifying machine
Focusing the stage
Amazement inside of me!
Christian Carlow, Grade 5
St Christopher's School, VA

Basketball
Orange sphere
Bouncing, playing, rounding
Ball goes to hoop
Playful
Jeremiah Jacob, Grade 4
Hebbville Elementary School, MD

Clouds Change
Vapor into crystals,
Crystals into clouds,
Big, white, and fluffy,
They have me wowed!
Olivia Wharton, Grade 4
St John Neumann Academy, VA

Pizza Man (A Man of Failure)
I make a phone call to that little shop
I order the crust and what goes on top
Pepperoni, ham, bacon, pineapple and extra cheese please.
I don't order sausage
Cause it makes me sneeze

They tell me
"Thirty minutes sir or your pizza is free"
So I sit and I wait
Hoping they bring me some paper plates.

10, 20 minutes went by and the thought of free pizza made me wanna cry.
I'd cry tears of joy as I'd eat my extra cheese
Oh pizza man take your time
Please, please, please

Another 15 minutes went through the clock
"Yes!" I cried
For my wallet will hurt not.

Heard a knock on the door,
"Dude, my bike broke down!" the pizza man roared.
I felt sorry for this funny dressed man,
So even though my pizza is free,
I will share all of one slice with this man of failure. I can I can.
Joshua Butler, Grade 5
Norwood Elementary School, MD

My Father
He is the one who pushed me through my first race,
I am the one who struggled with it.

He is the one who taught me to ride my bike without training wheels,
I am the one who kept falling off.

He is the one who taught me how to dance,
I am the one who was dancing by 9 months.

He is the one who held me when I was first born,
I am the one who was born September 5.

He is the one who will always love me,
He is my father.
Hannah Walsh, Grade 5
Claymont Elementary School, DE

Love
Looks like a soft fluffy red heart shaped pillow from your secret valentine.
Tastes like a warm, just out of the oven, chocolate chip cookie.
Smells like a cupcake.
Sounds like a cat purring.
Feels like someone cares for you.
Love, it's a wonderful thing,
But sometimes a sad thing.
Bethany Kasbohm, Grade 4
Waller Mill Fine Arts Magnet School, VA

High Merit Poems – Grades 4, 5, and 6

My Dad
My dad
He is rad
His middle name is Nad
He's a young lad
But he makes me glad!
Solana Cokenour, Grade 4
Angelus Academy, VA

Hockey
Hockey
Fast moving fun
Chasing the puck on ice
It is awesome to skate so fast
Rough sport
Luke Lucas, Grade 4
Waller Mill Fine Arts Magnet School, VA

Paper
P aper can be
A nything such as hats or paper airplanes
P aper can be colorful and
E legant, and can come with
R ewards that are fun!
Devin Rooney, Grade 5
St John Neumann Academy, VA

Cubs
Cub
Playful, fun
Chasing, speeding, Eating
There are so many different types of cubs.
Tigers
Mikey Pierce, Grade 6
Floyd T Binns Middle School, VA

Shark
Shark
Lurking blue
Jumping, biting, diving
Scary sharp toothed predator
Reef dweller
Bryan Cotellese, Grade 6
St John Neumann Academy, VA

Fighter Jet
Fighter jet
Speedy, soaring
Barrel roll, 768 mph, supersonic
Wing span is wide
Flying fortress
Caleb Branscome, Grade 5
St John Neumann Academy, VA

Winter
A million tiny snowflakes
falling from the sky,
and a far away snow owl
makes a silent cry.

All ice shards and no snow plows
snow's a delight,
humans or animals
are nowhere in sight.

Pit, pat, pit, pat,
the flakes dance in the wind,
mother nature forgiving
to all who have sinned.

Wind picks up,
and gives us a storm
and here comes the end
to all things warm.
Jake Bennett, Grade 5
Nottingham Elementary School, VA

The Moon
The moon is a
big,
bright
lamp
with moths longing to be soaring up
and be comforted by its light.
Deer take walks
in its pale,
milky
light
while bats feast overhead.
Snowflakes are guided
by that lamp of a moon
as they fall down
to earth
to rest
as they're guided safely
through the night
with the moon at their side.
Josie Krasny, Grade 4
Greenville Elementary School, VA

My Life
My life is hard
I have to do all sorts of things
like school, dance, and step class
This is my life.

The significant things in my life
are setting and achieving goals.
This is my life.
Elishia Ford, Grade 6
Magnolia Elementary School, MD

Feeling
I see autumn I see
fall I see you and your
reflections through the window
up in the sky brightness in
my eyes shine shine and you
will be mine.
Lisa Peoples, Grade 4
Featherbed Lane Elementary School, MD

Poverty
Poverty is bad
Poverty is sad
People in poverty are gracious
Poverty is hard
Poverty is owning little things
Poverty needs to change
RJ Wilkinson, Grade 5
St Christopher's School, VA

Cat
Cat
Cute, fussy
Scratching, climbing, drinking
Too soft to cuddle
Pet
Aaron Johnson, Grade 4
Hebbville Elementary School, MD

Dog
Dog
Cute, cuddly
Barking, jumping, playing
Beautiful four legged creature
Mammal
Jada Martin, Grade 4
Hebbville Elementary School, MD

Summer
Summer
Hot, sunny
Swimming, playing, running
Hot fun joyful times
Season
Akira Williams, Grade 4
Hebbville Elementary School, MD

People
People
Mean, nice
Playing, helping, eating
Fun loving caring people
Mammals
David Rufai, Grade 4
Hebbville Elementary School, MD

A Different World
Whenever I go to the beach
and stick my feet in the warm sand
it feels like I'm in a different world…
   where world peace is taking place
   dogs don't chase cats
   people don't have to be afraid at night
   adults and kids won't go hungry
   people aren't jealous
   and there is no violence
Gia Butler, Grade 6
St Columba School, MD

Music
Music can be fun
Music can be good
Music is a sweet sound

Sometimes music can be bad
Music can give doubts or hopes
Music can be created
Music is for me
Antonio Slyke, Grade 6
Magnolia Elementary School, MD

Chef
If I were a chef
I would cook fast
Compete in a competition
I would bake
And work in a restaurant
Maybe on a show
Even be famous
If I were a chef
Chris Schroeder, Grade 4
St Christopher's School, VA

Octopus
O verly dramatic with ink,
C uter than a pug,
T otally cool,
O cean creature,
P erfectly purple,
U nique,
S uper cool eight legs
   for an octopus.
Jade Clyburn, Grade 5
Rocky Gap Elementary School, VA

Kids
Kids
Playful, happy
Sharing, talking, learning
Fun to be young
Children
Christina Gambrell, Grade 4
Hebbville Elementary School, MD

Yellow
Yellow tastes like sharp American cheese
Yellow smells like yellow roses.
Yellow sounds like a lemonade truck.
Yellow feels like the sun's hot rays.
Yellow looks like my baseball jersey.
Yellow makes me feel hungry.
Yellow is bright.
Michael Pilozzi, Grade 5
St. Mary's School, RI

Green
Green tastes like pears.
Green smells like freshly cut grass.
Green sounds like swaying leaves on a tree.
Green feels like the soft grass.
Green looks like outside.
Green makes me smile.
Green is a good color.
Gino Mazzenga, Jr., Grade 5
St Mary School, RI

The Ground
Grumpy
Always there
Every place you go it's there
It goes up, down and all around
Many personalities
Strong and tough
Always has something on it
James Caza, Grade 4
American International School, VA

White
White tastes like vanilla ice cream.
White smells like a daisy blooming
White sounds like the big clouds of thunder.
White feels like fuzzy polar bears.
White looks like snow falling.
White makes me calm and shy.
White is soothing.
Emilienne English, Grade 5
St Mary School, RI

I Wish Monkeys Were EVERYWHERE!
Monkeys are like me
I like bananas
They have brown fur not hair
I have brown hair not fur
We have many things in common
I love monkeys
They love me
Hayleigh Burket, Grade 4
Courthouse Road Elementary School, VA

Spring Is Calling
Spring is calling
Calling
Through the midst
Of winter's frost

Spring is calling
For the blossoming
Of flowers
Spring is calling
For the animals
To awaken

Spring is calling
For crisp blue
Skies

Spring is calling
Whispering
Waiting
Emily Zheng, Grade 5
Claymont Elementary School, DE

How to Ski
Pull on, strap on, velcro on, zip on
Helmet, gloves, jacket, and boots
In your boots spread your toes
Tight is just right
Grab your skis
Step outside
Look up at the slopes to slide
Sit down in a chair
That will lift you
Waaaaay up there
While you're in the sky
Put your sun glasses on
Because you're going to fly
Head down the slope
Leaving tracks like a curvy rope
Turning quick, going straight
Watch out for those skiers, trees, and lake
At the bottom you will stop
Gently, smoothly, and without a chop
Omie Hogle, Grade 4
American International School, VA

Sunset
A sunset is like a fire,
hot and orange,
in a colorful furnace,
above an imaginary world.

The human slowly pours
water on it and turns it
into the ashes of night.
Hannah Sokolowski, Grade 4
Greenville Elementary School, VA

Birdsong

They are hidden,
Hiding in the trees,
Perched on a branch,
Avoiding us.
Singing songs as
A faithful chorus;
Chirping out their
Own verses,
One by one.
Even if just
Looking for a mate,
Or to communicate,
Birdsong
Is always
Beautiful.

Abigail Bischoff, Grade 5
Charles Barrett Elementary School, VA

Winter

I look outside,
and see the snow glistening
the kids laughing and yelling,
and the shovels and sleds everywhere.
I look in the closet
and see heavy coats,
mittens,
and snow pants.
I look in the kitchen,
and taste the warmth of hot cocoa.
I look in the fire place,
and see the fire burning.
I warm up and feel like I am melting.
Then I slither down in my bed
and slowly fall asleep.

Olivia England, Grade 5
Nottingham Elementary School, VA

Portrait of a Mystery

A very long tail,
Long black hair,
But doesn't move like a snail.
Unusually short,
With very small paws,
But has a scissor bite.
Has pointy ears,
Also very rare,
Like an ancient Roman glass jewel.
From the Isle of Skye,
During the day,
Chases and socializes.
But in the end,
Sleep and dreams come,
Until a new day begins.

Sydelle Davis, Grade 5
Forcey Christian School, MD

Playoff Game

Playoff Game
Our score starts the same
They score
We need more!
Score keeps going up
Our spirit goes down
This team is too good!
If we lose we are out
Our coaches keep shouting
The others are cheering
One minute left until the game ends
Tick tock goes the clock
The whistle screeches to a stop
Our game is gone and we lost our chance
Ending score: 14-18, them.

Katherine Barnes, Grade 5
Nottingham Elementary School, VA

I'm Talking Extraordinary!

I'm talking extraordinary!
I'm talking absurd!
I'm talking bizarre, crazy,
Extravagant!
I'm talking fanciful, foolish,
Insane, nonsensical!
I'm talking preposterous, unreal,
Wild, inconceivable, incredible!
I'm talking excellent, fantastic,
Exotic, ridiculous, extreme,
Far-fetched!
I'm talking imaginative, eccentric,
Ludicrous, peculiar, erratic,
Illusive, irrational!
I'm talking EXTRAORDINARY!

Mody Kutkut, Grade 4
Blacksburg New School, VA

That Spring Feeling

Roses
dancing in the pastures
on a warm, beautiful day.

Gardens
with plants ready to sprout.
The buds are popping.

The songs of birds
bring glory to my ears.

It was like…
    a dream.
It relaxes me.

Laney Thompson, Grade 5
Francis Asbury Elementary School, VA

Wind

Can you hear the wind,
Whistling through the trees?

Can you see the wind,
Blowing around the leaves?

Can you feel the wind,
Blowing through your hair?

Can you sense the wind,
Soaring through the air?

The wind is an extraordinary thing.
If you pay attention to it,
It may whisper in your ear.

Megan Tucker, Grade 5
Nottingham Elementary School, VA

I Am

I am someone who cares.
It's in my heart not what I wear.
I am loud and lovely.
Just like a swan.
As the grass lifts on
someone's old lawn.
Love is love, and that's official.
Be who you want to be
that's my last initial.
Black or white purple or blue.
It's what's in you.
I am a girl
as pretty as can be,
but best of all
I am…me.

Ciera Stephanie Bailey, Grade 4
Featherbed Lane Elementary School, MD

The Night's Secrets

When night and day fight at dusk,
    silence rises.
When roses peak into bloom,
    the moon's reflection
    on the glistening water
    lights the night with
    peace and hope.
But alas, not everything can
    last forever.
The sun begins to wake
    the sleepy animals
and the moon's secrets are once again
    hidden by the sun's
        light.

Payton Grubb, Grade 5
Francis Asbury Elementary School, VA

Blue

Blue tastes like crystal clear cold water
Blue smells like freshly picked flowers.
Blue sounds like the birds chirping in the morning.
Blue feels like the hot sun.
Blue looks like the summer nights.
Blue makes me want to jump in a pool.
Blue is the calm sky.

Marc Mansolillo, Grade 5
St Mary School, RI

Love

Love is beautiful
It is everything a person could want and more
Love isn't about holding hands, kissing, or going on dates
It's about two people that really mean something to each other
When you find love you put aside all your differences to become one
You're like magnets that can't be separated no matter what
Because you love each other so much

Tolu Akintoba, Grade 6
St Columba School, MD

Jaguar

Oh jaguar oh jaguar
How do you climb so high in the trees?
Where do you go at night to sleep?
What do you eat for food?
I climb with my front and back paws.
At nighttime I go to a safe place where I won't be bothered.
I eat the meat from the animals that I killed.

Huntley Davenport, Grade 4
St Christopher's School, VA

Yellow

Yellow tastes like a sweet glass of lemonade.
Yellow smells like a newly blossomed marigold.
Yellow sounds like a soft tweet of a canary.
Yellow feels like the warm rays of the sun.
Yellow looks like a tasty yellow cake.
Yellow makes me smile all day.
Yellow is like a warm sunny Saturday.

Conor Milson, Grade 5
St Mary School, RI

Dark and Light

Dark,
Despicable, twinkling eyes
Detecting and destroying light, overlapping
Jealousy, hearts filled with hatred
Gleaming on the pavement, optimistic feelings
Enchanting, not irritating, intention to be energetic
Light

Eliana Abraham, Grade 5
Lowes Island Elementary School, VA

Life

Life is hard and has many obstacles
Life is too short to be a hater
When life gives you a hard fall
You just get back up and
Brush yourself off and keep walking
Just live your life right and you will be all right
Now this is life.

Hamirah Jones, Grade 6
Magnolia Elementary School, MD

Purple

Purple tastes like a fresh bunch of grapes.
Purple smells like a beautiful violet.
Purple sounds like the crunch of a juicy plum.
Purple feels like the lick of a grape popsicle.
Purple looks like Justin Bieber's outfits.
Purple makes me feel happy.
Purple is absolutely fantastic!!

Gabriella DeVincenzis, Grade 5
St Mary School, RI

Ocean Blue

Ocean Blue tastes like salt water at the beach
Ocean Blue smells like a hot summer day.
Ocean Blue sounds like palm trees swaying in the sky.
Ocean Blue feels like a refreshing drink of water.
Ocean Blue looks like a tide getting low
Ocean Blue makes me feel calm and cool
Ocean Blue is absolutely marvelous!

Olivia Kearns, Grade 5
St. Mary School, RI

The Colors of the Revolutionary War

R ed, the blood our soldiers shed.
B lue, a color of our flag.
O range, the fire that warmed our soldiers.
Y ellow, the gun fire that our soldiers shot.
B lack, the smoke that blinded their eyes.
W hite, the horses that carried them through.
G ray, the hair of our General Washington.

Alexandra Medina, Grade 4
Waller Mill Fine Arts Magnet School, VA

The Wonders of God

Sun
bright, life
burning, flaming, heating,
red, orange, gray, gloomy
relaxing, lighting, providing
holes, round
Moon

Daniel Sempertegui, Grade 5
Church of the Redeemer Christian School, MD

First Kiss
Deeply entranced by their eyes,
Both surrounded by love,
That's it — pop — a smooch in the night,
Masqueraded by the lone darkness,

Love looms in the air
A first time for both,
Keeping both caught in the moment,
Masqueraded by the lone darkness,

An understanding is not needed,
A bud blooms,
Two hearts open,
Masqueraded by the lone darkness,

Love keeps them going,
The smell of roses surrounds them,
Their love soaring,
Masqueraded by the lone darkness,

Masqueraded by the lone darkness.
Natasha Gengler, Grade 5
Claymont Elementary School, DE

Giraffe
The tall, crispy grass
Covers the ground
Like a blanket over a bed.

The giraffe grazes among the trees
Like a cow in a field.

The trees stand strong
Like a ninja to opponent.

The giraffe's neck seems to
Stretch as high
As a skyscraper in a city.

The ground looks thirsty
In need of water.

In the distance
No sunset
But a powdery blue sky.
Akaela Feng, Grade 5
Blacksburg New School, VA

Soccer
The teams are so good.
You kick a black and white ball.
The fans cheer for you.
You can score bunches of goals.
Soccer players love their coach.
Cameron Deyo, Grade 4
Battlefield Elementary School, VA

A Stadium
It looks huge
Loud on Sundays
Parking lots are filled
Tailgate parties
Teams playing
Long concession stand lines
Thousands of fans
People cheering
You can hear
The touchdown across town
It is a NFL Stadium
Jack Horsley, Grade 4
St Christopher's School, VA

Yin and Yang
Yin and Yang
Tooth and fang
Tie and tether
Sew and Seam
Light and beam
Some words seem
To go together
Out and in
Smile and grin
Some words fit right in
Together
Nick Stacy, Grade 4
Blacksburg New School, VA

Green
When I see green
It makes me think
Of a green tie
Or a green car going by
It could be lots of vegetables
Or many colored pencils
Green could be trees in the spring
And it is the color of mint ice cream
Green is nature
Or the color of green paper
When I see green
Bridger Thurston, Grade 4
St Christopher's School, VA

Snow
Falling down,
Lightly touching,
With its hand of cold.
Chill of breath,
On my skin,
It holds the key to winter.
Without the snow,
I would not know,
That winter has some light.
Elena Hervey, Grade 5
Nottingham Elementary School, VA

Ms. Sims
Ms. Sims loves to teach
She always wears the color peach

Ms. Sims loves to sing
I hear her cell phone ring

Ms. Sims is really fair
She has nice curly hair

Ms. Sims is really smart
And she is faster than a flying dart!
Savannah Anderson, Grade 4
Courthouse Road Elementary School, VA

Football
Coming right out of the blue
Like a light turned on in your head
You can bet I'm going to hit you
Hit you so hard
You're black and blue
The ball comes out,
Like slippery soap,
It's on the ground
A teammate's treasure
He has found
Touchdown.
Jack Franko, Grade 5
St Christopher's School, VA

Whisper
As silver shoots across the ice
the ice the sun shines down upon the blade
the skates twirl, and spin, and shake
the figure spins and jumps under
the expanding blue sky

The beaming smile,
the setting sun,
the world seemed peaceful
as the figure walked away,
Like a whisper.
Clare Mapes, Grade 6
Monelison Middle School, VA

Summer
Taste the juicy watermelon,
Water splashing on my face,
Freezing ice cold lemonade.
What is this? I will tell you more.
The birds flying everywhere,
Loud kids yelling at the pool,
Hot and humid air,
Ice cream trucks galore.
What is this? It is summer time!
Morgan Foy, Grade 5
Nottingham Elementary School, VA

Playing Basketball

I am a basketball
I wonder if it hurts when I bounce
I hear the whoosh, whoosh when they made the basketball.
I see the concrete on the court.
I want to go high in the sky
I am a hard basketball
I pretend to get up and run and make the goal
I feel myself thrown down the court
I touch the hands of people
I worry that I might go flat
I cry that I don't pop
I am almost a flat basketball
I understand that I might go flat
I say help me, help
I dream to not get stuck in a tree
I try to make the hoop
I hope nobody sticks a needle in me
I am a flat basketball now

Brian Hudgins, Grade 6
Page Middle School, VA

The Typewriter's Last Wish

I am a typewriter
I wonder if I have ribbon
I hear something smacking the paper
I see that the ribbon has ink
I want to go to the place that built me
I am like a keyboard
I pretend to be a printer
I feel like a printer, printing paper letters on a piece of paper
I touch like my keys are worn out
I worry that my keys might break
I cry when I don't have ribbon on me
I am sad when no one uses me
I understand that there is not much ribbon in America
I say that America needs to use typewriters again
I dream that I have a life supply of ribbon
I try to dream that I can write all around the world
I hope that no one throws me away in the trash can
I am a typewriter, but now I am a keyboard

Terry Davidson, Grade 6
Page Middle School, VA

Football Game

I am a football being thrown into the sky
I wonder if I will hit the soft ground
I hear the screams of the fans around me
I see the flashing of the cameras
I want to make the win but don't know if I can
I am the soft grass
I pretend I'm like a sea of green
I feel as small as rice and thin as paper
I touch the players hard feet
I worry I will get cut if I mess up
I cry when I think about it
I am the football player
I understand that I might lose
I say that I will win
I dream I will make it big like to the NFL
I try with all my might
I hope all dreams will come true
I am a football game

Hailee Fry, Grade 6
Page Middle School, VA

Fire

I am fire popping under the moonlit sky.
I wonder what its like it be the moon.
I hear popping and sizzling sounds
I see the moonlit sky
I want to soar across the sky like a shooting star
I am fire
I pretend that I'm as bright as the moon
I feel hot with my flames shining bright.
I touch nice dried leaves
I worry I will die out
I cry when you put more leaves in my pile and I get all smoky
I am fire
I understand I will burn out at one point
I say yay when you start the fire.
I dream that I will just keep burning
I try to be as high as the sky
I hope my flames stay bright
I am fire popping under the moonlit sky.

Tayla Martin, Grade 6
Page Middle School, VA

Spring B's

What would spring be without its B's,
Spring gives buds on beautiful flowers,
Thanks to the April showers,
Spring gives new bundled babies and
Bugs that are speckled ladies,
Birds with blue wings, that sings and sings.
Spring gives bees and sweet honey,
Birthday bashes that are oh so funny,
What would spring be without its B's?

Celeste Creef, Grade 5
Church of the Redeemer Christian School, MD

Dreams

Dreams come only to open minds…
Dreams come from the heavens from night skies…
Or in day times
Children's dreams lie in their special souls…
And sometimes dreams come from your friends…
To give to you…like myself…I have a dream…
Like you too…
With your soaring minds from your father God…
To pass those shining minds he gave to you…

Jorge Betancourt, Grade 6
Magnolia Elementary School, MD

Peaceful Outdoors
Every season leaves
change. Flowers bloom, kids climb trees,
Birds sing, and grass grows.
Anna Creammer, Grade 6
Monelison Middle School, VA

Nature's Sky
The grass is growing
Sweet beautiful skies blow spring
Petals from above
Alexis Martin, Grade 6
Monelison Middle School, VA

The Rain Forest
Birds sing peacefully
Over the green blanket trees
Near the golden sun.
Brittany Mays, Grade 6
Monelison Middle School, VA

As the Spring Comes
Birds chirp in the breeze
As the sky welcomes the sun
While the flowers bloom
Austyn Weaver, Grade 6
Monelison Middle School, VA

Spring Is Near
Flowers bloom birds sing
We see spring is very near
Oh beautiful spring
Clay Bryan, Grade 6
Monelison Middle School, VA

The Morning Forest
The morning grass sang
With the trees and the big birds
Like the branches grow
T. J. Creammer, Grade 6
Monelison Middle School, VA

Breeze
A soft breeze is here
It cools the earth naturally
The breeze blows slowly
Rayven Claytor, Grade 6
Monelison Middle School, VA

Friends
Friends are great to have
It is fun to play with them
They're really awesome!
Carolyn Young, Grade 4
Angelus Academy, VA

What I Love
I love to watch…
The sheer beauty of the crashing waves of the Ocean City bay
Or perhaps the blue skies and sunshine on a warm summer day
I love to smell…
Some freshly cooked delicious homemade food
Maybe a small rose when I'm in a joyous mood
I love to hear…
The sound of a catchy, upbeat, happy, Beatles song
Or the rowdy cheers at a Ravens' game when Boldin goes long.
I love to taste…
The cheesy goodness of mac n' cheese made in a pot
Or when I eat a yummy Five Guys burger without a single thought
I love to touch…
A small bumpy grain of sand
Or maybe the lush grass and crunchy leaves on the land
I love the way…
My life has been for all of my eleven years
Also the respectful way I am treated well by my family, friends, and peers
Alex Abbott, Grade 6
Most Blessed Sacrament Catholic School, MD

Trouble
Trouble follows me everywhere to school and back,
Even places without any rules goodness is what I lack.
It sometimes sneaks up on me,
My life is a circus; can't you see?
And other times it floats in my head like the wind,
I even tend to twist the rules a little bit my friend.
But even though I'm bad, I am still perfectly good,
Since second grade it's been nothing but trouble;
I think I should get better; yes I think I should.
But goofing off helps me no better than anything else;
in fact it makes it worse.
I don't know what makes me bad, but my dad says it's a curse;
I think it's something even worse!
Is there something wrong with me? Is there, or isn't there?
I don't know but I certainly do care,
Because I don't want to end up wired like Joey Pigza and have a bald
spot in the middle of my hair.
J.T. Sullivan, Grade 5
Lightfoot Elementary School, VA

Nature
Nature feels like a pillow,
Smells like the sweet nectar of a flower,
Looks like a big land of life!
If nature was an animal it would be a small bird of peace,
If nature was music it would be a flute of freedom!
Nature's past is being with family,
Nature wants love to roam.
Nature's fear is to let pollution roam.
Nature can teach us how to live.
If nature was magical I would have it cure peoples' hatred.
If I was nature I would defend my land like a rhino defends his young.
Ace Williams, Grade 5
Monocacy Elementary School, MD

Spring Flowers
Spring is so awesome
You could see lots of flowers
I love the spring time
Lily Tran, Grade 4
Angelus Academy, VA

River
A rippling rush
Flowing with luscious nature
It sounds like heaven
Jack Thompson, Grade 4
St John Neumann Academy, VA

The Spring Breeze
The birds singing in
the fields of green grass with the
sweet nature of earth
Ryan Dorr, Grade 6
Monelison Middle School, VA

The Sound of Night
Dusk is rolling in,
And the wind sings a calm tune
Then I grow silent
Ryan Marquis, Grade 6
Monelison Middle School, VA

Shark Attack!
Out of the water
There is a hammerhead shark
I am a goner
Isaiah Eddy, Grade 6
Monelison Middle School, VA

Earth at Morning
Insects gently rest
Birds chirping in the soft breeze
The earth has woken
Jacob Lloyd, Grade 6
Monelison Middle School, VA

My Peaceful Morning
Listen to birds sing
The forest is full of sounds
The sky is peaceful!!!
Curtis Witcher, Grade 6
Monelison Middle School, VA

Oceans
Surfers oh so high
Waves above us in the sky
Castles in the sand
Alex Vaught, Grade 4
St John Neumann Academy, VA

Katie Cohen
Katie
Athletic, energetic, outgoing
sibling of
Jamie and Jake
Lover of
Lacrosse, soccer, and the Ravens
Who feels
Excited, kindness, sensitive
Who needs
Chocolate, my family, my friends
Who gives
Generosity, friendship, my time to volunteer
Who fears
Death, getting injured, getting lost
Who would like to see
The sunset in Hawaii, a blizzard in Florida, Houshmanzedeh in person
Cohen
Katie Cohen, Grade 6
Immaculate Heart of Mary School, MD

The Doll in the Corner
The doll in the corner sat there all year long.
She sat there singing her sad, sad song.
She sat there drenched in her own tears.
Hoping someone would find her and all her fears would disappear.
The family that lived in the house never found her so she gave up hope.
All she did there was sit and mope.
One dark morning, the family was moving out.
The doll was filled with even more doubt.
Then she heard footsteps coming up to the attic.
Her heart all of the sudden started to feel dramatic.
The door opened wide.
A little girl's head looked in from outside.
The girl picked up the doll with care and love.
The little girl's touch had an effect like a warming glove.
The doll was put in the girl's backpack.
She was loved forever and never looked back.
Ellie Maus, Grade 5
Norfolk Collegiate Lower School, VA

My Mr. Bunny
He loves me so much and he knows just how to show it.
Today he helps when I'm sick and feeling down
Soon I won't need him anymore but again I will
Tomorrow he will be waiting for me after school in my bedroom on my pillow
I just can't be away from him!
Emma Brauner, Grade 5
St Clement Mary Hofbauer School, MD

Nature's Beauty
The girls love the summer sun beating down on them as they splash around in the water.
I enjoy the silent beauty of the butterflies heading home.
I love the silence of the creek under the midnight moon!
The owls hoot as we wind down for bed.
Sunshine Williams and Emily Dieffenbach, Grade 5
Francis Asbury Elementary School, VA

High Merit Poems – Grades 4, 5, and 6

Written Words
I spelled peace in the sand,
And the water washed it away too soon.

I wrote love inside a shell,
And it got lost.

You wrote hate at the bottom of the ocean,
And I smudged it.

You scratched the word revenge into a rock,
And I made a line through it.

I wrote the word love on my hand,
And it washed off.

You wrote life,
I wrote love,
And they stayed there,
For all eternity.
Daya Jessee, Grade 6
Friends Meeting School, MD

Littering Kills Sea Turtles
A man goes to the beach
With his picnic lunch.
He brings a soda, a sandwich
And bananas in a bunch.

He eats his lunch and
Leaves the trash on the beach.
It was close enough
For a big wave to reach.

A sea turtle comes along
Mistaking a bag for jelly fish.
Because you know this is
His favorite dish.

The sea turtle eats the bag
And gets a stomach ache.
Now we pray to the Lord
His soul to take.
Gregory Walker, Grade 4
St Clement Mary Hofbauer School, MD

New Year's Eve
Fireworks in the sky
Fireworks in my eye.
Hear the laughter so very loud
Seeing smiles in the crowd.
Seeing them from a mile away
Always hoping they would stay.
Now the sky is clear
And the ball drops to start the new year.
Dominic Kogok, Grade 6
St Columba School, MD

Florida
When I go to Florida,
I know it will be great.
I smell the hot dogs
Burning on the grill.
When I get to the beach,
I smell the salty water.
When I head to the pond
I hear all the animals making noises
As if they're having a party.
The smell of Florida is great!
I see many things when I go to Florida
I see people relaxing in the toasty pool
I see the animals calling to each other.
I see the lightning strike the ground
As if it's throwing a tantrum.
Fireworks burst in the sky
As if a million crayons were thrown up.
In Florida, I see the greatest things!
Dresden Ingegneri, Grade 6
Wyman Elementary School, RI

Birds
Birds chirping,
Birds chirping.

Making nests,
Up in a tree.

Catching worms,
For thee.

Interesting creatures,
Angry,
Happy.

They make me feel,
Like an average person.

Most of them are nice,
Like how I want them to be.
John Arnold, Grade 5
Charles Barrett Elementary School, VA

Summer Light
In the gold summer light
let the butterflies play
listen to the light breeze whisper
frogs hopping on the
shimmering water
for soon the moon will come out
so all the creatures will
lay asleep
waiting for the next
breath of LIGHT.
Christian Skaggs, Grade 5
Francis Asbury Elementary School, VA

Grandma Mary Lou
My grandma has fought
All the cancer she has had
To me she has taught
That having cancer is quite sad
In addition to the cancer
She also had a bad hip
Although not a dancer
Recent surgery restored her zip
Grandma has a wonderful life
She lives in her cozy home
To everyone she is so nice
But she is never alone
Even when she has the flu
I love my Grandma Mary Lou
Zack Papa, Grade 6
Immaculate Heart of Mary School, MD

Jace
As he waits he starts to lick
I am very happy to get a dog
Before he knew it he was picked
He went outside and lay like a log
Our relationship has grown since then
We love him so much
He is such a good friend
He loves to eat toys and such
I know he loves the family
Every time I see him I fill with joy
He has so much energy
He loves when I play with him and his toy
I love his cute little face
He is my wonderful dog, Jace
Christopher Carroll, Grade 6
Immaculate Heart of Mary School, MD

My Maddie Crawford
Let me never lose
The memories we shared
Before my tears came down in deluge
To the days when I brushed your hair
Miss you, miss you is all I ever do
Crying myself to sleep some nights
Just waiting 'til the day is through
Oh how I miss your delicate bite
I still see you smiling back at me
Pulling back your gums
Showing me all your teeth
The warmth in your smile still hums
Rest in magnificent peace
Your love will never cease
Katelyn Ziegler, Grade 6
Immaculate Heart of Mary School, MD

I Am a Tree

I am a tree
I wonder what type of birds perch on me
I hear the other trees swaying in the wind
I see the little children climbing on me
I want my leaves to change color this autumn
I am mighty and tall
I pretend I am an even bigger tree
I feel the warm air
I touch the wind with my leaves
I worry for the others
I cry when they get cut down
I am old
I understand time
I say it never goes back
I dream of new things and new people
I try to imagine who they might be
I hope to meet them
I am a tree

Emily O'Neill, Grade 6
Page Middle School, VA

Shining Fire

I am a fire as bright as the sun
I wonder about what happens on this planet
I hear the rain forest from far away
I see the tents of the camping team
I want to be who I was meant to be
I am a shining fire of the west
I pretend to be a normal campfire and cook food
I feel as fine as a silk dress
I touch the dirt of the road in the night
I worry that I'll only burn once
I cry when I hear the boom of thunder
I am a shining fire burning bright
I understand that fire can't last long
I say that fire can last forever
I dream about heaven in the sky
I try to be tall and strong
I hope to be the brightest
I am a fire that shines bright

Scott Drake, Grade 6
Page Middle School, VA

I Am a Basketball

I am a basketball flying towards the net,
I wonder if I'll go in the net,
I hear kids shouting as I near the net,
I see kids looking at me hoping that I'll fall through the net,
I want to feel the net all around me.
I am a basketball hoop,
I pretend that kids play with me when they really don't,
I feel the ball falling through my net,
I touch the ball when it bounces off my rim,
I worry that I'll fall down in a storm,
I cry when a kid doesn't make a shot.
I am a kid,
I understand that I won't make every shot,
I say "aw" when I don't make the shot,
I dream to be a NBA player,
I try my best to make the shot,
I hope to make every shot one day,
I am a kid.

Sean Haugdahl, Grade 6
Page Middle School, VA

The River

I am a rushing waterfall
I wonder when I will finally be still
I hear the sound of myself crashing at the rocks below
I see a lake beyond the tall trees
I want to be calm like the lake
I am the lake beyond the trees
I pretend I am the strong waterfall
I feel weak and puny
I touch the edge of the woods
I worry that I will never be strong and free
I cry because I am trapped in my little bowl
I am the river that connects the waterfall to the lake
I understand they want to be like each other
I say I don't have that kind of power
I dream that I can one day help them
I try to do it
I hope they understand
I am the three bodies of water, each one like the other

Sarah Thompson, Grade 6
Page Middle School, VA

Marshmallow Land

Marshmallow land is the place to be,
Marshmallow land is the place for me!
It's peaceful, beautiful, and majestic too!
The water falls are pouring out light purple water,
Which sounds like the ocean waves.
The whole land is covered with light blue,
Light pink, and cotton candy purple marshmallows!
Also there are palm trees too!
It's just so wonderful,
You can't imagine a better place to be!

Alexis Lawson, Grade 5
Rocky Gap Elementary School, VA

Summer

Sweet green grass growing on the ground,
Pink yellow and blue flowers all around.
A fresh cool breeze hits my face,
Like a single drop of water with such grace.
I hear the soft melody of the bluebird's song,
It makes me want to hum and sing along.
I play and laugh with all of my friends,
The time passes quickly and soon it ends.
The freedom of running and singing so free,
The freedom of summer belongs to me.

Sophia Rose Gary, Grade 5
Nottingham Elementary School, VA

Sometimes I Wish

Sometimes I wish!
Sometimes I wish war would end.
Sometimes I wish love was our friend.
Sometimes I wish people didn't have to die for our freedom.
Sometimes I wish no one had to be hungry.
Sometimes I wish no one felt pain.
Sometimes I wish it wouldn't happen again.
Sometimes I wish we floated on clouds,
Free of worry, free to come down.
Sometimes I wish hate would just end.
Sometimes I wish everyone had a good friend.
Sometimes I wish pain would cease,
Finally at peace.
Sometimes I wish!

McKayla McDaniel, Grade 6
Paul L Dunbar Middle School for Innovation, VA

All the Shades of Blue

Royal
like a princess in a castle,
Navy
like the people that protect our country,
Turquoise
like the color of the ocean in the sparkling sun,
Indigo
the darkest shade with all of your secrets,
Sky
like ice in the winter,
Sapphire
like the gemstone,
Blue
the color of the world.

Isabelle Simmons, Grade 4
Montessori International Childrens House, MD

The Forgotten Soul

When the night had come and the moon is dead,
That forgotten soul comes.
He goes to the one who laughs at him,
And turn dreams to nightmares.

When the dark rises and holy's not there,
The forgotten soul comes,
He makes human minds puzzled,
And hearts beat slower.

When the stars are beaten from the dark clouds,
The forgotten soul comes,
He makes a creative brain no more,
But he is no match to my creativity.

Simon Cooper, Grade 5
Monocacy Elementary School, MD

Pawtuxet Village

The sights in the village are old, very old.
The shops and restaurants are all lined up neatly,
With bits of peeling paint hanging off the shingles.
The shops are tiny, almost doll-sized.
I like to watch it spit water under the bridge.
But the really remarkable thing about the village,
Over all the other sights, are the houses,
Some being over 300 years old.
The park is also a lovely place,
With its green grass and children's playground.

You can also hear many things in the village.
I hear the familiar rhythm of the rushing river,
Combined with many other sounds of the village,
Making it a medley of the river, honking cars,
And groups of people laughing and conversing.

The air in the village smells fresh to me,
Even though I can smell the gasoline of cars.
I smell the scent of coffee as I go past the bakery.
The smells make the best combination of scents —
The kind I can only smell in one place —
PAWTUXET VILLAGE!

Mary Dolan, Grade 6
Wyman Elementary School, RI

The Ruler of the Antarctic Ice

Mostly black and white,
Not much in height.
Plumper than a ball,
Not too tall,
A built in pouch to carry,
The baby,
The ruler of the Antarctic ice.

It waddles along silently
With webbed feet
As far as my eye can see.
It's plump, feathery body provides it heat.
They waddle on in dead silence
Marching single-file is no coincidence,
Only tobogganing when they tire of walking.
The ruler of the Antarctic ice.

Its voice is a varied one.
It can choose to make a ton
Of its cawing honking call.
And now, our friend will say something,
"OOK! OOK!"
That will be all.

MeiJade Hsu, Grade 5
Forcey Christian School, MD

Football

I am a football
I wonder why I fly
I hear whistling in the air
I see birds flying
I want to see the ground
I am bouncing when I hit the ground
I pretend to sleep in a player's hand
I feel the ground on my leather
I touch people when they catch me
I worry I will get flattened
I cry when I get fumbled
I am in good hands
I understand I might get replaced
I say please NO!
I dream I am in a cloud
I try to dream
I hope to see the ground more than the sky
I am a flying football.

Bradley Amos, Grade 6
Page Middle School, VA

Questions

I am brightness, like a fire
I wonder what its like down there
I hear emptiness
I see darkness
I want to cool down
I am seen during the day
I pretend to be big
I feel hot
I touch nothing
I worry I'm going to grow
I cry about the freedom I will never get
I am the source of life
I understand the way you live
I say nothing
I dream of fire
I try to move
I hope I will
I am a puzzle for you

Evelyn Hronec, Grade 6
Page Middle School, VA

March

Flowers are blooming
And the sun is shining
As the winter snow is
Slowly melting away
You can smell the
Spring breeze in your face
And you can see the
Brand new grass growing
But once you see the sun out
You will know it's really spring

Alaysia Sum, Grade 6
Warwick Neck School, RI

Darkness

I lay down in bed
The darkness envelopes me
As I close my eyes
I leave.
I go into the dark world
That is my subconscious
I search for something
Anything
Besides the darkness.
It holds me
Pressing and squeezing
Caressing and holding
Loving and hating
Helping and hurting
Taking and giving.
At last, I surface
I see all the light around me
And miss the darkness.

Emma Stohlman, Grade 6
St Francis of Assisi School, VA

The Wind

I am something moving quietly,
I wonder if I can move people,
I hear people laughing,
I see people crying,
I want people not to cry; but to feel good,
I am the wind "Wish."
I pretend I am strong,
I feel weak,
I touch something weird,
I worry it will hurt me,
I cry I will die,
I am the wind "Wish."
I understand I break things during storms,
I say nothing,
I dream I am quiet,
I try to feel good,
I hope to find friends,
I am the wind "Wish."

Cameron Miller, Grade 6
Page Middle School, VA

Summer Beach

Feel the sand beneath your feet,
The golden rocks that feel like sleet.
Nothing better than the summer waves,
While fish swim by on those summer days.
But look over by that little kid,
Is that something that a jellyfish did?
No it is pink and floating away,
OH NO, it's heading right this way!
I'd better run, it's by my side,
Sorry the next victim is you! Bye-bye.

Tynea Swinton, Grade 4
Waller Mill Fine Arts Magnet School, VA

My Sweet Senses

I see the spectacular parade
Of cherry blossoms
Marching along the prairie.

I smell the amazing aroma
Of the enormous field
Of daisies, daffodils, and roses.

I hear the annoying
But calming sound of
Tweeting birds and buzzing Bees.

I feel the tender touch
Of the bright yellow sunflowers
And orange Lucifer Crocosmias.

I taste the delicious meal
Of my mom sitting at the window
Watching the colorful garden yelling
It's SPRINGTIME!

Brittany Amadi, Grade 6
Magnolia Elementary School, MD

The Fair

The smell of popcorn,
Cotton candy, and hot dogs
Linger in the air.
Children squeal as
They take on the challenge
Of the chair swings that
Rise above pretzel stands
And ice cream carts.
Everybody has smiling faces.
Some, though, are splattered
With blue remains of cotton candy
That sticks like glue.
They indulge themselves
With the tasty clump
Of sugary heaven.
Then at the end of
The delightful day,
Children exit not only
With captured plush prizes
But memories worth holding on to.

Maggie Maguire, Grade 6
Trinity School, MD

Storms

The thunder
was loud,
like beating drums,
the lightning
was bright,
like the glowing sun

Taylor Green, Grade 6
Page Middle School, VA

High Merit Poems – Grades 4, 5, and 6

The Hungry Fish
My fish is darting
Up and down the lovely tank
Scouting for his lunch
Zach Williams, Grade 4
Greenville Elementary School, VA

Spring Is Near
Spring is almost here
Pack away those winter coats
Go outside and play.
Sarah Padilla, Grade 4
St Joseph School-Fullerton, MD

Spring
The buds sprout flowers
They are colorful and bright
I enjoy the scene.
Abigail Kaiss, Grade 4
St Joseph School-Fullerton, MD

Easter
Many Easter eggs
children rushing to gather
for Easter prizes.
Jamie Murielle J. Iringan, Grade 4
St. Joseph School-Fullerton, MD

Spring
Flowers rise above
baby animals are born
rain sprinkles the land.
Gabrielle Aversa, Grade 4
St Joseph School-Fullerton, MD

Spring
The weather is warm.
Lots of flowers are blooming.
Raindrops are falling.
Stacy Villanueva, Grade 4
St Joseph School-Fullerton, MD

Rainbows
They are colorful
Blue's my favorite color
Come out after rain
Austin Romano, Grade 4
Battlefield Elementary School, VA

Easter
Bright colorful eggs
brought to all in a basket
a sign Spring is near.
Connor McSharry, Grade 4
St Joseph School-Fullerton, MD

Fish*
Fish
Fish
Fish
Pretty fish
Wonderful, amazing fish
Graceful, loving, beautiful fish
Flowing fish
Bubbly fish
Shiny small goldfish
Colorful flashy koi fish
Flittery fish, too
Glittery fish
Peaceful fish
Don't forget guppy fish
Last of all, best of all, I like beta fish
Julia Rocca, Grade 4
Greenville Elementary School, VA
*Patterned after "Beans, Beans, Beans" by Lucia & James L. Hymes

Substantial
The wallow of Dense Forest.
Canopies soaring high,

Numerous sources of His own wealth,

Through the Power
Of Indifference,

Can be found Intrigued
Less to a tiny Bud.

Of less creative, or Substantial Power.
Yet to the Machine.

More importance.
Brendan Shimizu, Grade 6
Heather Hills Elementary School, MD

The Learning Fox
The fox in my backyard.
Sitting.
Waiting.
Watching.
Seems so alert and patient.
He is my teacher.
He will always know if something is not right.
Sometimes I feel like him.
Looking.
Observing.
Understanding.
Getting to know the real world.
Not just learning the basic facts, but interpreting them into a brand new language.
Suddenly, he darts away, leaving me with my broken train of thoughts.
I silently say, "Goodbye, learning fox."
Zoe Westrick, Grade 6
St Jane De Chantal School, MD

The Cat

There was a cat that was frisky,
He always ran in the road which was risky.
He couldn't help himself because he ate and ate,
Which made him very overweight.

This very clever cat's name was Meatball,
But believe it or not he wasn't very tall.
Under the bed he would hide and attack,
And there were days I was afraid he would never come back.

Dogs and snakes would always make him frightened,
And other cats made his stomach tighten.
When chasing mice he could always show great speed,
If he was chasing me, he would take the lead.

This unique cat means the world to me,
But his favorite thing of all is green tea.

Charlie Dyer, Grade 5
Lightfoot Elementary School, VA

Noise in the City

Traffic in a busy city is anything but pretty,
Tipity Tap Tap
The working woman's shoes say
As she hurries across the street.
"Taxi! Taxi!" the concerned clan shouts.
The sound of honks and horns abound,
And an ambulance is around
WEEEEEEE OOOOOOOO WEEEEE OOOOOOO
As it zooms past.
Clickity clack clickity clack.
The horse's hooves sing,
As he pulls traveling tourists all over town.

The noise resounds,
And as I lie down,
My dreams will be filled
With the city's sounds.

Jenna Thompson, Grade 6
Trinity School, MD

Mother's Way

On a bad day sadness is everywhere I go
Here and there
So and so.

When I go home the sadness starts to simmer
But when mama talks to me
And gives me a big old hug
It makes me want to keep on going.
Now I'm watching the day go by
Waiting for what the next day is going to bring.
Wow what a good day
Thinking about mother's way

Dylan Cook, Grade 6
Magnolia Elementary School, MD

My Cuddly Puppy

My cuddly new puppy sat on my lap,
her name is Cynthia
looking out the murky colored window
as if she is in some other world.

I'm running down the blurred street.
My dog is clomping next to me faithfully
Her tongue rolls out the side of her yellow muzzle.

I frantically leap down the steep stairs,
almost tardy for the school bus.
My dog bounds blithely down the stairs after me
"thud thud thump thump"
clears a pile of books lying patiently in the hallway
and sweeps the corner,
she doesn't want to miss me leaving
I love my new cuddly puppy.

Joy Modozie, Grade 6
Magnolia Elementary School, MD

I Used to, But Now I

I used to live in the everlasting California sun
But now I live in Delaware with tons of terrific fun

I used to listen to silly songs
But now I gracefully sing along

I used to play with cute fashion dolls
But now I daringly play softball

I used to not know right from wrong
But now my mind is oh so strong

I used to listen to my mom's guiding voice
But now I am older and make my own choice

I used to watch such smart shows to help educate me
But now I watch the amazingly musical Glee

Sarah Reeves, Grade 6
Most Blessed Sacrament Catholic School, MD

Spring Is Here

Hip-Hop-Hooray!
Hear everyone cheer
April 18th everyone's going to sing
for here is spring and what it brings
Crazy weather, School Spring Concert, Easter
And everyone's favorite April Fool's Day

In spring it is always a child's day
Every day a child pleads to play
from sunup to sundown in every city and every town
So let's enjoy it while it lasts
Spring is here and we're out of class

Demetrius Smith, Grade 6
Magnolia Elementary School, MD

Keep Our Home Clean

Keeping the world clean
Is the right thing to do.
Recycling bottles and cans
Will keep Earth like new.

The environment we live in
Needs love and care.
Everyone help out
And clean up our air.

When you go shopping
Take reusable sacks.
Fill them to the top
With goodies and snacks.

Take care of our world
Have fun with it too.
Carpool and bike ride
So it will be here for you.
Bailey Mullen, Grade 4
St Clement Mary Hofbauer School, MD

Bird

Hidden
Waiting in the trees
Chirping
Annoying the heck out of me
Crowing
Turning my face red

Chirp chirp
Chirp chirp
Tweet tweet
Tweet tweet
Teasing
Testing me

Mysterious little bird
Where are you? Who are you?
What is your problem?

Why do you do this to me?
Benjamin Wilson, Grade 5
Charles Barrett Elementary School, VA

Red

Red is the color of fresh-picked cherries,
tulip petals and ripe strawberries.
I can see the red rusted metal,
and feel the gentle rose petals.
I walk along the red brick path,
the robin splashes in the bird bath.
Red is the color of many beautiful things,
like strawberry pie and cardinal's wings.
Morgan Ramsey, Grade 5
Norfolk Collegiate Lower School, VA

Light Bulb

Light bulb
Like UFO
"Alien" watching me
Light bulb or an invader?
Invader
William Rodriguez, Grade 5
St Christopher's School, VA

Stars

Stars are bright
Stars shine
You can see them in the night sky
Each star is different
And that is what makes them special.
Hannah Turner, Grade 4
Courthouse Road Elementary School, VA

Camp Seagull

Camp Seagull's amazing
With all the wind blazing
Sailing sunfish every hour
At your cabin taking a shower
Delicious food that you'll devour
Jack Whitmore, Grade 5
St Christopher's School, VA

Springtime

Blossoms here,
Birds there,
Snow melting in the warm air.
Sleeping mammals waking up,
And eating 'cause they haven't since fall.
Matthew Neuman, Grade 5
Nottingham Elementary School, VA

Credit Card

Credit card
Spending money
Buying many things
Makes me feel rich
Money
Will Forrest, Grade 5
St Christopher's School, VA

Dragon

Dragon
Fire breathing
Flies in the cloudy sky
It makes me feel like a dragon too
Scaly
Dakota Emery, Grade 4
Waller Mill Fine Arts Magnet School, VA

Peaceful Nature

The breeze sorts the air
The sun covers the rainbow
The chirping bird sings
Darrell Wade, Grade 6
Monelison Middle School, VA

Index

Abbott, Alex 193
Abbott, Valerie 125
Abraham, Annie 103
Abraham, Eliana 190
Abraham, Liesel 132
Adams, Noah 169
Addison, Mitchell 84
Adelhardt, Teri 65
Adenekan, James 31
Adkins, Amber 33
Akintoba, Morenike 88
Akintoba, Tolu 190
Akula, Vishal 61
Aldridge, Alyssa 156
Aleman, Angie 169
Allen, Kaitlyn 37
Allen, Mykia 42
Allen, Yanni 102
Allison, Maggie 92
Allison, Ryan 180
Alves, Mirian 42
Alvey, Kayla 103
Amadi, Brittany 198
Amar, Kathryn Irene 165
Ambrose, Birch 138
Amos, Bradley 198
Anderson, Alex 144
Anderson, Caroline 173
Anderson, Casey 15
Anderson, Hunter 179
Anderson, Megan 29
Anderson, Savannah 191
Anderson, Sean 55
Andruzzi, Amanda 85
Aneke, Chioma 77
Annamreddy, Havisha 103
Anvari, Parrisa 169
Applegate, Sydney 119
Apsley, Allie 106
Arbogast, Ally G. 26
Archibald, Angelo 77
Arena, Meghan 18
Armstrong, Ian 58
Arnett, Katherine 28
Arnold, John 195
Arruda, Rachel 144
Asad, Mahnoor 56
Asam, Christian 27
Asbury, Kayla 177
Asihene, Nana 36
Aversa, Gabrielle 199
Bachman, Dana 99

Bailey, Ciera Stephanie 189
Baldwin, David J. 97
Balog, Graham 59
Banks, Christian 165
Banks, Helena 63
Barcelos, Destiny 169
Barfield, Whitney 46
Barger, Erin Nicole 22
Barker, Drew 176
Barnes, Dante 132
Barnes, Justin 122
Barnes, Katherine 189
Barr, Jarred 156
Barrand, Chase 58
Barreto, Karine 45
Barreto, Xena 56
Barrett, Ariana 95
Barrett, Ben 53
Barrett, Peter 122
Barton, Jaden 181
Bauer, Kyle 39
Bayzie, Maria 13
Beach, Mary Beth 175
Beasley, Samuel 122
Beavers, Meredith 143
Bendfeldt, Hannah 27
Benetti, Catherine 50
Bennett, Jake 187
Bennett, Lauren 144
Bentivenga, Grace 172
Bergeron, Darius 35
Bernard, Matt 39
Beshai, Heba 118
Betancourt, Jorge 192
Beteck, Nkongho 30
Bhatia, Shreya 129
Bialozynski, Chloe 89
Bickford, Lily 106
Bischoff, Abigail 189
Bishop, Steve 67
Black, Britney 175
Blake, Kaitlin 91
Blanchette, Elizabeth 166
Blankenship, Ariel 13
Blow, Kennedy 179
Blye, Kennedy 125
Boatman, Riviera 14
Bohenek, Kendall 60
Bonaminio, Gia 143
Bonner, Annemarie 185
Booker, Antoine 173
Borowy, Sara 111

Bose, Elizabeth 110
Bosi, Nicholas 164
Bourne, Hali 173
Bowden, Brett 154
Bowlds, Sam 161
Bowman, Katelyn 32
Bowman, Nicole 127
Boyd, Christopher 13
Boyd, Matthew 144
Boyd, Miyah 59
Bracey, Teliza 142
Bracy, Sophie 162
Bradby, Rodney 25
Bradby, Whitney 13
Bragg, Nicole 17
Branch, Olivia 182
Branch, Whitney 38
Brannon, Jimmy 76
Branscome, Caleb 187
Brauner, Emma 194
Bray, Amanda 93
Briscoe, Camryn 144
Brito, Lady 32
Brobst, Nicholas 50
Brodsky, Rachel 66
Brooks, Alexis 102
Brothers, Garrett 128
Broughton, Cameron 75
Brown, Alex 138
Brown, Ally 93
Brown, Josie 77
Brown, Madeline 159
Brown, Sam 63
Brown, Shaina 181
Bruce, Ian 20
Brunner, Lauren 60
Bryan, Clay 193
Bubniak, Lydia 48
Buchanan, Kayla 176
Buck, Ryan 138
Budagov, Arnold G. 37
Budd, Aaron 151
Budd, Christian 54
Buethe, Nathan 43
Buka III, Richard 31
Burden, Tavia 35
Burger, Luke 150
Burke, Meghan 47
Burket, Hayleigh 188
Burns, Kelly 73
Butler, Cashae 54
Butler, Christian 143

Butler, Gia ... 188	Clark, Thomas ... 130	Dagnon, Ise-Oluwa ... 153
Butler, Joshua ... 173	Clayton-Schwartz, AnnaLea ... 28	Dahl, Pamela ... 123
Butler, Joshua ... 186	Claytor, Rayven ... 193	Dansereau, Angela ... 119
Butler, Sarah ... 99	Cleland, Sophie ... 181	Davenport, Adia ... 156
Butler, Shawn ... 45	Clemmey, Austin ... 135	Davenport, Huntley ... 190
Buzzerd, Landon ... 93	Clyburn, Jade ... 188	Davidson, Terry ... 192
Byers, Christina ... 22	Coates, KeiAsia ... 63	Davis, Alexis ... 51
Cabral, Darien ... 142	Cochran, Madeline ... 43	Davis, Amanda ... 174
Cabral, Leslie ... 74	Coffman, Sarah ... 185	Davis, Cristian ... 185
Cain, Zoe ... 38	Cohen, Aislinn ... 122	Davis, Diamond ... 175
Calder, Macy ... 157	Cohen, Katie ... 194	Davis, Ebony ... 40
Callaghan, Liam ... 54	Cokenour, Solana ... 187	Davis, Jasper ... 140
Calvache, Alejandra ... 160	Cole, Breanah ... 36	Davis, Loretta ... 118
Camarco, Kexxer ... 158	Coleman, Jennifer ... 86	Davis, Savannah ... 156
Canfield, Glenn ... 112	Collins, Christina ... 165	Davis, Sydelle ... 189
Caparaz, Catherin ... 94	Colturi, Jenna ... 130	Davis, Taylor ... 64
Capobianco, Jenna ... 19	Coluna, ErinLiz ... 54	Davis, Tyreek ... 181
Carlow, Christian ... 186	Comegna, Anthony ... 165	Deans, Jarad ... 43
Carr, Tamira ... 106	Compton, Emily ... 75	DeBandi, Ethan ... 23
Carr, William ... 88	Conde, Hajah ... 152	DeCastro, Miguel ... 100
Carreon, Lizeth ... 156	Connelly, Jessica ... 171	Delaney, Daniel ... 43
Carroll, Christopher ... 195	Conner, Kamryn ... 157	DelSanto, Sarah ... 18
Carroll, Emma ... 151	Conrad, Gannon ... 183	Deng, Kate ... 132
Carter, Brittani ... 44	Conrad, Heather ... 118	DePanise, Emma ... 81
Carter, Pj ... 184	Cook, Alexandra ... 79	Detweiler, Bennett ... 141
Casale, Candace ... 115	Cook, Dylan ... 200	Devarakonda, Pooja ... 53
Cash, Julia ... 174	Cook, Sydney ... 148	DeVincenzis, Gabriella ... 190
Castillo, Brandon ... 129	Cooper, Simon ... 197	Deyo, Cameron ... 191
Castleberry, Asa ... 140	Corbit, Ruby ... 89	Dias, Ieltsin ... 35
Castleberry, Ransom ... 153	Cordero, Rita ... 176	Dichoso, David ... 107
Castro, Alexa ... 171	Cornely, Brendan ... 18	DiCocco, Daniel ... 51
Castro, Nahela ... 166	Correll, Jordan ... 32	Dieffenbach, Emily ... 194
Caulk, Danielle ... 81	Corum, Kayla ... 87	DiLenge, Madison ... 89
Caza, James ... 188	Cote, Hannah ... 104	Dill, Victoria ... 88
Celozzi, Rosa ... 90	Cotellese, Bryan ... 187	Dimeck, Leah ... 41
Celseti, Alessia ... 181	Cotellese, Megan ... 131	Dixon, Glenn ... 107
Chalk, Ian ... 170	Cotman, Gregory ... 30	Do, Fiona ... 72
Chandi, Mohit ... 66	Courtney, Nyah K. ... 155	Doane, Madeline ... 123
Charity, Keirra ... 44	Courville, Landon ... 121	Dobson, Ryan ... 140
Charleus, Zenobia ... 124	Courville, Sydney ... 167	Dolan, Mary ... 197
Cheek, Andrea ... 88	Covington, Bria ... 138	Donaldson, Susan ... 60
Chester, Jaren ... 147	Cowen, Andrew ... 52	Dorr, Ryan ... 194
Cheung, Natalie ... 52	Cravotta, Caneel ... 178	Dorsey, Kendel ... 154
Chicas, Vilma ... 140	Creammer, Anna ... 193	Dow, Jonathan ... 81
Chiruvella, Neil ... 104	Creammer, T. J. ... 193	Dowell, Tatyana ... 164
Chmielewski, Courtney ... 62	Creef, Celeste ... 192	Dowling, Tori ... 56
Chow, Chin Yi ... 40	Crewe, Rickala ... 42	Doyle, Charlie ... 116
Chriscoe, Ryan ... 151	Cromer, Isaiah ... 114	Drake, Scott ... 196
Christian, Chanell ... 17	Crook, Conor ... 152	Drinkwalter, Georgia ... 73
Chu, Quinn ... 98	Crow, Brittany ... 116	Drury, Brianne ... 120
Chuang, Andy ... 146	Cuevo, Connor ... 141	Dubois, Meaghan ... 132
Chuang, Grace ... 58	Cui, Jake ... 92	Duetsch, Julie ... 99
Chuang, Rachel ... 26	Cunningham, Amy ... 27	Dunlop, Connor ... 164
Clark, Bailey ... 175	Curtis, Michelle ... 78	Duong, Nhu-Phuong ... 44
Clark, Griffin ... 160	Curtis, Nick ... 114	Dupre, Yalaina ... 108
Clark, Horace ... 59	Cyphers, Valerie ... 132	DuVal, Jamie ... 27
Clark, Meghan ... 142	D'Acchioli, Tiana ... 71	Dye, Crystal ... 172
Clark, Shiona ... 17	Dabo, Aly ... 176	Dyer, Charlie ... 200

Index

Ealey, Myranda 142
Earley, James 33
Eberhardt, Lauren 93
Ebubedike, Jonathan 160
Eddy, Isaiah 194
Edejer, Jenalyse 181
Edsall, Hailey 21
Edwards, Sophia 185
Ekambarapu, Leela 120
Elliott, Darius 110
Elliott, Maya 172
Ellis, Jonathan 171
Emery, Dakota 201
Emrick, Makayla 64
England, Olivia 189
English, Emilienne 188
Eskinder, Abigail 177
Espinoza-Jones, Adilia 145
Estriplet, Sebastien 23
Eubank, Mason 184
Evans, Benton 15
Eyre, Emma 148
Fan, Emily 122
Fan, Shanell 124
Farmer, Autumn 172
Farnum, Emily 104
Farr, Nick 83
Feng, Akaela 191
Fenton, Teddy 115
Ferares, Trevor 161
Ferguson, Aysia 180
Ferguson, Brittany 37
Ferguson, Monique 166
Fernandez, Caleb 179
Fernandez, Marlena 23
Fialon, Guillemette 132
Figueroa, Amanda 89
Finch, Robert Paul 19
Fink, Hailey 185
Finnessy, Emily 185
Flaherty, Jennifer 126
Fleenor, Hannah 165
Fleming, Trey 143
Fletcher, Taylor 158
Flores, Emmanuel 41
Floyd, Joy 131
Fogg, Isabella 164
Fong, Daphne 27
Ford, Elijah 154
Ford, Elishia 187
Ford, Isaiah 156
Ford, Kiarah 118
Ford, Russhell 117
Forrest, Justin 45
Forrest, Will 201
Foster, Hannah 80
Fournier, Eileen 20
Fournier, Jessica 46
Foust, Bailey 100
Foxwell, Nicole 18
Foy, Morgan 191
Franko, Jack 191
Franzel, Katie 47
Frazier, Demaj 22
Frazier, Henry 63
Freeny, Lauren 57
Fry, Hailee 192
Fuller, Kalisa 130
Furrowh, Dominique 24
Fusca, Carolyn 86
Gaitan, Angeline 159
Galbreath, Rachel 144
Galdamez, Steffany 13
Gallardo, Celena 167
Gambardelli, Sabrina 142
Gambrell, Christina 188
Gana, Cynthia 22
Ganley, Connor 96
Garcia, Victor 12
Gardner, Amber 39
Gartner, Katelyn 116
Gary, Sophia Rose 196
Garzon, Emily 61
Gaskill, Moriah 117
Gatto, Carly 180
Gausman, Kiersten 21
Gavrila, Adrian 72
Gazzelli, Megan 41
Gengler, Natasha 191
Georgieff, James 170
Gepilano, Elizabeth 154
Gershman, Tamar 184
Giancola, Abby 118
Gibbs, Benjamin 163
Gilday, Haley 151
Glenn, Christopher 152
Godwin, Joe 23
Goebel, Madison 12
Gold, Michelle 171
Golshani, Bita 99
Gomes, Ivanildo 12
Gomez, Jaime 116
Gonzalez, Jason 185
Gonzalez Lopez, Maria Clara .. 71
Gonzalez Lopez, Paula Andrea .. 89
Goossens, Martijn 109
Gordon, Madelyn 68
Gormley, Victoria 85
Gosnell, Heather 44
Gray, Ashley 59
Green, Dillon 175
Green, Dominique 164
Green, Peyton 116
Green, Sarah 135
Green, Taylor 198
Greening, Mary Kate 62
Gregory, Kori 146
Gretschel, Louise 18
Griffith, Tyler 113
Grubb, Payton 189
Gruszczynski, Emily 123
Gudavalli, Deepika 83
Guevremont, Ethan 92
Gulian, Ellen 146
Guo, Matthew 126
Gurung, Ellen 101
Gutierrez Cuadra, Sofia 79
Gutierrez Ribera, Natalia 122
Gwira, Laudina 146
Haas, Madison 134
Haddad, Izzy 93
Haddad, Jacob 50
Hagan, Cassandra 35
Haley, Jordan 60
Hall, Janelle 17
Hall, Matt 162
Hall, Meade 142
Halsey, Drew 159
Hamby, Meghan 180
Hamilton, Paige 154
Hanline, Jack 175
Harrell, Taylor 62
Harris, Madison 142
Harrison, Danyelle 177
Hartley, Franklin 175
Hartlove, Brianna 103
Haschert, Erica 94
Hastings, Adam 142
Hatcher, Brandon 186
Hatton, Courtney 55
Haugdahl, Sean 196
Hayes, Tabby 102
Haynes, Courtney 166
Heaps, Jack 101
Heddinger, Kaitlyn 154
Heinold, Katie 74
Heller, Daniel 65
Helms, Meigs 143
Henderson, Ja'Qwaun R. 152
Henenlotter, Rebecca 20
Henkel, Catherine 159
Herbert, Alexis 66
Herbert, Eletria 74
Herbert, Makayla 58
Herbertson, Alan 68
Hertenstein, Victoria 147
Hervey, Elena 191
Hickman, Isabeau 36
Higgins, Ben 66
Hill, Eric 56
Hill, Jabraughn R. 127
Hinton, Jessica 70
Ho, Valerie 150
Hoag, Casey 143

Hobson, Taylor 64	Johnson, Ciara 130	Knox, Keegan 185
Hogge, Austin 139	Johnson, Dekel 138	Kogok, Dominic 195
Hogle, Omie 188	Johnson, Jeffrey 36	Kolhof, Jacqueline 70
Holland, Hanna 86	Johnson, Marcus 164	Kominsky, Cecelia 180
Hollinger, Mary Claire 170	Johnson, Scotti 55	Korendyke, Mary 135
Holmes, Kyle 12	Johnson, Shelby 177	Kraettli, Andrina 119
Holsinger, Rebecca 152	Johnston, Thomas 124	Kramb, Sarah 30
Hood, Stephaine 12	Jones, Angel 103	Kramer, Austin 68
Hopkins, Caitlin 57	Jones, Baylee 161	Krasny, Josie 187
Horsky, Holly 33	Jones, Cailin 117	Kron, Kelsey 139
Horsley, Jack 191	Jones, Erica 121	Krykanov, Nicole 163
Hosamane, Neel 50	Jones, Hamirah 190	Krystkiewicz, Maegan 178
Housley, Miles 177	Jones, James 160	Ku, Justin 106
Howard, Jamie 43	Jones, Jessica 14	Kubli, Aliyah 165
Howard, Kimberly 184	Jones, Kanesha 34	KuKanich, Matthew 173
Howe, Grant 177	Jones, Olivia 158	Kulick, Eliza 31
Howell, Joseph 163	Jurkiewicz, Eric 174	Kulikowski, Joey 170
Howlett, Timothy Mark 131	Justice, Aric 57	Kumar, Akshay 107
Hronec, Evelyn 198	Kaiss, Abigail 199	Kumar, Nidhi 120
Hsu, MeiJade 197	Kanter, Natalie 110	Kurtz, Christopher 177
Hu, Margaret 28	Kappen, Demi 54	Kutkut, Mody 189
Huang, Andrew 109	Karar, Ythrip 76	L'Etoile, Dorian 169
Hudenburg, Emily 63	Kargbo, Fatima 151	LaBarge, Taylor 71
Hudgins, Brian 192	Karlin, Hannah 139	Ladd, Shay 173
Hudgins, Cheyenne 66	Karn, Anthony 134	Lafond, Renee 27
Hudler, Nicole 62	Kasbohm, Bethany 186	Lagonegro, Jack 182
Huffaker, Kailyn 95	Kataxenou, Eleni 156	Lally, Kayla 51
Hughes, Delaney 150	Kaur, Baldeep 55	Lamberti, Kyle 18
Hummel, Charles 109	Kaushal, Yashica 124	Lanasa, Ally 111
Hurd, Ashley E 168	Kavanagh, Steven 182	Lane, Hailey 29
Hurst, Tyler 153	Kearns, Olivia 190	Langham, James 28
Huseby, Tristan 154	Keepudi, Neswanth 67	Langston, DaNaisha 143
Hutchinson, Dale 28	Keighton, Lucas 170	Lareau, Caley 43
Huth-Scruggs, Tim 181	Kelahan, Casey 67	Larson, Elizabeth 67
Huynh, Thao 28	Keller, Christian 52	Lashbaugh, Alexis 168
Hydara, Mariam 143	Kelley, Sean 83	Laster, Helen 153
Iannantuono, Haley 139	Kelly, Katelynn 51	Laverdure, Evan 129
Iannucci, Ricky 109	Kennedy, Sarah 128	Lawrence, Perry 143
Imdad, Rumika 77	Kerns, Madison 101	Lawson, Alexis 196
Ingegneri, Dresden 195	Khan, Marida 130	Lawson, Will 178
Ipock, Kristin 172	Khan, Oneib 61	Lawson Jr., Michael 87
Iringan, Jamie Murielle J. 199	Khanna, Anjali 134	LeBel, PJ 151
Jackson, Amy 109	Khosla, Meghna 40	Leber, Brilee 175
Jackson, Hannah 164	Kidwell, Zachary 177	LeBlanc, Megan 181
Jackson, Jazmine 122	Kilby, Kyle 153	Lee, Jason 144
Jackson, Shayne 26	Kilson, Deonte 96	Leggette, Chyna Breshay 160
Jacob, Jeremiah 186	King, Dominique 142	Leighton, Kristen 85
James, Maria 81	King, Madelynn 128	Leinbach, Charlotte 129
Janneh, Sheku 37	Kirk, Jayna 110	Lepine, Christopher 71
January, Jennifer 107	Kirwan, Sydney 88	Lepine, Jennifer 119
Jayaram, Jennani 147	Kissam, Skylar 134	Levy, Jacob 180
Jenkins, Samantha 116	Kivrak, Lydia 100	Li, Alison 103
Jersild, Kira 33	Klavan, Rachel 125	Liacopoulos, Dina 144
Jessee, Daya 195	Kleczkowski, Jeremy 164	Lightfoot, Dalonte 154
Jha, Chandini 34	Klein, Carolyn 74	Lin, Kevin 102
Johnson, Aaron 187	Klemkowski, Chase 148	Lindberg, Dennis 26
Johnson, Amanda 101	Kluger, Peyton 139	Lindsay, Alison 52
Johnson, Brandon 161	Knowles, Michael 178	Lindsay, Joseph 155

Index

Link, Adam 16
Little, Briana 155
Livingstone, Alexa 172
Lloyd, Jacob 194
Lobo, Antonia 21
Lock, Shalah 20
Lockard, Brianna 128
Long, Dylan 173
Lorusso, Zoe 59
Lough, Ryan 143
Lounsbury, Jennifer 143
Love, Kenny 78
Lowery, Amber 63
Lucas, Luke 187
Luck, Lisa 46
Lughmani, Madeeha 78
Lui, Michelle 155
Luke, Brandon 97
Luong, James 154
Lusk, Garrett 185
Luzier, Makenna 179
Lyon, Jan 64
Mabray, Erin 38
Madison, Amber 186
Maduka, Favour 155
Magoffin, Molly 50
Magruder, Karima Christine .. 154
Maguire, Maggie 198
Malik, Noreen 104
Manalac, Maddie 163
Mananghaya, Zachary 185
Mangum, Lucy 155
Mankin, Hart 164
Mann, Amndeep Singh 25
Manning, Jessica 78
Mansolillo, Marc 190
Mapes, Clare 191
Mark, Ryan 140
Markey, Jack 84
Marlow, Ryan 62
Marquis, Ryan 194
Marsengill, Taylor 65
Marsh, Madison 84
Marshall, Alexa 39
Martin, Alexis 193
Martin, Christina 88
Martin, Jada 187
Martin, Julia 112
Martin, Susannah 51
Martin, Tayla 192
Martinez, Savannah 133
Martino, Katelyn 147
Maruca, Caroline 93
Masciola, Tamara 152
Massenberg, Destiny 85
Mattheiss, Colbee 122
Matthews, Bryce 168
Matthews, Emoni 33

Maus, Ellie 194
Maxwell, Hunter 156
Maynard, Andrew 27
Mays, Brittany 193
Mazzenga, Jr., Gino 188
Mazzulla, Jared 166
McCaffrey, Jimmy 107
McCormick, Jacob 43
McCoy, Geoffrey 87
McCulloch, Samantha 67
McDaniel, Erin 66
McDaniel, McKayla 197
McElhattan, Neal 68
McGainey, Ahmal 52
McIver, Cekiya 156
McKee, Tess 88
McKenna, Shannon 41
McLain, Jack 79
McMillan, Shawn 157
McNelis, Hailey 75
McShane, Abigail 99
McSharry, Connor 199
Medina, Alexandra 190
Medrano, Christopher 175
Meehan, Olivia 114
Megge, Matt 105
MehrRostami, Aundia 89
Mejia, Omar 33
Mekkes, Ben 134
Menezes, Meryl 57
Mengenhauser, Alexa 62
Menikheim, Brooke 174
Messier, Amanda 168
Meyer, Hana 34
Michael 101
Mikhailova, Katya 173
Mikulskis, Anthony 38
Mikutina, Natalia 47
Miles, Herman 36
Miles, Jazmyn 22
Miles, Madeline 111
Miles, Sara 37
Miller, Ariana 61
Miller, Cameron 198
Miller, Nathaniel Andrew 25
Miller, Promyce D'eja 84
Miller, Sharmayne 30
Miller, Tommy 74
Miller, Zachery Adam 93
Milligan, Christopher 165
Mills, Cole 58
Milson, Conor 190
Mina, Alexander 131
Mishoe, Anna 127
Mitchell, Justin 127
Mitchell, Marquita 29
Mitten, Kailee 123
Mizelle, Bethany 174

Mo, Evelyn 123
Modozie, Joy 200
Mohamad, Morsal 113
Mohr, Stephane 80
Monk, Madeline 34
Monroe, Elizabeth 88
Montano, Cristobal 21
Moody, Natalya 141
Moore, Landon 159
Moore, Olivia 97
Moore, Sylvan 150
Moore, Thurston 140
Morales, Noah 144
Morelli, Joanna 25
Morgan, Ty 158
Morgan, Zachary 147
Morris, Claire 166
Morritz, Delilah 163
Mort Ranta, Penelope 131
Mugford, Emma 96
Mukundi, Bakhita 134
Mullane, Mary 183
Mullen, Bailey 201
Murillo, Elise 119
Murray, Devyn 53
Myers, Dalton 185
Nachlas, Eli 166
Nachtman, Nicole 41
Naeem, Nimra 40
Nagai, Sano 108
Nagy, Emma 126
Nakroshis, Morgan 17
Nathan, Shama 104
Navolio, Maria 175
Neely, Jimmy 149
Negron, Waleska 42
Neuman, Matthew 201
Newbold, Anna 126
Newcombe, Rhys 167
Ng, Sandy 121
Nguyen, Ellen 16
Nicholas, Kyndall 77
Nikolaou, Stella 177
Niles, Alicia 131
Nitkowski, Daniele 107
Nobre, Alejandro 83
Noell, Ryan 61
Nokib, Tasnia 100
Nolan, Jata A. 177
O'Brien, Colin 165
O'Brien, Kaitlin 37
O'Connor, Tim 38
O'Neill, Emily 196
Ojha, Shashank 130
Okpodu, Elizabeth 24
Oliver, Jacob 105
Olivieri, Angelina 174
Olmsted, Tyler 92

Olson, Megan	175	
Orozco, Ethan	141	
Orr, Mariah	75	
Osmond, Haboon	91	
Osofsky, Gil	99	
Oumhand, Basheer	181	
Owens, Donae	32	
Pablo, Patricia	89	
Padilla, Sarah	199	
Pagliarini, David	144	
Paige, Daquan	182	
Palangdao, Dominique	92	
Palmer, Thomas	154	
Papa, Ben	171	
Papa, Zack	195	
Papelis, Sophia	68	
Papineau, Valerie	108	
Parkin, Heather	174	
Parris, Anna	115	
Parsons, Hope	139	
Passela, Sashini	82	
Patacsil, Victoria	177	
Patel, Reema	95	
Patel, Vraj	177	
Patron, Nicko	105	
Patterson, Miranda	41	
Payne, Rashonna	161	
Peace, Victoria	157	
Peck, Owen	181	
Pennington, Ashley	22	
Peoples, Lisa	187	
Pereira, Abigail	159	
Perkins, Hannah	156	
Perkins, Jacob	154	
Perrine, Meredith	65	
Peters, Claudia	12	
Peterson, Arion	152	
Peterson, Ross	44	
Peterson, Seth	142	
Petrillo, Nick	91	
Pettit, Lauren	51	
Pettus, Julia	146	
Petty, Ryan	172	
Pettyjohn, Sara	142	
Pfizenmaier, Neil	64	
Phillips, Amy	34	
Phillips, Jonie	173	
Phillips, Victoria	96	
Pickett, Daja	181	
Piedmonte, Lucas	186	
Pierce, Mikey	187	
Pietruszka, Charlie	154	
Pilkington, Brooke	105	
Pilozzi, Michael	188	
Pinnamaneni, Sravya	138	
Pipkin, Emily	145	
Pires, Cintia	42	
Plater, Jordan	148	
Platt, Robbie	180	
Pleasant, Kayla	114	
Plummer, Jane	38	
Poff, Emma	175	
Pohorence, Olivia	182	
Polk, Maxx	165	
Pontz, Erin	86	
Poore, Janie	79	
Poosson, Desiree	19	
Pope, Nadine	173	
Poplovski, Bethany	177	
Portillo, Joseph	111	
Posch, Rachael	76	
Pothapragada, Raksha	96	
Potter, Garrison	160	
Poudel, Mokshyada	97	
Pouliot, Alexandrea	164	
Powell, Grace	179	
Powell, Kien	173	
Price, James	146	
Price, Rachael	177	
Pritchett-Wilson, Niyala	184	
Prock, Matthew	23	
Protogyrou, Demetra	124	
Pruchniewski, Bethany	118	
Pruitt, Cassidy	154	
Pryor, Katelyn	25	
Quesnel, Paul	133	
Radiguet-Correa, Anne-Marie L.	73	
Raj, Andrew	135	
Ramesh, Swetha	127	
Ramos, Blonnie	23	
Ramsey, Morgan	201	
Randolph, Shianne	149	
Randolph, William	90	
Raparthi, Farheen	62	
Rappaport, Sammi J.	104	
Rawls, Darla	141	
Redden, Riley Anne	144	
Reddy, Sushma	61	
Reed, Alejandro	155	
Reeder, Nickolas	140	
Rees, Daniel	76	
Reeves, Sarah	200	
Reid, Becky	54	
Reis, Mary	58	
Remka, Peter	171	
Renesis, Katherine Alyssa	129	
Resh, Shelby	87	
Reyes, Beatrice	180	
Reyes, Erika	16	
Rhodes, Eli	138	
Rhone, Rasheen Omar	24	
Rich, Theodore C.	69	
Richards, Sabrina	97	
Ricks, Savannah	63	
Ridlon, Lauren	90	
Riehl, Nicholas	14	
Rijhwani, Narain	71	
Rijhwani, Simran	163	
Riley, Amber	51	
Riley, Clare	162	
Riley, Grace	76	
Ringer, Donté	55	
Ringgold, Richard	63	
Riordon, Julia	143	
Ritter, Trey	110	
Riva, Joe	171	
Rivera, Alicia	62	
Rivera, Elena	31	
Rivero Anez, Stephany	65	
Roach, Jennifer	78	
Roberson, Abigail	69	
Robertson, Claire	168	
Robinson, Alexis	20	
Robinson, Amaya	97	
Robinson, Becca Lynn	35	
Robinson, Kinnicko	75	
Robinson, Tashauna	42	
Rocca, Julia	199	
Rodrigues, Kristen	64	
Rodriguez, Austin	143	
Rodriguez, Henry	138	
Rodriguez, Mark	105	
Rodriguez, William	201	
Rogers, Kaniya	173	
Rogers, Rita	138	
Roman, Taisha	90	
Romano, Austin	199	
Rommel, Shannon	112	
Rooney, Devin	187	
Rosenthal, Ben	138	
Ross, Olivia	50	
Rostov, Joseph	19	
Rowland, Hunter	77	
Royal, Frank	138	
Rubin, Rhoderic	128	
Rubio, Luis Felipe	146	
Rufai, David	187	
Rust, Robert	26	
Ryan, Colin	14	
Ryan, Elizabeth	97	
Ryan, Patrick	110	
Saathoff, Alexandra	151	
Sacher, Max	122	
Sacks, Hannah A.	25	
Sadler, Josh	60	
Sakhi, Rania	159	
Salamone, Genevieve	31	
Salassi, Kevin	61	
Samuda, Kyra	108	
Sanford, Virginia	85	
Santee, Emma	165	
Santos, Matt	74	
Sarza, Stephanie	63	
Sass, Cecily	117	

Index

Sass, Will 146
Saviano, Matthew 103
Schanck, Carley 88
Schauf, Mary 157
Schlott, Maxwell 66
Schmitt, Amy 91
Schroeder, Chris 188
Schroeder, Christopher 139
Schultz, Nathan 171
Schwartz, Valeria 169
Schwartzman, Becca 124
Scott, Rebecca 143
Sears, Drayce 180
Sechler, Bethany 160
Sechler, Brittany 117
Seerden, Sydney Anne Celestine 121
Selig, Lex 56
Sellars, DeAndre 93
Sempertegui, Daniel 190
Sengpraseuth, Theresé 80
Settle, Meghan 133
Shapard, Kai 95
Sharieff, Sidra 55
Shearer, Hannah 91
Sheehan, Julia 119
Shenoda, Marian 133
Shepherd, Mia 161
Shields, Shirley 102
Shimizu, Brendan 199
Short, Amber 15
Shuklis, Victoria 29
Shumate, Julia 17
Sidney, Zakiya 93
Silva, Briana 43
Simmons, Isabelle 197
Simmons, Olivia 147
Sindhwani, Anika 129
Singh, Avanthika 117
Singh, Manish 159
Singh, Sai 94
Sistrunk, Trinnity 184
Skaggs, Christian 195
Slavnik, Morgan 148
Sloat, Nicholas 170
Slyke, Antonio 188
Small, Emily 150
Small, Grace 174
Smith, Ayreanna 165
Smith, Carissa 101
Smith, Cheyanne 67
Smith, Cody 139
Smith, David 108
Smith, Demetrius 200
Smith, Sarah E. 174
Sokolowski, Hannah 188
Solomon, Nakia 30
Sorresso, Gabrielle 167
Soucy, Peter 85

Souranis, Maria 59
Spicer, Korey 168
Spickler, Jackson 73
Spirtas-Hurst, Claire 186
Spriggs, Savannah 125
Springfield, Tyler 176
Sprouse, Ashley 174
St.Germain, Erika 108
Stacy, Nick 191
Steendam, Evelien 112
Stephens, Benjamin 125
Stevens, Austin 62
Stevens, Natalie 113
Stitik, Seth 135
Stohlman, Emma 198
Stowe, Eliza 182
Strauss, John 125
Stroh, Joshua 111
Sturla, Meagan 98
Sulecki, Kyle 30
Sullivan, Emily 90
Sullivan, J.T. 193
Sullivan, Molly 112
Sum, Alaysia 198
Sun, Virginia 80
Swinton, Tynea 198
Szpisjak, D. Scott 133
Tabb, Joe 26
Tadeo, Anthony 135
Tadlock, Mary 14
Tappen, William 142
Tate, Hayley 106
Taylor, Jenna 179
Teague, Christine 112
Tharp, Abbey 150
Thomas, Alexis 82
Thomas, Cole 68
Thomas, Nicholas 103
Thomas, Shantaya 132
Thompson, India Zhane' 138
Thompson, Jack 194
Thompson, Jenna 200
Thompson, Laney 189
Thompson, Sarah 196
Thornten, Sara 70
Thrower, Dequante 180
Thupukari, Sashank 130
Thurston, Bridger 191
Tobin, Kayla 158
Tocco, Joseph 153
Tompkins, Kyle 83
Toomey, Jillian 154
Torbert, Matthew 183
Torres, Ava 145
Totten, Eric 57
Touafek, Gaston 39
Trail, Savannah 139
Tran, Lily 194

Traversari, Angelina 84
Trees, Brittany 148
Tremper, Jr., Kenneth 156
Tuck, Dylan 44
Tucker, Megan 189
Tucker, Taylor 151
Tumminello, Frankie 149
Turack, Steven 75
Turner, Catherine 21
Turner, Hannah 201
Turner, Mackenzie 95
Tyler, Shania 22
Ubago, Samantha 13
Uher, Katrina 115
Urquia, Sara 35
Vaccaro, Gabriella 114
Valentine, Catherine 175
Valentine, Kevin 66
Valverde, Zachary 140
Van Pelt, Angelica Bonnie 71
Van Winter, Andrew 69
Vanasse, Zachary 112
Vanik, Kayla 73
Vaughan, Molly 171
Vaught, Alex 194
Vazquez, Pedro 144
Vemulapalli, Krishna 126
Villanueva, Stacy 199
Vinson, Ruthie 106
Waddell, Katelyn 164
Wade, Brittany 19
Wade, Darrell 201
Wajda, Ann 171
Walker, Gregory 195
Walker, Wilbert 31
Wallace, Alexander R. 128
Walsh, Hannah 186
Walsh, Lexus 15
Walsh, Michael 87
Walsh, William 45
Walters, Stephanie 19
Wan, Enxin (Mary) 60
Wang, Max 132
Waters, Juatonia 159
Watson, Cameron 111
Watson, Monet 96
Watts, Jeremiah 36
Watts, Sarah Kerr 40
Weatherwalks, Alexa 100
Weaver, Austyn 193
Weaver, DeAndre 29
Webb, Sandra 126
Weber, Callahan CB 157
Weinstein, Michael 167
Weiss, Spencer 86
Wellington, Paige 73
Wells, James 47
Wenz, Ashley 53

West, Maranda	53
Westrick, Madeline	91
Westrick, Zoe	199
Whalen, Ian	174
Wharton, Marissa	98
Wharton, Olivia	186
Wheeler, Jenn'Asia	34
Whitaker, Kendall	184
White, Jeannette	105
White, Katrina	123
White, Lauren	79
White, Shane	19
White, Taylor	151
White-El, Daesani Ali	155
Whitmore, Jack	201
Whitsitt, Jadyn	156
Whitsitt, Justen	115
Whorley, Dale	167
Wieczorek, Leah	178
Wiles, Alyssa	181
Wilkinson, RJ	187
Williams, Ace	193
Williams, Akira	187
Williams, Alexis	83
Williams, Baldwin	114
Williams, Kearson	180
Williams, Quentin	32
Williams, Sunshine	194
Williams, Zach	199
Williamson, Keyonia	45
Williard, Samuel	173
Wilson, Benjamin	201
Wilson, D'Asia	175
Wilson, Jacquelyn	115
Wilson, Mitchell	79
Wilson, ShaJhea	40
Windrum, Willow	66
Wise, Fuller	152
Wise, Millicent	105
Witcher, Curtis	194
Wojciechowski, Kelly	105
Wolf, Abbie	56
Woller, Alexandra	152
Wong, Caitlyn	183
Woodard, Courtney	14
Wooleyhan, Jesse	21
Wooten, Molly	82
Wright, Tiffany	127
Wyland, Kristi	156
Xia, Jeffrey	58
Xin, Christie	132
Yeager, Jake	70
Young, Carolyn	193
Young, Riley	130
Young, Shaune	32
Young, Zachary	179
Zang, Colton	142
Zhao, Helen	158
Zheng, Emily	188
Zhu, Sara	133
Ziegler, Katelyn	195
Zittle, Anna	174
Zopp, Jett	87